THE SHEATHED SWORD

BLOOMSBURY INDIA
Bloomsbury Publishing India Pvt. Ltd
Second Floor, LSC Building No. 4, DDA Complex, Pocket C – 6 & 7,
Vasant Kunj, New Delhi, 110070

BLOOMSBURY, BLOOMSBURY ACADEMIC INDIA and the Diana logo
are trademarks of Bloomsbury Publishing Plc

First published in India 2022
This edition published 2022

Bloomsbury Academic
An imprint of Bloomsbury Publishing Plc

ISBN: HB: 978-93-54355-80-6; eBook: 978-93-54356-98-8

Typeset in Manipal Technologies Limited
Printed & bound in India by Replika Press Pvt. Ltd.

THE SHEATHED SWORD

From Nuclear Brink to No First Use

Edited by
Lieutenant General Prakash Menon
Aditya Ramanathan

B L O O M S B U R Y
NEW DELHI • LONDON • OXFORD • NEW YORK • SYDNEY

CONTENTS

Foreword by Ambassador Shivshankar Menon vii
Introduction 1

Part I: Understanding the Role of Nuclear Weapons in Global Security
Chapter 1: Superpower and World Order 7
Colin S. Gray
Chapter 2: The Seven Deadly Sins of Nuclear Strategy Dogmata 15
Lt General (Dr) Prakash Menon
Chapter 3: Is Nuclear Deterrence a Cost-effective Policy? 23
Bruno Tertrais
Chapter 4: Nuclear Weapons and the Global Security Environment 34
Rajesh Basrur
Chapter 5: Nuclear Weapons, Geopolitics, Emerging Technologies and Oppositional Nationalism 48
Sadia Tasleem

Part II: The Uses and Perils of Nuclear Weapons
Chapter 6: Nuclear Coercion—Evaluating Insights from Academic Scholarship 63
Walter C. Ladwig III
Chapter 7: Asia Treads the Nuclear Path, Unaware that Self-assured Destruction Would Result from Nuclear War 83
Owen B. Toon, Alan Robock, Michael Mills and Lili Xia

Part III: The Dilemmas of No First Use
Chapter 8: It's Time for a US No-First-Use Nuclear Policy 111
Nina Tannenwald
Chapter 9: The Purposes of Nuclear Weapons 123
Rajesh Rajagopalan
Chapter 10: Nuclear No First Use in Theory and Practice 135
Keir Lieber and Daryl Press

Part IV: States, Nuclear Weapons and the Prospects for Global No First Use
Chapter 11: US Nuclear Strategy, No First Use and the Return of Great Power Competition 143
Matthew Kroenig

Chapter 12: Russia's Nuclear Doctrine Journey 155
Petr Topychkanov
Chapter 13: Less Possible, More Necessary? No-First-Use Policy for France and Europe 166
Damien Cusey and Olivier de France
Chapter 14: China's No First Use as a Litmus Test for Global No First Use 177
Lora Saalman
Chapter 15: China's No-First-Use Policy and the Prospect of the Global No-First-Use Treaty—A Chinese Perspective 200
Zhong Ai
Chapter 16: The Desirability and Feasibility of Global No First Use—An Indian Perspective 211
Manpreet Sethi
Chapter 17: Israel and a 'No-First-Use' Declaration 224
Emily B. Landau
Chapter 18: Deterrence Unsheathed—Pakistan and the Prospects of Global No First Use 231
Brigadier (Retd) Feroz Hassan Khan
Chapter 19: No-First-Use Policy of a New Nuclear Weapons State—The Case of North Korea 250
Jina Kim
Chapter 20: Tokyo's Reluctance over No First Use, for Now 264
Hirofumi Tosaki
Chapter 21: On Turkey's Stance towards Nuclear Weapons and Global No First Use 276
Mustafa Kibaroglu

About the Editors and Contributors 293
Index 301

FOREWORD[1]

I am grateful to the Takshashila Institution for rekindling the discussion about no first use (NFU) and contextualising it globally, rather than just within the Indian situation. There has been sporadic discussion in India about its own NFU pledge, which was made after the 1998 nuclear tests. Three reviews of that doctrine by successive governments of India have concluded that it is a pledge that serves the needs of India's deterrent capability and security. In the present situation, when India and China are the only nuclear powers that have made categorical (if different) NFU pledges, I think it only sensible that the Government of India would periodically review the pledge in the light of circumstances and developments.

What this volume seeks to do is broader and more significant—examining the theoretical and practical implications of a Global No-First-Use pledge in the present context.

Mentioning the present context is relevant because contemporary deterrence theory is largely the product of a particular time, place and situation that no longer exists—the Cold War dyad of the US and the USSR on opposite sides of the globe. Today's nuclear powers are no longer in that situation—not even Russia and the USA.

The direction of global politics is hardly reassuring as the world becomes more contentious and security dilemmas involving nuclear powers multiply. The multilateral arms control and disarmament processes are at a standstill or going backwards. The effectiveness of multilateral regimes is increasingly in question. Besides, technologies have changed drastically, with great advances in conventional weaponry, autonomy and artificial intelligence. The risks of miscalculation and mistakes involving nuclear weapons have, as a consequence, risen in this century. This is, therefore, probably a good time to review the question of whether a GNFU would strengthen or stabilise nuclear deterrence and move the atomic clock back.

Anything we can do to lessen the risks is useful and necessary. A GNFU agreement is one such step, no more or less, in several ways:

1. It is useful as a confidence-building measure (CBM). It is politics that has driven states to build and deploy nuclear weapons. A political gesture like a GNFU agreement would be an attempt to reduce such political motivations. I believe that there is no such thing as a purely nuclear strategy, since nuclear weapons are political weapons.

2. The nuclear posture and force structure that would result from a GNFU agreement would be more stable and less offensively threatening than that required by states committed to first use of nuclear weapons. It is also probably cheaper, though that is not necessarily the criterion to adopt.
3. A GNFU agreement would reduce the chances of an inadvertent and unwanted nuclear escalation.
4. Reinforcing the taboo against the use of nuclear weapons, which has worked so far since 1945, would be an important gain.
5. A GNFU agreement would also be a useful first step towards a nuclear weapons-free world, a goal that was attractive enough for President Obama to support when he visited India in 2010.

Several arguments are also made against NFU pledges. A pledge is just that, a pious declaration of intent that can be broken. Will it stand the test of crisis or the imminent threat of war? These are valid considerations but they should not prevent us from doing what we can to strengthen the commitment not to use nuclear weapons to the extent possible and to make such a commitment legally binding.

Some believe nuclear weapons can be war-fighting weapons and suggest military utility for nuclear weapons, such as pre-empting an imminent attack, deterring conventional threats, extended deterrence reassurance to allies and as a guarantee of independence.

Let us consider each of these in a little more detail.

With the increased precision and lethality of conventional weapons today, both pre-emption and deterrence of conventional attacks can now be done with conventional and other weapons.

As for extended deterrence, this is a concept that is hard to believe after developments on the Korean Peninsula.[2] It stretches credulity to believe that a state would invite or risk a nuclear attack on its population and cities for the sake of an ally, no matter how loyal or valuable. That, at its heart, is what extended deterrence asks us to believe.

As for nuclear weapons as a guarantee of independence, they could indeed guarantee against nuclear blackmail and coercion. However, beyond that, it is hard to envisage realistic scenarios for the use of nuclear weapons to guarantee independence. As someone once remarked, there is little point in being independently dead. Fortunately, no military scenarios involving nuclear weapons have ever been tested in practice. The discussion of nuclear strategy and warfighting is, therefore, thankfully, just theory. May it always remain so—a GNFU agreement would certainly help in ensuring that.

Of course, even those who believe that nuclear weapons are not war-fighting weapons and have pledged NFU must consider the possibility of others, who do not share their convictions, actually using their nuclear weapons. As nuclear weapons get smaller, more tactical and easier to use and handle, the greater the temptation will be to use them.

A legally binding taboo on their use, or at least on their first use, could be a first step towards limiting this problem, de-incentivising their use and de-legitimising tactical nuclear weapons.

Another issue to consider is the effect of technological developments on deterrence and NFU pledges. Have sensing improvements made survivability an issue and therefore increased the temptation to undertake decapitating first strikes? What about the effects of artificial intelligence, machine learning and autonomy on nuclear deterrence, and the sort of pressures that they are generating on the taboo against the use of nuclear weapons?

The list of questions and issues is long. However, it all boils down to the credibility of deterrence with an NFU pledge and the broader implications of that pledge today. As a practitioner, I feel that to be credible, deterrence must first be credible to oneself. If we only go by our perception of what potential adversaries think of our deterrence, we would have handed over control and agency of our nuclear weapons doctrines to them. Therefore, there is value in the periodic soul-searching and debate on no first use.

Ambassador Shivshankar Menon

NOTES

1 A version of this text was previously delivered by Ambassador Menon as a keynote address at the author round table for this volume on 2 November 2019 in Bengaluru.

2 For extended deterrence to work in the Korean Peninsula, South Korea would have to believe that the USA is willing to lose its cities to protect South Korean territory.

INTRODUCTION

In the time since we began putting together this book, the world has experienced both a devastating pandemic and a major interstate war. The novel coronavirus upended societies and economies around the world and the Russia-Ukraine war set off a chain of events that are likely to have a lasting impact on international order. Together, these two events offer us harsh lessons on the challenges of maintaining peace and prosperity. The pandemic is a forceful reminder that catastrophes are not a thing of the past, while the war makes it abundantly clear that the salience of nuclear weapons will endure. The fine contributors to this anthology are principally concerned with the politics of nuclear catastrophe. At its heart, nuclear strategy, as practised since 1945, is a study of how the fear of these weapons, and the devastation they inflict, can be used by governments for political ends. The peril of nuclear strategy is that when it fails, the consequences can potentially be world ending.

Nearly eight decades since nuclear weapons were last used in anger, it has become possible for governments and the wider public to become complacent about the danger of nuclear war. This is happening even as international politics coarsens and technological developments threaten strategic stability. The international order established after the Second World War continues to exist in form but is increasingly fragile in substance. Major states have embraced great power competition at a time in which precision-guided munitions are becoming ubiquitous and innovations in space, cyber and artificial intelligence technologies are boosting both offensive and defensive capabilities.

Unsurprisingly, recent efforts at nuclear arms control have failed, as existing agreements fall apart or fade away and attempts at crafting new deals falter. Also, unsurprisingly, some nuclear weapons states are looking for a more pervasive role for the ultimate weapon and other states are hedging their bets, keeping open the option of going nuclear in the future.[1]

If traditional arms control does not offer easy solutions for reducing nuclear dangers, what can we do? At the Takshashila Institution, we propose a GNFU agreement. Such an agreement could help lower alert levels, slow down nuclear arms races and provide some measure of safety and security in political relationships.

Unlike traditional arms control agreements that are focused on hardware and complex verification mechanisms, a GNFU agreement is focused on a simple declaration. However, any such declaration also requires a shift in thinking about nuclear weapons from one that involves manipulating risk to achieve broader political goals to one centred on deterring the use (or threat of use) of these weapons by an adversary. In the future, as virtual technologies like artificial intelligence become deeply embedded in strategic systems, this cognitive shift may prove more effective at reducing nuclear risks than traditional arms control mechanisms.

To consider the feasibility and desirability of a GNFU agreement, our contributors consider a wide range of nuclear issues. In the first of four sections, the late Colin S. Gray, Bruno Tertrais, Rajesh Basrur, Sadia Tasleem and one of us, Lt General Prakash Menon, look at the role of nuclear weapons in global security. In the second section, Walter C. Ladwig III examines the literature on nuclear coercion. We also reproduce a landmark paper by Owen B. Toon and his co-authors from *The Journal of Asian Studies* in which they consider the devastating effects of a limited nuclear war on the world's climate.

In the third section, our contributors look at the issues around no first use. Nina Tannenwald makes the case for a multilateral NFU pledge. Rajesh Rajagopalan looks at how considerations like state survival and the balance of conventional military forces influence how states use nuclear weapons. Keir Lieber and Daryl Press examine whether NFU has helped or hindered India in dealing with Pakistan-based sub-conventional attacks.

The last and largest section is a series of studies of how individual states view nuclear weapons and the desirability of a GNFU agreement. This section includes chapters on both nuclear powers and some non-nuclear powers. Matthew Kroenig discusses the realities of US nuclear strategy in an era of great power competition. Petr Topychkanov delves into the question of whether Russia, in fact, has an 'escalate-to-de-escalate' strategy. Damien Cusey and Olivier de France argue that while a GNFU agreement is needed, France's compulsions will make it less likely. In separate chapters, Lora Saalman and Zhong Ai consider the state of China's NFU pledge. Manpreet Sethi concludes that NFU has served India well and should be adopted worldwide. The late Emily B. Landau walks us through the evolution of Israel's nuclear policy and Feroz Hassan Khan describes how Pakistan uses its nuclear weapons to deter perceived Indian assertiveness. Jina Kim seeks to dispel common misperceptions about how North Korea thinks about using its arsenal in a conflict.

The last two chapters are on Japan and Turkey. Hirofumi Tosaki argues that Japan would not want the USA to declare an NFU for the foreseeable future and Mustafa Kibaroglu lays out the conditions under which Turkey could consider backing a GNFU agreement.

While some of our contributors back the idea of a GNFU, many others express varying degrees of scepticism towards it. This not only highlights the challenges that lie ahead for a GNFU agreement but also the need for a continuing debate on the subject. If this volume informs readers and stimulates discussion, it will have achieved its purpose and perhaps brought us closer to understanding the forces that draw us towards nuclear calamity.

Lt General (Dr) Prakash Menon, PVSM AVSM VSM
Aditya Ramanathan

NOTES

1 A portion of this text draws from a concept note for this volume that was circulated among prospective authors via email. The note laid out the case for a consideration of the proposal for a global no-first-use agreement. It has not been published anywhere else.

Part I

UNDERSTANDING THE ROLE OF NUCLEAR WEAPONS IN GLOBAL SECURITY

Chapter 1

SUPERPOWER AND WORLD ORDER

Colin S. Gray

CONSTANCY AND CHANGE IN HISTORY

Honest scholars tend to find and acknowledge that their own thoughts and discoveries had precedents. Of course, never truly precise ones but unquestionably similar thoughts and findings will be awaiting rediscovery. This can be a disturbing, even alarming recognition that the very idea of human progress might be less important, even possibly less true, than we have believed, were we not educated to recognise and even expect, and anticipate in advance, progress in human affairs. It can prove shocking for students today to be obliged to confront the anarchic seeming idea that the very notion of human progress may be seriously bereft of merit. In this essay, I shall dare to suggest that real and important though change most certainly is, there are elements all too relevant to our human condition that appear scarcely to change at all. The grand scope of this atavistic appearing idea can be quite startling upon those who have never encountered it before.

To argue, at least suggest, that human progress is substantially illusory could be misunderstood. The argument presented here is thoroughly respectful of some change. Modernisation emphatically is not the issue. Humankind can secure and even celebrate change. The real issue is best revealed by posing the brutal-sounding question, so what? My approach is better explained by my recognition that there appears to be a rhythm to the history of human affairs, recognition of which warrants respect. We live with—indeed, seemingly require—change in many aspects of our lives and environment. This change, typically, is exploited by politicians who seek to sell it as meaning some material, or even moral, advance. What is remarkable, however, is the limited reach that pertains to this human realm of near-constant change today.

The monumental achievements of humankind are only an ornamental evidence of change in the context of a cultural parentage that has not altered markedly over the few millennia of the past that can be studied. This discovery can prove to be all but embarrassing to those among us who strive to advance the argument that we humans are bound on a long journey towards truly significant moral progress. Ironically, perhaps, there is good news as well as bad amidst the details of our species' historical narrative. Specifically, from such evidence as we can glean from history, it seems unlikely we humans are bound on any epic journey to some fantastic paradise or other. If true, this means we are obliged, for want of alternatives, perhaps, to strive to cope with conditions substantially as we find them here. Alas, it seems extremely unlikely that there is a radically different, morally better, future world awaiting our arrival and appreciation. The argument that I am making amounts to nothing less than the proposition that nothing very significant changes in the course of our history. I take no satisfaction from noting that we have achieved only a single advance in science and subsequent technology that threatens civilisation as we know it. Specifically, I refer, of course, to the militarisation of atomic physics. The atomic, then the much more powerful hydrogen bomb, is unique in the entire history of human disagreements and warfare. The use of nuclear weapons alone is capable of terminating the entire human enterprise and achievement on planet Earth. Familiarity with the danger of such peril is evidence of nothing very substantial. Good luck and courage, all too appropriately born of fear, have served well enough to date. This abominable creation by human science and technology may yet succeed in teaching that some human challenges would have been better left unexplored and unexploited. Later in this essay, I will address briefly the subject of nuclear strategy and its dilemmas explicitly.

GEOGRAPHY, HUMANITY AND STRATEGY

The important concept of geopolitics has had a much-chequered past for many years in the last century. In order to rescue the core idea from much irrelevant, often politically motivated, comment, it is useful to think of the concept of geopolitics fundamentally as referring simply to the meaning that both physical and ideational geography has for politics. Obviously, this concept is a highly permissive one, with reference to the wide range of beliefs and desires that geography can bestow upon particular people and indeed whole peoples. In truth, it is difficult to know for many historical cases just where the responsibility most potently was borrowed, possibly subsequently sustained, for a while. If, as here, we are particularly interested in possible, even probable, futures, the total absence of direct evidence drives us to endeavour to understand the past. This may be attempted not in the belief that the future will be the past, only with different clothes. Instead, we can postulate that particular behaviours will be probable for not much better reason than because the agents for decision and consequent action will all be human. At times, people largely do what they do for no better reason than that they can do it. Scholars are apt to neglect explanations as elementary as this.

It is tempting to settle upon physical geography as the foundation that inspires and, sometimes, frustrates all that we humans strive to accomplish on it. No matter how appealing such reasoning may appear to be, at first sight, it is almost certainly mistaken. Throughout the history of our species, it has been possible, evidently beyond room for plausible argument, for man (and woman) to succeed in building civilisation literally almost anywhere and everywhere on Earth, save for in the truly extreme high and low latitudes of the polar regions. Certainly, physical geography poses challenges; moreover, these may prove to be significantly disabling for human progress. Nonetheless, we should be careful not to exaggerate the relative significance of the physical environment.

GEOGRAPHY AND STRATEGY

As a general rule, it is prudent to be more impressed by what people do rather than by physical geography that both enables and hinders their activity. It is all too easy for us to exaggerate the probable influence of physical geography upon human thought and apparently consequent behaviour. It is admittedly difficult to identify cause and effect and to know with high confidence just which is what. There can be no doubt that all human activity has some geographical context. To be very blunt about it, everything, actually done or even just considered, must have some geographical context: everything that happens to us happens somewhere, but so what?

Theories of statecraft and strategy have been forged and matured resting evidentially upon the world as it has been, to the best of our knowledge necessarily. However, there is some value to be secured from some anthropological consideration. Scholarship often can tell us who did what, and even plausibly, why. We are ever likely to forget the very nature of our subject: humankind itself. Our human history is ever-changing, or so it may seem. Historical narratives inadvertently may conceal as much as they reveal to scholars. The physical and ideational artefacts from past centuries may be revealed for our contemporary admiration or derision. But for honest and perhaps accurate reappraisal, they all need to be considered and assessed by minds that are temporally maximally tolerant. We need to respect past human behaviour in its true authenticity of the past. What this means for contemporary analysis of both the past and the future is the recognition that little of great importance to mankind has changed for centuries, even millennia.

The truly great changes made by human will and action have been, near exclusively, matters of the mind, even calculation. Expressed in rather military terms, we have usually changed, at least adjusted, our tactics and operations in order to attempt to secure a better fix with our circumstances. However, there has been a persistent difficulty with which we could not, indeed cannot, cope substantively. Specifically, I refer to the enduring reality of human conflict.

Students may notice that the genuinely rich panoply of our history truly is propelled by the contemporary manifestation of values that have long endured. It can be more than a little dispiriting to be obliged by an overwhelming body of historical evidence to recognise that humanity simply is what it is and always was. The entirety of our past has been governed by an unimproved, unchanged humanity. The same emotions and values link the whole human narrative. Not for nothing have some careful scholars chosen to characterise the course of human history as a great stream of time; always in motion but also, rather worriedly, going nowhere in particular. From time to time, notable political, religious, indeed cultural leaders will claim to have discovered a goal for us all but as a general rule, such prophets and other seers are not to be trusted. It is not necessarily the case that such people are probably wrong but rather that they tend to have the ability to require that the rest of us should rest or even retire our critical faculties. A persisting problem for our species is that achievements typically are as plain to see and commonly understand as the motives that galvanised them into life tend to be obscure, hidden even.

Of course, culture influences behaviour. However, cultural preference almost invariably is shaped, sometimes reshaped, and disciplined by external forces. While physical geography is one such, human behaviour, perhaps merely presence, is likely to be more significant.

THE RHYTHM OF HISTORY

Human advance in science and understanding during the past two centuries has been truly remarkable. The particular climatic range permitted the geographical diversity that enabled political communities in Europe to mature, plunder and profit for centuries, in part, inevitably, at the expense of less fortunate others. Humanity, however, has not changed significantly. Students can find it challenging to believe that changes in the tools we use provide no key worth noting as to the values we espouse and profess. As best we honestly can determine, the human race has not altered—evolved perhaps—in any time period of relevance to us today. If this claim is assessed to be persuasive, the implications for our future are profound. Whereas the geography that yields unmistakable context to all our lives is ever-present and obvious, the culture of our distinctly human values usually will be more or less concealed. These values typically will be fed by emotion.

If we wish prudently to consider the future, we will soon discover that there is no guide superior to Thucydides, who was writing 2,400 years ago. The concern of states today is expressed with full empathy in the familiar triptych first written, to our current knowledge that is, by the great Greek historian literally millennia in the past. Thucydides told us that the motives behind all statecraft are captured well enough in just three ideas: fear, honour and interest. I have no good reason to seek to improve on this admittedly ancient formula. In the course of my fifty years of study and teaching, I have failed to come across anything superior to this decidedly ancient triptych. Common sense and accessible historical evidence tell us that the world, in the politics of its statecraft, simply is what it is and is beyond systemic reform. What I am striving to say clearly is that there is truly an essential unity to our great historical narrative. Furthermore, it is difficult to resist the idea that ours truly must be understood to be a strategic history.

The proposition that ours unavoidably must be expected to be a conflict-ridden future is strongly troubling because of the judgement just offered here concerning history's strategic character. The argument is not that war is a certainty in the future but rather that that is a permanent feature of life (and death) on our planet Earth. If we are interested in knowing what we are able about the future, we are obliged to be respectful of the laws of science. Of course, there are other, non-scientific, even anti-scientific, approaches that one may choose to adopt for guidance about the future. These sundry approaches may have some merit but as the product of rational education, I doubt it. My decades of both study and experience lead me inevitably to the conclusion that the future will be very like the past, and it was ever so. If we discard the conceit that our species is bound on some mystical journey, the human situation becomes clearer. Our future helpfully can be appreciated in full historical context. Such an approach provides the kind of historical context that should enable us to cope more effectively with the challenges of today and tomorrow that are new, to us at least.

States, political communities, tribes and so forth rise and fall today, as they have always done. The idea that needs to be accepted, though many people will resist its logic, is the master proposition that we are moved inexorably by circumstance along a great stream of time, a motion that had no beginning known to us, nor any objective we can determine.

Geopolitics, understood strictly and correctly simply as the political meaning of geography, is hugely significant because usually, it can change only slowly. Historical record tells us that great wealth serves as potent fuel for political ambition, which, in its time logically, will be held to require a large scale of military power for support and other protection.

The historical record that tells us about the dangerous temptations of great, particularly unbalanced economic wealth also typically advises, perhaps even reassures us with the generally well-evidenced argument that greatness on a politically significant scale tends, happily, to prove ironically self-defeating. This rather reassuring point is illustrated throughout recorded history. What it means is that the rise of any and indeed every state eventually will be ended, either essentially for reasons of domestic turmoil or because an unmatched greatness of power eventually fuels effective foreign resistance. We know that in our global human history many states have both risen and fallen. To be rather blunt on the subject, since all polities in our history, without exception, have both risen and eventually fallen, we know that there is a relative power rhythm to history, always. It should be needless to say that a very long-term dynamic to relative power relations does, of course, offer little reassurance to people who feel insecure today. As the rather depressing truism reminds us, in the long run, we are all dead. All too understandably it can prove a substantial challenge to cope with the demands of the present day, while keeping in mind, simultaneously, the rhythm of history's long term. We require of our statesmen that they deal satisfactorily with the demands of the moment, all the while not losing touch with forces and influences that need years or even decades to mature.

THE OLD FAMILIAR STORY? WORLD ORDER TODAY AND TOMORROW

Political error or technical mistakes have raised greatly the potential cost of risks in our human narrative. Books, reports and studies have all been done, revised and done again on both the pragmatic and also the operational meaning of nuclear weapons, both for national security and also for the world order (WO). The latter idea is as attractive as it is notably indistinct. It is probably true to claim that WO is as favoured around the world as it is strongly various in the meanings attributed to it; above all, no one is likely to favour disorder. There are two lethal problems with the seemingly innocuous master concept of WO: (*a*) its practical meaning is almost wildly permissive; (*b*) the entire history of the human race is one, the most destructive conflict in all human history was conducted barely 70 years ago. One may be inclined by the power of an optimistic spirit to claim all things in the future are possible. But anyone animated by some respect for the past, as well as by some alternative dreams for the future, must be inclined to respect the evidence we find readily enough. If we endorse a holistic view of our past, declining to be swayed unduly by plain evidence either of conflict or tranquillity, we discover the continual fuelling of the long-term shift in history's rhythm. The sole stand-out exception to the timeless motion of humans in history lurks still, all but unused in our nuclear arsenals. Together with climate change, nuclear weapons, and only nuclear weapons, would have the potential global consequence of an adverse effect upon all human life. I must admit that here I simply ignore the potentially global catastrophe that the impact of a truly rogue asteroid certainly would cause.

Returning to more familiar fields, we do know a great deal about the 21st century already. There should be no denying the risks, which, probably fairly, can be ascribed to nuclear possession. However, it has not escaped our notice that although nuclear acquisition may have offered statecraft and strategy at the most senior political and military levels, that still leaves very considerable scope for the energetic conduct of hostile intention. It is entirely evident that there have been no systemic changes in statecraft and strategy in recent decades (indeed, if ever!). The great powers of today, of necessity nuclear-armed, conduct their grand strategies in a manner with which the leading statesmen of the 19th century were thoroughly familiar. We need to be careful lest we exaggerate the consequences of the nuclear revolution. Whatever it was that the military application of atomic physics altered, it is not entirely self-evident that the political relations among states should be counted among them. It is very noticeable that only one of the current superpowers finds it desirable to seek to exploit nuclear aversion among rivals—the very recently much-reduced former USSR, Russia. Only Russia anticipates deriving high political worth from its undoubtedly impressive military nuclear establishment. Moreover, the Russians are alone internationally in boasting of nuclear might. The Russian military establishment has succumbed to the fantasy of believing in nuclear strategy. This is a dangerous chimaera. There may be some political value in the fear that nuclear weapons quite inevitably and sensibly induce but mature adults should know better than to profess to believe that nuclear weapons could be used sensibly to secure any particular political goal. It has been no accident that mutual nuclear deterrence has been our practice for decades.

CONCLUSION

The basic structure of world politics in the 21st century is now reasonably plain to see. While there are many relatively minor antagonisms to note, there are going to be just three true superpowers. The political relations among this trio—comprising the USA, China and Russia—will influence much else. What does appear to be beyond benign change is the prevalence of truly dangerous international conflict. Since Germany's dark dream of hegemony mercifully failed to be realised in the Second World War, there has been only one true, pre-eminent superpower—the USA. We know that international pre-eminence is so highly desirable a quality that it will always be challenged and that it has to decline over time. How can we be so confident in predicting a relative decline in American power? The answer lies quite unambiguously in the thoroughly reliable evidence of history. When power ranking considers the fairly long term, it is really unarguable that the recent number one power in the world on many scores can only shift its necessarily competitive hegemony in one direction—downwards. This is not to predict the near-term collapse of the USA. It is, however, to register with some confidence that the grand course of all our human history should be permitted to tell us that the American future internationally is certain to be one characterised by all our human history as a process of decline and fall.

Chapter 2

THE SEVEN DEADLY SINS OF NUCLEAR STRATEGY DOGMATA

Lt General (Dr) Prakash Menon

In October 1962, the US military outlined its plan to deliver an 'immaculate strike' against its adversaries. But despite the significant military superiority, there were mixed assurances from then President John F. Kennedy's advisors. His final decision betrayed his lack of conviction in the military's ability to deliver a strike that could guarantee zero nuclear retaliation. This decision, familiar to anyone working on nuclear strategy, has since figured in a particular line of thinking—that as far as nuclear deterrence is concerned, even a small probability of retaliation with a couple of nuclear weapons is sufficient to achieve deterrence. With the 'minimum deterrence argument', numbers matter less than the ability to create uncertainty about retaliation. North Korea's ability to withstand American pressure to shut down its nuclear weapons merely confirms the point.

The primary challenge confronting mutually armed nuclear powers today is the achievement of political objectives without bringing nuclear weapons into use. This challenge has defied resolution despite the intellectual heft of two generations of nuclear strategists—and also because the field remains dominated by the conflation of military think and expectations of coercive value.

Military think is a set of beliefs originated by military leaders that privilege the destructive power of nuclear weapons with little or no consideration for political outcomes. In practice, military think tends to maximise the destructive effect on the adversary in order to improve chances of self-preservation. Operationally, the emphasis was on counterforce that targeted nuclear assets. In contrast, civilian strategists who dominated the arena of nuclear strategy sought political utility in nuclear weapons by leveraging their coercive value, which translated into achieving credibility to threaten value targets like population centres and industrial capacity.

The coupling of military think and the pursuit of coercive value that shapes the contours of nuclear belief systems determines the deployment, growth and postures of nuclear arsenals. However, the unease that exists because of the political caveat—that essentially no weapons can be used unless there is certainty that no nuclear retaliation will occur—has defied the operational virtuosity of the military.

Military leaders have created a plethora of operational practices to make deterrence work but none of them can withstand the query, 'What will happen if deterrence fails?' Unless one jettisons perspectives that underpinned the first nuclear age (broadly defined as 1945–1990), the world might repeat the dangers in the second nuclear age (1990 to the present) as well.

Thus, I identify the seven deadly sins of nuclear strategy dogmata that require common global understanding and that point the way to adopt a safer path, one that has some scope of achieving the goal of nuclear disarmament.

NUCLEAR WAR MUST BE WON

The first deadly sin is the idea that nuclear war can be fought and won. George P. Schultz writes of a moment in Geneva in November 1985 when President Ronald Reagan and General Secretary Mikhail Gorbachev met in Geneva and jointly stated, 'Nuclear wars must never be unleashed and that there can be no winners in it.'[1] Towards the end of the Cold War, over 30,000 deliverable weapons existed in the inventory of both countries. Calculations were based on artillery firepower logic and catered for surprise attacks, interceptions and failures inter alia. The idea was to win and was described by some as 'to make the rubble bounce'. Instead of trying to win, the operational focus should be on survivability. Therefore, to meet commitments under the Nuclear Non-Proliferation Treaty (NPT), the idea that nuclear wars cannot be won and should not be fought should be accepted by all nuclear powers.

FIRST STRIKE IS THE BEST DEFENCE

The natural proclivity of military think is to strike first to minimise damage to oneself; this drives the operational imperative to keep weapons on high alert. During a crisis, the most dangerous element is the one in which opposing sides think that they can win if each struck first. Any posture or military technology that demands haste to succeed increases the very probability of war itself. It may be feasible to observe the movement of nuclear assets but it is impossible to judge real intent, especially amidst a nuclear crisis. Defensive preparations can be mistaken for offensive moves, and intelligence and surveillance inputs may be contradictory or unfathomable. All of this could easily overwhelm the judgemental capacity of military and political leaders who, in all probability, will be weighing their decisions after being evacuated to an underground facility or be aboard an aircraft with most of their families facing death on ground. The red line for crisis decision-making is, therefore, placing nuclear weapons on alert. Once nuclear weapons are alerted, every move that is noticed, even if it is defensive, could seem offensive. History is beset with instances of such military thinking being the cause of war itself, the First World War being a prime example. Belief in a first strike also drives the technological search for a greater number of weapons with more accuracy in the name of counterforce. Counterforce is highly questionable in terms of its ability to contain weapons' impact to the adversary's nuclear wherewithal as nuclear effects can neither be easily predicted nor contained. No better proof is required than the ongoing USA–North Korea confrontation, where the effect of nuclear weapons use on North Korea, depending on the quantum of weapons used, could affect China, South Korea and Japan at the very least.

The desire to strike first is also strengthened by the fear of 'bolt from the blue' attacks. Such attacks rest on the assumption that a strike can be launched even without a build-up of political hostilities. While visualising such threats is germane to military thinking, it completely disregards the fact that a bolt from the blue must be massive enough to prevent retaliation. This is impractical, for, with the advent of ballistic missile submarines (SSBNs), it is extremely difficult to be confident about destroying all retaliatory capacity with one massive strike. During the Cold War, this line of thinking spawned dangerous nuclear deployment postures like 'Launch-on-Warning' and 'Launch-under-Attack', which resulted in rapid response and systems on the ready. Several officially acknowledged accidents and near misses of the Cold War bear testimony to the dangers engendered by keeping delivery systems in these postures. The practice of keeping nuclear weapons on alert has endured with a concomitant impact on safety and crisis stability. Military leaders should use the experience of the Cold War to enlighten their political leadership and seek a global agreement on de-alerted postures.

NUCLEAR ESCALATION CAN BE CONTROLLED

The third deadly sin is the belief that nuclear escalation can be controlled. Once nuclear weapons are used, how does one determine that more are not on the way? The natural reaction would be to hit back in revenge in a manner that limits damage to oneself. Some reports indicate that the USA will be soon developing lower-yield warheads, ostensibly to increase the credibility of first use. The moot question is whether the use of low-yield weapons will freeze the exchange or cause the adversary to react in ways that are impossible to anticipate? The idea of projecting a greater probability of use to strengthen deterrence is another instance of military think where the slippery slope of escalation is unacknowledged. Herman Kahn's escalation ladder[2] may be impressive in theory but is impractical for practitioners who have to operate under what the Prussian general and military theorist Cal von Clausewitz described as 'friction', where uncertainty, chance and fog of war are the dominant elements. Escalation control of the type propagated by Herman Kahn ultimately depends on successfully signalling your intentions, which remain unpredictable at best.[3] In addition, escalation control requires bilateral cooperation that is not easy once nuclear weapons are used. Therefore, the idea of a limited nuclear war that can be waged through controlled escalation is a dangerous and impractical illusion.

LIMITED CONVENTIONAL WAR CAN BE FOUGHT UNDER THE NUCLEAR OVERHANG

Conventional wars between nuclear opponents can indeed be fought but the larger point is that such a war cannot achieve any substantial political objectives due to the dangers posed by escalation. If major political objectives are to be achieved, there has to be an increase in the military effort and, therefore, a concomitant rise in escalation dangers. Operational doctrines like 'Anti-Access/Anti-Denial', which supposedly relies on conventional missiles to blind, deafen and destroy major assets like aircraft carriers, will have to account for the adversary's countermeasures. With the impossibility of distinguishing cruise and ballistic missiles carrying conventional or nuclear warheads, the momentum of combat could bring nuclear weapons into play and increase the potential for misjudgement, miscommunication, misperception or accidents. There is also a misplaced faith in conventional firepower that is supposed to deliver victory before nuclear weapons come into play. Firepower on target misses the point that winning battles does not automatically mean winning the war—a fact proven by conflicts in Vietnam, Iraq and Afghanistan. Globally, the professional military education system for senior military leadership must be reoriented to enlighten them about the nuances of the vital link between the application of military force and political outcomes. It has also resulted in military advice that has blindsided the political leadership to the incapacity of military force to achieve political outcomes, particularly within nuclear contexts.

IGNORING LONG-TERM EFFECTS OF NUCLEAR WAR

The fifth deadly sin has been to restrict the view of the impact of nuclear weapons' use to its immediate effects. Targeting calculations were based on blast effect. Such a focus ignored the deadly medium- and long-term climatic consequences despite the fact that by the mid-1970s, studies indicated the potentially catastrophic range of atmospheric, climatic and radiological consequences.[4] These studies took into consideration the longer-term biological effects caused by the enormous amount of dust and smoke generated[5] and also the resultant fires. It meant that even a successful first strike by either adversary would bring about climatic changes[6] that could pose an existential threat to the victor. More recent investigations into catastrophic climate changes make it evident that[7] the quantity of nuclear weapons required to neutralise retaliation capacity makes first strike suicidal. This is an inconvenient truth that has been brushed aside by the military and gives birth to the sixth deadly sin.

NUCLEAR TARGETING IS THE EXCLUSIVE PRESERVE OF THE MILITARY

The sixth deadly sin is the military arrogation of nuclear targeting as its exclusive preserve and its weakening of any attempt at political oversight through obfuscation and secrecy—a point raised by General Lee Butler in his autobiography, *Uncommon Cause*.[8] At one point in the Cold War, Moscow was targeted with 400 nuclear weapons[9] and as late as 1991, Kiev had forty weapons aimed at it.[10] Arguably, there is no one who can carry out nuclear targeting other than military professionals who are required to have credible plans for deterrence failure. However, even if they do, they apply the principles of conventional firepower targeting for which they cannot be blamed as their professional turf is about destruction, derived from a conventional paradigm. The effects on climate, health, environment and food security require different expertise that is barred in the name of secrecy. The military cannot solve this problem and it is only expanded political oversight that should address this.

BALLISTIC MISSILE DEFENCE (BMD) IS USEFUL

The seventh deadly sin is the belief that BMD systems can improve deterrence capability. Deterrence through mutual vulnerability is the cornerstone of stability and the Anti-Ballistic Missile Treaty (ABMT) that was signed in 1972 between the USA and the Soviet Union stipulated that BMD systems be deployed at only two Anti-Ballistic Missile (ABM) complexes, each with a hundred missiles. The underlying logic was that BMD systems could reduce the vulnerability of the command-and-control system, which is the weakest link in nuclear wherewithal. But by 2001, the USA under George W. Bush withdrew from the ABMT based on the argument that a national missile defence was required against rogue states. Since then, most nuclear powers have attempted to develop BMD capability and have invested enormous resources to overcome the challenges posed for creating an effective shield against ballistic missiles. Overall, BMD systems have not been able to cope with the fact that all systems can be overwhelmed by counter-capability. The development of the Hyper Glide Vehicle (HGV) and Multiple Independently Targetable Reentry Vehicle (MIRV) are recent illustrations that BMD systems cannot provide the necessary degree of confidence for successful defence. Retrospectively, all that the US withdrawal has achieved is the triggering of an arms race that has had a chain reaction on Russia, China, India and Pakistan. However, the rogue state argument has some merit, in the sense that rogue actors within a state could fire a small quantum of missiles against an adversary state. Limited BMD on the lines of the lapsed ABMT could cater to this rogue actor threat. There is great merit in the argument that the world will be much safer with a global ABMT on the lines similar to the earlier treaty, which permitted two ABM sites, which should preferably be sited to cater to the rogue threat.

It is not too late to resurrect the ABMT as, by now, the illusion that BMD will provide reasonable protection has proven illusory. The old treaty caters to the rare possibility of rogue actors getting hold of nuclear weapons and attempting to launch them. The technological ability to perennially overcome BMD must find global acceptance and, therefore, pave the way towards an ABMT. This should immediately halt the BMD ripple effect that today encompasses the USA–China–Russia–India–Pakistan scenarios.

SEVEN DEADLY SINS—SO WHAT?

The USA–North Korea confrontation and several earlier historically recorded nuclear threats have proved beyond doubt that coercion based on first strike is a paper tiger. Politically and militarily, nuclear weapons inhibit nuclear powers from fighting wars. Instead, they opt to achieve their political objectives by other means. The methodologies adopted by Russia, China and Pakistan in the Crimea/Ukraine, the South China Sea and India–Pakistan confrontation are illustrative of the other means that combine the covert and the overt to keep a distance from the big fight.

Nuclear powers should revisit the role of nuclear weapons and realise that nuclear weapons have, at best, only a core deterrence role. Once this is accepted politically, the most suitable policy option is no first use (NFU) and an agreement on a global no-first-use (GNFU) treaty. While the NFU offers no silver bullet during crises, it lowers nuclear dangers and makes the world safer, especially during peacetime by promoting operational postures that focus more on survivability than rapid reaction. To a limited extent, NFU can bolster crisis stability if a nation declares that its force application will be restricted to the conventional sphere. The USA declaring an NFU policy before striking North Korea with conventional weapons would hold at least some limited promise that nuclear weapons will not come into play. But any perception that nuclear weapons have been alerted by the USA could hold the danger of nuclear use by North Korea. This would amount to North Korea committing suicide due to the fear of death. Ultimately, the better option is to refrain from the big fight wherever nuclear weapons are involved and avoid the fourth deadly sin of fighting a conventional war under the nuclear overhang.

The lessons of the first nuclear age encapsulated in the seven deadly sins provide the seeds of wisdom and the opportunity to make the world safer by distancing ourselves from outdated dogmas anchored in discredited military think and the futile pursuit of coercive value. If the present global momentum towards nuclear catastrophe is to be reversed, a deeper dialogue on the seven deadly sins between military and political leaders at both the national and international levels is needed. Interrogating nuclear strategy through the lens of experience derived from the follies of the first nuclear age could significantly increase the chance for peace in the second nuclear age. A major milestone in the process could be a GNFU treaty.

NOTES

1 George P. Shultz, "The War That Must Never Be Fought" (Defining Ideas, Hoover Institution, March 12, 2015), accessed on July 23, 2020, https://www.hoover.org/research/war-must-never-be-fought-0.

2 Herman Kahn, *On Escalation: Metaphors and Scenarios* (London and New York: Routledge, 2009).

3 Stephen J. Cimbala, "Nuclear Deterrence and Escalation: Strategy without Control, Arms Control," 11, no 1 (1990): 5–48, doi: 10.1080/01440389008403920.

4 Matthew R. Francis. "When Carl Sagan Warned the World about Nuclear Winter," *Smithsonian Magazine*, November 15, 2017, accessed on July 23, 2020, https://www.smithsonianmag.com/science-nature/when-carl-sagan-warned-world-about-nuclear-winter-180967198/, accessed March 31, 2022.

5 R.P. Turco, Owen B. Toon, T.P. Ackerman, J.B. Pollack, and Carl Sagan, "Nuclear Winter: Global Consequences of Multiple Nuclear Explosions," *Science*, 222, no 4,630 (December 23, 1983): 1283–1292, doi: 10.1126/science.222.4630.1283.

6 A. Barrie Pittock, Thomas P. Ackerman, Paul J. Crutzen, Michael C. MacCracken, and Charles S. Shapiro. *Environmental Consequences of Nuclear War: Volume I – Physical and Atmospheric Effects* (Chichester, New York, Brisbane, Toronto, Singapore: John Wiley & Sons, 1986), accessed on March 31, 2022, https://scope.dge.carnegiescience.edu/SCOPE_28_1/SCOPE_28I.html.

7 Michael J. Mills, Owen B. Toon, Julia Lee-Taylor, and Alan Robock, "Multidecadal Global Cooling and Unprecedented Ozone Loss Following a Regional Nuclear Conflict," *Earth's Future* Volume 2, Issue 4 (February 2014): 161–176, accessed on March 31, 2022, https://agupubs.onlinelibrary.wiley.com/doi/full/10.1002/2013ef000205.

8 Janne E. Nolan, "Cold Combat: The Memoir of a Nuclear Convert," *Bulletin of the Atomic Scientists* 73, no 3 (2017): 192–195, doi: 10.1080/00963402.2017.1315042, accessed on March 31, 2022, https://www.tandfonline.com/doi/abs/10.1080/00963402.2017.1315042?tab=permissions&scroll=top.

9 Hans M. Kristensen, Matthew G. McKinzie, and Robert S. Norris, "The Protection Paradox," *Bulletin of the Atomic Scientists* 60, no 2 (2004): 68–77, doi: 10.1080/00963402.2004.11460771, accessed on March 31, 2022, https://www.tandfonline.com/doi/abs/10.1080/00963402.2004.11460771.

10 Ike Jeanes, *Forecast and Solution: Grappling with the Nuclear, a Trilogy for Everyone* (Pulaski: Pocahontas, 1996), 305.

Chapter 3

IS NUCLEAR DETERRENCE A COST-EFFECTIVE POLICY?

Bruno Tertrais

We propose here a net assessment of nuclear deterrence, that is, a balance of its real and possible costs and benefits in all domains, at the national and global levels. The conclusion will suggest that while a rational calculation of said costs and benefits is impossible given the number of unknown and hardly quantifiable elements, there are good arguments to state that it remains overall a reasonable policy, even though it is, to some extent, an act of faith.

THE BENEFITS OF NUCLEAR DETERRENCE

Benefits at the National Level

For a country, the primary benefit of acquiring nuclear weapons is, of course, to ensure the protection of its very existence and/or its most vital interests. There are many ways to define those (which, in turn, help to delineate the nuclear threshold) but a good benchmark is the late Sir Michael Quinlan's apt formula that 'a nuclear state is a state that no one can afford to make desperate'.[1]

But nuclear acquisition can also include significant collateral benefits. The possession of nuclear weapons reinforces a country's independence and freedom of action. A country also gains strategically and politically by being *perceived* as independent. This includes reducing dependence on a foreign security guarantor. Examples in this respect include France, China, Israel, Pakistan and North Korea. Alternatively, nuclear weapons can be used as a means of influence on a key partner: historically speaking, the UK conceived its nuclear deterrent as a means to maintain a close strategic relationship with the USA.

From a strictly military standpoint, nuclear weapons provide 'more bang for the buck', which essentially is more overall explosive power per monetary unit spent. Because of the demanding nature of nuclear deterrence, the national development of a nuclear arsenal also contributes—to varying degrees depending on the level of technological and operational ambition—to scientific, industrial and military excellence.

The Nuclear Peace: Statistical Evidence

Have nuclear weapons made a decisive contribution to world peace? The answer is almost certainly 'yes'. The statistical evidence rests on the absence, since 1945, of major power war, major war between nuclear-armed countries and major military attacks against nuclear-armed or nuclear-protected countries.

Exhibit A in support of nuclear deterrence is the absence of major power war since 1945.[2] If one defines great powers as the five permanent members of the United Nations Security Council (UNSC), which are also the five nuclear weapons states in the sense of the NPT, clearly there was never any open military conflict between them, even less a major war (1,000 battle-related deaths in a single year). A broader definition to include Germany and Japan, which are protected by the US nuclear umbrella, also makes the cut.

John Lewis Gaddis forged the expression 'Long Peace' forty years after the end of the Second World War; it is now more than seven decades old. No comparable period of great power peace has ever existed in the history of modern states—perhaps not even since the Roman Empire. For instance, there were two dozen conflicts among major powers in the equivalent amount of time following the Treaties of Westphalia (1648), and nine between the Vienna Congress (1815) and the First World War. Is there not here an exceptional proposition that deserves an explanation?

The idea of a Long Peace has been challenged on the grounds that it was not so exceptional. Here, coding (i.e., What is a major power war? What is the relevant duration of the Long Peace?) is the bone of contention. Some would mark its beginning only in 1947 (the Iron Curtain speech), in 1949 (the first Soviet nuclear test) or even in 1953 (the end of the Korean War). Some would end it as early as 1989: the narrowest definition thus leads to a 'Short Long Peace' of only thirty-six years. If one simultaneously discounts some past events as being non-major power wars, then previous periods of non-war become lengthier, thus negating the exceptionality of the Long Peace.[3] Two authors claim that 'historical periods of major power peace are frequently as long as forty-two years'.[4] This is unpersuasive: the coding of the Korean War as a major power is debatable, and most importantly, there is no reason to conclude the Long Peace in 1989 or any posterior year. Even if one uses 1953 as a starting point and demotes several past major power wars, sixty-six years without a great power war is an exceptional duration.[5]

Exhibit B is the absence of any major war between two nuclear-armed states. Recent studies have shown that the possession of nuclear weapons by two countries significantly reduced—all things equal—the likelihood of war between them.[6] Events in Asia since 1949 provide an interesting test case. China and India fought a war in 1962 but have refrained from resorting to arms against each other ever since. There were three India–Pakistan wars before both the countries became nuclear; but since the late 1980s (when the two countries acquired a minimum nuclear capability), none of the two has launched any *significant* air or land operations against the other. Neither the Ussuri crisis of 1969 nor the Kargil conflict of 1999 qualify as major wars (none caused the death of more than 1,000).[7]

Exhibit C is the fact that no nuclear-armed country has ever been invaded, nor has its territory been the object of a major military attack. The 1973 Yom Kippur War and the 1982 Falklands War are often suggested as counterexamples. But these are not persuasive. Israel was invaded in 1948 but in 1973, Arab nations deliberately limited their operations to disputed territories. Likewise, India refrained from penetrating Pakistani territory at the occasion of the South Asian crises of the 1990s and the 2000s, whereas it had done so in 1965 and 1971. The Falklands Islands were a British Dependent Territory for which nothing indicates that it was covered by nuclear deterrence; it would be erroneous to take these two events as evidence that extended deterrence does not make sense, since the latter is meant to cover interests that are much more important to the protector than non-essential territories. During the Cold War, Germany was much more 'vital' to the USA than, say, Puerto Rico.[8]

The statistical evidence makes a good case for the fact that for nearly seventy years, there has not been any major power war, that nuclear-armed countries have not gone to war against each other and that non-nuclear-armed countries have refrained from going to war against them or their allies. There seems to be correlation. But is there causation?

The Nuclear Peace: Analytical Evidence

The dominant view is that nuclear deterrence has indeed been a key, if not *the* key, to the decline of major war. It worked mostly by fear and to some extent by interest.

Nuclear weapons, when mated with ballistic missiles (and even more with thermonuclear weapons), brought a revolution in warfare: the near-certainty of fast, massive, large-scale retaliation. Due to planning, targeting and command, control, communications and intelligence (C3I) advances, the ability to retaliate became less and less contingent on whom the aggressor would be and where he would attack. The peculiar effects of nuclear weapons and the memories of Hiroshima have given them a specific aura, which has been made even stronger by the development of thermonuclear weapons, the theory of 'nuclear winter' and various apocalyptic scenarios associated with escalation to the extremes. The absence of any precedent for a true nuclear war makes it even more unpredictable than conventional war.

It is possible that nuclear balances of power, models and equations of nuclear use were much less relevant to the success of nuclear deterrence than the mere combination of a significant arsenal and the apparent will to use it. John Lewis Gaddis made the most forceful case for nuclear deterrence: major powers feared nuclear war and took deliberate precautions to reduce the risks of direct conflict.[9] It is indeed likely that nuclear deterrence has limited the scope and intensity of possible conflict among the major countries. If crises in Europe, as well as wars in Asia and the Middle East, did not turn into global conflicts, it is probably due largely to nuclear weapons.

Without nuclear weapons, Washington might have hesitated to guarantee the security of Europe and might have returned to isolationism. Without US protection, the temptation for Moscow to grab territory in Western Europe would have been stronger. To assert that nuclear deterrence was key in the preservation of major power peace, one does not need to postulate a Soviet desire for war: as Quinlan put it, it is enough to argue that 'had armed conflict not been so manifestly intolerable the ebb and flow of friction might have managed with less caution, and a slide sooner or later into major war, on the pattern of 1914 or 1939, might have been less unlikely'.[10]

Unconvincing Alternative Explanations

Those supporting alternative explanations generally do not rule out a role for nuclear weapons but argue that they played, at best, a marginal and non-necessary role in the preservation of peace.

'Realists' often argue that the stability of the Cold War system was the dominant factor. But that might be a reversal of cause and effect. Nuclear weapons were a central element of the US commitment to European security. They did as much to consolidate alliances as to break them: the US nuclear guarantee (and access to nuclear sharing) was a non-trivial dimension of the attraction and staying power of the North Atlantic Treaty Organization (NATO), and France stayed in the Atlantic Alliance after developing its nuclear force. Regarding the post-Cold War period, the US hegemony might very well be a key cause of the absence of major war but it remains underwritten by the US nuclear primacy.

The construction of a new global institutional order based on collective security is insufficient as an explanation: the order based on the League of Nations—the first international organisation set up to ensure global peace—did nothing to prevent the Second World War. Economic interdependence is not a satisfying explanation regarding the Cold War: there was no such thing between the Western and Communist blocs. Neither is the progress of democratisation around the world: the risk of major power war was, and remains, between democracies and authoritarian regimes. Perhaps the creation of the European Community in 1957 became a powerful barrier against the return of war on the continent? The argument confuses cause and effect: the integration process would have been much more difficult without the USA/NATO umbrella.

The delegitimisation of armed violence since the Second World War is a more powerful argument. It rests on the observation that the number of wars and war-related deaths has been steadfastly declining since 1945. If true, then one does not need the hypothesis of nuclear deterrence. A related argument is the consolidation of a norm against territorial conquest and annexation of territory by force. In the three decades that followed the end of the Second World War, there were still many instances of territorial conquests and post-conflict annexations but much less so in the past four decades. In addition, some of the most significant attempts to conquer territory by force have failed, such as the Iran–Iraq War, the Falklands War and the Iraq War; this may have contributed to the dissuasion of forceful territorial aggrandisement. It has also helped that decolonisation and the creation of several dozens of new countries have reduced the number of pro-independence and secession movements. Perhaps the behaviour of Russia in Ukraine, and of China in its maritime environment, will put an end to this era; but generally speaking, it seems indeed that wars of territorial conquest are no longer considered a normal instrument of external policies.

However, such cultural arguments have limitations.

If war fatigue existed, one would have to argue that it did not exist in Europe after 1870, or after 1918. (It did.) One would have to posit the existence of a 'threshold effect' in 1945; to assume that war fatigue was transmitted from one generation to another—given that the Second World War generation is now gone—and to discard the many minor wars and military interventions of the post-1945 era deliberately initiated by former parties to the 1939–1945 conflict.

The claim that war is on the decline has been challenged on statistical and analytical grounds. It is argued that the usual metric of battle-related deaths may be misleading, either because the downward trend reflects improvement in preventive care, battlefield medicine, military and soldier protection; or because it does not represent the true overall costs of collective armed violence. Additionally, the realist, liberal and constructivist explanations can hardly account for the absence of major war involving Israel and its neighbours since 1973, or between India and Pakistan since these countries became full-fledged nuclear-armed countries in the late 1990s.

As Lawrence Freedman puts it:

> Given the undoubted existence of deep antagonism between East and West, it seemed grudging not to attribute at least part of the credit for avoiding yet another total war to the dread of global confrontation involving nuclear exchanges and to the policies adopted, at times by both sides, to reinforce this dread by means of deliberate deterrence.[11]

Explaining the Long Peace *mostly* by nuclear deterrence might be an implementation of Occam's Razor: sometimes the simplest answer is the best one.

Other Global Benefits

Extended deterrence has also contributed to the Long Peace. No country covered by a nuclear guarantee has ever been the target of a major attack. Here again, evidence can be found *a contrario*. The USA refrained from invading Cuba in 1962 but did not hesitate in invading Grenada, Panama or Iraq. The Soviet Union invaded Hungary, Czechoslovakia and Afghanistan but not a single US treaty ally. China has refrained from a full-scale invasion of Taiwan, which benefits from a US de facto defence commitment, even if ambiguous. North Korea invaded its southern neighbour in 1950 after Washington had excluded it from its 'defensive perimeter' but has refrained from doing so since Seoul has been covered with a nuclear guarantee. The USA's allies South Vietnam or Kuwait were not covered by US nuclear protection. Russia could afford to invade Georgia or Ukraine because they were not NATO members.

By shielding Western European countries from possible Soviet aggression, extended deterrence allowed for the peaceful reconstruction of the continent.[12] At the end of the day, nuclear deterrence is perhaps even a form of global common good. For instance, without nuclear peace, would Asia as a whole—including those countries not protected by nuclear weapons—have known the peace and stability that allowed for its massive transformation and development, leading to hundreds of millions of human beings being lifted out of poverty?

The existence of nuclear weapons has forced great powers to sit down and talk to each other. The dangers of nuclear war have contributed to the realisation that dialogue is necessary—notably through arms control negotiations. The fear of nuclear war led the two superpowers to create a mesh of cooperative security arrangements including the establishment of 'hotlines', the Strategic Arms Limitations Talks (SALT) process, the drafting of the NPT, the conclusion of the Helsinki Final Act, etc. Patrick Morgan goes so far as saying that nuclear weapons may have hastened the end of the Cold War—by giving confidence to Soviet leaders that the country's survival would be assured even after the loss of the Eastern European *glacis.*[13]

THE COSTS OF NUCLEAR DETERRENCE

The Costs of Nuclear Acquisition

Budgetary costs of nuclear acquisition have been significant for all countries. Such costs vary, of course, depending on the degree of external assistance that a country has received and of its operational ambitions. Maintenance costs are significant, too, especially when seeking a reliable, permanent and up-to-date deterrent. Nuclear acquisition can also have various externalities: effects of atmospheric testing (which is no longer practised) on the biosphere or accidents. It can have reputational costs, for countries that are not nuclear weapons states (an NPT) or which have violated their international commitments. In such a case, sanctions can be significant; however, sanctions have never led any State to give up its nuclear arsenal.[14]

Extended deterrence can weigh on the security provider. He may have to acquire specific types (e.g., dual-capable aircraft for deployment abroad) or numbers (e.g., 'staying first') of nuclear weapons to ensure both reassurance and deterrence. Do positive nuclear security assurances also create a 'commitment trap'? This is dubious. It is very hard to imagine that a nuclear-armed country would feel compelled to use nuclear weapons just for the sake of maintaining the global credibility of its security commitments.

In fact, another category of costs is the responsibilities that a nuclear country may have to have regarding maintaining the tradition of non-use as well as the promotion of disarmament and non-proliferation. As the saying goes, with great power comes great responsibilities—and this is particularly true in the nuclear domain. The latter two are legally mandated responsibilities for the NPT nuclear weapons states, but voluntary for the others.

Are nuclear weapons alliance-breakers? This was a USA fear during the Cold War. However, the acquisition of nuclear weapons by the UK and France ended up being recognised by their NATO allies as making a positive contribution to the overall security of the Atlantic Alliance, including through the existence of three separate nuclear decision centres (Washington, London and Paris) which, arguably, reinforces the uncertainty about a NATO reaction to aggression—and thus deterrence.

The Strategic Costs of Nuclear Relationships

If nuclear weapons have lowered the risk of major war, they may also have contributed to increasing the risk of lower-scale conflict. The stability/instability paradox conceptualised by Glenn Snyder in 1965 seems to have been a reality: if nuclear weapons did prevent major armed conflict between nuclear-armed adversaries, *but* this came at the price of the multiplication of bloody indirect wars and sub-conventional conflicts, from the East–West context (the Berlin crises) to the India–Pakistan theatre.[15] Fear of war may have moderated superpower behaviour and restrained Washington and Moscow during major crises, but at the same time, encouraged them to take dangerous initiatives, as Richard Ned Lebow and Janice Gross Stein suggest.[16] They may, as suggested by the work of Robert Jervis, have incited fear, hubris and misperceptions, making them inherently destabilising.[17] The argument made above by Patrick Morgan is also valid in reverse: nuclear weapons may have contributed to ending the Cold War peacefully and subsequently, made it easier for Moscow to challenge Georgia's and Ukraine's turn westwards.

Other possible strategic costs are more debatable.

Do nuclear weapons help in coercing opponents or allies? This would be the downside—or a security dilemma illustration—of the 'freedom of action' described above: a gain for one country would be a loss for others. However, this remains a disputed claim. 'Our analysis of nineteen historical cases demonstrated that nuclear coercion rarely works at all,' write two authors.[18]

Lebow and Stein, as well as John Lewis Gaddis, argue for their part that nuclear weapons may have perpetuated the Cold War.[19] Maybe they made détente and peaceful coexistence easier but real peace more difficult, in addition to extending the life of communism.

Finally, the action-reaction dynamics of nuclear weapons acquisition, generally called the arms races, can weigh heavily on national budgets as shown by the USA–Soviet competition of the Cold War. But the mad competition of that time is far from being an inevitable by-product of nuclear acquisition. And most importantly, this is not a nuclear-specific problem.

The Ultimate Cost: Nuclear Weapons Use

There remains, of course, the ultimate possible cost of nuclear deterrence: the consequences of nuclear use, which, in some scenarios, would be regional or even global, as testified by the 2010s debate on the so-called 'humanitarian consequences' of the use of nuclear weapons.

Leaving aside the question of a possible accidental detonation, there are three broad scenarios of nuclear use: unauthorised nuclear employment, inadvertent nuclear escalation due to a false alert or alarm and deliberate nuclear employment.

Any discussion of these scenarios must begin with the obvious: no such event has taken place since 1945. This suggests, at a minimum, that the risk is probably not as high as some fear-mongering commentators would have it. In a 2017 publication, this author took an in-depth look at the various incidents that took place since the end of the Second World War; he suggested that there is, in fact, little empirical basis for the claim that the world has stood many times 'on the brink' of nuclear catastrophe and that 'luck' is not a necessary hypothesis to explain the absence of nuclear use.[20]

This does not close the discussion—far from it. But we propose, as food for thought, the following metaphor: a very small daily probability of a deadly car accident has to be balanced against the benefits of driving to work every day.[21] The risk of nuclear use is real, and that is the very basis of nuclear deterrence. The latter remains a fragile construct. During the Cold War, the nuclear balance was never as 'stable' as some retrospectively suggest.[22]

Nuclear weapons are a valuable investment: only one country (South Africa) has given up, indigenously developed weapons; also, some of those who gave them up, sometimes seem to regret it. What about the net assessment of nuclear deterrence at the global level? There is no possible rational calculation here: there are too many factors at play, including non-quantifiable ones.

Calculations about the value and stability of nuclear deterrence also depend on doctrines and their perceptions: for instance, a universal NFU doctrine would vastly decrease the risk of nuclear war if, and only if, it was universally believed. However, on the contrary, uncertainties about the real nuclear intents of an adversary having declared an NFU doctrine can make a strategic situation unstable. Thus, NFU declarations can be beneficial from a diplomatic standpoint—signalling nuclear restraint—but detrimental from a strategic standpoint.

Ultimately, nuclear deterrence is an act of faith. Nuclear weapons are an imperfect instrument and nuclear deterrence has significant downsides. It is a 'powerful but very dangerous medicine'.[23] A reasonable conclusion would thus be to see it as a useful evil and a provisional, imperfect measure, or as an insurance against the failure of the liberal order. As Winston Churchill put it at a time when the nuclear age was just a few years old: 'Be careful above all things not to let go of the atomic weapon until you are sure and more than sure that other means of preserving peace are in your hands.'[24]

NOTES

1 Michael Quinlan, "Thinking about Nuclear Weapons" (Whitehall Paper, The Royal United Services Institute, London, 1997), 30.
2 John Lewis Gaddis, *The Long Peace* (New York: Oxford University Press, 1990).
3 Discounting the Franco-Spanish War of 1823 and the First Russian–Turkish War of 1828–1829 leads to thirty-three years of great power peace (1815–1848); discounting the Second Russian–Prussian War of 1877–1878 and the Russian–Japanese War of 1905 leads to forty-three years of peace (1871–1914).
4 Randolph M. Siverson and Michael D. Ward, "The Long Peace: A Reconsideration," *International Organization* 56, no 3 (Summer 2002).
5 Ibid. Another argument is that it is statistically irrelevant. See Pasquale Cirillo and Nassim Nicholas Taleb, *What Are the Chances of a Third World War?*, www.fooledbyrandomness.com; Cirillo and Taleb, "On the Statistical Properties and Tail Risk of Violent Conflict," *Physica A: Statistical Mechanics and its Applications*, vol. 452, June 15, 2016. However, Cirillo and Taleb do not limit their analysis to great power wars and do not address whether or not the absence of *any* great power war (be it one that caused 1,000 or 10,000,000 deaths) in the past sixty-three years is a statistical anomaly.
6 James F. Pasley, "Chicken Pax Atomica: The Cold War Stability of Nuclear Deterrence", *Journal of International and Area Studies* 15, no 2 (December 2008); Robert Rauchhaus, "Evaluating the Nuclear Peace Hypothesis: A Quantitative Approach", *Journal of Conflict Resolution* 53, no 2 (April 2009).
7 Although the Correlates of War (CoW) data set lists Kargil as a major war, the sum of the official tally of battle-related deaths is under 1,000.
8 This does not mean that *any* absence of open conflict between two nuclear-armed nations can be explained by nuclear deterrence. India and China have fought over disputed territory in 1962 but have refrained from doing so since then—but there may be other factors at work.
9 John Lewis Gaddis et. al., ed., *Cold War Statesmen Confront the Bomb: Nuclear Diplomacy Since 1945* (New York: Oxford University Press, 1999).

10 Quinlan, *Thinking about Nuclear Weapons: Principles, Problems, Prospects* (Oxford: Oxford University Press, 2009), 28.

11 Lawrence Freedman, *Deterrence* (Cambridge: Polity Press, 2004), 13–14.

12 Extended deterrence is also a powerful nuclear non-proliferation instrument: countries which benefit from a nuclear 'umbrella' are less likely to develop nuclear weapons.

13 Patrick M. Morgan, *Deterrence Now* (Cambridge: Cambridge University Press, 2003), 27.

14 It can be argued that sanctions on South Africa contributed to the downfall of the apartheid regime and, indirectly, to its renunciation of nuclear weapons. Such sanctions were not imposed because of nuclear weapons acquisition (which was kept secret at the time).

15 Robert Rauchhaus, "Evaluating the Nuclear Peace Hypothesis: A Quantitative Approach," *Journal of Conflict Resolution* 53, no 2 (April 2009).

16 Richard Ned Lebow and Janice Gross Stein, "Deterrence and the Cold War," *Political Science Quarterly* 10, no 2 (Summer 1995): 180.

17 Robert Jervis, *The Meaning of the Nuclear Revolution: Statecraft and the Prospect for Armageddon* (Ithaca, New York: Cornell University Press, 1989).

18 Todd S. Sechser and Matthew Fuhrmann, *Nuclear Weapons and Coercive Diplomacy* (Cambridge: Cambridge University Press, 2017), 239.

19 John Lewis Gaddis, *We Now Know: Rethinking Cold War History* (New York: Oxford University Press, 1997); Richard Ned Lebow and Janice Gross Stein, *We All Lost the Cold War* (Princeton: Princeton University Press, 1994).

20 Bruno Tertrais, "A Deux Doigts de la Catastrophe? Un Réexamen des Crises Nucléaires Depuis 1945," (Recherches & Documents [April 2017], Fondation pour la Recherche Stratégique, Paris, 2017). A shorter version of this text was published in English as Bruno Tertrais, "On the Brink, Really? Revisiting Nuclear Close Calls Since 1945," *The Washington Quarterly* 40, no 2 (Summer 2017).

21 In a conversation with the author, Lt General Prakash Menon cogently argues that extended deterrence is the equivalent (for the guarantor) of driving faster. I share this view—the more the countries protected by a nuclear umbrella, the higher the chances of a deterrence breakdown involving the guarantor.

22 Archives show that the Soviet Union did believe that NATO would use nuclear weapons in a major war and thus planned for massive pre-emptive nuclear operations against its forces. If war had broken out despite nuclear deterrence, then the risk of early escalation might have been greater than thought at the time. The same phenomenon could be at work today in South Asia despite the apparent success of nuclear deterrence so far.

23 Lebow and Stein, "Deterrence and the Cold War," 180.

24 Winston Churchill, "Address to the US Congress," January 17,1952.

Chapter 4

NUCLEAR WEAPONS AND THE GLOBAL SECURITY ENVIRONMENT

Rajesh Basrur[1]

After the optimism of the early post-Cold War era, the hope that nuclear weapons might be relegated to a relatively marginal role in international politics has receded. In the quarter century from 1986 to 2011, the global total of stockpiled nuclear warheads had fallen from a peak of 64,099 to 10,565. Since then, the momentum has slowed, with numbers down to 9,220 in 2017.[2] Long after the end of the Cold War, some 2,000 remain on high alert.[3]

Moreover, the structure of arms control built during and immediately after the Cold War is breaking down. The USA walked out of the 1972 Anti-Ballistic Missile (ABM) Treaty in 2002 and quit the 1987 Intermediate Nuclear Forces (INF) Treaty in August 2019. The then President Donald Trump labelled the New Strategic Arms Reduction Treaty (START) of 2010 'a bad deal'.[4] The Comprehensive Test Ban Treaty (CTBT) lies comatose; negotiations on the Fissile Material Control Treaty languish; and none of the nuclear-armed states is willing to sign on to the 2017 Treaty on the Prohibition of Nuclear Weapons. Analysts have drawn attention to the onset of a 'second nuclear age', said to be characterised by a high degree of instability as a result of the proliferation of nuclear powers and the development of new technologies.[5]

The commonplace impression that the present nuclear strategic landscape is less stable than that of the Cold War era is not quite grounded in fact, at least, not yet. During the Cold War era (1945–1991) there were nine nuclear powers: five overt (the USA, the Soviet Union, the UK, France and China) and four covert (Israel, India, Pakistan and South Africa). The total remains the same in the post-Cold War period (1991–2019), with one subtracted (South Africa) and one added (North Korea). The number of significant military confrontations in which nuclear war has loomed large is four for the first period: the US–Soviet Berlin crisis of 1961; the US–Soviet

Cuban Missile Crisis of 1962; the air-to-air and ground-to-air combat between Chinese and American forces during the Vietnam War in the mid-1960s; and the Sino-Soviet border clashes of 1969. In the current era, there have been five crises under the nuclear shadow: the India–Pakistan crises of 1999 (Kargil), 2001–2002 (Operation Parakram) and 2019 (the Balakot strikes), and the India–China crises of 2017 (Doklam) and 2020 (Ladakh).

It is sometimes argued that the current era is less stable because, whereas the Cold War antagonists were distant from each other, the same is not the case with, say, India and Pakistan or with India and China. But this is not an accurate depiction of the two realities. The risks pertaining to the two time frames are comparable. True, major cities in South Asia are extremely close to enemy nuclear-weapons systems; but the same was true of the USA and the Soviet Union, which targeted each other with high-speed, land-based systems (notably late-Cold War intermediate-range missiles) as well as sea-based systems. We tend to forget that Pershing II missiles fired from West Germany had the capacity to hit Moscow in six minutes. Moreover, for both periods, the distinction between the so-called theatre and strategic weapons is largely meaningless. The pace and speed of escalation once the nuclear threshold is crossed cannot be known in advance and decision-makers would perforce have had to assume the worst at the outset of any conflict.

While these examples show an even distribution between the two time frames, a truly significant difference is that three of the Cold War crises mentioned above (all except the US–China case) involved the overt mobilisation of nuclear forces, whereas that has not been the case in the present period. Threats to use nuclear weapons against adversaries were made periodically then but none has been made in the current age. From this perspective, the nuclear environment appears much less dangerous than it was earlier.

But even if we live in a relatively safer nuclear world, there is no room for complacency given the cataclysmic capacity of nuclear weapons, which obliges us to worry about low-probability, high-consequence events. And there is certainly a good reason to be troubled about current trends and what they might augur for the future. Despite the drawing down of tensions in comparison with the Cold War era, the USA and Russia have continued to keep substantial numbers of their nuclear weapons on hair-trigger alert.[6] Beyond this, there are two major factors that generate uncertainty today: (a) changes in the distribution of power among states; and (b) the emergence of new technologies that fall under the rubric of the 'fourth industrial revolution'.[7]

POWER SHIFTS

It is a truism that major changes in the distribution of military and economic power tend to produce tectonic effects in international politics, often war.[8] The decline of the British Empire and the rise of Germany produced two world wars. The rise of the Soviet Union to challenge American dominance led to a 'cold' war because an actual war was too terrible to contemplate (though the prospect of it occurring remained prominent). Today, the world appears to be undergoing another major power transition. Though the USA still remains preponderant, its power is steadily waning in relative terms—a process that has become evident in the twenty-first century. In 2000, the gross domestic product (GDP) of the USA was 30.53 per cent of world GDP; by 2018, it had dropped to 23.88 per cent of world GDP.[9] In contrast, China's GDP grew during the same years from 3.61 per cent to 15 per cent of world GDP. Put another way, China's GDP as a proportion of US GDP during this time frame grew from 11.81 per cent to 66.40 per cent.

In military spending, the USA outspends other major powers but a similar trend is visible.[10] In 2000, Chinese military spending ($22.9 billion) constituted just 7.6 per cent of USA's ($301.7 billion). By 2018, the gap was significantly narrower: Chinese military expenditure ($250 billion) was now 38.53 per cent of American spending ($648 billion). The difference in their respective rates of growth is remarkable: China's military spending during this period grew by 990 per cent as compared to the growth in US spending (115 per cent).

This power shift has brought growing friction between the two states. Indeed, the spurt in China's economic growth and military spending has been a source of apprehension for others as well, causing rising tension between China and other major powers, notably India and Japan. A pattern of intensified balance-of-power politics among nuclear (and non-nuclear) powers has been apparent. The chief areas of focus are the South China Sea and the East China Sea, where China has territorial and maritime disputes with several Southeast Asian states and Japan, with the USA—playing the role of global policeman—rejecting Chinese boundary claims, actively displaying its military power in the region and insisting on freedom of navigation and a 'rules-based-order'.[11] At a lower level of intensity, similar tensions have arisen in the Indian Ocean, with China, India and the USA as the main players.

On another front, the revival of the Russian power has brought renewed tensions between Washington and Moscow. Initially, the post-Cold War weakening of Russia enabled NATO and the European Union (EU) to expand their presence eastwards, which was perceived as threatening by the Kremlin. Vladimir Putin, who came to power in 2000, has been able to stabilise Russia's economy and revive its military power, the latter with a strong focus on nuclear weapons. Russia's 'blowback' action in asserting control over Eastern Europe and annexing Crimea has ratcheted up the tension between it and NATO and led to Cold War-type competition in other areas as well, notably Syria.

In Asia, the India–China rivalry has come under a nuclear overhang after India's 1998 nuclear tests. With the rise of China and the dismantling of the Soviet Union, India has moved to forge a closer defence relationship with the USA even as it seeks arms from other countries as well. Growing India–China tension has resulted in regular border confrontations, including major ones in in the summer of 2017 at the India–Bhutan–China tri-junction area known as Doklam, and a more violent one that began in 2020.[12] China, unwilling to accept India as a potential peer, has sought to contain it by tightening its alliance-like relationship with Pakistan. The latter, though a nuclear-armed state, has nevertheless been increasingly worried by India's rapid economic and military growth after the 1990s. Seeing the prospect of gaining control over Jammu and Kashmir fading, it has adopted a strategy of actively backing jihadis based on its soil,[13] which has increased the tension between the two countries and led to a series of fresh military engagements along their border, most notably Indian ground and air strikes on Pakistani territory.[14]

Finally, the growth of North Korean nuclear capability has had two effects. First, it has raised tensions between Washington and Pyongyang, though no major crisis has occurred thus far.[15] And second, it has led to a new interest in crossing the nuclear threshold in Japan and South Korea.[16] While the potential for new nuclear powers to emerge remains low today, it cannot be ruled out. An expanded membership of the club of nuclear powers would undoubtedly complicate the already weak universe of arms control.

The big picture is one of considerable uncertainty. The waning of American power brings up the possibility that states which had hitherto relied on the US nuclear umbrella might, at some point, decide to go nuclear themselves. In addition to Japan and South Korea, Europe might be tempted to decrease its reliance on Washington and embark on a unified 'Eurobomb'.[17] Meanwhile, as tensions associated with Iran's possible nuclear ambitions grow, the acquisition of nuclear weapons by Saudi Arabia and the United Arab Emirates (UAE) somewhere down the road cannot be ruled out. In addition, it could be argued that, in a world where social media plays an expanding role, considerations of image and status may also drive political leaderships to be less amenable to compromise.[18]

While there is no immediate cause for alarm, there is undoubtedly a rise in tensions all around, more specifically, among several nuclear powers in Asia. This sets the stage for other factors to add more layers to a situation already fraught with the prospect of military conflict.

On the positive side, the constraints imposed by nuclear weapons are better understood with the experience of the Cold War, particularly the excessive pursuit of marginal advantage in the fiercely competitive relationship between its chief interlocutors. Today's nuclear powers are not engaged in the kind of unrestrained pursuit of capability that produced multiple overkill capacity in the USA and the Soviet Union earlier. The reversal of the relationship between war and politics has been firmly embedded in the thinking of political leaderships (if not always in the minds of some strategic experts). In a nuclear weapons environment, war is not an instrument of politics so much as politics is the critical instrument for minimising the risk of war. In a sense, while the possibility of war remains an instrument of politics (in the form of deterrence as well as coercion), that possibility itself shapes strategic behaviour differently from the past.

As the history of periodic confrontations between nuclear rivals shows, the likelihood of war produces abundant caution. Would-be belligerents invariably cooperate in two ways: implicitly, by means of unilateral actions to avoid large-scale combat; and explicitly, by establishing informal and/or formal channels of negotiations to reduce tensions.[19] But the fact remains that, while nuclear weapons impose restraint on those who wield them, they have a great limitation. Nuclear weapons tell us what we *cannot* rationally do (wage war, except in a marginal sense) but they do not tell us what we *can*. This leaves open the question of how policymakers respond to a threatening environment. Hence, while nuclear rivals behave with great circumspection in crises, they tend to return to 'normal' competition when immediate pressure to avoid war is absent. This impels them towards arms racing.

That tendency is visible in the current phase of power transition. To it is added the pressure exerted by changes in technology relating to military affairs.

TECHNOLOGICAL CHANGE

The emergence of new technologies has had a powerful impact on strategic competition among states. Decision-makers regularly face a security dilemma. The adoption of a new military technology may be counter-productive in terms of costs and risks since it may generate accelerated competition in the form of arms racing; but not adopting it may undermine security if a competitor acquires an edge by taking the lead.[20] New technologies tend to produce fresh arms-race cycles. With respect to nuclear weapons, Alexey Arbatov has identified four such cycles during the Cold War period.[21] Competition in the early phase of the Cold War (the late 1940s and 1950s) revolved around bombers and medium-range missiles. The focus shifted to long-range sea- and land-based missiles in the 1960s and early 1970s, then moved on to multiple independently targetable reentry vehicles (MIRVs) in the 1970s and early 1980s. Finally, in the 1980s, the spotlight was on medium-range cruise missiles and long-range missiles with hard-target penetration capability.

We can find elements of these in arms development today, though with variations. For instance, MIRV-ing is not in vogue in the USA but it is being pursued in Russia and China.[22] India is pursuing the technology as well. But the new cycle is centred on the technologies of the fourth industrial revolution. These are likely to have profound effects on the strategies, acquisitions and organisations of military forces. In short, technological insecurity and competition are heating up.

One such technology—by no means new, but picking up pace—is missile defence.[23] The US has the lead, which has propelled Russia and China, followed by India, to follow suit. Arms-racing effects are visible in two areas: defending against enemy missiles and penetrating enemy missile defences. Russia, in response to the deployment of the American missile defence systems, has been building both: a set of integrated air defence–missile defence systems and advanced transoceanic nuclear torpedoes and hypersonic vehicles (HSVs).[24] The constant tension accompanying this technology is its perceived impact on the balance of capabilities between rival powers. The argument usually made about its destabilising nature is that the possession of a strong missile defence gives its possessor an incentive to strike first, while the weaker side will have a powerful incentive to launch first in order to avoid losing a large proportion of its assets if the other side strikes first. MIRV-ing is a response not only to uncertainty about accurate targeting but also to the need to penetrate missile defences.

HSVs are a leading technology producing military competition.[25] They have the capacity to achieve speeds of Mach 5 and over, which reduces the time to react to them, and are hard to target because of their high degree of manoeuvrability. There are three main types of HSVs: ballistic missiles already in existence, boost-glide vehicles and hypersonic cruise missiles, the latter two having a much lower trajectory than the first. Shorter-range hypersonic gun-launched weapons are also under development.[26] In American parlance, these are considered 'non-strategic' but they are certainly strategic in areas such as the

India–Pakistan border, where distances between the border and major cities are, in many instances, short. Like missile defences, HSVs generate a strong sense of vulnerability that drives the quest to possess them a balancing response.

Space has long been militarised through the presence of satellites for remote sensing, navigation and communication.[27] Since command and control is the central nervous system of any military structure, anti-satellite (ASAT) technology is a critical aspect of contemporary arms racing. The technology encompasses a range of approaches: physical kinetic (hit-to-kill), non-physical kinetic (e.g., lasers), electronic (e.g., jamming), and cyber (e.g., disrupting communications). Unsurprisingly, states have long (from Cold War days) sought ASAT capabilities. Restricted to only the main competitors at the time, the technology has now spread to China and India. Pakistan has a long-term plan to follow suit under its Space Vision 2047 programme, which envisions the eventual acquisition of this capability.[28] Falling behind in the race for ASAT weapons may well leave states at risk of possessing a dysfunctional military structure. Also under study is the development of space-based weaponry, such as drones with lasers and space-based interceptors for missile defence.[29]

As with most of the technologies outlined above, cyber technology may be seen as a military instrument in a broad sense as well as one pertinent to the narrower ambit of nuclear weapons. Cyber warfare, in a relatively early stage of use, already occupies a prominent place in current research and development as well as future planning for militaries.[30] It can be utilised to disrupt communications, compromise warning systems, obtain data from information networks and/or corrupt them, send false warnings and so on. Cyber risks are so pervasive and grave that states are scrambling to develop their capacities to defend against as well as to attack with this technology.

Artificial intelligence (AI) or 'the use of computing power, in the form of algorithms, to conduct tasks that previously required human intelligence', has broad military utility.[31] It can be used for, among other things, image recognition, tracking, targeting and the development and deployment of lethal autonomous weapons systems (LAWS), which can make critical battlefield decisions at high speed, such as assessing warnings of incoming missiles and responding to them. Like cyber technology, in some ways even more so, AI has profound implications for the planning and conduct of war, indeed even for the making of decisions that may lead to war. Hence, its attractiveness is likely to be immediate. Adam Lowther and Curtis McGiffin, writing on the website War on the Rocks, recommend that given the speed and complexity of the new technologies, the US decision-making process is too slow and should be replaced by 'an automated strategic response system based on artificial intelligence'.[32] Moving in the same direction, the Indian government established in February 2018 a Task Force on AI, which handed in its report that June. The report, according to a press release, recommended the application of AI for 'making India a significant power of AI in defence specifically in the area of aviation, naval, land systems, cyber, nuclear, and biological warfare'.[33] Clearly, India does not want to be left behind.

Other areas of technology that are likely to be enormously impactful include submarine-tracking technology, which has the potential to pull the rug out from beneath the notion that nuclear submarines constitute the foundation of assured deterrence[34];and 3D printing technology, which offers the promise of speedy reduced-cost production of weapons systems, including nuclear weapons.[35] These and other technologies carry strong incentives to compete in order not to become vulnerable as the new technologies forge ahead.

As of now, the new technologies identified in this section are largely 'conventional' (i.e., non-nuclear) technologies, though they can also be adapted for direct application to nuclear weapons. It is sometimes argued that these technologies can make existing nuclear arsenals vulnerable to first strikes or that, more generally, they can confer an advantage on those who possess them. But such arguments are specious extensions of the reasoning that prevailed in the conventional era. What conceivable 'advantage' in terms of political gain is worth the 'small' risk of nuclear retaliation against an attempted first strike? In any case, nuclear and conventional weapons are increasingly integrated into a seamless whole and the notion that they can be practically separated into clearly defined segments is no longer tenable. Low-probability events carry high potential costs, which makes the two inseparable.

CONCLUSION: ARMS CONTROL, ANYONE?

We live in an age of nationalism, when policymakers are prone to portray themselves as tough leaders of volatile publics. The rapid spread of social media adds to the pressures imposed on political leaders to act quickly and decisively when crises break out. As the combination of rising international tensions and the technological imperative propels nuclear-armed states toward the harnessing of new technologies, we are at the cusp of another cycle of competitive nuclear weapons-related development. There are, moreover, impatient critics who are unhappy with what they see as the internal contradictions of current doctrines, which they believe must be jettisoned in favour of more robust principles and instruments. Calls for new weapons systems and for a 'flexible' approach to deterrence that would encompass a range of options are growing. The new buzzword is 'tailored deterrence'—a reincarnation, more or less, of the Cold War doctrine of flexible response that allows for limited war and, possibly, nuclear warfighting. What, then, are the prospects of arms control?

The situation is not as dire as it might seem. In the first place, military and civilian leaders are rarely willing to countenance unrestrained technological leaps into the dark when large numbers of lives are at stake. The loss of control that tends to go hand in hand with the new technologies is bound to give pause. In London, in 2018, a series of war games aimed at understanding escalation risks in the context of AI demonstrated policymakers' awareness of the serious risks involved and their unwillingness to choose aggressive options in conflict environments.[36] Second, a previous technological revolution—the nuclear revolution—exacerbated risks without world leaders succumbing to them. There has been some learning from that experience. That is why nuclear powers today do not feel it necessary to brandish their weapons or to project overt threats of nuclear use, as was the case in the Cold War era. Third, technologies have historically created no more than enabling conditions for escalation.[37] The decision to wield arms in pursuit of national security has always been, and remains, a political and moral choice. There is no reason to believe that this does not apply to the new military technologies.

Fourth, the new technologies have positive stabilising effects as well. Some, such as 'packet-switching', which involves disaggregating components of a digital message and reassembling them at the desired destination, enhance strategic stability.[38]

Fifth, advanced surveillance technologies enhance stability by improving early warning and by strengthening verification for arms control. Other possibilities for arms control involving the new technologies are already being discussed. For instance, there is a scope for 'asymmetric arms control' as was done with respect to weapons systems during the Cold War where equity rather than equality was the abiding principle. This could be applied to single weapons systems, such as HSVs, but could conceivably be applied across domains (i.e., between and among weapons systems based on different technologies).[39] There has been a fresh interest of sorts in the concept of no first use (NFU) in the USA, following the decline of elite interest in the movement to completely abolish nuclear weapons.[40] It has been suggested that, given their common interest in avoiding disasters, nuclear powers might consider an NFU agreement on cyber weapons as well.[41]

And yet, we ought not to underestimate the difficulties involved in curbing arms races. Since the advent of nuclear weapons, significant arms control has been limited. And, whether in the form of quantitative weapons-related agreements or of confidence-building measures (CBMs) involving better transparency and communication, arms control agreements have usually been triggered either by crises or by the ending of tension. The US–Soviet arms control process took off only after the Berlin and Cuban crises. Similarly, India–Pakistan CBMs were preceded by periods of high tension. And a flurry of arms-control agreements took place when the Cold War ended. From this perspective, arms control at the beginning of a period of rising competition may be difficult. It may take a crisis—only that, one hopes—to set in motion the next round of arms control.

NOTES

1 The author would like to thank Lt General Prakash Menon, Anit Mukherjee and the participants of the Takshashila Institution workshop for their valuable comments on an initial draft of this paper.

2 "Nuclear Arsenals of the World," *Bulletin of the Atomic Scientists* (n.d.), accessed on October 9, 2019, https://thebulletin.org/nuclear-notebook-multimedia/#. Data is available for 2019 from the Stockholm Peace Research Institute (SIPRI) but is not comparable since the classification methods are different. See "6. World Nuclear Forces," (*SIPRI Yearbook*, 2019), accessed on October 9, 2019, https://www.sipri.org/yearbook/2019/06.

3 "Modernization of World Nuclear Forces Continues Despite Overall Decrease in Number of Warheads: New SIPRI Yearbook Out Now," (Data, SIPRI, Stockholm, June 17, 2019), accessed on October 9, 2019, https://www.sipri.org/media/press/release/2019/modernization-world-nuclear-forces-continues;despite-overall-decrease-number-warheads-new-sipri.

4 Rakesh Sood, "An End to Arms Control Consensus," *The Hindu*, August 24, 2019, accessed on October 9, 2019, https://www.thehindu.com/opinion/lead/an-end-to-arms-control-consensus/article20236033.ece.

5 Paul Bracken, *The Second Nuclear Age: Strategy, Danger, and the New Power Politics* (New York: Henry Holt–Times Books, 2012); Gregory D. Koblentz, *Strategic Stability in the Second Nuclear Age* (New York: Council on Foreign Relations, 2014).

6 "*Frequently Asked Questions about Taking Nuclear Weapons Off Hair-Trigger Alert,*" Union of Concerned Scientists, January 2015, accessed on January 20, 2020, https://www.ucsusa.org/sites/default/files/attach/2015/01/Hair-Trigger%20FAQ.pdf.

7 Klaus Schwab, "The Fourth Industrial Revolution," *Foreign Affairs*, December 12, 2015, accessed on October 10, 2019, https://www.foreignaffairs.com/articles/2015-12-12/fourth-industrial-revolution.

8 Robert Gilpin, *War and Change in World Politics* (New York: Cambridge University Press, 1981); Ronald Tammen et. al., *Power Transitions* (New York and London: Chatham House, 2000).

9 The GDP figures used here and below (percentages calculated by the author) are taken from the World Bank, "GDP Current US$, China, United States, World" (World Bank, Washington DC), accessed on October 7, 2019, data.eorldbank.org/Indicator/NY.GDP.MKTP.CD?locations=CN-US-1W.

10 All military spending figures (and calculations from them) are taken from SIPRI; see "Military Expenditure Database," (SIPRI), accessed on October 7, 2019, sipri.org/databases/milex.

11 Idrees Ali, "U.S. Won't 'Tiptoe' around China with Asia Stability at Threat: Defense Chief," Reuters, June 1, 2019, accessed on October 9, 2019, https://www.reuters.com/article/us-asia-security/u-s-wont-tiptoe-around-china-with-asia-stability-at-threat-defense-chief-idUSKCN1T22T4.

12 Manoj Joshi, "Doklam: To Start at the Very Beginning," (Observer Research Foundation, New Delhi, August 2017), accessed on May 25, 2019, https://www.orfonline.org/wp-content/uploads/2017/08/ORF_SpecialReport_40_Doklam.pdf; Ankit Panda, "The Political Geography of the India–China Crisis at Doklam," *The Diplomat*, July 13, 2017, accessed on May 25, 2019, https://discuss.forumias.com/uploads/editor/8u/5uh8rbmzqms4.pdf; Niharika Mandhana, Rajesh Roy, and Chun Han Wong, "The Deadly India-China Clash: Spiked Clubs and Fists at 14,000 Feet,' *Wall Street Journal*, June 17, 2020, accessed on August 20, 2020, https://www.wsj.com/articles/spiked-clubs-and-fists-at-14-000-feet-the-deadly-india-china-clash-11592418242.

13 S. Paul Kapur, *Jihad as Grand Strategy: Islamist Militancy, National Security, and the Pakistani State* (New York: Oxford University Press, 2017).

14 Karthika Sasikumar, "India's Surgical Strikes: Response to Strategic Imperatives," *Round Table* 108, no 2 (2019): 159–174; Rohan Mukherjee, "Climbing the Escalation Ladder: India and the Balakot Crisis," War on the Rocks, October 2, 2019, accessed on October 9, 2019, https://warontherocks.com/2019/10/climbing-the-escalation-ladder-india-and-the-balakot-crisis/.

15 Van Jackson, *Rival Reputations: Coercion and Credibility in U.S.–North Korea Relations* (Cambridge: Cambridge University Press, 2017); Jonathan D. Pollock, *No Exit: North Korea, Nuclear Weapons and International Security* (Abingdon and New York: Routledge, 2011).

16 On Japan, see Jake Adelstein, "Is Japan about to Hit Its Nuclear Tipping Point?" *Daily Beast*, February 15, 2018, accessed on October 11, 2019, https://www.thedailybeast.com/is-japan-about-to-hit-its-nuclear-tipping-point.

On doubts about Japanese public opinion, see Joseph Grieco, Atsushi Tago, and Naoko Matsumura, "Understanding What the Japanese Public Think of Nuclear Weapons," *MHE Blog*, April 9, 2019, accessed on October 11, 2019, https://www.macmillanihe.com/blog/post/japanese-nuclear-weapons-joseph-grieco/.

On South Korea, see Jeff Daniels, "South Koreans Want Their Own Nuclear Weapons but Doing So [sic] Risks Triggering a Wider War," CNBC, August 25, 2017, https://www.cnbc.com/2017/08/24/south-koreans-want-their-own-nukes-but-doing-so-risks-wider-war.html; Jung Suk-yee, "Liberty Korea Party Demands Nuclear Armament," *Business Korea*, August 13, 2019, accessed on August 14, 2019, http://www.businesskorea.co.kr/news/articleView.html?idxno=34867.

17 Bruno Tertrais, "Will Europe Get Its Own Bomb?" *Washington Quarterly* 42, no 2 (Summer 2019): 47–66.

18 On the dynamics of status-driven policies, see T.V. Paul, Deborah Welch Larson, and William C. Wohlforth, eds. *Status in World Politics* (New York: Cambridge University Press, 2014).

19 Benjamin Miller, *When Opponents Cooperate: Great Power Conflict and Collaboration in World Politics* (Ann Arbor: University of Michigan Press, 2002).

20 Richard Burt, "Technology and East–West Arms Control," *International Affairs* 53, no 1 (1977): 51–72, at 54– 55.

21 Alexey Arbatov, "Mad Momentum Redux? The Rise and Fall of Nuclear Arms Control," *Survival* 61, no 3 (2019): 7–38, at 19.

22 Tertrais, "A Second Nuclear Age? A View from France," in *Nuclear Order in the Twenty-First Century*, ed. Rakesh Sood (New Delhi: Observer Research Foundation, 2019), 45–54, at 49.

23 Stephan Frühling, "Managing Escalation: Missile Defence, Strategy and U.S. Alliances," *International Affairs* 92, no 1 (January 2016): 81–95; Columba Peoples, "Technology and Politics in the Missile Defence Debate: Traditional, Radical and Critical Approaches," *Global Change, Peace and Security* 19, no 3 (October 2007): 265–280.

24 "Russian Air and Missile Defence" (Center for Strategic and International Studies, Washington, DC, June 15, 2018), accessed on October 9, 2019, https://missilethreat.csis.org/system/russian-air-defense/; David C. Gompert and Martin Libicki, "Cyber War and Nuclear Peace," *Survival* 61, no 4 (2019): 45–62, at 56.

25 *Hypersonic Weapons: A Challenge and Opportunity for Strategic Arms Control*, United Nations Office for Disarmament Research, New York, 2019; Richard M. Harrison, "Welcome to the Hypersonic Arms Race," *National Interest*, January 19, 2019, accessed on October 9, 2019, https://nationalinterest.org/blog/buzz/welcome-hypersonic-arms-race-42002; Dean Wilkening, "Hypersonic Weapons and Strategic Stability," *Survival* 61, 5 (2019): 129–148.

26 Wilkening, "Hypersonic Weapons and Strategic Stability," 129.

27 *Competing in Space*, United States National Air & Space Intelligence Center, Wright-Patterson, Ohio, December 2018, https://www.nasic.af.mil/News/Article-Display/Article/1733201/usaf-nasic-releases-unclassified-competing-in-space-assessment/, accessed on July 22, 2022; Todd Harrison et al, *Space Threat Assessment 2019*, Center for Strategic and International Studies, Washington, DC, April 2019, accessed on

October 9, 2019, https://aerospace.csis.org/wp-content/uploads/2019/04/SpaceThreatAssessment2019-compressed.pdf.

28 Ahmed Saeed Minhas, "Indian ASAT Capability and Its Impact on South Asian Strategic Stability," *Pakistan Politico*, June 16, 2019, accessed on October 9, 2019, http://pakistanpolitico.com/indian-asat-capability-and-its-impact-on-south-asian-strategic-stability/.

29 Aaron Mehta, "Space-Based Interceptors with Drones and Lasers: The Pentagon's Missile Defense Review Wish List Revealed," Defense News, January 16, 2019, accessed on October 10, 2019, https://www.defensenews.com/breaking-news/2019/01/17/space-based-interceptors-and-drones-with-lasers-the-pentagons-missile-defense-review-wish-list-revealed/.

30 Kartik Bommakanti, "The Impact of Cyber Warfare on Nuclear Deterrence: A Conceptual and Empirical Overview," *ORF Issue Brief*, no 266 (2018), accessed on October 9, 2019, https://www.orfonline.org/wp-content/uploads/2018/11/ORF_Issue_Brief_266_Cyber_Warfare.pdf; Stephen J. Cimbala, "The INF Treaty and New START: Escalation Control, Strategic Fatalism, and the Role of Cyber," *Cyber, Intelligence, and Security* 3, no 1 (May 2019): 41–69; Andrew Futter, *Hacking the Bomb: Cyber Threats and Nuclear Weapons* (Washington DC: Georgetown University Press, 2018); Andrew Futter, "Cyber Threats and Nuclear Weapons: New Questions for Command and Control, Security and Strategy," (Royal United Services Institute, London, July 2016), accessed on October 9, 2019, https://rusi.org/sites/default/files/cyber_threats_and_nuclear_combined.1.pdf; Gompert and Libicki, "Cyber War and Nuclear Peace"; Jon Lindsay, "Cyber Operations and Nuclear Weapons," (Nautilus Institute, Berkeley, June 20, 2019), accessed on October 9, 2019, https://nautilus.org/napsnet/napsnet-special-reports/cyber-operations-and-nuclear-weapons/.

31 Michael C. Horowitz, "When Speed Kills: Lethal Autonomous Weapons Systems, Deterrence and Stability," *Journal of Strategic Studies* 42, no 6 (2019): 764–788, at 767. See also Vincent Boulanin, ed., *The Impact of Artificial Intelligence on Strategic Stability and Nuclear Risk, Vol. 1: Euro-Atlantic Perspectives*, SIPRI, Stockholm, May 2019, accessed on October 9, 2019, https://www.sipri.org/sites/default/files/2019-05/sipri1905-ai-strategic-stability-nuclear-risk.pdf; Edward Geist and Andrew J. Lohn, "How Might Artificial Intelligence Affect the Risk of Nuclear War?" (RAND Corporation, Santa Monica, 2018), accessed on October 9, 2019, https://www.rand.org/pubs/perspectives/PE296.html.

32 Adam Lowther and Curtis McGiffin, "America Needs a 'Dead Hand,'" War on the Rocks, August 16, 2019, accessed on October 9, 2019, https://warontherocks.com/2019/08/america-needs-a-dead-hand/.

33 Ministry of Defence Report, "AI Task Force Hands over Final Report to RM," (Ministry of Defence, Government of India, New Delhi, June 30, 2018), accessed on October 9, 2019, https://pib.gov.in/newsite/PrintRelease.aspx?relid=180322.

34 Rajesh Basrur, "India's Nuclear Doctrine and Strategic Stability at Sea" (Paper, Annual Convention of the International Studies Association, San Francisco, April 2018(.

35 Tristan A. Volpe, "Dual-Use Distinguishability: How 3-D Printing Shapes the Security Dilemma for Nuclear Programs," *Journal of Strategic Studies* 42, no 6 (2019): 814–840.

36 Mark Fitzpatrick, "Artificial Intelligence and Nuclear Command and Control," *Survival* 61, no 3 (2019): 81–92.

37 Caitlin Talmadge, "Emerging Technology and Intra-War Escalation Risks: Evidence from the Cold War, Implications for Today," *Journal of Strategic Studies* 42, no 6 (2019): 864–887.

38 Gompert and Libicki, "Cyber War and Nuclear Peace," 48.

39 Heather Williams, "Asymmetric Arms Control and Strategic Stability: Scenarios for Limiting Glide Vehicles," *Journal of Strategic Studies* 42, no 6 (2019): 789–813.

40 For a recent summary of the debate, see Brad Roberts, "Debating No-First-Use, Again," *Survival* 61, no 3 (2019): 39–56. See also Nina Tannenwald, "It's Time for A U.S. No-First-Use Nuclear Policy," *Texas National Security Review* 2, no 3 (August 1, 2019): 130–137.

41 Cimbala, "The INF Treaty and New START," 57.

Chapter 5

NUCLEAR WEAPONS, GEOPOLITICS, EMERGING TECHNOLOGIES AND OPPOSITIONAL NATIONALISM

Sadia Tasleem

In April 2009, US President Barack Obama made his now-famous Prague speech pledging his commitment to free the world of nuclear weapons. Obama's commitment generated hope in many circles around the globe. A world without nuclear weapons began to look like a possibility.[1] A decade later, Washington DC continues to maintain an active and robust nuclear arsenal.[2] Similar trends can be observed in other nuclear-armed states, which are pursuing qualitative and, in some cases, even quantitative upgradation of their respective arsenals. It is not difficult to infer that nuclear weapons are here to stay for the foreseeable future. What is driving this continued commitment to the changes in the size and sophistication of nuclear arsenals of the nuclear-armed states? How are these trends going to affect the geopolitical environment? Will more states contemplate building nuclear weapons due to growing geopolitical tensions?

Even though the contemporary geopolitical conditions are unique in some ways and the emerging threats cannot be undermined, I argue that the situation today is not completely divorced from nuclear history. However, the complexity of the nuclear question has been further accentuated because of how nuclear weapons have become entangled with geopolitics, evolving technology and most importantly, oppositional nationalism. This chapter will investigate the contemporary security landscape. It will then attempt to untangle the intricate relationship between nuclear weapons, geopolitics, evolving technologies and the domestic political dynamics within the nuclear-armed states.

THE NUCLEAR DISORDER

The world is going through a phase of acute instability. The situation is not unprecedented but it is not entirely familiar either. The Cold War between the USA and the Soviet Union was marked by both arms races and crisis instability. However, some noticeable differences between the past and present deserve a mention here.

The predominant fears during the Cold War emanated from the possibility of a war between the USA and the erstwhile Soviet Union—most likely initiated in Europe to later engulf the entire world. The fear of the unknown was omnipresent, resulting in caution as well as restraint. Leaders on both sides of the Iron Curtain made serious efforts to reduce the sources of instability. Hotlines were established and arms-control regimes were instituted. Although these measures were imperfect and did not eliminate the possibility of crises or nuclear war, the recognition of nuclear dangers was obvious.

Today, the nuclear flashpoints are far more widely spread out. The danger of a nuclear confrontation is not restricted to Europe anymore. Asia is becoming a hotbed of conflicts. The growing tensions between India and Pakistan—the two nuclear-armed South Asian neighbours—as well as the uncertainty on the Korean peninsula, are daily reminders of a looming danger.

The Middle East is under duress. Civil wars, unstable regimes, growing rivalry among regional actors and foreign interventions undermine any chances of peace in the region.[3] The presence of nuclear-armed Israel in the region has long been a source of frustration for the regional actors. On the other hand, the US withdrawal from the Joint Comprehensive Plan of Action (JCPOA) under former president Donald Trump only exposed further the fragility of multilateral negotiations, not only creating a serious trust deficit but also undermining diplomacy as a trusted way of carrying out negotiations and reaching compromises. Consequently, the future of both the nuclear deal and Iran's nuclear programme is far from clear irrespective of the Biden administration's renewed efforts to engage with Iran.

Meanwhile, the more familiar threats of great power rivalry are also resurfacing on two fronts with the growing tensions between the USA and Russia on the one hand, and the USA and China on the other.

Russia's resurgence and the inflated threat perception it has caused in the Western imagination is ringing alarm bells in NATO headquarters. NATO's moves in turn raise Russian fears.[4] The withdrawal of the USA from the INF Treaty is yet another major blow to the international 'nuclear order'.[5] This indicates that the commitment as well as the frameworks that helped manage the arms race in the past, are considered superfluous. This breakdown of commitment can have serious consequences.

Meanwhile, the blatant disregard for the Treaty on the Prohibition of Nuclear Weapons, commonly known as the Nuclear Weapon Ban

Treaty, by the major powers is only going to increase the friction between the nuclear haves and the have-nots at the next NPT review conference.The future of NPT itself is also uncertain. Even if the treaty manages to withstand the stress, it will be increasingly seen as dormant, if it fails to get the nuclear-armed states to make serious commitments.

Under these circumstances, and the growing geopolitical tensions in various parts of the world, even tactical issues can have strategic implications. A case in point is the concern that the news of the presence of roughly fifty American nuclear weapons at the Incirlik airbase in Turkey generated across the world, only two years ago when the Turkish government had wilfully pushed itself into the throes of a war.[6]

Today, the danger comes from the confidence shared by all nuclear-armed states that they can play with fire without harm. What does this mean for global security and the role of nuclear weapons therein? Will the contemporary nuclear trends aggravate geopolitical tensions? Will the geopolitical tensions increase the incentives for nuclearisation?

NUCLEAR WEAPONS AND GEOPOLITICS

The relationship between nuclear weapons and geopolitics is intricate. Neorealists led by Kenneth Waltz maintained that geopolitical tensions incentivize states to build nuclear weapons and acquisition of nuclear weapons by hostile states locked in a security competition reduces the chances of war.[7] This assumption indicated a rather simple relationship between geopolitics and nuclear weapons, suggesting that geopolitical tensions result in nuclear proliferation, and nuclear weapons in turn dampen geopolitical tensions. Evidential support for this claim was drawn from the Cold War between the USA and Soviet Union not turning hot. Some scholars also noted changes in China's foreign policy after its nuclear tests as indicative of a shift from belligerence to caution.[8]

But the assumption that nuclear weapons tame the aggressive propensities of states and thereby reduce geopolitical tensions was subjected to scrutiny in the aftermath of the Kargil crisis between India and Pakistan. The post-nuclearisation instability that ensued in South Asia resulted in rethinking the impact of nuclear weapons on geopolitical tensions. Paul Kapur, a noted expert on South Asia, drew attention to what he called the 'instability–instability paradox', referring to a situation where the possibility of nuclear war is exploited by a nuclear-armed state to seek strategic advantage against a conventionally stronger adversary.[9]

Meanwhile, mainstream Western discourse on nuclear weapons over the past two decades was heavily overshadowed by the US preoccupation with the so-called 'war on terrorism'. Much of the debate about nuclear weapons focused on the danger of nuclear weapons falling into the 'wrong' hands.

More recently, however, the US nuclear posture review under former president Donald Trump highlighting China and Russia as the USA's competitors shifted the focus back to nuclear weapons and geopolitics.[10] The nuclear posture review under the Trump administration categorically declared great power competition to be the focus of the US national security strategy. In the nuclear policy realm, the primary focus has shifted from arms-control-led strategic stability to a categorical commitment to establish qualitative superiority of the US nuclear arsenal over its competitors, Russia and China.

Does this mean that the growing geopolitical competition among major powers is incentivising the modernisation of existing nuclear arsenals? Or nuclear weapons are fuelling competition between the USA and China on the one hand, and the USA and Russia on the other?

A careful examination of nuclear history reveals that nuclear weapons as well as geopolitics affect different states' behaviours differently.[11] Some states justify their nuclear choices by alluding to geopolitical tensions whereas others have abstained from building nuclear weapons despite being at the centre of international tensions.

There is no gainsaying the fact that no region in the world is undergoing the kind of volatility that exists in the present-day Middle East. From a realist logic, states like Egypt, Turkey, Saudi Arabia and Iran should have had by now built the bomb or at least should have shown a serious commitment towards building one. The fact that the Middle East is so central to the global geopolitical landscape has, however, dissuaded these states from seriously pursuing nuclear weapons. What happened to Iraq and Libya is not lost on other states in the Middle East.

Although realist logic suggests that the cases of Iraq and Libya would have created an urgency in the Middle East to acquire the bomb, that doesn't seem to be the case. Rhetorical statements by leaders like the President of Turkey, Recep Tayyip Erdoğan[12] and speculative analysis about Saudi Arabia contemplating buying a bomb off the shelf from a state like Pakistan aside, there is no serious evidence to indicate any steps taken by these states in pursuit of nuclear weapons. Iran stands out as the only exception with, most likely, an inclination to pursue hedging as opposed to building the bomb itself.[13] Nonetheless, this also reveals how states facing geopolitical turmoil respond to the exogenous circumstances differently.

Geopolitical tensions on the Korean peninsula reveal a contrary trend. The supreme leader of the Democratic People's Republic of Korea (DPRK) Kim Jong-un seems undeterred, despite threats from Washington, in his ambition to continue expanding his country's nuclear arsenal.[14] The US administration's inability to effectively negotiate an acceptable solution with the DPRK is accentuating the possibility for the North Korean leadership to continue building more weapons and delivery vehicles.

Meanwhile, South Asia is experiencing a period of heightened tensions. Nuclear-armed rivals, India and Pakistan, escaped an outbreak of war in the early 2019. Both states once again faced the possibility of escalation of tensions after India's decision to dilute Jammu and Kashmir's special status. The presence of nuclear weapons, it seems, has accentuated the risk-taking behaviour as well as the propensity of crises in South Asia.[15] The line of control (LOC) perpetually goes through cycles of violence without much respite for the soldiers manning it. The ceasefire announced on 25 February 2021 by the armies on both sides is a welcome development, yet the lack of a formal agreement outlining an agreed-upon code of conduct keeps the situation uncertain and fragile. Meanwhile, both India and Pakistan, like other nuclear-armed states, are relentlessly expanding their nuclear-weapon capabilities. These technologically advanced capabilities become part of a feedback loop that perpetuates uncertainty and anxiety, consequently fuelling geopolitical tensions. It is, therefore, imperative to consider technological modernisation and its likely implications for the future of nuclear weapons.

TECHNOLOGICAL IMPERATIVES

The world is witnessing major technological breakthroughs and military transformations both in the nuclear and non-nuclear realms with serious implications for the future of warfare as well as nuclear doctrines and postures.

In the nuclear realm, massive advancement has been made by the major powers in technologies related to ballistic missile defence systems, hypersonic boost-glide vehicles and cruise missiles,[16] satellites and other space-based systems and anti-submarine warfare capabilities. The development and deployment of the US missile defence system have resulted in fuelling anxieties in Russia and China. As a result, both these states have opted to diversify their response options by investing in hypersonic missiles.[17]

Meanwhile, India and Pakistan are also caught up in a debilitating arms competition, mainly emulating the technologies developed by the major powers. Along with the consistent increase in the production of fissile material to sustain a sizeable nuclear arsenal, India is building up its ballistic missile defence programme.[18] Moreover, India also followed the Chinese in successfully conducting an anti-satellite missile test.[19] Pakistan, on the other hand, is countering India's capabilities by building MIRVs, cruise missiles and short-range ballistic missiles.[20] Both states are also heavily investing in their sea-based nuclear capabilities.[21]

A mix of all these technologies generates a high degree of uncertainty, resulting in instability. It needs to be stated here that the development of destabilising technologies is not unique to contemporary times. The world has witnessed several cycles of technological modernisation generating incentives for war. The Cold War was a period of intense great-power competition. The arms race between the USA and the erstwhile Soviet Union generated unprecedented risks of nuclear annihilation. Nuclear planners contemplated nuclear warfighting and counterforce targeting as real possibilities. Technologies were aimed at enabling the two superpowers to build sufficient capabilities to undertake a decapitating first strike against each other in event of a nuclear crisis.

Today, too, nuclear doctrines and respective postures are articulated keeping in view similar objectives. Then, what has changed now? Some changes are too significant to be ignored.

Firstly, technological maturation in recent times has tremendously increased the precision, accuracy and efficiency of weapons systems. Some of the risky decisions, particularly involving targets that could have inflicted heavy collateral damage in the past, might be conceivable now.[22] Technologies involving counterforce capabilities have improved significantly, making warfighting doctrines a real possibility. The potential US ability to carry out a decapitating strike against its adversaries while protecting its territory with the missile defences have alarmed both China and Russia, resulting in their pursuit of new weapons. Pakistan's development of short-range ballistic missiles capable of carrying nuclear warheads and medium-range Shaheen III missiles aimed at targeting the Indian bases in the Andaman and Nicobar islands and the successful testing of Ababeel—a MIRV-capable missile—also indicate a gradual shift from countervalue targeting strategy to a combination of countervalue and counterforce targeting choices. In India's case, the preference to move away from countervalue to counterforce capabilities is becoming more obvious. The development of a ballistic missile defence system, a successful demonstration of nuclear submarine *Arihant*'s 'deterrence patrol' in the Indian Ocean, sea-based and land-based cruise missiles, ballistic missiles ranging from 150 km to 5,000 km and the development of MIRVs suggest India's growing counterforce targeting potential. South Asia analysts

Vipin Narang and Christopher Clary claim, 'South Asia is already facing a counterforce feedback loop' where India's missile defence programme has resulted in Pakistan's development of countermeasures like MIRVs.[23] Regardless of how the feedback loop functions, the presence of counterforce capabilities can, on the one hand, generate incentives for India to undertake a pre-emptive strike against Pakistan early in a crisis, whereas the classical 'use it or lose it' dilemma can push decision-makers in Pakistan to lower the threshold to use nuclear weapons first.

Secondly, these technologies are being developed in a diplomatic deadlock. In the absence of bilateral and multilateral negotiations and arms-control agreements, the risks are getting higher.

Thirdly, nuclear weapons-related technologies are not advancing in a vacuum. Technological developments, particularly in the context of cyberspace, AI and machine learning are changing the nature of warfare. Lethal autonomous weapons, killer robots and drones put the technologically advanced states at an overwhelming advantage. Evolving technologies are decreasing the likelihood of causing collateral damage and might change the fundamental character of military operations.[24]

Technologically advanced states like the USA should have little incentives to modernise their arsenals, given the reduced military utility of nuclear weapons in the wake of more precise military technologies. However, the ongoing technological developments can have two peculiar impacts in the context of nuclear weapons.

Firstly, the uncertainty created by the developments in AI will likely be used to rationalise a continuous commitment to nuclear weapons. This is evident in the nuclear modernisation programmes of the major powers.

Secondly, technologically less developed states that possess nuclear weapons like, Pakistan and DPRK will likely invest more in nuclear weapons as a certain kind of 'insurance strategy' against the threats emanating from developments taking place in the realm of AI and autonomous weapons. Although nuclear weapons won't be able to prevent or even deter calibrated, pointed attacks against given targets in states, the likelihood of these states finding some hope in nuclear weapons would dominate.

Another important aspect of these developments is the greater integration of these technologies in nuclear weapons programmes. If integrated with nuclear weapons command and control systems, these technologies will tremendously enhance operational readiness, target precision and likely produce better coordination.[25] A higher degree of confidence in a state's ability to neutralise the enemy's military infrastructure or a high degree of fear of being attacked first can result in a crisis.

Having said that, technology alone is not a sufficient condition for crisis escalation or war.[26] Also, technological determinism is a deeply contestable idea to explain the causes of proliferation. Technically, with more accuracy and precision, the incentives to reduce the number of nuclear weapons should increase. However, these decisions are not always rational and logical. Depending upon the peculiar characteristics of decision-making dynamics within the nuclear-armed states, these decisions would vary as has been the case in the past.

It is also important to highlight here that the decisions to invest in specific technologies as well as foreign policy choices relating to coercion, blackmail, belligerence and restraint are all heavily, if not exclusively, determined by the decision-making elite in each state. In the case of established democracies, it is the political leadership that determines such choices. As a result, popular politics may influence strategic choices. This means that the availability of destabilising technologies at the hands of populist leaders, interested in risk-taking, can increase the risk of an actual nuclear confrontation.

In sum, responses to geopolitical tensions as well as technological imperatives are deeply embedded in domestic political structures.

DOMESTIC POLITICS AND THE BOMB

As mentioned above, domestic political dynamics remain at the heart of strategic decisions. In his seminal work, Jacques Hymans persuasively argued that proliferation decisions are deeply influenced by the national identity conceptions that the decision-makers have of their state. Hymans defines national identity conception as 'an individual's understanding of the nation's identity—his or her sense of what the nation naturally stands for and of how high it naturally stands, in comparison to others in the international arena'.[27] Hymans broadly categorised national leaders into four types. He claimed that the only type that is highly likely to decide in favour of the bomb is the oppositional nationalist leadership. It is because the oppositional nationalist leaders combine the emotions of fear and pride and find in nuclear weapons a response to both.[28]

The rising regimes of oppositional nationalists—to borrow Jack Hymans' terminology—in democratic states like the USA, India and the UK as well as in others like Russia, have implications for arms build-up and geopolitical tensions. These oppositional nationalists tap into the masculine narratives of the bomb to fuel nuclear nationalism. Nuclear weapons become a rallying point, a weapon to make electoral gains. This, in turn, creates an environment of uncertainty, giving birth to calls for military modernisation in all those states that are interlocked in military conflicts.

The case of India–Pakistan tensions merits attention here. The Balakot crisis right before the Indian election exposed the fraught fault lines in the domestic political order that brought two nuclear-armed states to the brink of war.[29] At the height of the crisis, the Indian government threatened to launch a missile attack against Pakistan.[30] Two months later, in an election rally, the Indian prime minister Narendra Modi, told his people, 'India has stopped the policy of getting scared of Pakistan's threats. Every other day they used to say "we have nuclear button, we have nuclear button". What do we have then? Have we kept it for Diwali?'[31] In a democracy, this kind of political rhetoric can bind the leadership in a commitment trap. The demand for tough action can be very high in a future escalation.

This is worrisome because the tensions between India and Pakistan endure. The crisis after the Balakot strikes temporarily diffused when Pakistan unconditionally released India's fighter pilot, who was captured after an Indian fighter aircraft was shot down during a dogfight between Indian and Pakistani warplanes.[32] But the Bharatiya Janata Party (BJP) government's decision to revoke the special status granted to Jammu and Kashmir, under Article 370 of India's Constitution, once again locked India and Pakistan in a deadly confrontational stalemate. The Indian government under the BJP's leadership has been testing Pakistan's limits. Within the Modi regime, there is a clear realisation that Pakistan is constrained by its financial and political circumstances. Consequently, the BJP government is trying to reverse the status quo in Kashmir in its own favour. Constrained by its challenging circumstances, the Government of Pakistan has so far exercised restraint. However, BJP's militaristic policies vis-à-vis Pakistan have strengthened the already overwhelmingly powerful nuclear establishment in Pakistan. The consensus on the significance of nuclear deterrence is only going to grow under the current circumstances. This implies that a further build-up of nuclear arms will be considered essential.

Similar political trends have plagued many other parts of the world.

Nowhere is this more significant and pronounced than in the USA. The legacy left by former president Donald Trump is difficult to undo, —with consequences that are far-reaching and go well beyond the US territory. The rhetoric of 'America First', nuclear modernisation, increased defence spending, a highly provocative nuclear-posture review mixed with a weakening resolve for extended deterrence and assuring allies, generated deep uncertainty in states like Japan, South Korea and Australia. Trump had repeatedly urged the allied states to increase financial contributions to NATO or build means to defend themselves. This strengthened the narrative of conservative politicians in the allied states. Talk about a Euro deterrent was a direct consequence of the oppositional nationalism exhibited in Trump's politics.

Conversely, it is difficult to make sense of the US nuclear modernisation in the wake of its waning interest in extended deterrence. Trump claimed that the USA will outspend its competitors because it can.[33] This oppositional nationalism revealed dangerous tendencies in the US nuclear policy. This narrative was built around opposition, not only to Russia and China but also to the US allies in some ways. The narrow calculations of Trump's White House and the resultant nuclear policy made nuclear weapons regain political currency. This memory of Trump's tenure in the White House will not fade away quickly. Even though he is out of office, the implications of his policies and the possibility of his comeback in the next US elections are major impediments to any possibility of a global consensus against nuclear weapons. Under the present circumstances, arguing against the 'value' of nuclear weapons appears an insurmountable task.[34]

Is this process irreversible? Are there ways to slow down and eventually stop nuclear weapons development? What can be done to stabilise the geopolitical tensions and arms competition in various parts of the world?

Literature on nuclear weapons is replete with brilliant proposals aimed at reducing global tensions and dampening arms competitions. Scholars have offered exhaustible accounts of CBMs, nuclear risk reduction measures (NRRMs), policy suggestions like an NFU pledge to prevent inadvertent, accidental and unauthorised use of nuclear weapons. All such proposals carry some value. The challenge, however, is to generate the political will in the concerned capitals of the world to implement these proposals. The question then is how to persuade the like of former president Donald Trump to rethink the US nuclear modernisation plan? How to persuade the military leadership in Pakistan or Kim Jong-un in DPRK—both convinced that they are faced with disproportionately stronger conventional armies—to agree to an NFU pledge when a military superpower like the USA insists on retaining its first-use option against its adversaries?

The prospects for arms control, CBMs and NFU appear bleak in the near future. With the withdrawal of the USA and Russia from the INF treaty, arms-control diplomacy is losing traction among other nuclear-armed states as well. Domestic political and institutional imperatives encouraging nuclear arms build-up in the USA and elsewhere are unlikely to change without a major shift in the mindset that perpetuates weaponisation. Such a shift will require more than the change of the ruling political parties. Political leaders from non-nuclear states, as well as the civil society across the world, need to challenge the growing trends in favour of oppositional nationalism and the hegemonic discourses that normalise nuclear weapons.

Only a strong transnational anti-nuclear movement can create a conducive political environment to coax nuclear-armed states to pursue major policy shifts, including NFU and nuclear disarmament.

NOTES

1 Tom Sauer, "A Second Nuclear Revolution: From Nuclear Primacy to Post-Existential Deterrence," *Journal of Strategic Studies* 32, no 5 (2009): 745–767.
2 Kate Hewitt and Bruce Jones, eds, *Managing Risk: Nuclear Weapons in the New Geopolitics—A Brookings Interview* (Washington DC: Brookings, 2019), accessed on November 22, 2019, https://www.brookings.edu/wp-content/uploads/2019/02/FP_20190211_nonproliferation_interview.pdf.
3 Robert Malley, "The Unwanted Wars: Why the Middle East Is More Combustible than Ever," *Foreign Affairs*, October 2, 2019, accessed on December 20, 2019, https://www.foreignaffairs.com/articles/middle-east/2019-10-02/unwanted-wars.
4 James Marson and Thomas Grove, "U.S., NATO Moves in Baltics Raise Russian Fears," *The Wall Street Journal*, June 14, 2019, accessed on October 15, 2019, https://www.wsj.com/articles/u-s-nato-moves-in-baltics-raise-russian-fears-11560543426.
5 "INF Nuclear Treaty: US Pulls Out of Cold War-Era Pact with Russia," BBC News, August 2, 2019, accessed on November 10, 2019, https://www.bbc.com/news/world-us-canada-49198565.
6 "Turkey's Syria Move Highlights America's Tactical Nukes in Europe," *The Economist*, November 28, 2019, accessed on December 3, 2019, https://www.economist.com/europe/2019/11/28/turkeys-syria-move-highlights-americas-tactical-nukes-in-europe.
7 Kenneth Waltz, "The Spread of Nuclear Weapons: More May Be Better," *Adelphi Papers* (London: International Institute for Strategic Studies, 1981), 171, accessed on July 23, 2022, https://www.tandfonline.com/doi/abs/10.1080/05679328108457394.
8 Francis J. Gavin, "Same as It Ever Was: Nuclear Alarmism, Proliferation and the Cold War," *International Security* 34, no 3 (Winter 2009): 15–16.
9 Paul Kapur, *Dangerous Deterrent: Nuclear Weapons Proliferation and Conflict in South Asia* (Stanford University Press, 2007).
10 US Department of Defense, "Nuclear Posture Review 2018" (Report, US Department of Defense, Washington DC), 6–14, accessed on July 23, 2022, https://media.defense.gov/2018/Feb/02/2001872886/-1/-1/1/2018-NUCLEAR-POSTURE-REVIEW-FINAL-REPORT.PDF.

11 Mark S. Bell, "Nuclear Opportunism: A Theory of How States Use Nuclear Weapons in International Politics," *Journal of Strategic Studies* 42, no 1 (2019): 3–28.

12 Borzou Daragahi, "Turkey's Erdogan Hints He Wants Nuclear Weapons," *Independent*, September 5, 2019, accessed on October 23, 2019, https://www.independent.co.uk/news/world/europe/turkey-nuclear-weapons-erdogan-missiles-uae-saudi-arabia-russia-a9092711.html.

13 Wyn Q. Bowen et. al., *Living on the Edge: Iran and the Practice of Nuclear Hedging* (UK: Palgrave Macmillan, 2016).

14 "North Korea Claims Successful 'Crucial Test' at Long-Range Rocket Site," *The Guardian*, December 14, 2019, accessed on December 15, 2019, https://www.theguardian.com/world/2019/dec/14/north-korea-test-long-range-rocket-site.

15 For India's willingness to resort to risk-taking after Pulwama attacks, see Manpreet Sethi, "Lessons from the Indo-Pak Crisis Triggered by Pulwama," *South Asia Post-Crisis Brief* (Nuclear Crisis Group, June 2019), 6–8.

16 Dean Wilkening, "Hypersonic Weapons and Strategic Stability," *Survival* 61, no 5 (2019): 129–148.

17 Ivan Oelrich, "Hypersonic Missiles: Three Questions Every Reader Should Ask?" *Bulletin of the Atomic Scientists* (December 17, 2019), accessed on December 30, 2019, https://thebulletin.org/2019/12/hypersonic-missiles-three-questions-every-reader-should-ask/.

18 Shishir Gupta, "India's First Floating Test Range Ready, Ballistic Missile Defence Trails On Cards," *Hindustan Times*, October 27, 2019, accessed on October 28, 2019, https://www.hindustantimes.com/india-news/new-age-weapons-set-to-add-to-india-s-arsenal/story-SUcRAjtwyZRej8Fq0SHSJJ.html.

19 Kelsey Davenport, "Indian ASAT Test Raises Space Risks," *Arms Control Today*, May 2019, accessed on October 10, 2019, https://www.armscontrol.org/act/2019-05/news/indian-asat-test-raises-space-risks.

20 For Pakistan's testing of MIRV, see "ISPR Press Release No PR-34/2017-ISPR" (Press Release, Inter Services Public Relations, Rawalpindi, January 24, 2017), accessed on January 05, 2020, https://www.ispr.gov.pk/press-release-detail.php?id=3705; For the latest testing of HATF IX, see Ankit Panda, "Pakistan Conducts Test of Nuclear-Capable Nasr Missile," *The Diplomat*, January 26, 2019, accessed on December 10, 2019, https://thediplomat.com/2019/01/pakistan-conducts-test-of-nuclear-capable-nasr-missile/.

21 Hans M. Kristensen and Matt Korda, "Indian Nuclear Forces, 2018," *Bulletin of the Atomic Scientists* 74, no 6 (2018), accessed on July 23, 2022, https://www.tandfonline.com/doi/full/10.1080/00963402.2018.1533162?af=R; Hans M. Kristensen, Robert S. Norris, and Julia Diamond, "Pakistani Nuclear Forces, 2018," *Bulletin of the Atomic Scientists* 74, no 5 (2018) accessed on July 23, 2022, https://www.tandfonline.com/doi/full/10.1080/00963402.2018.1507796.

22 Keir A. Lieber and Daryl G. Press, "The New Era of Counterforce: Technological Change and the Future of Nuclear Deterrence," *International Security* 41, no 4 (2017): 9–49.

23 Christopher Clary and Vipin Narang, "India's Counterforce Temptations: Strategic Dilemmas, Doctrine, and Capabilities," *International Security* 43, no 3 (2019): 7–52, doi: https://doi.org/10.1162/isec_a_00340.

24 Matt Field, "As the US, China, and Russia Build New Nuclear Weapons Systems, How Will AI Be Built In?" *Bulletin of the Atomic Scientists* (December 20, 2019), accessed on July 23, 2022 https://thebulletin.org/2019/12/as-the-us-china-and-russia-build-new-nuclear-weapons-systems-how-will-ai-be-built-in/.

25 Field, "As the US, China, and Russia Build New Nuclear Weapons Systems, How Will AI Be Built In?"

26 Caitlin Talmadge, "Emerging Technology and Intra-War Escalation Risks: Evidence from the Cold War, Implications for Today," *Journal of Strategic Studies* 42, no 6 (2019): 864–887.

27 Jacques E.C. Hymans, *The Psychology of Nuclear Proliferation: Identity, Emotions, and Foreign Policy* (Cambridge: Cambridge University Press, 2006), 13.

28 Hymans, *The Psychology of Nuclear Proliferation: Identity, Emotions, and Foreign Policy*, 35.

29 Soutik Biswas, "'War' and India PM Modi's Muscular Strongman Image," BBC News, March 6, 2019, accessed on November 23, 2019, https://www.bbc.com/news/world-asia-india-47439101.

30 Shishir Gupta, Rezaul H. Laskar, and Yashwant Raj, "India, Pakistan Came Close to Firing Missiles at Each Other on February 27," *Hindustan Times*, March 23, 2019, accessed on October 23, 2019, https://www.hindustantimes.com/india-news/india-pakistan-came-close-to-firing-missiles-at-each-other-on-february-27/story-rVsBjZ5qmxXMprktzDNqcM.html.

31 *India Today* Web Desk, "Our Nuclear Weapons Are Not for Diwali: PM Modi on Pakistan's Nuclear Button Threat," *India Today*, April 21, 2019, accessed on October 25, 2019, https://www.indiatoday.in/elections/lok-sabha-2019/story/our-nuclear-weapons-are-not-for-diwali-pm-modi-on-pak-nuclear-button-threat-1506893-2019-04-21.

32 Helen Regan, Sophia Saifi, and Tara John, "Pakistan Releases Indian Pilot in an Effort to Diffuse the Kashmir Crisis," *CNN* March 1, 2019, accessed on January 13, 2022, https://www.cnn.com/2019/03/01/india/india-pakistan-pilot-release-intl/index.html.

33 Bloomberg, "Trump Says US Will Outspend Rivals on Its Nuclear Arsenal," *The Irish Times*, October 23, 2018, accessed on December 10, 2019, https://www.irishtimes.com/news/world/us/trump-says-us-will-outspend-rivals-on-its-nuclear-arsenal-1.3672678.

34 Peter Hayes, "Trump and the Interregnum of American Nuclear Hegemony," *Journal for Peace and Nuclear Disarmament* 1, no 2 (2018): 225.

Part II

THE USES AND PERILS OF NUCLEAR WEAPONS

Chapter 6

NUCLEAR COERCION—EVALUATING INSIGHTS FROM ACADEMIC SCHOLARSHIP

Walter C. Ladwig III

A prominent view in the field of international relations suggests that international politics was fundamentally altered by the introduction of the atomic bomb in 1945. The tremendous destructive power of nuclear weapons and the speed with which they achieved their effect upended the traditional strategic calculations between ends and means, undermining the role of force as a central tool of statecraft. As Bernard Brodie famously exhorted, 'Thus far the chief purpose of our military establishment has been to win wars. From now on its chief purpose must be to avert them. It can have almost no other useful purpose.'[1]

One of the main difficulties facing scholars who investigate the political effects of nuclear weapons on international relations is the comparative lack of empirical evidence on which to base claims: nuclear weapons have only been used in anger twice and seventy-five years after their advent, fewer than ten countries are believed to possess a nuclear capability. Consequently, many traditional beliefs about the effects of nuclear weapons on international politics rest on limited evidence or deductions based on theories drawn from other fields of social interaction.[2]

Recent years have seen a resurgence of academic interest in nuclear issues. New scholarship on the political effects of nuclear weapons, often employing quantitative methods, have challenged some traditional beliefs while confirming others. Since neither security challenges nor nuclear status is randomly distributed across the international system, these 'large-n' studies are ultimately based on observational data. Promising though they are, their results can only report correlations, not concrete causal claims.[3] Consequently, while definitive conclusions remain elusive, a much more nuanced understanding of how international politics has been shaped by the nuclear era is emerging.

This chapter examines the academic literature on nuclear coercion and crises. To do so, it proceeds in three parts. The first section explores the empirical evidence undergirding three schools of thought on nuclear coercion. The second section identifies the factors that scholars report affect the efficacy of nuclear threats. The last section explores the logic of nuclear first use.

EVALUATING NUCLEAR COERCION

Most scholars who study coercion in international relations employ Thomas Schelling's framework which divides the subject into two distinct sub-categories: deterrence and compellence.[4] Although both are forms of coercion, they differ in their objectives and have different dynamics.

From a conceptual standpoint, deterrence involves preventing a target from undertaking a particular act by convincing them that the perceived costs outweigh the expected benefits. This can be achieved by persuading the target that they will not accomplish their objective in the first place (deterrence by denial) or by threatening severe retaliation against something the opponent holds dear if they undertake the specified act (deterrence by punishment). Irrespective of the approach, the target is expected to respond rationally to the threats on the basis of an educated cost-benefit calculation. Whereas deterrence seeks to preserve the status quo and prevent changes, compellence employs threats to force a target to alter its conduct. The objective may be to oblige an adversary to do something specific they have not done or to reverse an action they have already taken.

Aside from the objective, deterrence and compellence also differ in terms of where the initiative lies, the time scale for action and the reputational effects incurred. With deterrence, the threatening state outlines the proscribed action and only executes the promised punishment if the target undertakes the undesirable act. The trigger for punishment is in the hands of the target. With compellence, on the other hand, the hostile state threatens or commences a punishing action that only ceases when the target complies with the coercer's wishes. Deterrent threats could exist more or less indefinitely. As long as the target avoids acting in a specified manner, the threat can remain latent. With compellence, on the other hand, a clear deadline for action is typically part of the threat. If no time frame is specified, the target could delay action forever.

Since it involves a concrete action on the part of the target—reversing something they have already done or doing something they would otherwise not wish to—complying with a compellent threat is far more visible than compliance with the deterrent threat. Consequently, acceding to a compellent threat can involve a reputational or prestige cost for the target. With deterrence, on the other hand, complying with a threat literally requires the target to do nothing. There is no need for them to indicate they were deterred or even acknowledge the deterrent threat in the first place. Thus, deterrence does not necessarily carry with it the 'loss of face' that is inherent in compellence. Consequently, deterrence is often seen as an easier objective to accomplish than compellence.

The literature on nuclear weapons has produced at least three major schools of thought regarding the efficacy of these devices as tools of coercion. The first, the so-called nuclear revolution, is the dominant view in most international relations scholarship and contends that deterrence with nuclear weapons is comparatively easy, while compellence is quite hard. The second school of thought, nuclear irrelevance, takes issue with the concept of nuclear deterrence, arguing that nuclear weapons are ineffective in warding off challengers who are cowed by robust conventional forces instead. The third school of thought, brinksmanship, is far more optimistic about the prospects of compellence via nuclear threats than the nuclear revolution literature suggests. The remainder of the section explores each of these perspectives in more detail and assesses the degree to which their theoretical predictions are upheld or challenged by existing scholarship.

The Nuclear Revolution

In line with Brodie's comments in the introduction, the dominant view in much of the international relations literature sees the development of the atomic bomb as a transformational development in the history of warfare. According to adherents of what Robert Jervis termed the 'nuclear revolution' viewpoint, these devices are primarily defensive weapons: the threat to retaliate with a nuclear strike is a powerful tool in the hands of a state that wished to preserve its territory and independence in the face of an adversary who sought to deprive them of it.[5] With just a handful of survivable weapons, Waltz argued, a nuclear-armed state could defend itself from most challenges.[6] Once protected in such a manner, a state can ensure its security via nuclear deterrence more or less indefinitely, 'because thwarting a first strike is easy....'[7] Since the requirements for effective deterrence are seen to be so low, when crises between nuclear-armed states do occur, the outcomes are not expected to be determined by the nuclear balance.[8] In Stephen Walt's words, 'nuclear superiority was a meaningless concept'.[9]

The defensive power of nuclear weapons is presumed to be so great that the costs of attempting an offensive against a nuclear adversary rise to unthinkable levels.[10] Consequently, the political utility of nuclear weapons, Jervis argued, is much greater for those with defensive aims, such as deterring threats and preserving the status quo.[11] They are less useful for pursuing revisionist objectives and compelling states to act in specific ways, particularly if the target also possesses nuclear weapons.[12] Thus, nuclear deterrence is relatively easy and nuclear compellence is very difficult. With the non-violent end of the Cold War, it was easy to accept arguments such as that of John Gaddis, that the nuclear stalemate explained the 'long peace' between heavily armed, ideologically antagonistic superpowers.[13]

This body of literature suggests that the risks of a catastrophic nuclear exchange mean that nuclear-armed states will be reluctant to initiate military crises with each other and non-nuclear states will avoid triggering a confrontation with a nuclear-armed state as well. As John Mearsheimer contends, 'the presence of nuclear weapons makes states more cautious about using military force of any kind against each other'.[14] Consequently, threats of violence and the use of force should no longer be seen as viable tools of international politics, at least between nuclear powers.[15]

Perhaps reflecting its dominance in academia, surveys of former US national security official find that a majority hold views in line with the nuclear revolution thesis.[16] What evidence do we have to support the nuclear revolution thesis? Empirical analysis of inter-state disputes between 1945 and 1976 by Bueno de Mesquita and Riker reports that 'the presence of an explicit or underlying nuclear threat constrains conflict by reducing its likelihood of escalating into war'.[17] More recent work by Rauchhaus examining both the outbreak of war and militarised interstate disputes between pairs of states from 1885 to 2000 also finds that nuclear-armed states are less likely to fight wars with each other.[18] The assumption that nuclear weapons result in less risky behaviour is borne out by Asal and Beardsley who find that the involvement of a nuclear-armed state in a crisis increases the chances of a non-violent resolution, an effect that is magnified the more nuclear-weapon states are involved.[19] All of these findings are in line with the expectations of nuclear revolution literature.

Does the presence of nuclear weapons on both sides of a crisis make the participants more cautious? Multiple studies by Asal and Beardsley fail to conclude that the presence of nuclear weapons deters the outbreak of crises between nuclear-armed states, even if those crises are less likely to escalate into full-blown war. Similarly, separate studies by Geller and Rauchhaus find that the chances of a crisis escalating short of war are significantly greater when both sides possess nuclear weapons, compared to disputes between pairs of non-nuclear states.[20] In contrast to the expectations that nuclear weapons on both sides of a conflict have a pacifying effect on belligerents, Bell and Miller report that nuclear-armed states are no less likely to go to war with each other than non-nuclear states are.[21]

Indeed, the most significant challenge to the nuclear revolution comes from the 1999 Kargil war between India and Pakistan. Instead of inhibiting risk-taking, as the nuclear revolution theory would suggest, Paul Kapur argues that possession of nuclear weapons actually encouraged Pakistan's military leaders to mount a high-risk operation to seize territory from their larger neighbour, secure in the belief that their nuclear capability would protect them from retaliation.[22] Admittedly, this is the only example of a war between nuclear-armed states. However, its existence undermines much of the certitude associated with the predictions of the nuclear revolution school of thought.

While not challenging the idea of nuclear deterrence per se, some scholars have questioned the presumptions that nuclear revolution theorists make about the survivability of nuclear forces and, therefore, the durability of deterrence and mutually assured destruction (MAD). During the Cold War, the limits of sensor technology and missile accuracy made counterforce targeting a difficult prospect, which, in turn, led scholars to presume it was relatively easy for the two superpowers to develop survivable arsenals that could provide the kind of secure second-strike capability that allowed a MAD stalemate to set in.[23] The validity of that claim has been challenged by recent scholarship. Green and Long call into question the degree to which Cold War policymakers, such as Soviet leaders, actually saw the stalemate MAD supposedly imposed as a stabilising and enduring factor of international politics.[24] The reason? Technological advancement rendered MAD a delicate balance which, in turn, led the two superpowers to pursue nuclear supremacy.[25] In the contemporary era, Lieber and Press argue that increasingly accurate nuclear-delivery systems, paired with persistent real-time sensor networks, are reducing the survivability of nuclear arsenals by weakening the effectiveness of the key means of defending nuclear weapons: concealment and hardening.[26] In a similar vein, Long and Green contend that the USA was far more successful than commonly believed at tracking mobile missile launchers and nuclear-armed submarines, which raises questions about the survivability of second-strike nuclear forces.[27] Thus, according to this point of view, counterforce strikes to disarm an opponent are an increasingly plausible undertaking. This, in turn, suggests that maintaining a secure second-strike capability to ensure deterrence may be more difficult than the nuclear revolution literature suggests.

On balance, there is a reasonable amount of evidence to support the predictions of the nuclear revolution thesis. This is particularly true with respect to the expectations that nuclear-armed states will rarely, if ever, go to war. In seven decades, we have only one example of a conventional war between two nuclear-armed states. Some of the other expectations of the nuclear revolution literature appear to rest on less solid ground. Empirical analysis of the behaviour of nuclear-armed states indicates that crises occur at a rate of frequency far beyond what much of the nuclear revolution literature would expect and that crisis escalation is more, not less, likely when nuclear weapons are possessed by both parties to a dispute. Moreover, there are increasing questions as to whether the assumptions made in much of this literature about the ease of achieving deterrence stability is a universal truth or is simply the result of the limitations of existing technology in the 1970s and 1980s.

IRRELEVANCE OF NUCLEAR WEAPONS

Challenging the orthodoxy of the nuclear revolution thesis is the view that nuclear weapons are actually irrelevant for deterrence and, in some instances, may actually exacerbate crises. Scholars such as Michael Gordin contend that when the first atomic bombs were used against Japan, their revolutionary strategic potential was not perceived by the US military and other key decision-makers.[28] Rather than being a fundamentally different type of weapon, they were simply seen as bigger and more effective versions of what came before them. Surprising though this view may be, given the way in which international relations scholarship has reified nuclear weapons as fundamentally different from their conventional counterparts, there are those who claim that their effects on strategy, coercion and international politics more broadly are overstated.

The most prominent proponent of the view that nuclear weapons have little relevance for either deterrence or explanations of the broad geopolitical patterns of the Cold War is the political scientist John Mueller. He attributes the lack of major-power war since 1945 not to the presence of nuclear weapons, as Gaddis does, but to the intense destructive power of conventional militaries, which render inter-state war between great powers useless as a tool of statecraft.[29] Thus, fears of an escalation in crisis and unwillingness by either of the two superpowers to use force against each other cannot be attributed to their nuclear arsenals. These tools may have contributed to keeping the peace on the margins. However, events would have played out in exactly the same manner if they had been absent. In a related view, deterrence sceptics like Lebow and Stein have challenged the idea that the nuclear stalemate contributed to peaceful relations between the USA and the

Soviet Union. Examining key nuclear flashpoints, such as the Cuban Missile Crisis and the 1973 Arab–Israeli war, the duo concludes that nuclear deterrence strategies, as employed by the superpowers, were more provocative than pacific, and ultimately contributed to prolonging the Cold War.[30]

Is there evidence to support Mueller's assertion that the conventional military balance is more salient than the balance of nuclear capabilities explaining crisis behaviour or outcomes? Blechman and Kaplan's study of more than 200 uses of force by the USA finds that in episodes involving the USA and the Soviet Union, the outcome of confrontations was determined primarily by the conventional military balance at the local level, rather than the size of each superpower's strategic nuclear arsenal.[31] This finding is echoed by Kugler's examination of crisis escalation in clashes involving China, the Soviet Union and the USA, which finds that conventional military force levels, rather than nuclear capabilities, are the main factor shaping crisis outcomes, irrespective of their severity.[32]

Are there concrete reasons to believe that nuclear weapons might, in fact, not have significant deterrent value? A study of militarised interstate disputes involving great powers, which was carried out by Huth, Bennett and Gelpi, determined that challengers are not precluded from initiating military confrontations against major powers armed with nuclear weapons.[33] This finding is echoed by a more recent scholarship carried out by Gartzke and Joe, who expressly investigate the connection between patterns of militarised interstate disputes and nuclear weapons.[34] The conclusion they reach is that dispute initiation is not affected by possession of nuclear weapons. Significant conventional military capabilities, existing security challenges and broader geopolitical interests, not nuclear weapons, make states more likely to undertake military challenges against each other.[35] In line with these arguments is the aforementioned study by Bell and Miller which concludes that pairs of nuclear-armed states are no more or less prone to war than non-nuclear states.[36]

Evidence questioning the relevance of nuclear weapons for deterrence is most striking in a series of studies examining the interaction between pairs of states where only one side possesses nuclear weapons. In such scenarios, Geller finds that non-nuclear states are willing to assertively escalate a crisis with a nuclear-armed opponent.[37] Historically, Kugler reports non-nuclear states have prevailed over their nuclear-armed opponents in a number of 'extreme crises' occurring between 1946 and 1991, while Organski and Kugler find that nuclear-armed states were defeated by non-nuclear opponents in six of seven armed conflicts between 1945 and 1979.[38] Echoing previously discussed research, both of these studies conclude that the successful party was the one with the superior conventional military force, not a nuclear arsenal.

These various studies provide mixed support for claims that nuclear weapons are irrelevant at best and destabilising at worst. Scholars found that, in interactions between pairs of nuclear-armed states, conventional military capabilities rather than the size of a nuclear arsenal is the primary predictor of both the initiation of interstate disputes and crisis outcomes bolster Mueller's argument.[39] Lebow and Stein's claims are supported by findings by Geller and Rauchhaus discussed previously, that disputes between pairs of nuclear-armed states are more likely to escalate versus those carried out by pairs of non-nuclear states.[40] Claims about the irrelevancy of nuclear weapons for deterrence are further strengthened by the conclusion that possession of nuclear weapons has little relevance for explaining the outcomes of crises or conflicts between a nuclear-armed state and a non-nuclear opponent.[41] Once again, the conventional military balance between the two parties best explains crisis outcomes, which most often favoured the non-nuclear state.[42] Instead of dampening the chances of conflict, non-nuclear states in a dispute with a nuclear power are more likely to escalate the clash and the likelihood of war is greater in comparison to conflicts involving two nuclear powers.[43] Taken together, these studies suggest that even when only one party has nuclear weapons, that fact will not affect the likelihood that a dispute will be initiated, its escalation potential, nor its outcome. This, in turn, raises big questions about the deterrent power of nuclear weapons and the assumptions of deterrence put forth by proponents of the nuclear revolution thesis.

The main challenge to claims of nuclear irrelevancy comes from the multiple studies demonstrating that war is substantially less likely to occur between pairs of states when both sides possess nuclear weapons than when neither possess them.[44] The conclusion that nuclear status does lead to different patterns of behaviour, however, is inconsistent with Mueller's argument that the presence of nuclear weapons has no bearing on interstate interactions. Although the claims of nuclear irrelevancy are only partially upheld by the research reviewed here, this scholarship also suggests that the case for the transformative effects of nuclear deterrence on international politics made by proponents of the nuclear revolution thesis remains, in the Scottish verdict, 'not proven'.

BRINKSMANSHIP

Whereas the nuclear irrelevance school questions the viability of deterrence, brinksmanship questions the nuclear revolution literature's assumption that nuclear weapons cannot easily compel an opponent. Scholars embracing this line of reasoning see nuclear weapons as narrowly useful for deterring nuclear first use by an opponent but question the ability of nuclear weapons to ward off conflict at other levels.[45] A range of work from the 1960s examined tactics that could be employed to allow nuclear weapons to compel an opponent.[46] A key means by which nuclear-armed states could leverage their strategic arsenals to achieve offensive political objectives is by engaging in high-risk behaviour, which Schelling referred to as a strategy of brinksmanship.[47] Although in general, compellent nuclear threats may not appear to be credible, Schelling suggests states can take actions to purposefully increase the risk that events spiral out of control, resulting in a devastating outcome that no side would rationally choose. The metaphor often invoked is the classic game of chicken where two drivers drive directly at each other at high speeds until one party loses its nerve and swerves out of the way (or both cars crash). In a similar manner, by manoeuvring the other side into a position where their only choice is to capitulate or to risk experiencing reciprocal devastation, brinksmanship can allow a state to leverage non-credible threats to achieve real gains.[48] Actions such as deploying low-yield nuclear weapons on the battlefield and pre-delegating launch authority to local commanders can increase the risk of accidental nuclear exchange, which would not be strictly rational. By escalating the chances that a mutually catastrophic outcome would occur, an aggressor can push a target to the point where they lose their nerve and back down, conciliating the aggressor rather than risking devastation.

Strategies of brinksmanship may give nuclear weapons far greater utility for achieving 'offensive' political objectives than the nuclear revolution school suggests. In other words, nuclear weapons could be effective tools of compellence. As discussed above, calibrated escalation in a crisis, what Herman Kahn referred to as 'a competition in risk-taking', is a key means of weakening an adversary's resolve.[49] Since the consequences of a nuclear conflict are so profound, a number of scholars contend that states on the receiving end of nuclear threats will be highly motivated to avoid conflict and manifest an extensive trade space when it comes to meeting an aggressor's demands.[50] Virtually, any bargaining outcome leaves the target better off than it would be from suffering a nuclear strike. From a rationalist standpoint, nuclear weapons and nuclear threats can enhance a state's bargaining effectiveness relative to non-nuclear-weapon states.

The logic of brinksmanship is rooted in game theory and draws analogies from risky strategic interactions in other walks of life, like the aforementioned game of chicken. In practice, is it a viable means of leveraging nuclear arsenals to make compellence possible? Sechser and Fuhrmann contend it is unlikely to do so for two key reasons.[51] First, signalling to an adversary in the middle of a crisis can be difficult. Military signals are infamously vague. The 'message' being sent by the movement of delivery vehicles, the conduct of flight tests or the mating of warheads may not be noticed or may be misconstrued. During the 1999 Kargil war, for example, the USA believed it detected Pakistani efforts to operationalise its nuclear arsenal but Indian sources were split as to whether this alleged nuclear signalling was real and how credible a threat it represented.[52] Pakistani observers allege that US national technical means failed to detect similar preparations by India and suggest that information provided by reconnaissance satellites lacked context, and therefore confused defensive preparations by Pakistani missile forces for offensive ones.[53] The second constraint on employing a strategy of brinksmanship is a given leader's appetite for risk. The danger that events can spin out of control may be intolerable for an opponent but it can also be unbearable for the triggering side as well. An extremely high level of risk tolerance is necessary to engage in nuclear brinksmanship, which may not be possessed by most national leaders.

Is there evidence that nuclear-armed states are willing to engage in Kahn's risk-taking competition and, more importantly, that such behaviour leads them to triumph in a crisis? Both Asal and Beardsley as well as Rauchhaus report that pairs of nuclear-armed states engage in crises at a much higher rate than non-nuclear states.[54] Geller finds that compared to pairs of non-nuclear states, confrontations between nuclear-armed states are more likely to escalate short of war, a finding echoed by Rauchhaus.[55] In line with the brinksmanship thesis, Kroenig's examination of fifty-two crises involving pairs of nuclear-armed states reports that states possessing a clear nuclear superiority are willing to accept more risk in a confrontation and employ brinksmanship strategies.[56] In turn, these states are more likely to prevail over their opponents without resorting to a full-scale war. Similarly, De Mesquita and Riker contend that possessing an asymmetric nuclear advantage over another state allows one to employ its arsenal for offensive political gains.[57] A related study by Beardsley and Asal looks at crisis bargaining between nuclear-armed and non-nuclear states, which concludes that nuclear powers are more likely to prevail.[58] Thus, these studies indicate nuclear weapons can be a source of leverage in international politics and accrue political benefits to their possessors quite apart from their military utility.

Sechser and Fuhrmann's neo-orthodox 'nuclear skepticism theory' has raised questions about the value of nuclear weapons for compellence[59] The duo contends that nuclear weapons are a weak tool of compellence.

The ideal instruments of compellence are those that allow a state to: (a) effectively force a target to do what it wants and (b) inflict significant harm comparatively cheaply. Neither of these characteristics applies to nuclear weapons. In line with nuclear revolution theorists, Sechser and Fuhrmann contend that nuclear weapons have limited usefulness for wresting control of contested objectives or terrain from an adversary. Moreover, the cost to the aggressor state of following through on a nuclear threat is a significant one. Not only would the target respond with full force but the use of nuclear weapons would be expected to provoke the opprobrium of the international community as well, which could endanger its longer-term interests. In the face of an existential threat to a country's survival or independence, the cost of using nuclear weapons may be worth paying. When it comes to a compellent threat, however, the balance of resolve often favours the defender. States are willing to fight harder and suffer more to defend things they already have. Conversely, aggressors have lived without the contested objective; therefore, possessing it cannot be an existential issue. Thus, they assert that nuclear-armed states can deliver credible deterrent threats but are not any more likely to compel an adversary than non-nuclear states. In fact, their statistical analysis of 210 compellent threats delivered between 1918 and 2001 finds that states equipped with nuclear weapons are actually less effective at compelling adversaries than non-nuclear states, even when possessing a nuclear monopoly.

Paul Bracken adds nuance to the debate. He argues that it is necessary to distinguish between nuclear compellence of the type studied by Kroenig and Sechser and Fuhrmann, and compellence in a nuclear context, which, he asserts, is quite different.[60] The former involves explicit nuclear threats to compel a target to act, whereas the latter is compellence by a state possessing nuclear weapons where no explicit atomic threat is issued. As long as a state has nuclear weapons, Bracken contends, compellence targets have to assume their use is 'on the table', which renders any threat an implicit nuclear one.[61] Thus, the study of 'nuclear blackmail' needs to be broadened beyond the 'narrow' set of instances where explicit nuclear threats are issued to capture the full range of situations in which nuclear weapons affect the dynamics of coercion.

How well does the brinksmanship thesis fare in the literature reviewed here? Multiple studies report that pairs of nuclear-armed states engage in a large number of crises and that they are more likely to escalate those crises than non-nuclear states. This provides a strong indication that states can and do engage in competitive risk-taking. The evidence is much more mixed with respect to the utility of nuclear weapons in general and this risk-taking crisis behaviour in particular to achieve superior compellence results, with some studies concluding nuclear superiority is associated with compellence success and others contesting that conclusion.

FACTORS INFLUENCING THE EFFICACY OF NUCLEAR COERCION

Early nuclear theorists tended to adopt a binary understanding of nuclear status: states either had nuclear weapons or they did not, and the coercive effects of such weapons were seen to operate irrespective of what anyone else did.[62] This point of view, which Narang refers to as the 'existential bias' in nuclear scholarship, has been challenged by other scholars who demonstrate that how states structure and deploy their nuclear arsenals has an effect on their coercive potential.[63]

One factor that can affect the coercive effects of nuclear weapons is the size and configuration of a state's arsenal. Does having more nuclear weapons than your opponent strengthen your ability to coerce them? The nuclear revolution thesis personified by Jervis suggests that the nuclear balance is immaterial. In order to deter an adversary, a state really just requires a secure second-strike capability. Anything beyond that is unnecessary. In contrast, other scholars contend that nuclear coercion is only effective when the aggressor state has such an overwhelming superiority that it need not fear an adversary's atomic retribution.[64] This view on the benefits of nuclear supremacy is echoed by Kroenig who reviews more than four dozen nuclear crises and reports that the size of a state's nuclear arsenal is correlated with the likelihood of prevailing in a crisis.[65] Consensus on this point does not exist in the scholarship, however, as Sechser and Fuhrmann's examination of 210 interstate compellent threats reports the opposite conclusion—a nuclear advantage has no bearing on the success of coercive efforts.[66]

A second issue influencing the coercive effect of a state's nuclear arsenal is the particular configuration of its delivery systems. Gartzke, Kaplow and Mehta report that states possessing a diversified portfolio of nuclear delivery systems have greater success in deterring conventional conflict.[67] This holds true in disputes with both nuclear and non-nuclear states and is more important for explaining deterrence outcomes than either possessing survivable nuclear forces or nuclear superiority. If this is true, why don't all states pursue a broad range of nuclear delivery vehicles? The ability to do so is limited by both the need to simultaneously contend with conventional military threats and the state's overall resource constraints.[68] However, states with nuclear-armed allies or rivals pursue diversification, which also tends to increase the longer a state possesses nuclear weapons.

The nuclear posture adopted by a state is a third factor that can affect the efficacy of their nuclear threats. Narang identifies a typology of nuclear postures pursued by emerging nuclear-armed states in the second nuclear age.[69] The first approach, catalytic, primarily focuses on using nuclear arsenals to attract third-party intervention in a crisis. The primary 'target' of the strategy is not an adversary but an ally or neutral one is pressing to intervene on one's behalf. Pursuing this strategy requires only a nuclear force in being—a survivable second strike is not essential. Israel's behaviour during the 1973 Yom Kippur war is a prime example of this approach. The second posture, assured retaliation, seeks to deter nuclear coercion by threatening a guaranteed nuclear response. Possessing a secure second-strike capability, the state can guarantee a response to any first strike against it, punishing aggressor cities or other countervalue targets. Assured retaliation only requires a small nuclear arsenal and is the basic nuclear strategy traditionally pursued by India and China. The final posture, asymmetric escalation, focuses on deterring threats by undertaking the first use of nuclear weapons against enemy forces or strategic targets in the event of a crisis. Echoing US experiments with massive retaliation and flexible response in the 1950s and 1960s, asymmetric escalation is the nuclear posture pursued by France during the Cold War and Pakistan today. Of these three nuclear postures, Narang reports that only asymmetric escalation is effective at deterring the outbreak or intensification of conventional war.[70] In contrast, assured retaliation and catalytic postures have historically been associated with deterrence failure. Thus, states possessing similarly sized nuclear arsenals achieve different deterrence outcomes based on the nuclear posture they adopt.

THE LOGIC OF NUCLEAR FIRST USE

There are several reasons why a state would retain an option of nuclear first use, or not be willing to move beyond a merely rhetorical commitment to NFU.[71] The first reason is to pre-empt an impending nuclear threat by an adversary. If the state believes that an opponent is preparing to strike it with nuclear weapons, countless lives might be saved by eliminating or reducing the antagonist's arsenal in a pre-emptive strike. The ability to undertake a pre-emptive strike requires a country's nuclear arsenal to have a high degree of readiness so that decision-makers can quickly respond to a warning. As noted previously, changes in technology may be making a counterforce strike a more realistic or effective possibility.

The second reason why states might wish to retain a first use option is to deter against the use of other weapons of mass destruction. If a state feels that its conventional military offers insufficient retaliatory options to adequately punish an actor for using biological or chemical weapons against it, the nuclear option may be retained for such purposes. The USA is a prime example of a country that appears to find utility in a first-use option for these purposes. Despite arguments against the use of nuclear weapons to deter chemical and biological threats, neither the Clinton, Bush or Obama administrations were willing to publicly rule out this possibility.[72]

A third plausible reason for maintaining a first-use option is to deter conventional military threats. If a state faces an adversary that is believed to have a major conventional military advantage, tactical or strategic nuclear weapons could be a key means of raising the anticipated cost to an attacker of undertaking a military adventure. As noted previously, Narang's research on alternative nuclear postures found that only asymmetric escalation—which explicitly retains the option of nuclear first use—was effective in deterring conventional military threats.[73] The threat of battlefield nuclear weapons has a secondary benefit in that should deterrence fail, hostile forces will have to disperse themselves on the battlefield to minimise the consequences of a nuclear strike, which can negatively influence their military effectiveness. During the Cold War, the overwhelming numerical superiority of the Soviet Red Army and its proximity to Western Europe led the USA and its NATO allies to adopt a nuclear-based deterrent strategy to dissuade a presumed Soviet conventional attack on Western Europe.

Related to the point above, nuclear first use may be seen as having utility not just for deterring an attack on oneself but on allies as well. American security guarantees to Japan, South Korea and its NATO partners are based on an alleged willingness to employ US nuclear weapons against an aggressor who threatens them. Since nuclear escalation could mean that an adversary would respond with an attack on the USA itself, the credibility of such guarantees was always an issue, as exemplified by the infamous question: Would the USA trade Boston for Berlin? A range of actions was undertaken to enhance the credibility of such promises, including the forward deployment of nuclear weapons on allies' soil. Fuhrmann and Sechser report that the latter approach has no effect on deterring aggression; what matters is possessing an alliance with a nuclear-armed state, not the basing of their nuclear weapons in your country.[74] US allies remain strongly opposed to an NFU pledge, illustrating their perceptions of the importance of the nuclear option in their defence.

Finally, the first use of nuclear weapons can be seen by a state as the ultimate guarantee of its independence and freedom. As a last resort in the face of near-certain defeat, employment of nuclear weapons might salvage an otherwise untenable situation and avert catastrophe. The threat of first use may also prevent a hostile power from pushing for a nuclear-armed state's unconditional surrender and even create some kind of bargaining space in post-conflict negotiations. The so-called Sampson Option, an alleged Israeli nuclear strategy of massive retaliation in the event the country was being overrun, is an example of this 'last resort' logic.[75]

CONCLUSION

Although nuclear weapons have been with us for more than seven decades, scholars are still coming to grips with their effect on international politics. Traditional views on the ease of nuclear deterrence have been called into question by changes in technology as well as recent research indicating that the choices states make regarding their nuclear posture and portfolio of delivery systems affects the ability to dissuade adversaries, if indeed, nuclear weapons deter at all. When it comes to predictions about nuclear crises and coercion, what theoretical propositions are supported by empirical study and which have been found wanting? The expectations found in the nuclear revolution literature, that wars between nuclear states should be infrequent occurrences, is upheld by the fact that the 1999 Kargil war is the only example of such a clash between two nuclear-armed states in more than seven decades. The expectation that the presence of nuclear weapons will lead states to avoid crises and minimise escalation, however, is not upheld. In fact, both crises and escalation are a common phenomenon when nuclear weapons are on both sides of a dispute. Suggestions that nuclear weapons are irrelevant for coercion and crisis are bolstered by the finding that the possession of nuclear weapons does not prevent an opponent from initiating a dispute, escalating a crisis or using force against a nuclear-armed defender. Indeed, non-nuclear states have prevailed over nuclear opponents in conflict and crisis with surprising frequency, raising questions about the ability of nuclear weapons to deter conventional threats. The broader claims that nuclear weapons cannot explain patterns of state behaviours is undermined by multiple studies indicating that pairs of nuclear, non-nuclear and mixed states do exhibit differing likelihoods of escalating crises and fighting wars. Finally, the conclusion that pairs of nuclear-armed states are more likely to escalate a crisis—short of war—validates aspects of the brinksmanship literature. The possibility of nuclear blackmail remains a concern. Early thinking on the irrelevance of nuclear weapons for compellence has been challenged by revisionist scholars who contend that nuclear threats can be used to intimidate targets into capitulation. In turn, these revisionist views have been contested by neo-orthodox scholarship, which contend that nuclear threats lack credibility and nuclear weapons are not capable of changing the status quo. Despite hopes that in the twenty-first century, a norm of nuclear NFU might be adopted, few states have been willing to move beyond a rhetorical commitment to that cause; arguments remain for retaining the first-use option. As the field of international relations sees a resurgence of scholarly research on nuclear weapons, our understanding of all of these issues will continue to improve. The first generation of nuclear theorists shaped our thinking about the political effects of nuclear weapons. The challenge for contemporary scholars is to understand which of these insights are timeless and which no longer apply in the second nuclear era.

NOTES

1 Bernard Brodie, *The Absolute Weapon: Atomic Power and World Order* (New York: Harcourt, Brace, 1946), 76.
2 For example, Scott Sagan's concern about the effect of nuclear proliferations draws its insights from organization theory. Scott D. Sagan, "The Perils of Proliferation: Organization Theory, Deterrence Theory, and the Spread of Nuclear Weapons," *International Security* 18, no 4 (1994): 66–107.
3 Vipin Narang, "The Use and Abuse of Large-N Methods in Nuclear Security," in James McAllister and Diane Labrosse, eds, *What We Talk about When We Talk about Nuclear Weapons*(H-Diplo/ISSF Forum, no 2, 2014), 95, http://issforum.org/ISSF/PDF/ISSF-Forum-2.pdf.
4 Thomas C. Schelling, *Arms and Influence* (New Haven: Yale University Press, 1966).
5 Stephen Walt, "Rethinking the 'Nuclear Revolution,'" *Foreign Policy*, August 3, 2010, https://foreignpolicy.com/2010/08/03/rethinking-the-nuclear-revolution
6 Kenneth N. Waltz, "The Spread of Nuclear Weapons: More May Be Better," Adelphi Papers, 21, no 171 (London: International Institute of Strategic Studies, 1981), 171.
7 Scott D. Sagan and Kenneth N. Waltz, *The Spread of Nuclear Weapons: A Debate Renewed, with New Sections on India and Pakistan, Terrorism, and Missile Defense* (Manhattan: W.W. Norton & Company, 2003), 30.

8 Richard K. Betts, *Nuclear Blackmail and Nuclear Balance* (Washington, DC: Brookings Institution Press, 1987), 218–219; Robert Jervis, *The Meaning of the Nuclear Revolution: Statecraft and the Prospect of Armageddon* (Ithaca: Cornell University Press, 1989), 42.
9 Walt, "Rethinking the 'Nuclear Revolution.'"
10 Stephen Van Evera, *Causes of War: Power and the Roots of Conflict* (Ithaca, New York: Cornell University Press, 1999), 178.
11 Jervis, *The Meaning of the Nuclear Revolution*.
12 Sagan and Waltz, *The Spread of Nuclear Weapons: A Debate Renewed*, 17.
13 John Lewis Gaddis, *The Long Peace: Inquiries into the History of the Cold War* (London: Oxford University Press on Demand, 1987). See also, George H. Quester, *The Future of Nuclear Deterrence* (Lanham, MD: Lexington Books, 1986); McGeorge Bundy, *Danger and Survival* (New York: Random House, 1988).
14 John J. Mearsheimer, *The Tragedy of Great Power Politics* (Manhattan: W.W. Norton & Company, 2001), 129.
15 Jervis, *The Meaning of the Nuclear Revolution*; Lawrence Freedman, *The Evolution of Nuclear Strategy* (New York: Springer, 1989); Kenneth N. Waltz, "Nuclear Myths and Political Realities," *American Political Science Review* 84, no 3 (1990): 730–745.
16 Paul C. Avey, "MAD and Taboo: US Expert Views on Nuclear Deterrence, Coercion, and Non-Use Norms," *Foreign Policy Analysis* 17, no 2 (2021): 1–14.
17 Bruce Bueno De Mesquita and William H. Riker, "An Assessment of the Merits of Selective Nuclear Proliferation," *Journal of Conflict Resolution* 26, no 2 (1982): 291.
18 Robert Rauchhaus, "Evaluating the Nuclear Peace Hypothesis: A Quantitative Approach," *Journal of Conflict Resolution* 53, no 2 (2009): 258–277.
19 Victor Asal and Kyle Beardsley, "Proliferation and International Crisis Behavior," *Journal of Peace Research* 44, no. 2 (2007).
20 Daniel S. Geller, "Nuclear Weapons, Deterrence, and Crisis Escalation," *Journal of Conflict Resolution* 34, no 2 (1990): 291–310; Rauchhaus, "Evaluating the Nuclear Peace Hypothesis: A Quantitative Approach."
21 Mark S. Bell and Nicholas L. Miller, "Questioning the Effect of Nuclear Weapons on Conflict," *Journal of Conflict Resolution*, 59, no 1 (2015): 74–92.
22 Paul S. Kapur, *Dangerous Deterrent: Nuclear Weapons Proliferation and Conflict in South Asia* (Stanford: Stanford University Press, 2009), 124.
23 Jervis, *The Meaning of the Nuclear Revolution*, 10.
24 Brendan R. Green and Austin Long, "The MAD Who Wasn't There: Soviet Reactions to the Late Cold War Nuclear Balance," *Security Studies* 26, no 4 (2017): 606–641.
25 Brendan R. Green, *The Revolution That Failed: Nuclear Competition, Arms Control, and the Cold War* (Cambridge University Press, 2020); Keir A. Lieber and Daryl G. Press, *The Myth of the Nuclear Revolution: Power Politics in the Atomic Age* (Cornell University Press, 2020).
26 Keir A. Lieber and Daryl G. Press, "The New Era of Nuclear Weapons, Deterrence, and Conflict," *Strategic Studies Quarterly* 7, no 1 (2013): 3–14.

27 Austin Long and Brendan R. Green, "Stalking the Secure Second Strike: Intelligence, Counterforce, and Nuclear Strategy," *Journal of Strategic Studies* 38, nos 1–2 (2015): 38–73.
28 Michael D. Gordin, *Five Days in August: How World War II Became a Nuclear War* (Princeton: Princeton University Press, 2007).
29 John Mueller, "The Essential Irrelevance of Nuclear Weapons: Stability in the Postwar World," *International Security* 13, no 2 (1988): 55–79; John Mueller, *Atomic Obsession: Nuclear Alarmism from Hiroshima to Al-Qaeda* (London: Oxford University Press, 2009).
30 Richard Ned Lebow and Janice Gross Stein, *We All Lost the Cold War* (Princeton: Princeton University Press, 1995).
31 Barry M. Blechman, Stephen S. Kaplan, and David K. Hall, *Force without War: U.S. Armed Forces as a Political Instrument* (Washington DC: Brookings Institution Press, 1978).
32 Jacek Kugler, "Terror without Deterrence: Reassessing the Role of Nuclear Weapons," *Journal of Conflict Resolution* 28, no 3 (1984): 501.
33 Paul Huth , D. Scott Bennett, and Christopher Gelpi, "System Uncertainty, Risk Propensity, and International Conflict among the Great Powers," *Journal of Conflict Resolution* 36, no 3 (1992): 478–517.
34 Dong-Joon Jo and Erik Gartzke, "Determinants of Nuclear Weapons Proliferation," *Journal of Conflict Resolution*, 51, no 1 (2007).
35 Jo and Gartzke, "Determinants of Nuclear Weapons Proliferation," 221.
36 Bell and Miller, "Questioning the Effect of Nuclear Weapons on Conflict."
37 Geller, "Nuclear Weapons, Deterrence, and Crisis Escalation."
38 Kugler, "Terror without Deterrence; A.F.K. Organski and Jacek Kugler, *The War Ledger* (Chicago: University of Chicago Press, 1981).
39 Blechman, Kaplan, and Hall, *Force without War*; Kugler, "Terror without Deterrence"; Huth, Bennett, and Gelpi, "System Uncertainty, Risk Propensity, and International Conflict among the Great Powers"; Jo and Gartzke, "Determinants of Nuclear Weapons Proliferation."
40 Geller, "Nuclear Weapons, Deterrence, and Crisis Escalation."
41 Geller, "Nuclear Weapons, Deterrence, and Crisis Escalation."; Rauchhaus, "Evaluating the Nuclear Peace Hypothesis: A Quantitative Approach."
42 Organski and Kugler, *The War Ledger*; Kugler, "Terror without Deterrence."
43 Geller, "Nuclear Weapons, Deterrence, and Crisis Escalation;" Rauchhaus, "Evaluating the Nuclear Peace Hypothesis."
44 Mesquita and Riker, "An Assessment of the Merits of Selective Nuclear Proliferation"; Geller, "Nuclear Weapons, Deterrence, and Crisis Escalation"; Asal and Beardsley, "Proliferation and International Crisis Behavior"; Rauchhaus, "Evaluating the Nuclear Peace Hypothesis."
45 Henry A. Kissinger, *Nuclear Weapons and Foreign Policy* (New York: Harper & Row, 1957).
46 Thomas C. Schelling, *The Strategy of Conflict* (Cambridge: Harvard University Press, 1960); Herman Kahn, *On Thermonuclear War* (Princeton: Princeton University Press, 1960); Kahn, *On Escalation: Metaphors and Scenarios* (New York, NY: Praeger, 1965); Schelling, *Arms and Influence.*
47 Schelling, *Arms and Influence.*

48 Schelling, *The Strategy of Conflict*, 200.
49 Kahn, *On Escalation: Metaphors and Scenarios* (New York: Praeger, 1965), 3.
50 Kyle Beardsley and Victor Asal, "Winning with the Bomb," *Journal of Conflict Resolution* 53, no 2 (2009): 278–301; Christopher R. Dittmeier, "Proliferation, Preemption, and Intervention in the Nuclearization of Second-Tier States," *Journal of Theoretical Politics* 25, no 4 (2013): 492–525; Bradley A. Thayer and Thomas M. Skypek, "Reaffirming the Utility of Nuclear Weapons," *Parameters* 42, no 4 (2013): 41–45.
51 Todd S. Sechser and Matthew Fuhrmann, *Nuclear Weapons and Coercive Diplomacy* (Cambridge: Cambridge University Press, 2017).
52 Michael Krepon and Liv Dowling, "Crisis Intensity and Nuclear Signaling in South Asia," in Sameer Lalwani and Hannah Haegeland, eds, *Investigating Crises: South Asia's Lessons, Evolving Dynamics, and Trajectories* (Washington DC: The Henry L. Stimson Center, 2018), 202.
53 Feroz Hassan Khan, "Nuclear Signaling, Missiles, and Escalation Control in South Asia," in Michael Krepon, Rodney W. Jones, and Ziad Haider, eds, *Escalation Control and the Nuclear Option in South Asia* (Washington DC: The Henry L. Stimson Center, 2004), 85–86.
54 Asal and Beardsley, "Proliferation and International Crisis Behavior"; Rauchhaus, "Evaluating the Nuclear Peace Hypothesis."
55 Geller, "Nuclear Weapons, Deterrence, and Crisis Escalation."
56 Matthew Kroenig, "Nuclear Superiority and the Balance of Resolve: Explaining Nuclear Crisis Outcomes," *International Organization* 67, no 1 (2013): 141–171.
57 Mesquita and Riker, "An Assessment of the Merits of Selective Nuclear Proliferation."
58 Beardsley and Asal, "Winning with the Bomb."
59 Sechser and Fuhrmann, *Nuclear Weapons and Coercive Diplomacy*.
60 Paul Bracken, "Blackmail under a Nuclear Umbrella," War on the Rocks, February 7, 2017, https://warontherocks.com/2017/02/blackmail-under-a-nuclear-umbrella.
61 For an earlier articulation of the same view, see Paul H. Nitze, "Atoms, Strategy and Policy," *Foreign Affairs* 34, no 2 (January 1956): 187.
62 Bernard Brodie, *Strategy in the Missile Age* (Princeton: Princeton University Press, 1959), 275; Waltz, *The Spread of Nuclear Weapons*; John J. Mearsheimer, "Nuclear Weapons and Deterrence in Europe," *International Security* 9, no 3 (1984): 19–46; Jervis, *The Meaning of the Nuclear Revolution*.
63 Vipin Narang, "What Does It Take to Deter? Regional Power Nuclear Postures and International Conflict," *Journal of Conflict Resolution* 57, no 3 (2013): 478–508.
64 Robert A. Pape, *Bombing to Win: Air Power and Coercion in War* (Ithaca, New York: Cornell University Press, 1996).
65 Kroenig, "Nuclear Superiority and the Balance of Resolve."
66 Sechser and Fuhrmann, *Nuclear Weapons and Coercive Diplomacy*.

67 Erik Gartzke, Jeffrey M. Kaplow, and Rupal N. Mehta, "Nuclear Deterrence and the Structure of Nuclear Forces," unpublished manuscript (San Diego: University of California, 2015).

68 Gartzke, Kaplow, and Mehta, "The Determinants of Nuclear Force Structure," *Journal of Conflict Resolution* 58, no 3 (2014): 481–508.

69 Narang, "What Does It Take to Deter?"

70 Ibid., 480.

71 For a general discussion of the utility of nuclear weapons, see Thayer and Skypek, "Reaffirming the Utility of Nuclear Weapons."

72 Scott D. Sagan, "The Commitment Trap: Why the United States Should Not Use Nuclear Threats to Deter Biological and Chemical Weapons Attacks," *International Security* 24, no 4 (2000): 85–115; Amy F. Woolf, "U.S. Nuclear Weapons Policy: Considering 'No First Use'" (Washington DC: Congressional Research Service, March 1, 2019).

73 Narang, "What Does It Take to Deter?."

74 Fuhrmann and Sechser, "Nuclear Strategy, Nonproliferation, and the Causes of Foreign Nuclear Deployments."

75 Avner Cohen, *Israel and the Bomb* (New York: Columbia University Press, 1998), 273–4; Louis René Beres, "Israel's Uncertain Strategic Future," *Parameters* 37, no. 1 (2007): 41.

Chapter 7

ASIA TREADS THE NUCLEAR PATH, UNAWARE THAT SELF-ASSURED DESTRUCTION WOULD RESULT FROM NUCLEAR WAR

Owen B. Toon, Alan Robock, Michael Mills And Lili Xia[1]

Of the nine countries known to have nuclear weapons, six are located in Asia and another, the United States, borders the Pacific Ocean. Russia and China were the first Asian nations with nuclear weapons, followed by Israel, India, Pakistan and North Korea. Most of the world's nuclear powers are reducing their arsenals or maintaining them at historic levels, but several of those in Asia—India, Pakistan and North Korea—continue to pursue relentless and expensive programmes of nuclear weapons development and production. Hopefully, the nuclear agreement reached in July 2015 between Iran, the European Union and the five permanent members of the United Nations Security Council will be a step towards eliminating nuclear weapons throughout Asia and the rest of the world. As we will discuss below, any country possessing a nuclear arsenal is on a path leading towards self-assured destruction, and is a threat to people everywhere on Earth.

Nuclear-armed countries are a threat to people everywhere partly because of the destructive power of single weapons—one weapon is enough to destroy a small city—and partly because of the growing ability of nations to launch missiles across the globe. Nuclear powers such as India and North Korea, the latter of which is thought currently to have a very small nuclear capability that is not in the form of useful weapons, are working on the means to deliver weapons globally. Each has capabilities now to launch weapons from submarines and both are working on intercontinental ballistic missiles. India has already

---

1 Toon, Owen B., Alan Robock, Michael Mills, and Lili Xia. "Asia Treads the Nuclear Path, Unaware That Self-Assured Destruction Would Result from Nuclear War." *The Journal of Asian Studies* 76, no. 2 (2017): 437–56. doi:10.1017/S0021911817000080.

launched satellites to the moon and Mars but these missiles are not thought to be suitable for India's current nuclear warheads.

However, it is not just the brute force attack, which kills people in the geographically limited target zone, that threatens people everywhere. Most people have forgotten nuclear winter. Many think that the theory was disproven, or that the end of the nuclear arms race and the subsequent reduction of Russian and American nuclear arsenals eliminated the dangers of global nuclear war. But they are wrong. Nuclear winter is an assault on the global climate system caused by smoke from fires ignited by the bombs. As the smoke rapidly spreads globally in the stratosphere, it will reduce temperatures and rainfall and destroy the global ozone layer, which shields us from harmful ultraviolet radiation from the sun. Recently it has been shown that even the smoke created by the use of 100 weapons of the size used on Hiroshima in the Second World War, comparable to the arsenals of India or Pakistan, could cause environmental damage that would extend glob-ally, threatening the world food supply and creating mass starvation worldwide (Mills et al., 2014; Özdog˘an, Robock, and Kucharik 2013; Robock and Toon 2012; Xia and Robock 2013; Xia et al., 2015). The effects of food loss would also be felt in the aggressor nation. Hence, being a nuclear aggressor is suicidal and destruction is self-assured. The deaths from these environmental changes would likely be a factor of ten or more larger than the direct casualties from the explosions—potentially threatening the bulk of the human population—and would not be limited to the combatants.

The acquisition of nuclear weapons may initially be driven by military considerations, and primarily involve a nation's scientists and engineers. However, the reasons for having nuclear arsenals go far beyond defensive needs or scientific and engineering capability. The rationale for nuclear weapons touches on politics, economics, cultural identity, religion and many other aspects of human society. As a result, reducing nuclear arsenals requires political, cultural and other changes that in turn demand contributions from many sectors of society and potentially the entire populations of countries with arsenals.

The primary reason cited by nations for building an arsenal is national protection. For example, the United States argued that it needed to develop nuclear weapons to be prepared in case Germany developed them during the Second World War. Once it had nuclear weapons, the United States argued that it needed to use them in the first nuclear war, the Second World War, to save the lives of large numbers of allied military personnel who might otherwise have died invading Japan. Like dominoes falling, Russia argued that it needed nuclear weapons to protect itself against the United States and other Western nations. Similar arguments were made by China and North Korea. India may have built weapons initially as a counter to China, while Pakistan built them to counter India. Israel built them to defend itself from surrounding hostile states. The concept of mutual assured destruction (MAD) lies at the heart of using nuclear weapons for national protection. Under MAD, it is assumed that an aggressor will not attack you because they fear nuclear retaliation.

Protection from potential enemies is not the only reason that nuclear arsenals have been built, however. As discussed by Tim Oakes and Emily Yeh in this volume, a wide variety of people are involved in understanding catastrophes within Asia. Some insight into reasons for building nuclear arsenals comes from critical self-examinations by Indian and Pakistani intellectuals—including journalists, scientists, social psychologists, filmmakers and poets—and schoolchildren, among others, in the aftermath of the nuclear tests by India and Pakistan in 1998, perhaps stirred by the conflict between the peaceful resistance image of Mahatma Gandhi and nuclear weapons (Kothari and Mian 2001). Analytical studies of India's motivations for having a nuclear arsenal have been discussed by historians, political scientists, defense analysts and others (e.g., Sardesai and Thomas 2002).

One reason, discussed in these works, for having a nuclear arsenal is the demonstration of scientific and technical capability in order to enhance national image. Another set of reasons for having a nuclear arsenal is to be seen as a major power in the world, to prevent current nuclear states from meddling in your affairs, and to take a place in world decision-making. For instance, the first five nuclear nations—the United States, the United Kingdom, the Soviet Union (now Russia), France and China (the P5)—are the permanent members of the UN Security Council, but now India, with a significant fraction of the world's population, wants a seat. Many nations have a desire to be freed from external interference in internal affairs. This latter rationale is particularly important to many countries. For example, Indian writers cite US President Richard Nixon sending an aircraft carrier into the Bay of Bengal during the 1971 conflict between India and Pakistan as interference and favouritism of (former) Western Pakistan that should be prevented in the future. Another goal is to obtain freedom of action that is external to the country. The idea is that nuclear states can do whatever they please, because other states would be afraid of triggering a nuclear response if they resist. Sagan (2012), following earlier insights by others, pointed out that soon after Pakistan tested its first nuclear weapon in 1998 it invaded part of Kashmir, apparently under the mistaken assumption that India would not counter the invasion for fear of triggering a nuclear response. At the time, there were threats and counter-threats between Pakistan and India concerning the use of nuclear weapons. However, India did repel the Pakistani invasion. The recent Russian annexation of Crimea, and its potential expansion across other former Soviet states, may involve a similar assumption that the rest of the world will be afraid to respond because of the possibility of triggering a nuclear conflict.

The Cold War nuclear stand-off between the West and the East, which was based on MAD, may be slowly evolving into a nuclear free-for-all (e.g., Evans 2014). Former US Secretaries of State George Shultz and Henry Kissinger, former US Secretary of Defense William Perry, and former US Senator Sam Nunn founded the Nuclear Security Project, 'an effort to galvanize global action to reduce urgent nuclear dangers and build support for reducing reliance on nuclear weapons, ultimately ending them as a threat to the world' (Nuclear Security Project, n.d.). These warriors of the Cold War argue in a series of editorials in the *Wall Street Journal* that in a world with many nuclear powers, each capable of destroying any country on Earth, and terrorist groups with increasing potential to gain control of nuclear weapons, MAD no longer works and one can no longer assume that peace can be maintained through rational analysis, careful control of weapons, or successful negotiation between well-defined states with clear national interests. The only solution, they argue, is to create a world without nuclear weapons (Shultz et al., 2007, 2008, 2010, 2011).

While most of us are oblivious to the power of the arsenals of India and Pakistan, they are, in fact, at the levels of the Soviet Union and the Western powers in the early 1950s. If the weapons were used, they could destroy a large fraction of the infrastructure of any country on Earth. India, North Korea and Iran are developing ballistic weapons-delivery systems that can send nuclear warheads over intercontinental scales. In the coming decades, it is possible that there will be a global nuclear gridlock caused by multiple nuclear-armed Asian, American and European states, each with differing goals and aspirations, and each with the capability to purposefully destroy any adversary and to inadvertently destroy much of the rest of the world.

Against this backdrop of expanding nuclear states, the concept of self-assured destruction (SAD) has been introduced (Robock and Toon 2012). According to this concept, it is suicidal to use nuclear weapons, even the not-so-modest arsenals of Pakistan and India. Everyone recognises that immense damage and loss of life will occur in the combatant countries due to the explosions of the weapons. However, it is not as well understood that worldwide environmental damage from even a regional conflict could be much worse than the direct effects of the explosions. The fires started from weapons exploding in cities will flood the upper atmosphere with smoke. Smoke absorbs sunlight, heating the upper atmosphere and destroying the protective ozone layer. The light-absorbing smoke also prevents sunlight from reaching the Earth's surface, driving global temperatures down enough to damage agriculture at mid-latitudes. The loss of agricultural productivity will create mass starvation globally, including in those countries that used the nuclear weapons. To reiterate, the deaths from these environmental changes would likely be a factor of ten or more larger than the direct casualties from the explosions—potentially threatening the bulk of the human population—and would not be limited to the combatants.

HOW DO ASIAN ARSENALS COMPARE WITH OTHERS?

Figure 7.1 illustrates the history of the number of warheads on the planet, and those in Russia and the United States, which currently control more than 90 per cent of the weapons (Kristensen and Norris 2014). The world total peaked at around 70,000 warheads in 1986, five years before the disintegration of the Soviet Union. The downward trend in

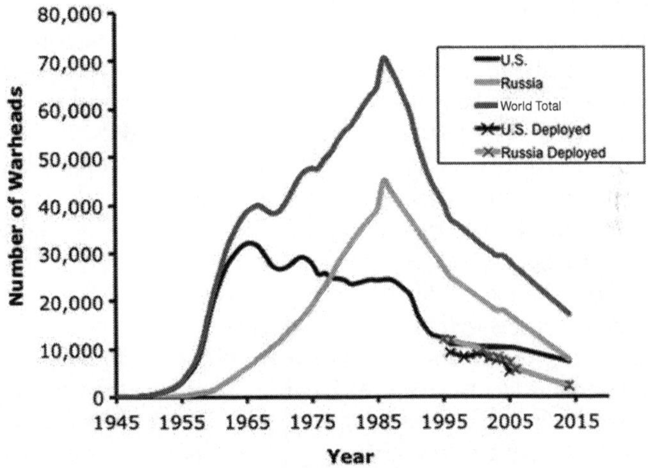

Figure 7.1 The number of nuclear warheads since the Second World War based on data from Kristensen and Norris (2013). Shown are the arsenals of the United States, Russia and the world. After about 2000, Russia and the United States began to base treaties on the number of deployed strategic warheads, rather than the total number of warheads. Deployed strategic warheads are shown with symbols. In 2013, there were about 16,300 warheads in the world. About 6,200 of these were retired and ostensibly waiting to be destroyed. The United States and Russia had about 3,750 deployed strategic warheads, which are covered by treaties negotiated under the Bush and Obama administrations. Another 5,380 warheads were in storage, or considered not to be strategic, and therefore not covered in recent treaties.

nuclear weapons begun in 1986 has continued to this day, with the 2014 world arsenal being near 16,000 weapons, about 23 per cent of the peak in 1986. The Strategic Offensive Reductions Treaty (SORT) reached by Presidents George W. Bush and Vladimir Putin, and in place from 2003 to 2011, regulated the number of strategic warheads to not exceed 1,700 to 2,200 for each country by 31 December 2012. The New Strategic Arms Reduction Treaty (New-START), developed under Presidents Barack Obama and Dmitry Medvedev and in place after 2011, results in similar numbers of deployed strategic warheads as in the SORT. Certain types of warheads were not counted in either the SORT or New-START. Of the 16,000 total warheads believed to exist among all nuclear powers, only about 3,750 deployed strategic weapons are regulated under New-START. The remainder includes about 7,000 weapons waiting to be dismantled in the United States and Russia, and more than 5,000 weapons in the United States and Russia that are not considered deployed or strategic (many are strategic warheads in storage, others are tactical weapons). Both Russia and the United States are embarked on expensive upgrades to their nuclear capabilities.

Figure 7.2 outlines the history of nuclear proliferation. Up until the mid-1980s, about one new nuclear state appeared every five years. Following the start of the build-down of nuclear weapons by the United States and Russia in 1986, a number of states abandoned their arsenals or stopped nuclear weapons programmes that were under consideration or development. South Africa developed a small nuclear arsenal and then abandoned it in the 1990s, the only country to ever abandon a self-developed nuclear arsenal. A number of countries inherited nuclear weapons from the former Soviet Union, but gave them up, including Kazakhstan in Asia as well as Belarus and Ukraine in Europe.

Unfortunately, proliferation was renewed in 1998 when India and then Pakistan tested nuclear weapons. As Figure 7.2 indicates, the world now may be back on the trend of one new nuclear state about every five years.

Figure 7.3 illustrates the arsenals of the countries with nuclear weapons other than the United States and Russia (Kristensen and Norris 2013). It is very difficult to determine the numbers of weapons in most of these countries. While Britain and France have been slowly reducing their arsenals, and China seems to have maintained a constant level, Pakistan, India and possibly Israel seem to be increasing their arsenals. The yields of the weapons in most of the programmes are not known. Britain, France and China have weapons with yields above 100 kilotons[1]; however, it is likely, based on their nuclear tests, that India and Pakistan have weapons with yields similar to those of the US weapons used in the Second World War, around 10–20 kilotons, or even less.

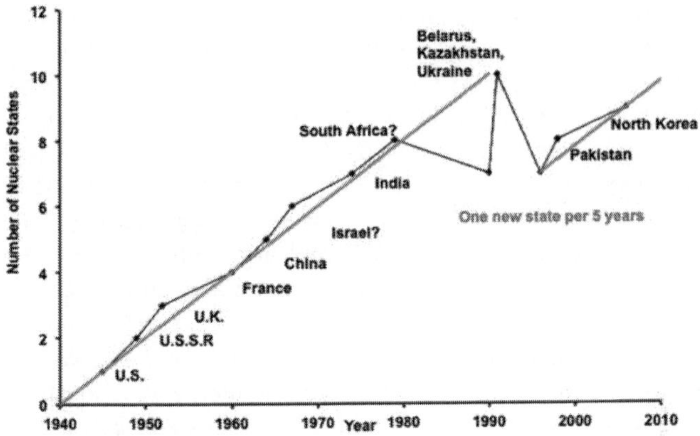

Figure 7.2 The dates when various nations obtained a nuclear warhead, mainly based on when they first tested a weapon. For Israel and South Africa, the evidence for tests is controversial, so an estimate for when they had a useable weapon is given. Belarus, Kazakhstan and Ukraine inherited weapons from the Soviet Union and transferred them to Russia in the 1990s. South Africa gave up its weapons in the 1990s. The straight lines represent one new nuclear state every five years.

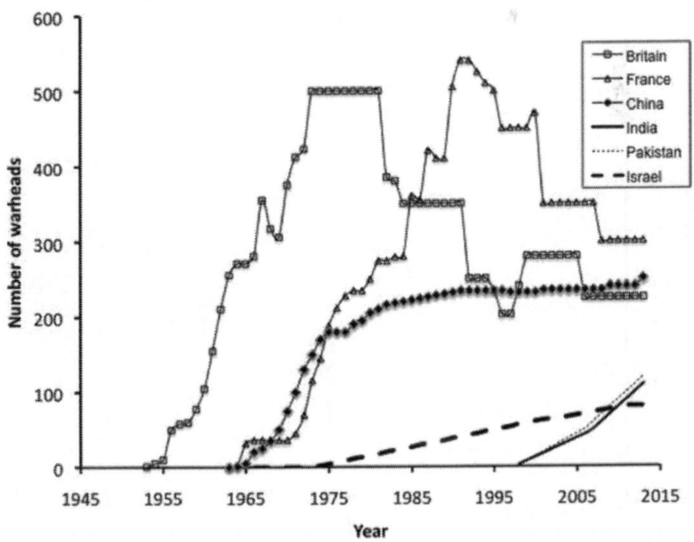

Figure 7.3 The number of warheads thought to be in the arsenals of Britain, France, China, India, Pakistan and Israel based on data from Kristensen and Norris (2013). North Korean weapons are not shown because it is uncertain that it has an arsenal of useable weapons.

In contrast to some parts of Asia where nuclear proliferation and arsenal growth are occurring, much of the world is ridding itself of nuclear weapons. Figure 7.4 shows the history of the development of Nuclear-Weapon-Free Zones. Almost one-third of the human population now lives in regions in which the UN has recognised treaties banning nuclear weapons. The Treaty for the Prohibition of Nuclear Weapons in Latin America and the Caribbean, also known as the Treaty of Tlatelolco, went into effect in 1968, and was eventually signed by all thirty-three independent nations of Latin America and the Caribbean, including Cuba. However, Brazil and Argentina reserved the right to conduct 'peaceful nuclear weapons explosions', and islands such as Puerto Rico, British Virgin Islands and Guadeloupe, associated with Nuclear Weapons States, are excluded. Africa established a Nuclear-Weapon-Free Zone under the Treaty of Pelindaba, which took effect in 2009. As a result of the additional treaties for Antarctica and the Rarotonga Treaty—involving Australia, New Zealand and a number of island nations in the Pacific—the entire Southern Hemisphere (with the exception of the islands associated with states with nuclear weapons and international waters) is a Nuclear-Weapon-Free Zone. The Association of Southeast Asian Nations, including Brunei Darussalam, Cambodia, Indonesia, Laos, Malaysia, Myanmar, Philippines, Singapore, Thailand and Vietnam, became a Nuclear-Weapon-Free Zone in 1997 under the Bangkok Treaty. There is also a Central Asian nuclear-free treaty

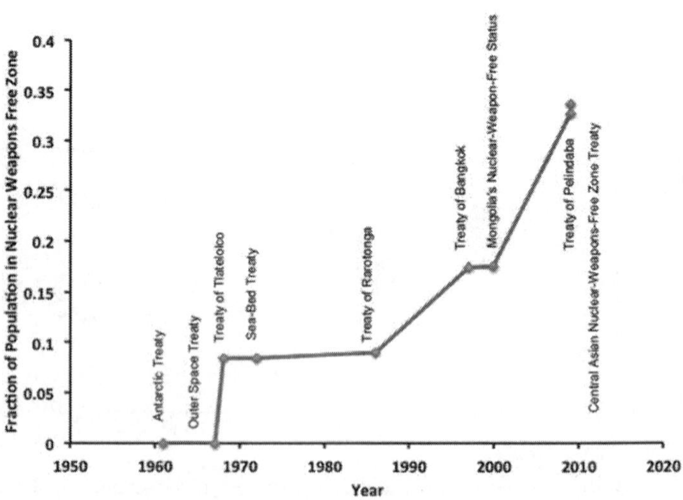

Figure 7.4 The fraction of the world's current population that lives in Nuclear-Weapon-Free Zones, as recognised through UN treaties. Currently about one-third of Earth's population lives in a nuclear-free zone.

signed by Kazakhstan, Kyrgyzstan, Tajikistan, Turkmenistan and Uzbekistan, which entered into force in 2009. Mongolia declared itself a Nuclear-Weapon-Free Zone in 1992, and it was formally recognised as a Nuclear-Weapon-Free Zone in 2012 by the five original Nuclear Weapons States: the United States, China, France, the United Kingdom and Russia. In total, there are at least sixteen countries in Asia that are free of nuclear weapons, which is almost three times as many as Asian Nuclear Weapons States.

HOW MANY WEAPONS ARE ENOUGH?

A comparison of Figure 7.1 and Figure 7.3 raises the question—how do you know how many weapons are enough? None of the Nuclear Weapons States has stated its criteria for answering this question.

In the case of the United States, analyses in the late 1940s reported by Eden (2004) identified militarily important industrial sites for the Soviet Union and concluded that these could be destroyed by the delivery of 100 atomic weapons, which were similar in yield to the weapons in the arsenals of present-day Pakistan, India and North Korea. Of course, weapons may not explode, or may never reach their target, so it was estimated that 200 weapons would be needed for the United States to destroy the Soviet Union. Despite this estimate, the US arsenal rose to more than 150 times this many weapons, and with typically more than ten times the yield per weapon. One reason for the bloated number of weapons may be the competition between Russia and the United States and attempts to dominate the other so that a first strike might overwhelm the adversary (e.g., Lieber and Press 2006). In the case of a first strike, each missile of the adversary must be targeted with multiple warheads. The opponent must then obtain even more warheads so that it can attack each of the other country's missiles with more than one warhead. This competition to outnumber the other side leads to exponential growth in warheads. Alternative suggestions for the large numbers of weapons include competition for funding to support the nuclear infrastructure, political posturing, lack of planning or lack of thought about the size of the arsenal needed, or concern that there would be a high failure rate of the weapons.

Toon, Robock and Turco (2008) analysed a modern attack on the urban areas in a number of countries. They found that in an attack on US urban areas—based on population density, with 1,000 weapons of 100-kiloton yield—48 per cent of the US population would be within 5 km of ground zero, 20 per cent of the population (about sixty million people) would be killed outright, and another 16 per cent injured (about forty million people). They also found that a war between India and Pakistan using fifty weapons with 15-kiloton yield on each country, exploded on cities based on population, would kill or injure about forty-five million people.

The eventual build-up to over 30,000 American warheads and 40,000 Soviet warheads, most with more than ten times the yield of the Hiroshima weapon, was gross overkill. There are simply not that many targets. It is supposed to be US policy to attack military and industrial targets, not civilian population centres. However, recently revealed nuclear targeting documents show that in 1959, population was treated as a distinct target for US nuclear weapons (Shane 2015). Yet, even this stance that population is not directly attacked is clearly misleading because military and industrial targets are both located in urban areas. For instance, Bush et al. (1991) and Small (1989) considered a counterforce attack by Russia on 3,030 leading US targets, such as US Army, Navy and Air Force bases; fuel storage locations; refineries; and harbours (but not missile silos or launch-control facilities) with 500-kiloton warheads.[2] In fact, due to the significant area destroyed by a nuclear bomb explosion, there were only 348 unique targets in these studies that were on average each attacked by 8.7 weapons when 3,030 weapons were used. While cities were not targeted directly, 50 per cent of the US urban areas were destroyed.

There are only about 300 cities in the United States and 180 in Russia with a population greater than 100,000. There are about 60 cities in Pakistan, 365 in India, and 445 in China with a population greater than 100,000. It might require more than one weapon to destroy some large cities, and there are some important targets in rural areas. Nevertheless, the 2,000 strategic deployed weapons in both the American and the Russian arsenals under current treaties still allows them to destroy the bulk of any adversary's infrastructure and population, given the likely assumption that the majority of the weapons detonate. The current arsenal of India is great enough to attack almost every moderate-sized city in Pakistan two times.

This sort of gruesome calculation of the numbers of weapons needed to destroy an adversary has likely been repeated in many nations. Based on the numbers of weapons in Figures 7.1 and 7.3, and the numbers of cities in the world that might be targets, the number of weapons is being chosen by most countries to ensure they can bomb every moderate-sized city of any country in the world that they choose. The emphasis in sizing nuclear arsenals is on ensuring a level of destruction, not a level of survival.

Unfortunately, the collateral damage from using these weapons may be much greater than the direct damage. Therefore, ensuring the destruction of any adversary, and giving no consideration to how many might survive, may lead to the accidental deaths of most of the world's population.

SELF-ASSURED DESTRUCTION FOLLOWING AN ASIAN WAR

Nuclear weapons cause damage through prompt and delayed nuclear radiation thermal radiation, and shock waves. Prompt radiation comes from the nuclear fireball and the nuclear reactions producing the detonation. Delayed radiation comes from the fallout containing the radioactive daughter products of the nuclear explosion. Thermal radiation is a bright pulse of light emitted by the explosion. Shock waves are high winds and associated pressure fluctuations that occur over very short periods of time. It is difficult to untangle the direct damage from prompt radiation, thermal radiation and shock waves because their zones of influence overlap near ground zero. Delayed radiation could kill large numbers of people in areas downwind of ground bursts, which might be used to attack missile silos. Ground bursts near the surface (as opposed to being deeply buried) lift relatively large soil particles into the air. Radioactive particles attach themselves to these dust particles, and when they fall out of the atmosphere onto the ground (hence the name 'fallout') within hours or days, they can expose the population at the surface to dangerous levels of radiation. However, even with ground bursts, the casualties from delayed exposure to radiation are likely to be less than those from the other direct effects in an attack on a city. An attack on a missile silo, or an other unpopulated area, might have the majority of casualties from delayed radiation. Airbursts are generally more destructive than ground bursts because the area impacted by prompt radiation, thermal radiation and shock waves is larger. Therefore, combatants are likely to use airbursts unless they are attacking buried targets. The debris from airbursts generally contains little material of large enough size to fall out of the atmosphere quickly. Therefore, the nuclear radiation largely decays before it reaches the surface and is less of a hazard to people than material that falls out rapidly. If your goal is killing people, an airburst over a city is more effective than a ground burst that kills less with prompt radiation, thermal radiation and shock waves and more with delayed radiation.

Following a nuclear explosion, the shock waves knock down structures. These ruptured buildings will experience myriad small fires, which can coalesce into a firestorm. The thermal radiation from the fireball can also set fires over a wide area. One does not need a nuclear weapon to initiate a firestorm. For example, the United States and its allies purposefully set many firestorms in urban areas during the Second World War, including at Dresden, Hamburg, Tokyo and several other Japanese cities, using hundreds of aircraft carrying incendiary bombs. There have also been damaging firestorms after earthquakes, such as the 1906 San Francisco earthquake. It is believed that fires rather than the earthquake caused the vast majority of the damage to that city. The energy released in firestorms is immense. For instance, Toon et al. (2007) estimated that the energy released in the Hiroshima firestorm, which reached full strength several hours after the nuclear explosion, was about 1,000 times greater than the energy released in the nuclear explosion.

Firestorms are self-feeding fires that suck air into themselves and generate immense columns of rising smoke. There are many observations of stratospheric injections of smoke from large, intense forest fires, which are similar to urban firestorms (e.g., Fromm and Servranckx 2003). Once the smoke is 10 km (6 miles) above the ground, sunlight will heat the smoky air and it will rise, which is called self-lofting. Observations may have recorded smoke from forest fires rising by self-lofting to 20 km above the surface (de Laat et al., 2012), and models suggest large smoke injections in a nuclear conflict could reach 50 km above the ground by self-lofting. At altitudes above 20 km it never rains, so the smoke would remain in the air for years. The clouds from very large volcanic eruptions are observed to remain in the stratosphere for a few years, but they have only a small amount of self-lofting because their semi-transparent particles do not absorb much sunlight.

The most recent study of the aftermath of a nuclear conflict (Mills et al., 2014) used an Earth system climate model including atmospheric chemistry, ocean dynamics and interactive sea ice and land components to investigate the environmental damage from a limited, regional nuclear war between India and Pakistan. Mills et al. (2014) assumed each side detonates fifty weapons with 15 kilotons of yield for each weapon over urban areas. One hundred total weapons is about half of the existing arsenals of India and Pakistan. These urban explosions are assumed to start 100 firestorms, which would produce a total of slightly more than five million tons of smoke. In the computer simulation, this smoke self-lofted to the stratosphere, where it spread globally, producing a sudden drop in surface temperatures, because the smoke blocked sunlight from reaching the surface, and intense heating of the stratosphere, because the smoke absorbed sunlight. The results showed that about one-third of the smoke was removed after about nine years. In the hot stratosphere, ozone was destroyed by chemical reactions. Global ozone losses of 20–50 per cent over populated areas, levels unprecedented in human history, would accompany the coldest average surface temperatures since the waning phases of the last ice age, thousands of years ago. Ozone in the stratosphere protects us from the harmful effects of solar ultraviolet light. Mills et al. (2014) calculated summer enhancements in ultraviolet solar exposure indices of 30–80 per cent over mid-latitudes, suggesting widespread damage to human health, agriculture and terrestrial and aquatic ecosystems, though the effects of enhanced ultraviolet light are poorly under-stood since such enhancements have never been observed. Killing frosts would reduce growing seasons by ten to forty days per year for five years at mid-latitudes. Surface temperatures would be reduced for more than twenty-five years. The long period of cold temperatures is due to thermal inertia from the cooled ocean waters and to extra reflection of sunlight back to space by expanded sea ice.

Large global decreases in ozone have not been observed in human experience, though there is a significant latitudinal gradient in ultraviolet intensity. It is known, for instance, that the incidence of skin cancer in people with light-coloured skin increases with decreasing latitude as a result of increasing ultraviolet light. The ultraviolet light is greatest in the tropics because the sun is more intense there and because there is less ozone in the tropics than elsewhere. While we know that enhanced ultraviolet light is hazardous, its effects are not included in agricultural models, so it is not possible to gauge its impact on food supplies or the environment. On the other hand, we have a lot of experience with the effects of changes in temperature and precipitation on agriculture. Table 7.1 provides some calculated crop losses due to temperature and precipitation changes following a regional war with 100 weapons. The crop declines are mainly due to reduced temperatures and shortened growing seasons.

There are no studies on the effect on human society of crop losses such as those shown in Table 7.1. However, there are several reasons to think the effects would be devastating. The world does not recognise the Biblical warning by Joseph to the Pharaoh of Egypt to store grain for seven years of famine. Instead, the total world grain storage would be consumed in around seventy days at the current rate of consumption (see Figures 7.5 and 7.6). As shown in Figure 7.5, consumption has steadily risen since 1960 as world population increased, but ending food stocks, which represent food storage, have leveled out since about 1985. Food production and consumption are closely balanced, and the food surplus or deficit is a small fraction of ending stocks (less than 23 per cent) in the past fifty years, as shown in Figure 7.6. The small ups and downs of the ending stocks curve in Figure 7.5 represent the accumulation of the year-to-year variations in the production of grains relative to their consumption. Recently, food consumption has tended to exceed production slightly, so ending stocks are slowly trending downward in Figure 7.5. Given the rising population, the days of food on hand has declined by about a factor of two in the past decade to less than seventy days at present, as shown in Figure 7.6.

Table 7.1 Loss of agricultural productivity following a regional nuclear conflict with 100 warheads (Özdog˘an et al., 2013; Xia and Robock 2013; Xia et al., 2015).

	First Five Years	**Second Five Years**
US maize	– 20%	– 10%
US soybeans	– 15%	– 10%
China maize	– 15%	– 12%
China middle-season rice	– 26%	– 21%
China spring wheat	– 26%	– 20%
China winter wheat	– 38%	– 23%

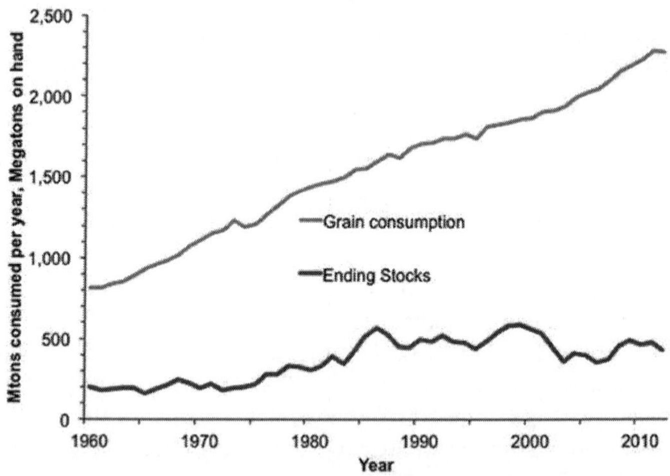

Figure 7.5 The worldwide consumption of grains and the ending stocks from 1960 until 2012. Data from Earth Policy Institute (2012).

Table 7.1 suggests, from the limited studies done so far, that a regional nuclear conflict between India and Pakistan might reduce global grain production by 20 per cent for five years and 10–15 per cent for another five years. A 20 per cent reduction in grain production today would represent about 450 metric tons of grain each year, which is comparable to the ending stocks on hand in 2012. This would be an unprecedented loss of food, exhausting the global food storage in one year, and could not be made up, since the loss would continue for a decade.

How would the world respond to a sudden global decline in food? Some clues are given in Figure 7.7, which illustrates an inflation-corrected food price. The Food Price Index is an estimate of the relative costs of meat, dairy, grains, oils and sugar. Historically, the highest price was in the early 1970s, which corresponds to a time when, as indicated in Figure 7.6, the minimum number of days of food consumption neared fifty-six days. We are currently experiencing a new period of a relatively high Food Price Index with peaks in 2008 and 2011 and a new minimum of days of food consumption.

Analysis of the 1970s peak in the price of food indicates that a major cause was a drop in agricultural production, particularly in Russia, that was partly compensated by the United States selling Russia the equivalent of 30 per cent of the US wheat production in the previous few years. The food price jump was exacerbated by decisions made by various political bodies (e.g., Schnittker 1973). Although apparently unrelated in cause, the Arab oil embargo coincided in time and drove energy prices to record levels, causing rationing and other disruptions across the globe.

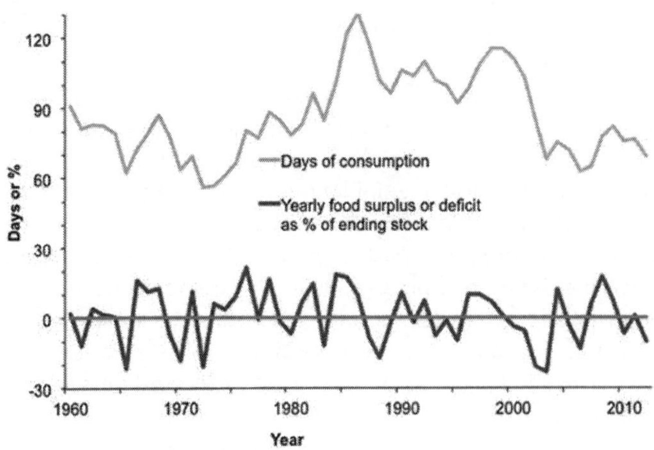

Figure 7.6 The number of days that the ending stocks could supply world food consumption, and the surplus or deficit of food as a percentage of the ending stocks. Data from Earth Policy Institute (2012).

Figure 7.7 UN Food and Agriculture Food Price Index, based on data from Earth Policy Institute, Monthly Food Price Indexes, January 1990–January 2014, updated February 6, 2014.

The 2008 food price peak followed another low point in the days of food consumption near sixty-three, and another run-up in energy prices. These changes were coupled with the increased use of biofuels, which diverted about 100 million tons of maize away from food; wheat-growing failures in Australia; an increased consumption of meat in China; and various types of speculation and political manipulation. In the case of rice, India and Vietnam stopped exporting rice, which may have been due to internal political manipulations in India and speculation in Vietnam. The loss of two of the world's largest rice exporters caused a cascade of panic in rice-importing nations (Slayton 2009). Whatever the cause, the rise in food prices coincided with food riots in a number of countries and significant numbers of deaths in those riots (Lagi, Bertrand and Bar-Yam 2011). The government of Haiti was overthrown in 2008 during food-related riots, and there were bread riots in Egypt in 2008 (Sternberg 2013).

The 2011 spike in the Food Price Index may have had even more dramatic impacts on world affairs. In 2010, Russian wheat production fell 32.7 per cent, Ukrainian wheat production fell 19.3 per cent, Canadian wheat production fell 13.7 per cent and Australian wheat production fell 8.7 per cent (Sternberg 2013). In the fall of 2010, China experienced drought and began to purchase wheat, which drove up prices. People in Middle Eastern and North African countries spend large fractions of their income on food. Libya, Jordan, Algeria, Tunisia, Yemen and Egypt are each in the range of 35–44 per cent of income spent on food. A large fraction of the food is bread. A significant causal factor in the Arab Spring uprisings, beginning in December 2010 and still ongoing, was food insecurity due to the wheat failures in 2010 (Sternberg 2013). Since 2010, rulers have been forced out of power in Tunisia, Egypt, Libya and Yemen. There have been uprisings in Bahrain and Syria, and major protests in Algeria, Iraq, Jordan, Kuwait, Morocco and Sudan.

The production failures in recent decades pale in comparison to those that might follow a nuclear conflict between India and Pakistan. In that case, the world grain storage might be eliminated in the first year after a war, and a deficit of 10–20 per cent might then occur for a decade. Helfand (2013) has estimated that two billion people who are now only marginally fed might die from starvation and disease in the aftermath of a nuclear conflict between India and Pakistan. A conflict in the future with more weapons, or between other powers with more weapons, could be much worse.

SCENARIOS FOR WAR

People have grown comfortable with nuclear weapons, and few are concerned about the possibility of nuclear conflict. Unfortunately, this lack of concern is not justified by the facts. We are only an accident, a mistake or a deranged politician away from killing most of the world's population now. As arsenals continue to grow, the threat of a nuclear exchange is bound to grow in the future.

The United States and Russia remain in 'launch-on-warning status', which means that the leaders of these countries are constantly prepared to launch some of their nuclear missiles within a few moments of learning that missiles from the other side are headed their way. This is a very dangerous situation. There are numerous examples of each side mistakenly thinking the other has initiated an attack, and war has been narrowly averted by identifying or discounting the mistake.

In Asia, a number of analyses have been conducted on how a war might start. For instance, Lavoy and Smith (2003) discuss three plausible scenarios for a nuclear war between India and Pakistan. India has conventional military superiority. India is also geographically much larger than Pakistan, so parts of its nuclear arsenal are currently out of range of Pakistan's forces, while all of Pakistan is easily reached from India. One possible route to nuclear war involves a conventional conflict between India and Pakistan. If Pakistan perceived that India were about to invade, that could put pressure on Pakistan to launch its nuclear weapons before it was overrun by the superior Indian forces. Another possibility for starting a nuclear conflict is that India or Pakistan could lose control of its command and control structures due to an attack on it by the other side, or possibly an attack by terrorists. In such a scenario, it is not clear who might be in control of the nuclear forces and what steps they might take. A third possibility for starting a nuclear conflict is that India or Pakistan might mistake an attack by conventional forces, or even military exercises, for an attack by nuclear forces. Both countries have ballistic missiles and aircraft that are potentially dual-use between conventional and nuclear weapons, making any attack ambiguous.

Another point of future conflict could involve North Korea. It is not clear that North Korea currently has operational nuclear weapons, though it has tested nuclear explosives. It is also not certain that North Korea has nuclear-capable missiles (Kristensen and Norris 2014), though it continues to test long-range missiles and submarine-launched missiles and does have nuclear-capable aircraft. Fortunately, no other countries with nuclear weapons are near North Korea, except for China, with which North Korea is allied. Factors that might trigger a nuclear conflict involving North Korea have some parallels with the Pakistan–India situation. North Korea has a much larger military than South Korea, including the US troops stationed in South Korea, and Seoul is only 35 miles from the North Korean border. It would, therefore, be possible for North Korea to overrun South Korea in a sudden attack, possibly triggering a nuclear attack by the United States. Hayes and Cavazos (2015) have analysed some of the many possible scenarios for a nuclear conflict involving North Korea. Generally, they conclude that North Korea does not have the capability to launch an attack at present, but may have in the near future. While North Korea is expanding its capabilities, it is difficult to find a scenario in which it could launch a first-strike nuclear conflict and win, even in the future. However, the North Koreans may not analyse the situation in the same ways that are done in the West: their leadership might not be rational; there is the potential for the regime to be overthrown, leading to nuclear weapons use in North Korea itself; and it is possible that its continuing provocations of its neighbours might lead to an attack on North Korea. Any of these possibilities, and several others, might lead to the use of nuclear weapons.

There are numerous other scenarios that could lead either to a nuclear conflict or to destabilising Asia further. For example, Japan or South Korea could develop nuclear weapons to defend against North Korea, likely because they lose confidence that the United States will continue to protect them. Iran could obtain nuclear weapons, which would likely trigger Saudi Arabia and other countries in the Middle East to obtain them. Hopefully, the 2015 agreement with Iran will prevent the Middle East from becoming a warren of nuclear states.

Unless the world does something to build-down the existing arsenals further, and stops proliferation, the remainder of the twenty-first century is likely to involve increasing risk of nuclear confrontations.

WHAT CAN ASIAN COUNTRIES DO?

No government, anywhere, is conducting studies to determine the damage that might be done to them in a nuclear conflict in which they were a combatant, or a bystander. There is no evidence that any current leader of any nuclear power is aware of the potential harm that might occur due to the environmental damage from a nuclear conflict. However, the cold temperatures and the destruction of the ozone layer caused by the smoke from burning cities following a nuclear conflict, even between powers such as India and Pakistan with modest numbers of weapons compared with other Nuclear Weapons States, could devastate agricultural productivity, leading to mass starvation across the globe. It is dangerous not to discuss these issues and risks openly in society.

Calculating the direct casualties from a nuclear conflict is very straightforward. The major uncertainties are the number and yields of the weapons used and their targets. There is also uncertainty about extrapolating the casualties from Hiroshima and Nagasaki to those that would occur in modern cities at various distances from ground zero. It is more difficult to compute the environmental impacts from nuclear conflicts and their consequences. However, the major uncertainties are the same for the direct effects, the number and yields of the weapons used and their targets. The size and duration of resulting firestorms is uncertain, since we have no modern examples. In addition, the amount of fuel burned, the amount of smoke emitted and the amount of smoke removed in local precipitation are uncertain. Uncertainty does not mean that the impacts have been overestimated. It is just as likely that the effects have been underestimated. Like many other areas of human endeavour, uncertainty is unavoidable when predicting the outcome of possible nuclear wars. However, when gambling with the future of human civilisation, it is not wise to ignore the possibility of nuclear winter by hoping that no country will ever use its arsenal.

Donna Goldstein argues in this volume that politicians do not care about the predictions of models, and use science only to manipulate events. However, the Montreal Protocol, which is based on modelling showing that the release of certain chemicals is destroying the ozone layer, has reduced industrial emissions of ozone-destroying chemicals. The Intergovernmental Panel on Climate Change, which is largely based on models for future climate, is currently pushing a revision of the Earth's energy production system. These are very large changes caused by scientific recognition of a problem, and wrought by statespersons who have taken science very seriously. Of course, in both these examples, there was also evidence that the Earth was being impacted, such as the Antarctic ozone hole, melting glaciers, rising sea levels and rising temperatures. Nuclear war is not approachable by experiment or observation. Nevertheless, there is no reason to be pessimistic and assume that politicians cannot understand the advice about the dangers of nuclear wars from their scientific establishments, or will not act on that advice. History shows, even in the case of nuclear weapons, that statespersons will understand these dangers if they are told of them, and act appropriately.

In the early 1980s, studies of the environmental effects of a nuclear conflict played a role in causing the leaders of the United States and of the Soviet Union to reduce their arsenals. Mikhail Gorbachev observed, 'Models made by Russian and American scientists showed that a nuclear war would result in nuclear winter that would be extremely destructive to all life on Earth: the knowledge of that was a great stimulus to us, to people of honor and morality, to act' (Hertsgaard 2000). And Ronald Reagan noted:

> [A] great many reputable scientists are telling us, that such a war could just end up in no victory for anyone because we would wipe out the earth as we know it. And if you think back to … natural calamities—back in the last century, in the 1800's, … volcanoes—we saw the weather so changed that there was snow in July in many temperate countries. And they called it the year in which there was no summer. Now if one volcano can do that, what are we talking about with the whole nuclear exchange, the nuclear winter that scientists have been talking about? It's possible. (*New York Times* 1985)

As a first step towards a world that is free of the threat of a global nuclear catastrophe, we suggest that the nuclear-armed states, perhaps led by those in Asia, collectively engage in a dialogue on the impacts of nuclear conflicts. There is precedence for such a dialogue in two formats. Just prior to the build-down in nuclear weapons illustrated in Figure 7.1 and the pause in the creation of new nuclear states, as illustrated in Figure 7.2, the scientific academies of the world conducted a study of nuclear conflicts under the umbrella of the UN Scientific Committee on Problems of the Environment (Harwell and Hutchinson 1986;

Pittock et al., 1986). Of course, it is not just scientists that need to participate in this discussion, as discussed by Yeh in this volume. During the early 1980s, a vibrant debate about nuclear weapons took place among a wide variety of interest groups, including physicians, politicians, philosophers and poets. More recently, an environmental disaster was avoided when the nations of the world agreed to limit ozone-destroying chemicals in the Montreal Protocol on Substances that Deplete the Ozone Layer. Currently the Intergovernmental Panel on Climate Change is working to achieve international agreement on regulations related to climate change. We suggest that there be a new study of the consequences of nuclear conflict.

The study should not only consider the consequences of conflicts but should also address whether the reasons cited to develop nuclear weapons are valid. For example, Japan and South Korea do not have nuclear arsenals, while North Korea does. There is no evidence that North Korea is technologically superior in any way, has a greater place in any facet of world decision-making or has a greater influence on any aspect of world affairs. Nor is North Korea any safer due to nuclear technology. The same opposing army is still in South Korea that was there prior to North Korea testing nuclear weapons. Indeed, sanctions placed on North Korea because of its nuclear weapons programme, which may not have impacted its nuclear weapons programme, have damaged its economy. Likewise, India has not gained entry to the UN Security Council because of its nuclear arsenal, and while India is recognised for its many prominent scientists and thinkers in a variety of peaceful fields of study, its nuclear programme has done nothing to gain it respect as a technological power in the rest of the world. Pakistan's nuclear weapons have not helped it solve its dispute with India over Kashmir, nor has it prevented other nations from bombing its citizens and making armed military raids to seize militants located in its territories.

India and Pakistan are engaged in a rapid build-up of nuclear weapons, which is a danger to them both and to the rest of the world. While dialogues between these nations, and others, have taken place for decades, little progress has been made. Possibly a detailed analysis by their own scientists and scientists of other nations of the consequences of a war would aid them in constructive discussions. Of course, these studies should include an analysis of conflicts involving all the nuclear-armed nations and consider all of their arsenals.

History shows that nuclear weapons do not achieve the goals envisioned by the states that have them. Not even a single nuclear weapon can be used, given the potential for escalation to employ many more weapons, leading to a nuclear winter. Such escalation is particularly likely due to the 1,800 weapons on high alert in the United

States and Russia that could be used on a short notice. A nuclear war cannot be fought, given the adverse impacts on the food supply of all nations of the world, including the ones that used them. The case of Pakistan's invasion of Kashmir after its test of nuclear weapons, and the entire Cold War, show that nuclear arsenals do not provide cover for unopposed conventional warfare. The Argentinean invasion of the Falklands and the Yom Kippur War show that possession of nuclear weapons does not stop invasions of nuclear nations by non-nuclear nations. The Vietnam War and the Soviet War in Afghanistan show that nuclear weapons do not help win wars, since in both wars the nuclear power lost. The weapons do not confer immunity from meddling by others in internal affairs, nor give countries with them enhanced access to world government. On the contrary, the weapons are very expensive to obtain and maintain. The weapons expose their possessors, and the rest of the world, to the potential for terrorists to obtain and use them. There is a significant risk, particularly between India and Pakistan, of nuclear conflict starting from misunderstanding, or misinterpretation of the other country's actions. A large fraction of the world's population, inside and outside of the combat zone, could die from such errors. It would behoove each Nuclear Weapons State, in Asia and elsewhere, to get rid of its nuclear weapons before it is too late.

ACKNOWLEDGMENTS

Alan Robock and Lili Xia are supported by National Science Foundation grants AGS-1157525 and GEO-1240507.

NOTES

1 The explosive energy released in a nuclear detonation is measured in relation to an explosion of the equivalent weight of the conventional explosive trinitrotoluene—TNT. The explosive power in the total of all bombs used in Second World War, including the atomic bombs dropped on Hiroshima and Nagasaki, was several megatons, which could now be released by just one high-yield nuclear weapon.

2 In the lexicon of military targeting, there are countervalue, counterforce and rational wars. Rational wars use a small number of weapons to attack targets of symbolic value. Countervalue wars use massive attacks on urban areas to destroy economic and social infrastructure. Counterforce wars involve massive attacks on military, economic and political targets. In reality, countervalue and counterforce wars end up attacking much the same targets, especially for large numbers of high-yield weapons.

LIST OF REFERENCES

Bush, Brian W., M.A. Dore, G.H. Anno, and Richard D. Small. "Nuclear Winter Source-Term Studies: Smoke Produced by a Nuclear Attack on the United States." Report no. DNA-TR-86-220-V6, 6 (1991). Alexandria, Va.: Defense Nuclear Agency.

De Laat, Jos, Debora C. Stein-Zweers, Reinout Boers, and Olaf N.E. Tuinder. "A Solar Escalator: Observational Evidence of the Self-Lofting of Smoke and Aerosols by Adsorption of Solar Radiation in the February 2009 Australian Black Saturday Plume." *Journal of Geophysical Research* 117(D4) (2012). doi:10.1029/2011JD017016.

Earth Policy Institute. "World Grain Consumption and Stocks as Days of Consumption, 1960–2012." (2012), accessed on July 23, 2022, http://www.earth-policy.org/data_center/C24.

Eden, Lynn. 2004. *Whole World on Fire: Organizations, Knowledge, and Nuclear Weapons Devastation* (Ithaca, N.Y.: Cornell University Press, 2004)

Evans, Gareth. "Nuclear Deterrence in *Asia and the Pacific." Asia and the Pacific Policy Studies* 1(1) (2014):91–111. doi:10.1002/app5.00011.

Fromm, Michael D., And Rene Servranckx. "Transport of Forest Fire Smoke above the Tropopause by Supercell Convection." *Geophysical Research Letters* 30 (10) (2003). doi:10.1029/2002GL016820.

Harwell, Mark A. and Thomas C. Hutchinson. *Environmental Consequences of Nuclear War: Volume II: Ecological and Agricultural Effects* (New York: Wiley, 1986)

Hayes, Pete, and Roger Cavazos. "North Korea's Nuclear Force Roadmap: Hard Choices." (2015), NAPSNet Special Reports, March 2, accessed on July 23, 2022, https://nautilus.org/napsnet/napsnet-special-reports/north-koreas-nuclear-force-roadmap-hard-choices/.

Helfand, Ira. Nuclear Famine: Two Billion People at Risk? 2nd ed. (Malden, Mass, 2013).

International Physicians for the Prevention of Nuclear War. Accessed on July 23, 2022, http://www.ippnw.org/pdf/nuclear-famine-two-billion-at-risk-2013.pdf.

Hertsgaard, Mark. "Mikhail Gorbachev Explains What's Rotten in Russia." *Salon*, September 7, 2000, accessed on July 23, 2022, http://www.salon.com/2000/09/07/gorbachev/.

Kothari, Smitu, and Zia Mian, eds. *Out of the Nuclear Shadow*. (London: Zed Books, 2001).

Kristensen, Hans M. and Robert S. Norris. "Global Nuclear Weapons Inventories, 1945–2013." *Bulletin of the Atomic Scientists* 69(5) (2014):75–81. doi:10.1177/0096340213501363.

——. (2014) "Worldwide Deployments of NuclearWeapons, 2014." *Bulletin of the Atomic Scientists* 70(5):96–108. doi:10.1177/0096340214547619.

Lagi, Marco, Karla Z. Bertrand, and Yaneer Bar-Yam. "The Food Crises and Political Instability in North Africa and the Middle East." (2011), accessed on July 23, 2022, https:arxiv.org/abs/1108.2455.

Lavoy, Petėr R and Stephen A. Smith. "The Risk of Inadvertent Nuclear Use Between India and Pakistan." *Strategic Insight*, February 3, accessed on July 23, 2022, https://apps.dtic.mil/sti/pdfs/ADA525408.pdf.

Lieber, Keir A. and Daryl G. Press. "The Rise of U.S. Nuclear Primacy." *Foreign Affairs*, March/April, accessed on July 23, 2022, https://www.foreignaffairs.com/articles/united-states/2006-03-01/rise-us-nuclear-primacy.

Mills, Michael J., Owen B. Toon, Julia Lee-Taylor, and Alan Robock. "Multidecadal Global Cooling and Unprecedented Ozone Loss Following a Regional Nuclear Conflict." *Earth's Future* 2(4) (2014):161–76. doi:10.1002/2013EF000205.

New York Times. "Transcript of Interview with President on a Range of Issues." February 12, 1985, accessed on July 23, 2022, http://www.nytimes.com/1985/02/12/world/transcript-of-interviewwith-president-on-a-range-of-issues.html.

Özdogˇ An, Mutlu, Alan Robock, and Christopher Kucharik. "Impacts of a Nuclear War in South Asia on Soybean and Maize Production in the Midwest United States." *Climatic Change* 116(2) (2013):373–87. doi:10.1007/s10584-012-0518-1.

Pittock, A. Barrie et al. *Environmental Consequences of Nuclear War: Volume I: Physical and Atmospheric Effects* (New York: Wiley, 1986).

Resource Collection. "Nucleur Security Project Resource Collection." September 20, 2021, accessed on July 23, 2022, https://www.nti.org/analysis/resource-collections/nucleur-security-project-resource-collection/.

Robock, Alan and Owen B. Toon. "Self-Assured Destruction: The Climate Impacts of Nuclear War." *Bulletin of the Atomic Scientists* 68(5) (2012):66–74.

Sagan, Scott D. "Policy: A Call for Global Nuclear Disarmament." *Nature* 487 (7405) (2012):30–32.

Sardesai, Damodar R. and Raju G. C. Thomas, eds. *Nuclear India in the Twenty-First Century* (New York: Palgrave Macmillan, 2002).

Schnittker, John. "The 1972–73 Food Price Spiral." *Brookings Papers on Economic Activity* 2 (1973):498–507.

Shane, Scott. "1950s U.S. Nuclear Target List Offers Chilling Insight." *New York Times*, December 22, accessed on July 23, 2022, https://www.nytimes.com/2015/12/23/us/politics/1950s-us-nuclear-target-list-offers-chilling-insight.html.

Shultz, George P., William J. Perry, Henry A. Kissinger, and Sam Nunn. "A World Free of Nuclear Weapons." *Wall Street Journal*, January 4, 2007, accessed on May 28, 2014, http://online. wsj.com/article/SB116787515251566636.html.

——. "Toward a Nuclear-Free World." *Wall Street Journal*, January 15, 2008, accessed on July 23, 2022, http://online.wsj.com/article/SB120036422673589947.html.

——. "How to Protect Our Nuclear Deterrent." *Wall Street Journal*, January 19, 2010, accessed on July 23, 2022, http://online.wsj.com/article/SB10001424052748704152804574628344282735008. html.

——. "Deterrence in the Age of Nuclear Proliferation." *Wall Street Journal*, March 7, 2011, accessed on July 24, 2022, https://www.wsj.com/articles/SBI10001424052748703300904576178760530369414..

Slayton, Tom. "Rice Crisis Forensics: How Asian Governments Carelessly Set the World Rice Market on Fire." CGD Working Paper 163. Washington, D.C.: Center for Global Development. 2009, accessed on July 24, 2022, https://www.cgdev.org/publication/rice-crisis-forensecs-how-asian-governments-carelessly-set-world-rice-market-fire.

Small, Richard D. "Atmospheric Smoke Loading from a Nuclear Attack on the United States." *Ambio* 18(7) (1989):377–83.

Sternberg, Troy. "Chinese Drought, Wheat, and the Egyptian Uprising: Howa Localized Hazard Became Globalized." In *The Arab Spring and Climate Change: A Climate and Security Correlations Series*, eds. Caitlin E.Werrell and Francesco Femia. Center for American Progress. 2013, accessed on July 24, 2022, https://www.americanprogress.org/article/the-arab-spring-and-climate-change/.

Toon, Owen B., Alan Robock, and Richard P. Turco. "Environmental Consequences of Nuclear War." *Physics Today* 61(12) (2008):37–42. doi:10.1063/1.3047679.

Toon, Owen B., Richard P. Turco, Alan Robock, Charles Bardeen, Luke Oman, and Georgiy L. Stenchikov. "Atmospheric Effects and Societal Consequences of Regional Scale Nuclear Conflicts and Acts of Individual Nuclear Terrorism." *Atmospheric Chemistry and Physics* 7 (2007):1973–2002.

Xia, Lili and Alan Robock. "Impacts of a Nuclear War in South Asia on Rice Production in Mainland China." *Climatic Change* 116(2):357–72. doi:10.1007/s10584-012-0475-8.

Xia, Lili, Alan Robock, Michael Mills, Andrea Stenke, and Ira Helfand. "Decadal Reduction of Chinese Agriculture after a Regional Nuclear War." *Earth's Future* 3(2) (2015):37–48. doi:10.1002/2014EF000283.

Part III

THE DILEMMAS OF NO FIRST USE

Chapter 8

IT'S TIME FOR A US NO-FIRST-USE NUCLEAR POLICY[1]

Nina Tannenwald

Beginning in the early days of the Cold War, the USA has been relying on the threat to use nuclear weapons first as a way to deter both nuclear and non-nuclear attacks. Yet, the world has changed significantly since then. In the contemporary era, the dangers and risks of a first-strike policy outweigh the hoped-for deterrence benefits. The USA should join China and India in adopting a declared no-first-use policy and should encourage the other nuclear-armed states to do likewise. A no-first-use policy means that the USA would pledge to use nuclear weapons only in retaliation for a nuclear attack. The sole purpose of US nuclear weapons would then be to deter—and, if necessary, respond to—the use of nuclear weapons against itself and its allies and partners. To be credible, this declaratory pledge would need to be reflected in a retaliatory-strike-only nuclear force posture.

The most important goal for the USA today should be to prevent the use of nuclear weapons. Since the country dropped atomic bombs on Hiroshima and Nagasaki in 1945—the only use of nuclear weapons in warfare—it has established a nearly seventy-four-year tradition of not using nuclear weapons. This tradition is the single most important fact of the nuclear age. Today, the risks of nuclear war are increasing. Heightened geopolitical tensions, a more complex calculus of deterrence in a multipolar nuclear world, renewed reliance on nuclear weapons, technological arms races in nuclear and non-nuclear systems, the collapse of arms control and the return of nuclear brinkmanship have all resulted in highly dangerous deterrence policies. Such policies, through miscalculation or accident, could plunge the USA into a nuclear war with North Korea, Russia or China. The nuclear-armed states urgently need to step back from this dangerous situation by adopting an NFU policy that would significantly reduce the risk of nuclear war.

INTERNATIONAL RELATIONS THEORY AND NFU

Several theoretical approaches in international relations help to illuminate why states choose to adopt a first use versus an NFU policy. A realist approach, which emphasises the central role of material capabilities, would generally be sceptical of NFU pledges, which it would view as 'cheap talk' and unenforceable. States that have made such pledges could still launch a nuclear weapon first in a conflict. Thus, NATO leaders and other observers expressed considerable scepticism during the final years of the Cold War that the Soviet Union's declaration of an NFU policy in 1982 had any real substance behind it.[2] Today, while India has made an NFU pledge, analysts debate how constraining it really is. In turn, Indian Prime Minister Narendra Modi is sometimes dismissive of China's NFU policy.[3]

But some states—India, China, and the Soviet Union for a period—have nevertheless pledged NFU and, in the cases of India and China, have attempted to make those pledges credible. What explains these choices? The empirical record suggests that a state's choice regarding a nuclear first-use policy tends to be strongly influenced by asymmetries in the conventional military balance between nuclear-armed adversaries. Nuclear-armed states that face a conventionally superior military adversary will threaten to use nuclear weapons first because they depend more heavily on nuclear threats to defend themselves. In contrast, nuclear-armed states that possess overwhelming conventional superiority are more likely to declare an NFU policy because it privileges their conventional advantage on the battlefield and might help to keep the conflict non-nuclear.

Thus India, which possesses a much larger conventional military than Pakistan, declared an NFU policy in 1999, following its nuclear test in 1998. Pakistan, which relies heavily on its nuclear deterrent for its defence against India, has rejected Indian calls to adopt an NFU pledge.[4] This logic also helps explain why, in 1993, Russia dropped its NFU pledge first made in 1982. After the collapse of the Soviet Union in 1989, as Russian conventional military forces deteriorated and the USA declined to reciprocate the NFU pledge, Russian leaders felt they had to rely more heavily on nuclear weapons.

Consistent with this logic, during the Cold War, the USA relied on a first-use threat to offset and counter the overwhelming conventional superiority of the Soviet conventional military threat in Europe. Today, the situation is reversed. The USA possesses overwhelming conventional superiority while Russia's conventional military has declined. Because conventional US military power now vastly exceeds that of its largest adversaries, Russia and China, many argue that America's first-use policy is now unnecessary to deter conventional threats.[5]

China's NFU policy, on the other hand, while consistent with its small nuclear force, is less well explained by asymmetries in conventional forces. China adopted an NFU policy at the time of its first atomic bomb test in 1964, when its peasant army was still transitioning to a modern military force. Part of the explanation for this decision has to do with Mao's thinking about the nuclear bomb as a 'paper tiger', but Chinese leaders have primarily seen an NFU policy as an effective way to signal the purely defensive nature of the small Chinese nuclear arsenal and to avoid a US–Soviet-style arms race.[6] An NFU policy also conveys the spirit of 'peaceful coexistence' to which China is committed.

The theory that adopting an NFU policy is based on asymmetries in conventional forces is further complicated by the existence of other weapons of mass destruction. During the George W. Bush and Barack Obama years, the strongest argument for the USA to retain the first-use option was that nuclear weapons are necessary to help deter and possibly retaliate against attacks with chemical, and especially biological weapons.[7] The Trump administration's 2018 Nuclear Posture Review (NPR) expanded the category of non-nuclear attacks that it will seek to deter with nuclear threats to include cyberattacks, a move that previous presidents had ruled out and that most observers view sceptically, given its dangerous escalatory potential.

A second theoretical perspective, 'liberal institutionalism', emphasises the role of rules and institutions, both domestic and international, in stabilising expectations and behaviour. According to this theory, even if NFU are unenforceable, they are not necessarily meaningless. To be meaningful, an NFU pledge must be built into domestic institutions, that is, the structure of operational military capabilities.[8] A genuine NFU policy would require that nuclear forces be consistent with an 'assured retaliation' posture that eschews counterforce objectives—the ability to destroy an adversary's nuclear arsenal before it is launched.

This perspective thus emphasises the value of an NFU pledge in structuring operational forces to make them smaller and less threatening. When US secretary of defence Robert McNamara, soon after entering office in 1961, sent a directive to the joint chiefs of staff about strategic force requirements, he stated that the first assumption shaping requirements was that 'we will not strike first with such weapons'.[9] McNamara's directive was undoubtedly partly an effort to stem air force demands for a first-strike capability and the vast procurement of weaponry it would require. This directive, in effect, repudiated the extended-deterrent doctrine that the USA would respond to a Soviet conventional attack in Europe with nuclear weapons.

At the international level, liberal institutionalists emphasise the value of rules and institutions to prevent nuclear war. They argue that NFU has become a de facto norm anyway and therefore should be declared publically and multilaterally. As Morton Halperin, who later became deputy assistant secretary of defence for arms control, wrote as early as 1961: 'There now exists a powerful informal rule against the use of nuclear weapons,' and it would be advantageous to the USA to transform this tacit understanding into a formal agreement.[10] Indeed, the 'negative security assurances' first issued by the USA and the other P5 countries (the United Nations Security Council's five permanent member countries) in 1978 and renewed periodically—commitments to non-nuclear states that are members of the NPT not to use or to threaten to use nuclear weapons against them—already constitute a partial NFU regime. Liberal institutionalists would also point out that constantly touting the value of a nuclear threat for security sends signals that nuclear weapons are useful and undermines non-proliferation goals.[11]

Finally, constructivists who focus on the role of norms, identity and discourse emphasise that a declared NFU policy is an important way to strengthen norms of nuclear restraint and the nearly seventy-four-year-tradition of non-use. Strong statements from leaders about the need to avoid using nuclear weapons can help reduce tensions, just as irresponsible tweets can increase them. In the constructivist view, an NFU policy is also a diplomatic tool that can be used to signal that a state is a responsible nuclear power. As Indian Prime Minister Narendra Modi recently put it: 'India is a very responsible state. We are the only country to have a declared NFU [sic]. It's not because of world pressure, but because of our own ethos. We will not move away from this, whichever government comes to power.'[12] Indeed, India's NFU pledge has proved useful for portraying Pakistan as a relatively irresponsible custodian of its nuclear arsenal. Likewise, Indian leaders use their NFU pledge as a way to resist pressures to sign any treaties that would restrict India's nuclear arsenal.

THE WEAK CASE FOR A FIRST-USE POLICY

A first-use policy is based primarily on the belief that the threat of nuclear escalation continues to serve as a deterrent to large-scale conventional war or the use of chemical and biological weapons.[13] Critics of NFU argue that the USA should not make any promise that might make it easier for an opponent to plan an effective military action, a strategy known as 'calculated ambiguity'. As the defence department recently explained,

> Retaining a degree of ambiguity and refraining from a no first use policy creates uncertainty in the mind of potential adversaries and

> reinforces deterrence of aggression by ensuring adversaries cannot predict what specific actions will lead to a U.S. nuclear response. Implementing a no first use policy could undermine the U.S. ability to deter Russian, Chinese, and North Korean aggression, especially with respect to their growing capability to carry out nonnuclear strategic attacks.[14]

In addition, sceptics believe that an NFU promise would be especially costly for the USA, given its wide-ranging extended deterrence commitments.[15]

These arguments are not compelling for four reasons. First, a policy of calculated ambiguity is unnecessary. Today, there are very few missions that the USA could not accomplish with conventional weapons. Indeed, the US conventional capabilities are more than sufficient to deter and respond to anything but a nuclear attack. None of the country's most likely adversaries—Russia, China, North Korea and Iran—can hope to defeat it and its allies in a protracted non-nuclear conflict.

Second, threats of first use are dangerous. As Michael Gerson has argued, they undermine crisis stability in multiple ways.[16] The large, highly accurate US nuclear arsenal, along with missile defences and new dual-use precision-strike weapons, may cause leaders in Russia and China to believe that the USA is capable of conducting a disarming first strike against them. Furthermore, the entanglement of nuclear and conventional weapons in deterrence strategies could inadvertently increase the chance of nuclear war, while new, smaller nuclear warheads, along with doctrines of 'escalate to de-escalate' appear to be lowering the threshold for nuclear use.[17] In a crisis, Russian or Chinese leaders might come to believe that the USA might attempt a disarming strike, forcing them, in turn, to contemplate acting pre-emptively.[18]

Third, although supporters of calculated ambiguity fervently believe it maximises deterrence, the evidence for such a claim is hardly definitive. Nuclear weapons did not deter the 9/11 attacks; the rise of the Islamic State; Russian interventions in Georgia, Ukraine or Syria; or North Korean nuclear and ballistic missile tests. Nor have Indian and Pakistani nuclear weapons deterred risky conventional crises between the two countries over Kashmir, most recently in February 2019. The calculated ambiguity argument gained some support from the perception that during the 1991 Gulf War, a US nuclear threat had helped deter Iraqi leader Saddam Hussein from using chemical weapons against the USA and coalition forces or Israel.[19] As Scott Sagan has persuasively argued, however, it is highly unlikely that a nuclear threat deterred Saddam from using chemical weapons.[20] Indeed, recent research suggests that the threat to use nuclear weapons first against non-nuclear states has little credible coercive power.[21]

Fourth, even in the very small number of scenarios where nuclear weapons might seem to be necessary—for example, knocking out North Korean mobile missiles or underground command centres—opening Pandora's box of nuclear use would likely lead to uncontrolled escalation. There is no scenario in which using nuclear weapons first can make a bad situation better. As James Doyle, a former staffer at Los Alamos National Laboratory has argued, 'It is folly to believe that the use of nuclear weapons could de-escalate a conflict.'[22]

As for threatening to use nuclear weapons first in support of extended deterrence commitments, such a policy lacks credibility because the costs of starting a nuclear war would vastly outweigh the benefits. As Henry Kissinger once said, 'Great powers don't commit suicide for their allies.'[23] Thus, as several analysts have persuasively argued, extended deterrence based on a conventional military response to a conventional threat is much more credible. Moreover, constantly arguing that nuclear weapons are necessary reduces the credibility of the USA's more usable conventional deterrent.[24]

THE BENEFITS OF AN NFU POLICY

As Kingston Reif and Daryl Kimball of the Arms Control Association have argued, 'a clear U.S. no-first-use policy would reduce the risk of Russian or Chinese nuclear miscalculation during a crisis by alleviating concerns about a devastating U.S. nuclear first-strike'.[25] This would mean that the USA would rely on nuclear weapons only to deter nuclear attacks. Adopting this approach would involve more than 'cheap talk', for it would require meaningful doctrinal and operational changes.[26] Specifically, it would allow the USA to adopt a less threatening nuclear posture. It would eliminate first-strike postures, pre-emptive capabilities and other types of destabilising warfighting strategies. It would emphasise restraint in targeting, launch-on-warning, alert levels of deployed systems, procurement and modernisation plans. In other words, it would help shape the physical qualities of nuclear forces in a way that renders them unsuitable for missions other than deterrence of nuclear attacks.[27]

Implementing these steps would significantly reduce the risk of accidental, unauthorised, mistaken or pre-emptive use. The removal of threats of a nuclear first strike would also strengthen strategic and crisis stability.[28] Of perhaps equal importance, adopting an NFU policy would help address humanitarian concerns and reduce the salience of nuclear weapons.[29] Likewise, it would 'be more consistent with the long-term goal of global nuclear disarmament and would better contribute to US nuclear non-proliferation objectives'.[30]

A multilateral NFU pledge would have even more benefits. It would move Russia and Pakistan away from their high-risk doctrines and reduce a source of Russia–NATO tensions. A common NFU policy would help anchor the existing NFU policies of China and India and implicitly acknowledge their leadership in this area, a virtue when middle-power states are feeling disenfranchised from the global nuclear order.

Some analysts have questioned whether, in an asymmetric conflict, a US NFU policy would actually help reduce the risk of nuclear escalation by an adversary. The USA is so conventionally dominant, they argue, that in a crisis, a country like North Korea might employ nuclear weapons pre-emptively because the USA could take out North Korean targets even with just conventional weapons.[31] It is true that an NFU policy might make no difference in such a situation. Still, it might nevertheless remove at least one source of crisis instability. Most importantly, however, in the era of 'multi-front' deterrence, North Korea is not the only adversary and a US NFU policy would remain valuable in less asymmetric conflicts.

A second concern is that a real NFU strategy would require a greater commitment to a countervalue targeting strategy—targeting civilians rather than nuclear silos—and thus run up against moral and legal rules prohibiting the direct targeting of civilians.[32] This is a legitimate point. However, the current US counterforce targeting policy will likely result in massive civilian casualties as 'collateral damage', making the risk to civilians of an NFU strategy little different.[33]

IMPLEMENTATION

The USA ought to unilaterally adopt an NFU policy and ask other nuclear-armed states to do the same. This would constitute the formal adoption of what is already essentially de facto US policy.[34] An NFU policy adopted by the USA would create political space for Russia to follow suit: for Russia to consider NFU, its concerns about US ballistic missile defences, imbalances in conventional forces and issues of NATO enlargement would need to be addressed. The USA would also need to tackle the issue of extended deterrence with its allies and move towards conventional extended deterrence.[35] India and Pakistan would need a *modus vivendi* on Kashmir, while the USA and North Korea would need to sign a non-aggression pact. In fact, the USA could actually negotiate a mutual NFU agreement with North Korea. The former is extremely unlikely to use nuclear weapons first on North Korea; therefore, an agreement that provided a basis for imposing some restraint on the North Korean arsenal would be in America's interest.[36]

Doctrinal and operational changes would need to follow such a declaration. China's restrained nuclear arsenal provides the best example of an NFU pledge implemented in practice. Unlike the USA and Russia, China keeps its warheads and missiles separated. It has not developed precision-strike nuclear-warfighting capabilities, such as tactical nuclear weapons, and it does not keep its forces on 'launch-on-warning' alert. China has also invested heavily in conventional military modernisation so that it would not have to consider nuclear escalation in a conventional war.[37] India, too, keeps its warheads and missiles separate in support of its NFU pledge, though some analysts argue that India's NFU policy does not run especially deep and that it 'is neither a stable nor a reliable predictor of how the Indian military and political leadership might actually use nuclear weapons'.[38] Nevertheless, both countries' operational postures reflect (to some degree) their NFU policies.[39] The USA and the other nuclear powers should move in this direction.

CONCLUSION

What are the prospects for an NFU policy? On 30 January 2019, Senator Elizabeth Warren (the Democratic party representative from Massachusetts) and Representative Adam Smith (the Democratic party representative from Washington) introduced legislation that declared, 'It is the policy of the United States to not use nuclear weapons first.'[40] But Congress is divided on this.[41] Sceptics have objected that the geopolitical preconditions are not ripe for an NFU policy at this time. In 2016, the Obama administration seriously considered declaring an NFU policy but then hesitated at the last minute, largely because of pushback from the European and Asian allies, who are under the US nuclear umbrella.[42] Donald Trump, for his part, had been busy dismantling arms-control agreements, not creating them.[43]

Adoption of an NFU policy will require close consultation with allies, but the US administration should begin this task. As an initial step on the way to NFU, US leaders should consider the recent proposal by Jeffrey Lewis and Scott Sagan that the country should declare it will not use nuclear weapons 'against any target that could be reliably destroyed by conventional means'.[44] This policy would not solve the problem posed by highly asymmetric crises, as noted above. Nevertheless, it would represent an initial important declaratory statement of nuclear restraint.

The most important goal of the USA today is to prevent the use of nuclear weapons. The policy of relying on the threat to use nuclear weapons first is an outdated legacy of the Cold War. As even card-carrying realists such as the 'four horsemen' recognised, given US conventional capabilities, there are no circumstances in which the country ought to start a nuclear war.[45] Relying on the pretence that it might do so in order to deter a conventional threat unacceptably increases the chances of nuclear escalation. Moving towards declared NFU policies is the best way to reduce the risks of nuclear war.

NOTES

1 An earlier version of this chapter appeared as an essay in the *Texas National Security Review* 2, no 3 (2019): 131–137.

2 Ankit Panda, "'No First Use' and Nuclear Weapons" (Council on Foreign Relations, Manhattan, July 17, 2018), accessed on March 31, 2022, https://www.cfr.org/backgrounder/no-first-use-and-nuclear-weapons. In fact, there is some evidence that it was real and affected Soviet war planning. See *Soviet Intentions, 1965–1985*, (BDM Federal, Inc., 1995), chapter 3, 41–43; John Hines, Ellis M. Mishulovich, and John F. Shulle, *Soviet Intentions 1965–1985, Volume I: An Analytical Comparison of U.S.–Soviet Assessments during the Cold War*, (McLean: BDM Federal, Inc., 1995). Unclassified, excised copy, accessed on March 31, 2022, https://nsarchive2.gwu.edu/nukevault/ebb285/doc02_I_ch3.pdf.

3 Kumar Sundaram and M.V. Ramana, "India and the Policy of No First Use of Nuclear Weapons," *Journal for Peace and Nuclear Disarmament* 1, no 1 (February 2018): 152–168, accessed on March 31, 2022, https://www.tandfonline.com/doi/full/10.1080/25751654.2018.1438737.

4 Sadia Tasleem, "Pakistan's Nuclear Use Doctrine," (Carnegie Endowment for International Peace, Washington DC, June 30, 2016), https://carnegieendowment.org/2016/06/30/pakistan-s-nuclear-use-doctrine-pub-63913.

5 Although the Trump administration rejected an NFU pledge in its 2018 Nuclear Posture Review, increasing calls in recent years for the USA to adopt an NFU policy from former government officials, members of Congress and civilian analysts as well as serious consideration by the Obama administration itself in 2016, draw on this logic.

6 Zhenqing Pan, "A Study of China's No-First-Use Policy on Nuclear Weapons," *Journal for Peace and Nuclear Disarmament* 1, no 1 (May 2018): 124, doi: 10.1080/25751654.2018.1458415.

7 For its part, India has a carve-out in its NFU pledge for chemical and biological weapons attacks.

8 Ronald Mitchell, "Regime Design Matters: Intentional Oil Pollution and Treaty Compliance," *International Organization* 48, no 3 (Summer 1994): 425–458, https://www.jstor.org/stable/2706965.

9 McNamara to Chairman, Joint Chiefs of Staff, "Task Force Reports," Memo, February 20, 1961, US Nuclear History, 00307, National Security Archive, 1.

10 Morton Halperin, "Proposal for a Ban on the Use of Nuclear Weapons," (Special Studies Group, Study Memorandum No 4, Washington DC, 1961), 12, iv.

11 Scott D. Sagan, "The Case for No First Use," *Survival* 51, no 3, (2009): 163–182, doi: 10.1080/00396330903011545.

12 The interview can be seen at https://www.youtube.com/watch?v=-6tb2e8o9P4&feature=youtu.be.

13 Amy F. Woolf, "U.S. Nuclear Weapons Policy: Considering 'No First Use'" (Congressional Research Service, Washington DC, March 1, 2019).

14 US Department of Defense, "Dangers of a Nuclear No First Use Policy" (US Department of Defense, Washington DC, April 2019), https://media.defense.gov/2019/Apr/01/2002108002/-1/-1/1/DANGERS-OF-A-NO-FIRST-USE-POLICY.PDF.

15 Parris H. Chang, "No-First Use Would Only Embolden China," *Bulletin of the Atomic Scientists*, September 21, 2016, https://thebulletin.org/roundtable_entry/no-first-use-would-only-embolden-china/.

16 Michael S. Gerson, "No First Use: The Next Step for U.S. Nuclear Policy," *International Security* 35, no 2 (Fall 2010): 9, doi: 10.1162/ISEC_a_00018.

17 James M. Acton, "Escalation through Entanglement: How the Vulnerability of Command-and-Control Systems Raises the Risks of Nuclear War," *International Security* 43, no 1 (Summer 2018): 56–99, doi: 10.1162/isec_a_00320; Fiona S. Cunningham and Taylor M. Fravel, "Why China Won't Abandon Its Nuclear Strategy of Assured Retaliation" (Policy Brief, US–China Project, Institute for Security and Conflict Studies, Elliott School of International Affairs, Washington DC, February 2016).

18 Gerson, "No First Use," 9.

19 Keith B. Payne, "Strategic Hubris," in "Forum: The Case for No First Use: An Exchange," *Survival* 51, no 5 (October–November 2009): 27–32, doi: 10.1080/00396330903309840.

20 Sagan, "Reply: Evidence, Logic and Nuclear Doctrine," in Morton H. Halperin, Bruno Tertrais, Keith B. Payne, K. Subrahmanyam, and Scott D. Sagan, eds, (2009) Forum: The Case for No First Use: An Exchange, Survival: Global Politics and Strategy, 51:5, 17–4 "Forum: The Case for No First Use," 30–41.

21 Todd S. Sechser and Matthew Fuhrmann, *Nuclear Weapons and Coercive Diplomacy* (Cambridge, UK: Cambridge University Press, 2017).

22 James E. Doyle, "Nuclear No First Use (NFU) Is Right for America," Real Clear Defense, July 12, 2016, accessed on March 31, 2022, https://www.realcleardefense.com/articles/2016/07/13/nuclear_no-first-use_nfu_is_right_for_america_109556.html.

23 Quoted in Elbridge Colby, "If You Want Peace, Prepare for Nuclear War," *Foreign Affairs* 97, no 6 (November/December 2018): 30, https://www.foreignaffairs.com/articles/china/2018-10-15/if-you-want-peace-prepare-nuclear-war. China can afford to declare an NFU policy more easily than the USA because it lacks the kind of wide-ranging extended deterrence commitments of the former.

24 Sagan, "No First Use;" Steve Fetter and Jon Wolfsthal, "No First Use and Credible Deterrence," *Journal for Peace and Nuclear Disarmament* 1, no 1 (April 2018): 102–114, doi: 10.1080/25751654.2018.1454257.

25 Kingston Reif and Daryl Kimball, "Rethink Old Think on No First Use," *Bulletin of the Atomic Scientists*, August 29, 2016, accessed on March 31, 2022, https://thebulletin.org/2016/08/rethink-oldthink-on-no-first-use/.

26 Sagan, "No First Use."

27 Alberto Perez Vadillo, "Beyond the Ban: The Humanitarian Initiative and Advocacy of No First Use Nuclear Doctrines," (Report, British–American Security Information Council [BASIC], London, May 10, 2016), accessed on March 31, 2022, http://www.basicint.org/publications/alberto-perez-vadillo-eu-non-proliferation-consortium-researcher/2016/beyond-ban.

28 Bruce Blair, "How Obama Could Revolutionize Nuclear Weapons Strategy before He Goes," *Politico*, June 22, 2016, accessed on March 31, 2022, https://www.politico.com/magazine/story/2016/06/barack-obama-nuclear-weapons-213981.

29 Vadillo, "Beyond the Ban," 12.

30 Sagan, "No First Use."

31 Alexander Lanoszka and Thomas Leo Sherer, "Nuclear Ambiguity, No-First-Use and Crisis Stability in Asymmetric Crises," *Nonproliferation Review* 24, no 3–4 (2017): 343–355, doi: 10.1080/10736700.2018.1430552.

32 I thank Vipin Narang for this comment on Twitter.

33 Jeffrey G. Lewis and Scott D. Sagan, "The Nuclear Necessity Principle: Making U.S. Targeting Conform with Ethics and the Laws of War, *Daedalus* 145, no 4 (Fall 2016): 62–74, doi: 10.1162/DAED_a_00412.

34 Blair, "How Obama Could Revolutionize Nuclear Weapons Strategy."

35 Sagan, "No First Use."

36 Abigail Stowe-Thurston, "Why It's Time to Negotiate a Mutual No First Use Policy with North Korea," NK News, April 15, 2019, accessed on March 31, 2022, https://www.nknews.org/2019/04/why-its-time-to-negotiate-a-mutual-no-first-use-policy-with-north-korea/.

37 Pan, "China and No First Use," 117.

38 Sundaram and Ramana, "India and No First Use," 152.

39 Cunningham and Fravel, "Why China Won't Abandon Its Nuclear Strategy of Assured Retaliation."

40 US Senate, "A Bill to Establish the Policy of the United States Regarding the No-First-Use of Nuclear Weapons," (Senate Bill 272, 116th Congress, Washington DC, 2019–2020), https://www.congress.gov/bill/116th-congress/senate-bill/272; "To Establish the Policy of the United States Regarding the No-First-Use of Nuclear Weapons," (House Bill 921, 116th

Congress, Washington DC, 2019–2020), https://www.congress.gov/bill/116th-congress/house-bill/921.

41 "Fischer: 'A No-First-Use Policy Erodes Deterrence," (Office of Deb Fischer, United States Senator for Nebraska, January 30, 2019), https://www.fischer.senate.gov/public/index.cfm/2019/1/fischer-a-no-first-use-policy-erodes-deterrence.

42 Tannenwald, "The Vanishing Nuclear Taboo? How Disarmament Fell Apart," *Foreign Affairs* (November/December 2018), https://www.foreignaffairs.com/articles/world/2018-10-15/vanishing-nuclear-taboo.

43 Paul R. Pillar, "Trump's Demolition of Arms Control," *National Interest*, May 1, 2019, https://nationalinterest.org/blog/paul-pillar/trumps-demolition-arms-control-55317.

44 Lewis and Sagan, "The Nuclear Necessity Principle."

45 George P. Shultz, William J. Perry, Henry A. Kissinger, and Sam Nunn, "A World Free of Nuclear Weapons," *Wall Street Journal*, January 4, 2007, https://www.wsj.com/articles/SB116787515251566636.

Chapter 9

THE PURPOSES OF NUCLEAR WEAPONS[1]

Rajesh Rajagopalan

The idea of reducing nuclear danger, even before nuclear weapons are themselves abolished, is an attractive one. Though nuclear weapons may present some level of irreducible risk by their very existence, there can be no argument that we should attempt to find a path to reducing these dangers as much as possible. Indeed, even nuclear weapon states agree: in the immediate aftermath of the Cold War, the USA, followed by Russia, unilaterally eliminated a significant number of tactical nuclear weapons (TNWs)—which remains the largest single reduction in nuclear forces—because these very short-range weapons were considered far more dangerous than long-range strategic weapons. Though TNWs are once again slowly increasing in importance, the principle itself is no less valid. The proponents of NFU nuclear strategies hope that something similar can be achieved by moving current nuclear strategies towards a more responsible direction. If nuclear-armed states could be convinced to adopt NFU strategies, it could significantly reduce the risks associated with early-use or first-use nuclear strategies. But this would be a very difficult venture because adopting NFU strategies would undermine the fundamental purpose for which many of the current nuclear-armed states sought these weapons: a guarantee against perceived existential threats.

In this chapter, I will illustrate why adopting NFU policies will undermine the basic purpose for which *some* states acquire nuclear weapons, which would, in turn, make it highly unlikely that they would adopt NFU. I do this by first briefly examining the different purposes for which states have acquired nuclear weapons. I then focus on Pakistan, Israel and India. The first two demonstrate cases where either significant conventional military imbalance and/or existential threats require them to abjure NFU postures. India, in contrast, is a case that demonstrates the security conditions that permit the adoption of NFU. The penultimate section outlines the complex emerging security scenario that could make NFU more difficult.

SECURITY, SURVIVAL AND NUCLEAR WEAPONS

There are, of course, multiple reasons why states seek nuclear weapons. But while several scholars have pointed out that some states may pursue nuclear weapons for motivations other than security—such as domestic bureaucratic politics or status and identity, as Scott Sagan points out[2]—we can also further parse the security motivation. Even if security is the primary driver, it is possible to identify at least three variants of the security motivation: deterrence of nuclear threats, deterrence of conventionally superior adversaries and deterrence of non-nuclear existential threats.[3] The former is the more common assumption among scholars and policymakers. But all three are important in determining how states plan to use their nuclear weapons. This is particularly so when it comes to considering the feasibility of adopting NFU doctrines. NFU has important benefits. It reduces the pressure on command-and-control systems because it does not require nuclear forces to be kept constantly on alert, ready to be launched. It also reduces the pressure on early warning and surveillance systems. Early warning is considerably less important for NFU states since the NFU posture is based on retaliation after an attack has landed rather than responding to the detection of an attack in the extremely brief time between the detection and the landing of the attack. Though surveillance may still be important in determining the source of the attack, this does not create the dangerous pressures that could lead to the risk of catastrophic mistakes, which happened several times during the Cold War between the USA and the Soviet Union. There are other benefits too: not keeping nuclear weapons in a ready state is likely to be a lot less dangerous, though the prevalence of canisterised missiles in the hands of even NFU states such as China and India reduces the relevance of this particular point.

As Sagan has argued, there can be a number of good reasons for the USA adopting an NFU posture, and many of the objections to such an American declaratory policy may be overstated[4]; many, but not all. The US nuclear force is meant to assure American allies that they do not need to build their nuclear weapons, which is particularly important as many American allies face potential adversaries who are far stronger. Such allies would need to adopt nuclear weapons, and a first-use doctrine, if they did not have the US nuclear umbrella.

An NFU posture is a viable option for states of the first category, those that only need to deter nuclear threats or attacks. But it is not a viable posture for states that either face clearly conventionally superior adversaries or worse—states that face existential threats. For such states, NFU would make little sense. Below I consider two such states,

Pakistan and Israel, to illustrate the deterrence dilemma they face and its consequences for NFU.

PAKISTAN—CONVENTIONAL MILITARY INFERIORITY AND EXISTENTIAL ANXIETIES

There is little likelihood that Pakistan will be willing to adopt an NFU policy. Indeed, adopting an NFU policy would undermine the very purpose for which Pakistan acquired nuclear weapons at enormous national cost.

This purpose is the security condition that Pakistan faces, which is an enormous inequality in wealth and conventional military power vis-à-vis its adversary, India. Though Pakistan is a fairly large and powerful state on its own, its unfortunate location next to a gigantic India defines this condition. India is almost four times Pakistan's size today, with a population that is more than six times as large and an economy ten times as large. Such inequalities cannot be easily, if ever, overcome. Pakistan has had to deal with this inequality even before it built nuclear weapons. For almost three decades after Independence, Pakistan created myths to artificially claim parity with Indian power, by claiming, for example, that 'one Pakistani was equal to ten Indians'. Such myths were severely tested by the 1965 India–Pakistan war and finally put to rest by the 1971 war in which India used its conventional military superiority to vivisect the country.[5] Until the 1971 war, Pakistan's strategy also included balancing India's conventional superiority by leveraging a technological advantage with US weapons, acquired through a military alliance with the USA and by joining US-led anti-communist alliances such as the Central Treaty Organization (CENTO).

The 1971 war demonstrated that advanced weaponry, cultural myths and military allies could not compensate for the gross inequality between the two sides. Not surprisingly, within a few weeks of the military disaster in Bangladesh, Zulfikar Bhutto, Pakistan's new prime minister, called on Pakistan's scientific community to build nuclear arms for the country. This had little to do with India's nuclear capability: Mrs Gandhi's decision to test an atomic 'device' came months later, towards the end of 1972. Bhutto had argued for nuclear weapons even in the 1960s and he lost little time after he became prime minister to push for it. His consistent advocacy for nuclear weapons for Pakistan might appear to suggest that his decision to pursue nuclear arms was driven by personality factors rather than actual security conditions. However, this would be a mistaken assumption for two reasons. First, his advocacy was based on his fairly accurate reading of Pakistan's security context: he recognised that Pakistan faced a much stronger and larger adversary that could not be countered with 'a small, though highly efficient, armed forces equipped with conventional weapons'.[6] Second, his advocacy, which was dismissed by the Pakistan military in the 1960s, was embraced by it in the aftermath of the Bangladesh War because the unambiguous result of the 1971 war appears to have convinced them of the need for nuclear weapons to deal with Pakistan's conventional military weakness. Thus, though there is little doubt that India's 1974 nuclear test spurred Pakistan's own nuclear weapons programme, it is also equally clear that the programme itself originated in Pakistan's realisation that there was no other way it could deal with the conventional military inferiority it faced with India.

The gross inequality Pakistan faced with India led it to invest its nuclear weapons with two purposes: first, to prevent India from using its conventional military strength to defeat Pakistan by threatening nuclear escalation and second, to ensure Pakistan's survival in the face of what Pakistan considers an existential threat from India. Both require that Pakistan maintain at least the threat of using nuclear weapons first. Whether Pakistan would actually be willing to use nuclear weapons first is a legitimate question. It appears at least debatable that Pakistan will use nuclear weapons to prevent defeat at India's hands in a conventional war. Any Pakistani use of nuclear weapons will mean certain Indian nuclear retaliation. Such a nuclear conflict will mean, in turn, certain destruction for Pakistan. Though India will also possibly face destruction, that is likely to be of little consolation if the alternative to such an outcome is simply a conventional military defeat from which Pakistan could easily recover. Pakistan lost half the country in the Bangladesh War, and despite the humiliation it suffered, was able to recover fairly quickly. Even if Pakistan had nuclear weapons, it is difficult to imagine Pakistan actually using them to prevent that defeat, because the consequences for Pakistan would have been far worse. Of course, the stress here is on *combat* use: Pakistan can definitely be expected to 'use' nuclear weapons to threaten India with nuclear escalation. The question is whether Pakistan will actually carry out the threat, which is doubtful. In addition, in several instances where India has escalated—the Kargil war, the surgical strike (2016) and the Balakot strike (2019)— Pakistan showed little inclination to escalate, despite previously threatening such escalation.

The credibility of Pakistan's nuclear escalation threats rises when the context changes from defeat in a conventional war to national survival. If India puts Pakistan in a situation where its national survival itself is threatened, then the likelihood that Pakistan will use nuclear weapons first rises. In Pakistan's case, such a threat could arise not just from a nuclear attack on Pakistan, but even from India's far greater conventional military power. Though it is highly unlikely that India will put Pakistan in such a situation—Indian decision-makers, it can be presumed, will be rational enough to realise the dangers of making such an attempt—this is not something that Pakistani decision-makers can rule out. As Pakistan's Prime Minister Imran Khan stated recently at the United Nations, 'Supposing a country seven times smaller than its neighbour is faced with the choice—either you surrender or you fight for your freedom till death. What will we do? ... when a nuclear armed country fights to the end, it will have consequences far beyond the borders.'

Irrespective of which of these two scenarios for Pakistan's use of nuclear weapons is more likely, what is important to recognise is that both require Pakistan to be ready to use nuclear weapons first. It would make little sense for Pakistan to abjure the first use of nuclear weapons because the threat Pakistan faces is its inadequate conventional military power, which it compensates with nuclear weapons. Even more importantly, Pakistan's deterrence strategy requires it to *threaten* to use nuclear weapons first, irrespective of whether it actually will have the gumption to do so. Even if we assume for the sake of argument that Pakistan's leaders have decided internally that they would use nuclear weapons only to retaliate to a nuclear attack—in other words, an NFU policy—it would make little sense for them to state this publicly. Thus, for deterrence purposes, Pakistan's declaratory policy is far more important than its actual policy. This means that Pakistan will not formally adopt NFU as its policy for very good reasons: it would cripple its nuclear deterrence strategy and the very purpose for which it built nuclear weapons.

ISRAEL AND THE REQUIREMENTS OF EXISTENTIAL DETERRENCE

Israel's case is even clearer than Pakistan's because of Israel's even starker security circumstance. From the very beginning, there was little ambiguity about the purpose of Israel's pursuit of nuclear weapons. Israel has an understandable fear about national survival. This flows from both the experience of the Holocaust when about a third of the global Jewish population (and two-thirds of the European Jewish population) was exterminated by Nazi Germany as well as the hostility faced by the state of Israel from its Arab neighbours from the time Israel was established. As early as the mid-1950s, some Israeli leaders like David Ben-Gurion had decided that Israel's survival required Israel to build nuclear weapons, rejecting the idea of a military alliance with the USA (which was one alternative) as a solution to Israel's existential problem.[7] Indeed, the cooperation between Israel and France in nuclear technology began in the aftermath of the USA's opposition to the Suez War, which appeared to indicate to both countries that Washington could not be depended upon as an ally. As Vipin Narang points out, 'both nations embarked on a nuclear weapons program after being abandoned by the United States in Suez—France in pursuit of strategic independence, Israel seeking insurance.'[8]

Though there were significant internal debates in Israel about the utility of nuclear weapons for its defence, this was more about whether nuclear weapons could play additional roles in Israel's defence, not so much about the utility of nuclear weapons as a weapon of last resort.[9] As in Pakistan's case, once Israel developed nuclear weapons, they put them to other uses, specifically as a way of bargaining with the USA to convince it to step in when Israel needed its support, which is what Narang calls a 'catalytic nuclear posture'. Israel did this by signalling to the USA that it might be forced to use its nuclear arsenal, by undertaking preparations that only the USA could see, to convince the latter to resupply Israel with war material. It is important to point out, however, that Israel's 'catalytic' posture does not contradict its 'last resort' strategy but is in addition to it. Thus, in the 1973 Yom Kippur War, Israel's Defence Minister Moshe Dayan was convinced that Israel might lose the war and advocated using nuclear weapons to stop the Arab armies from advancing into Israel. However, other cabinet members, including Prime Minister Golda Meir disagreed with Dayan's assessment of the situation and refused to order nuclear weapons to be used. Though US assistance and the changing military fortunes on the frontlines made the issue moot, it is likely that Israel may have used its atomic arsenal if the USA had not stepped in and if the Arab armies had broken through the frontlines into Israel proper. The point is that though the catalytic posture explains some aspects of Israel's strategy, if this attempt had failed to catalyse US intervention, it is likely that Israel would have used nuclear weapons to first attempt to halt the Arab military advance on the battlefield, and if that failed, to probably threaten a massive nuclear attack on Arab states to force them to stop. The catalytic posture thus does not replace the 'last resort' option but is simply designed to postpone the last resort. Paradoxically, Israel's refusal to build TNWs can be seen as another indication that 'Israel treats its nuclear arsenal in existential terms'.[10]

For this chapter, what is essential to note is the fundamental nature of the existential threat that Israel perceives it faces, even if its centrality has to some extent reduced because of contemporary Israeli conventional military superiority. This fundamental problem has now been exacerbated because of the potential development of nuclear arms by some of Israel's adversaries, first Iraq, and more recently, Iran. Israel's development of a sea-based deterrent flows from this threat: it gives Israel the certainty that it will have a secure second-strike capability even in the face of nuclear threats. These threats mean that Israel has limited room to change its policies, despite its own fairly favourable conventional military balance as well as support from the world's most powerful nation. But Israel possibly recognises that both could change: its military superiority has already been eroded by groups such as Hezbollah (supported by Iran), and American support has always been less than certain.

An NFU posture would create multiple problems for Israel. To begin with, Israel would have to acknowledge that it possesses nuclear weapons, which it has so far been reluctant to do. But a much more important problem is that an NFU would make the very purpose of Israeli nuclear weapons meaningless. The country built nuclear weapons neither for status nor for battlefield use, but to correct a conventional imbalance. It is the ultimate guarantor that Israel will survive as a state. Adopting an NFU posture would be the equivalent for Israel of giving up its nuclear guarantee against existential threats. That makes it highly doubtful that Israel would ever do so.

INDIA

In contradistinction to Pakistan and Israel is India's nuclear doctrine and its NFU posture. Understanding why India can adopt NFU also tells us something important about the international security conditions that permit NFU postures. In brief, though India's nuclear weapons have a security purpose, India is a relatively strong conventional military power that does not face an existential threat. This comfortable security condition was what made India a reluctant nuclear power, to begin with, and it is what made India adopt a relatively relaxed nuclear posture, including the NFU policy.

India's nuclear pursuit has generally been described as haphazard and uncertain. Despite having a fairly robust nuclear programme even in the 1960s, Indian leaders were reluctant to build nuclear weapons.[11] Even China becoming a nuclear-armed state in 1964 did not lead India to build nuclear weapons, despite the fact India had suffered a massive military defeat at China's hands just two years earlier, and despite the fact that the border dispute that led to that war remained unresolved. Instead, India sought nuclear guarantees from the two superpowers and essentially settled for what is termed as 'implicit' security guarantees—

which was not much of a security guarantee—to avoid building nuclear weapons.[12] This decision becomes even more difficult to understand considering the development of new institutional architecture to promote nuclear non-proliferation in the form of the NPT, which ruled out the possibility of India legitimately acquiring nuclear weapons at a later date. Even when India did finally test an atomic 'device' in 1974, it refused to follow up with a full-fledged nuclear arsenal, basically shuttering the weapons programme for at least another decade. When New Delhi finally reluctantly resumed the nuclear weapons programme in the mid-1980s, it was driven by the development of nuclear weapons by Pakistan. But the reluctance continued, with India developing only a nascent weapons capability. Even the CTBT, which further threatened Indian efforts to test and perfect its nuclear arms, did not enjoin any urgency on India's part. When India finally went openly nuclear in 1998, it was at least as much of an ideological decision as a security one. And India's relaxed nuclear posture has continued subsequently: two decades later, the country has still not developed a deterrent capability that can target all of China, nor does it have a fully functioning nuclear triad. India's nuclear arsenal is possibly smaller than even Pakistan's but this has had little effect on accelerating India's nuclear weapons programme nor has it led to much comment in India. Simply put, India's nuclear weapons programme demonstrates that while India has determined that nuclear weapons are essential to its security, their role is quite limited. India sees nuclear weapons as nothing more than a deterrent against nuclear threats and nuclear attacks by adversaries.

In short, India adopted NFU because it is a relatively strong power that faces no existential threats. Though India faces a two-front threat, this has until now not been a coordinated threat. India has thus built sufficient conventional military strength to deal with both China and Pakistan separately. Moreover, the threat from each is territorial rather than existential (save for their nuclear capability). Neither Pakistan nor China threatens to eliminate the Indian state, nor is there any such threat perception from any section in India, elites or otherwise. Even if India should be defeated in a conventional war with each, the worst outcome it faces is the loss of Indian territory in Kashmir and Arunachal Pradesh and possibly elsewhere along the border. While these would be grievous blows, they do not threaten the existence of the nation itself. Indeed, it is difficult to imagine how the use of nuclear weapons would provide a solution to such an outcome. If such situations were to come to pass, Indian leaders would have to balance the loss of these territories against the even graver damage that could be caused if it retaliated with nuclear weapons. The point is that using nuclear weapons first would make little sense for India, given the military balance and the (relatively) limited nature of the threats it faces. This fairly comfortable security situation is an important reason for both the lackadaisical Indian pursuit of nuclear weapons, which has been a well-known puzzle in the literature on India's nuclear programme, as well as India's adoption of the NFU.

China represents an interesting case and one which, on the surface at least, might appear to negate the argument made above. China did face significant threats when it built its nuclear weapons but still adopted an NFU strategy. On the other hand, the threats that China faced from the USA were not considered existential from China's perspective. Indeed, Chinese military strategy, which underwent changes both in 1956 and in 1964, was based on a threat from the USA but one that Chinese leaders were fairly confident they could handle. In fact, the strategy that Mao adopted after 1964 of 'luring the enemy in deep' was designed to effect a decisive defeat on the US.[13] Indeed, after an initial phase of defensive war designed to deny the USA a quick victory, China expected to take the offensive to ultimate victory.[14] Thus, though China felt a significant threat from the USA, especially in the late 1950s, the country's leaders were confident they could defeat the threat, and these threats were not considered to be existential. Thus, China's adoption of NFU fits well within the proposition made earlier—that countries that do not face an existential threat can adopt NFU while countries that face existential threats are unlikely to adopt an NFU posture because such threats, whether or not these are nuclear, would require states to be prepared to use nuclear weapons first.

NFU AND THE EMERGING SECURITY CONTEXT

The prospects for NFU could quite possibly get worse because of the increasingly uncertain international security situation. China's rise and Russian aggressiveness have exacerbated international insecurity because most of their neighbours are relatively smaller and weaker, even if many of them are rich and technologically advanced. Many of them have had an interest in building nuclear weapons at some point in the past, and are technologically capable of building them if they decided to do so. Moreover, there have been recent debates in each of these countries about the issue, even if none of them have yet proceeded down this path. This includes states such as Germany[15] in Europe, as well as Japan,[16] Australia[17] and South Korea[18] in the Indo-Pacific. The USA's suspected withdrawal from its global commitments gives further impetus to such debates. All are countries that are protected by the US extended nuclear deterrent; if these countries begin to suspect that this commitment may not last, they will have an incentive to take this path.

The important point to note here is not whether these countries are likely to go nuclear, but about the prospects for NFU should these countries decide to take the plunge. All of them are, in the context of conventional military power, much weaker than their adversaries and their primary purpose in going nuclear would not be to deter nuclear threats but to counter potential conventional military threats. In other words, facing significant conventional imbalance and threats, these states would have an incentive to not only build nuclear weapons but may also be reluctant to adopt NFU doctrines. An NFU posture makes little military sense for states seeking to compensate for conventional military imbalance rather than deterring nuclear threats alone. Thus, should these states decide to build nuclear weapons, it is unlikely that they would adopt an NFU posture. This does not resolve all of their security dilemmas, of course. The objective of building nuclear weapons would be to deter existential conventional military threats primarily, but it is also possible that they may face a combined conventional and nuclear threat. For example, a Japan that builds nuclear weapons (in the absence of the USA or other allied extended nuclear commitments) would have to face both a Chinese conventional and nuclear military threat. At the point of decision, they will have to consider the possibility that using nuclear weapons to defeat a conventional existential threat would force them to face another kind of existential threat—a nuclear retaliation. The logic of nuclear first use in this context is twofold: first, that existential threats are indistinguishable and nuclear extinction is no worse than the extinction of the state through conventional military defeat and capture. Second, that even the threat of such a nuclear first use would prevent an adversary from attempting to defeat and capture the country. For both reasons, the option of using nuclear weapons first would need to be retained.

Of course, such threats of nuclear first use are unlikely to prevent all conventional threats and attacks, nor is it designed to do so. It would only be expected to prevent the most serious: those that threaten the very existence of the country. Another caveat is that some states—Iran comes to mind—may not face an existential threat but could pursue nuclear weapons for more limited purposes, such as prestige or even to simply deter nuclear threats from other nuclear powers. Such states may be willing to adopt NFU; indeed, an NFU posture may be seen as attractive in signalling their responsible behaviour and respectability. I must hasten to add that I am not predicting these countries would pursue nuclear weapons but only that if they did so, their posture would be dictated by the purpose for which they embark on this path.

The dominance of national security concerns also makes it unlikely that movement towards a GNFU will factor into state decision-making regarding acquiring nuclear weapons unless such a move also includes some manner of addressing the security threats that states face. If unilateral (extended nuclear umbrella) or multilateral (effective arms control or dispute resolution mechanism) efforts to reduce insecurity were undertaken, this could reduce the incentive of many states to pursue nuclear weapons. Alternatively, structural changes, such as a more stable and favourable distribution of power, could also reduce the security motivation for building nuclear weapons. But if security circumstances continue to slide, with a combination of both rapid changes in power balances and increasing doubts about alliance commitments, the incentives for nuclear acquisition are only likely to increase.

CONCLUSION

While NFU has significant benefits, it is not clear that these benefits are spread equally across all nuclear-armed states and potential nuclear powers. The strategic circumstances facing different states determines the kind of nuclear postures they adopt, which suggests that not all states may benefit from adopting an NFU posture. Thus, for states that face significant conventional military imbalance or existential threats, an NFU posture may not be viable. Indeed, an NFU posture may make their security condition worse. Thus, a GNFU proposal should take into consideration the peculiar security circumstances that these states face for such an initiative to be practical and to be able to find some traction.

NOTES

1 An earlier version of this chapter appeared as an essay in the *Texas National Security Review* 2, no 3 (2019): 131–137.

2 Scott D. Sagan, "Why Do States Build Nuclear Weapons? Three Models in Search of a Bomb," *International Security* 21, no 3 (Winter 1996–1997): 54–86.

3 Extended deterrence can be considered yet another security motivation but I am leaving this out because this applies only to the USA.

4 Scott D. Sagan, "The Case for No First Use," *Survival* 51, no 3 (June–July 2009): 163–182.

5 Sumit Ganguly, "Deterrence Failure Revisited: The Indo-Pakistani War of 1965," *Journal of Strategic Studies* 13, no 4 (1990): 77–93.

6 Zulfikar Ali Bhutto, *The Myth of Independence* (London: Oxford University Press, 1969), 129
7 Avner Cohen, *Israel and the Bomb* (New York: Columbia University Press, 1998), Chapter 3.
8 Vipin Narang, *Nuclear Strategy in the Modern Era: Regional Powers and International Conflict* (Princeton: Princeton University Press, 2014), Chapter 7.
9 For a discussion of these issues, see Yair Evron, *Israel's Nuclear Dilemma* (London: Routledge, 1994/2005).
10 Cohen, *The Worst-Kept Secret: Israel's Bargain with the Bomb* (New York: Columbia University Press, 2010), 83.
11 For some of these debates, see Yogesh Joshi, "Waiting for the Bomb: P.N. Haksar and India's Nuclear Policy in the 1960s," NPIHP Working Paper #10, September 2017.
12 Andrew B. Kennedy, "India's Nuclear Odyssey: Implicit Umbrellas, Diplomatic Disappointments and the Bomb," *International Security* 36, no 2 (Fall 2011): 120–153.
13 This section is based on M. Taylor Fravel, *Active Defense: China's Military Strategy since 1949* (Princeton: Princeton University Press, 2019), chapters 3 and 4.
14 See also, Sulmaan Wasif Khan, *Haunted by Chaos: China's Grand Strategy from Mao Zedong to Xi Jinping* (Cambridge: Harvard University Press, 2018), 105–107.
15 "Germans Are Debating Getting Their Own Nuclear Weapons," *The Economist*, March 4, 2017, accessed on January 14, 2022, https://www.economist.com/europe/2017/03/04/germans-are-debating-getting-their-own-nuclear-weapon.
16 Liubomir K. Topaloff, "Japan's Nuclear Moment," *The Diplomat*, April 21, 2017, accessed on January 14, 2022, https://thediplomat.com/2017/04/japans-nuclear-moment/.
17 Paul Dibb, "Should Australia Develop Its Own Nuclear Deterrent?" The Strategist, Australian Strategic Policy Institute, October 4, 2018, https://www.aspistrategist.org.au/should-australia-develop-its-own-nuclear-deterrent/.
18 Byong-Chul Lee, "Don't Be Surprised When South Korea Wants Nuclear Weapons," *The Bulletin of Atomic Scientists*, October 23, 2019, https://thebulletin.org/2019/10/dont-be-surprised-when-south-korea-wants-nuclear-weapons/.

Chapter 10

NUCLEAR NO FIRST USE IN THEORY AND PRACTICE

Keir Lieber and Daryl Press

The organisers of this anthology, along with many of its contributing experts, believe that the adoption of a GNFU policy would make the world a safer place by reducing the dangers of nuclear weapons use. Their hope is that the widespread adoption of a GNFU agreement might lower alert levels, slow the arms race, build confidence and trust and perhaps even soothe tense international relationships. Analysts and government officials often see India's existing NFU nuclear doctrine as a model for other countries to emulate as they proceed toward a GNFU agreement. Therefore, in this brief chapter, we examine the case for and against India's NFU policy as a window into the trade-offs associated with a GNFU agreement. We then link our conclusions about India's NFU policy to the broader debate about a GNFU agreement.

We make four principal arguments. First, we argue that the case for India's current NFU policy is weak. The policy is unlikely to build confidence or reduce tensions with Pakistan; in fact, the opposite outcome is at least as likely. Second, although we see little benefit accruing to India from its current NFU policy, publicly reversing course would be unwise. Third, debates about NFU and other aspects of India's nuclear declaratory policy may distract analysts from more fruitful debates over the critical deterrence dilemma in South Asia: how India can deter Pakistan from sponsoring anti-Indian terrorists without threatening or undertaking excessively escalatory military reprisals. And finally, we draw on our discussion of NFU in a South Asian context to draw broader inferences about the GNFU proposal.

THE CASE FOR AND AGAINST INDIA'S NFU POLICY

There are three major arguments in favour of India's NFU policy. First, NFU signals to the international community India's normative stance against nuclear weapons. The policy signals New Dehli's deep aversion to nuclear weapons and its support for practical steps towards a nuclear-free world. The core idea behind NFU—that the only role for nuclear weapons today is to deter nuclear weapons use by others—can be seen as one expression of a broader view that these are dangerous and unnecessary tools of statecraft.

The second argument for NFU is that it offers a clear sign to Pakistan (or any potential adversary) that India desires to reduce the salience of nuclear weapons in South Asia. NFU, according to this argument, is a helpful confidence-building measure, which—if met with reciprocal steps by Pakistan—can reduce the role of nuclear threats in the subcontinent and reduce fears of pre-emptive strikes. If two adversaries are truly committed to NFU, then neither side will need to build pre-emptive nuclear capabilities, place nuclear delivery systems on hair-trigger alert or otherwise behave in ways that will make each side nervous about the prospect of sudden nuclear attack.

Third, an official NFU policy signals India's various domestic political constituencies about the kinds of capabilities that are necessary—and unnecessary—for credible deterrence. Specifically, the policy suggests that sophisticated nuclear 'counterforce' capabilities are not merely dangerous and counterproductive but also unnecessary. If nuclear weapons exist only to deter nuclear attacks, then the only kind of capabilities needed are those that preserve India's ability to retaliate against 'countervalue' targets if India were attacked. In short, counterforce capabilities are incompatible with a NFU doctrine; thus, they need not be built or deployed.

We see significant weaknesses in all three of these arguments. First, NFU is not a powerful signal of India's normative stance against nuclear weapons. Any political benefit that India might gain from NFU by signalling its moral revulsion towards nuclear weapons is likely undone by its ongoing nuclear modernisation programme. This undertaking not only appears to increase the number of weapons in the country's arsenal but will also improve India's nuclear capabilities: specifically, by creating more survivable, longer-range and more accurate systems.[1]

To be clear, we are not criticising India for the nature of its nuclear modernisation. Indeed, India faces a range of threats, including those from a powerful and rising China, and Pakistan pursuing its own nuclear modernisation programme. India lives in a tough neighbourhood. Nor is the modernisation of India's nuclear force—including the enhancement of its counterforce capabilities— evidence that India intends to use those weapons *first* (in violation of its NFU pledge). In fact, India's growing capabilities may be intended as second-strike forces: to deter nuclear attacks on India by threatening a response against either countervalue or counterforce targets. But those subtleties have been lost on critics who see nuclear modernisation as evidence that India is wavering on NFU.[2] In fact, from the standpoint of India's adversaries, the combination of nuclear modernisation and NFU pledges might make New Delhi seem duplicitous, eroding trust with its rivals. As a tool to signal India's benign intentions, NFU is likely to be ineffective or even counterproductive.

Second, India's NFU policy is not a powerful confidence-building measure with adversaries. The goal of using NFU to reassure Pakistan seems unrealistic at best and cynical at worst. The strategic reality is that Pakistan requires nuclear weapons and a *first-use* option in order to counter India's superior conventional military capabilities. Nuclear weapons have always been a greater boon to weaker powers than stronger ones. Just as the USA and NATO used nuclear weapons to counter the Soviet Union's superior conventional capabilities during the Cold War, countries such as North Korea and Pakistan rely on them today to stalemate their conventionally superior foes—a doctrine that requires Pakistan to have a first-use doctrine.[3] As a result, even if India could guarantee that it would never use nuclear weapons first against Pakistan, which is, of course, impossible, doing so would not lead Pakistan to adopt an NFU policy of its own. After all, Pakistan's nuclear deterrent is postured to deter India's conventional power as much as New Delhi's nuclear forces.

In many respects, rather than NFU being a confidence-*building* measure, the policy could be seen as a confidence-*reducing* measure. Pakistani officials may view India's NFU as a hostile policy designed to isolate Pakistan in the international community—depicting Pakistan as one of those recalcitrant nuclear powers that still relies heavily on nuclear weapons for its national security. There is no evidence that the political pressure from NFU will convince Pakistan to eliminate its nuclear arsenal but it will reinforce Pakistan's suspicion that India seeks to weaken its neighbour.

Finally, NFU does not undermine the rationale for India to build counterforce capabilities. Advocates of Indian NFU might defend the policy as a means to prevent the development of counterforce capabilities that domestic defence hawks desire. That is, if the only mission for India's nuclear weapons is to retaliate against adversary countervalue targets after India suffers a nuclear strike (and hence, to deter such an attack in the first place), then there is no need for need for sophisticated intelligence, surveillance, and reconnaissance (ISR) capabilities, advanced nuclear C2 upgrades, or prompt and accurate offensive strike systems. The problem with this argument, however, is that there is a strong case for India developing these so-called offensive capabilities even if India were committed to following its

NFU policy. As we described above, India faces an enemy in Pakistan that plans to use nuclear weapons first in a range of circumstances, including conflicts in which India employs conventional forces to counter Pakistan's aggression. Even with NFU, India might logically seek the capability to conduct *second-use counterforce strikes* against Pakistan's nuclear forces if Pakistan has begun to use those forces against India.

SHOULD INDIA STEP AWAY FROM AN NFU POLICY?

Proponents of the Indian NFU might agree with our arguments and still advocate maintaining the current policy, given the costs of abandoning it. They might argue that abandoning NFU would be a step in the wrong direction. Regardless of its merits or lack thereof, Indian NFU exists as official policy; so reversing course would effectively increase the salience of nuclear weapons in South Asia, which is something that no Indian government should desire. According to this argument, stepping away from NFU and increasing the salience of nuclear weapons would be bad not only for broader ethical and humanitarian reasons but also for strategic reasons, since India is the conventionally dominant power in the region.

We tend to agree. If one is persuaded by our arguments that NFU is unhelpful but also persuaded that abandoning NFU is needlessly costly, then one might conclude that the Indian government should do exactly what it seems to be doing now: that is, maintaining NFU as official policy while simultaneously building strategically necessary capabilities that would improve India's ability to conduct nuclear counterforce operations. It is true that this policy may seem duplicitous to India's adversaries but reversing course and abandoning NFU would surely not improve New Delhi's relations with leaders in Islamabad and Beijing.

Viewed in this manner, advocates on both sides of India's nuclear policy debates may be taking their arguments too far. Critics of NFU may err in leaping from their criticisms of NFU to their conclusion that NFU should be scrapped—because the policy may be ineffective but better than the consequences of abandoning it. But defenders of the principle of NFU may be too quick to critique India's nuclear modernisation. They tend to conflate the terms 'pre-emptive' and 'counterforce'. In reality, not all counterforce capabilities are for pre-emptive use. Second-strike counterforce capabilities are entirely consistent with NFU and may be helpful for deterring nuclear escalation amid a crisis or war (or reducing the costs to India if escalation occurs).

INDIA'S PRESSING DETERRENCE DILEMMA

Taking a step back, the debate about NFU might be a distraction from the core deterrence dilemma that India faces. Pakistan has repeatedly allowed terrorist groups operating from its territory to attack India and then relied on the 'shield' of Pakistan's nuclear arsenal to limit India's military response. Pakistan's strategy has triggered a string of adaptations and responses that, overall, have worked to India's *dis*advantage. Specifically, India sought to develop limited, quick ground-force options to allow New Delhi to respond to limited provocations without triggering Pakistani nuclear escalation; Pakistan responded by building additional limited nuclear capabilities, which could be credible against India's limited ground-force options. This back-and-forth dynamic has not solved India's primary problem—its inability to respond decisively to Pakistan's aggression without triggering escalation—but it *has* increased the number and salience of nuclear weapons in South Asia, which is a bad outcome for India. Although we believe that improved counterforce capabilities (for second-strike counterforce) may be in India's interests, those capabilities do not adequately solve the dilemma India faces.

India might consider a different approach to the problem of deterring and responding to Pakistan's provocations. Rather than respond to Pakistan's attacks with the threat of major ground offensives (which may be too escalatory) or with 'tit-for-tat' reciprocal strikes (which may be too timid), India might develop a strategy for assertive conventional counter-coercion that focuses on inflicting pain on Pakistan for sponsoring attacks on India, but which does so without invading Pakistan's territory. The targets for India's retaliatory strikes need not be connected to the terror groups conducting the attacks on India, nor to the Pakistani forces protecting them. (It is likely that terror groups would have moved key personnel out of their camps before conducting a major attack on India, making the terror camp a poor target for retaliation.) Instead of retaliating in a predictable manner, India could retake the initiative by selecting targets that India wished to destroy in Pakistan and that Pakistan would be sorry to see attacked. Indian strikes could be modulated—they could be either relatively minor in response to minor Pakistani attacks, and much more consequential in response to larger Pakistani-supported strikes.

Of course, India would need to defend itself from retaliatory strikes from Pakistan. But if Pakistan continues to host terror groups that attack India, and if invading Pakistan is a non-starter, then India has little choice but to develop strategies of conventional counter-coercion. The challenge for Indian strategists is to identify the types of targets that, if destroyed, would be painful enough to coerce Pakistan—but not so painful as to trigger escalation. That is the difficult job India's strategists should be focused upon rather than debating the wisdom of India's NFU declarations.

In sum, India faces a difficult challenge of how to deter provocations under the shadow of nuclear stalemate. Solving that problem is not simple. But India's NFU policy is neither the source of the problem nor the solution.

India's current NFU policy is not ideal but abandoning it would probably be needlessly costly. The best course on nuclear matters would be to continue with a judicious nuclear modernisation programme to enhance the survivability of Indian nuclear forces against China, and give India second-strike counterforce options against Pakistan. The best course on deterring Pakistan's provocations probably lies in the realm of conventional deterrence, using long-range punitive strikes of India's choosing, rather than ground invasions or predictable tit-for-tat operations.

***

The complexity of NFU in a South Asian context should give pause to those who see India's declaratory policy as a model for a GNFU regime. All the problems associated with India's NFU apply even more broadly in the heterogenous deterrence environment around the world. Nuclear-armed states could sign on to GNFU principles but doing so is less likely to demonstrate their moral convictions and more likely to make them appear cynical.

The first problem is that every nuclear-armed country is currently modernising its force, resulting in increased numbers of weapons, improved delivery systems or both. Many of these new capabilities benefit from broader technological trends in the realm of weapons accuracy and remote sensing, rendering existing adversary arsenals more vulnerable than ever before.[4] Although those upgrades can be essential pillars of deterrence—by facilitating retaliatory threats against counterforce targets—critics of modernisation have painted those programmes as revealing first-strike policies. Framed in that manner, the purportedly normative signal of a GNFU agreement is likely to be seen by adversaries as disingenuous—meaning as a sign of duplicity rather than a foundation for reconciliation.

The India case also reveals a second reason that a GNFU seems unwise: many conventionally weaker countries face powerful incentives to make their adversaries believe that they have a first-use nuclear use policy. The goal of confidence- and trust-building through mutual

NFU declarations is incompatible with strategic realities that suggest the necessity of first use in order to deter or mitigate the consequences of conventional attack. Nuclear-armed but conventionally weaker countries—such as Pakistan (facing India), North Korea (vis-à-vis the USA and South Korea), Russia (relative to NATO) and potentially a future Iran (facing a conventional threat from Israel and the USA)—see their nuclear arsenals as a vital solution to their relative weakness. To them, a GNFU policy would not result in greater safety and security; instead, they see it as part of a coordinated effort by powerful countries to isolate and weaken them. Rather than build confidence, NFU will fuel division.

Finally, a GNFU policy would not prevent countries from developing counterforce capabilities, which proponents of a GNFU regime suggest are unnecessary and counterproductive for national and international security. For countries facing adversaries that plan to use nuclear weapons first in a conflict, the ability to conduct second-use nuclear counterforce strikes will be compelling. In short, if some countries feel compelled to build credible nuclear first-use capabilities to deter stronger enemies, those enemies will feel compelled to build counterforce capabilities, both for the purpose of deterring nuclear escalation in the first place and for mitigating the consequences should deterrence fail.

The tension inherent in India's NFU policy mirrors the global challenge of 'sheathing the sword' and moving towards a world where countries do not threaten each other with nuclear weapons. But just as Indian officials and analysts cannot square the circle and make Pakistan believe that India's NFU policy demonstrates India's benign intentions, countries around the globe will struggle to use GNFU as a tool to reduce global nuclear risks. In fact, if GNFU has any effect at all, it may ironically inflame tensions between the strong powers who say they abhor nuclear weapons and the weak who must cling to them dearly.

NOTES

1 Hans M. Kristensen and Matt Korda, "Indian Nuclear Forces, 2018," *Bulletin of the Atomic Scientists* 74, no 6 (2018): 361–366.

2 Kumar Sundaram and M.V. Ramana, "India and the Policy of No First Use of Nuclear Weapons," *Journal for Peace and Nuclear Disarmament* 1, no 1 (February 2018): 152–168.

3 For more on this argument, see Keir A. Lieber and Daryl G. Press, *The Myth of the Nuclear Revolution: Power Politics in the Atomic Age* (Ithaca, New York: Cornell University Press, 2020), Chapter 4; Lieber and Press, "The Next Korean War," *Foreign Affairs*, April 1, 2013, *Snapshot*, https://

www.foreignaffairs.com/articles/north-korea/2013-04-01/next-korean-war; Lieber and Press, "Coercive Nuclear Campaigns in the 21st Century: Understanding Adversary Incentives and Options for Nuclear Escalation," (Report Number 2013–001, Project on Advanced Systems and Concepts for Countering Weapons of Mass Destruction [PASCC], U.S. Naval Postgraduate School, Monterrey, March 2013).

4 Lieber and Press, "The New Era of Counterforce: Technological Change and the Future of Nuclear Deterrence," *International Security* 41, no 4 (2017): 9–41.

Chapter 11

US NUCLEAR STRATEGY, NO FIRST USE AND THE RETURN OF GREAT POWER COMPETITION

Matthew Kroenig

The 2017 National Security Strategy of the USA declares the return of great power competition with Russia and China to be the foremost threat facing the USA and its allies.[1] As competition with nuclear-armed powers has become the foremost priority of US foreign and defence policy, nuclear weapons, the ultimate instrument of military force, has once again become a high-priority issue.

This chapter will explain US nuclear strategy in an era of great power competition.[2] It will argue that the country facing multiple great power adversaries, cannot have a single nuclear strategy but rather needs a tailored and flexible strategy, able to simultaneously deter multiple rivals presenting diverse threats.

The chapter will also argue that the USA has never possessed an NFU policy and has always retained the option of using nuclear weapons first in order to deter substantial non-nuclear attacks on itself and its allies. The USA's reliance on nuclear deterrence is in part a result of its global defence commitments. Despite some support for a US NFU in the far left wing of the US political spectrum, it is unlikely the country will adopt NFU or support a GNFU treaty absent a fundamental reorientation of its grand strategy and foreign and defence policy objectives.

The rest of the chapter will continue in five parts. First, it will describe the changed strategic context facing the USA and its allies and partners. Second, it will define the goals for US nuclear strategy. Third, it will articulate the central tenets of a tailored and flexible US nuclear strategy. Fourth, it will discuss the capability requirements for such a strategy. Next, it will explain why NFU would be contrary to core tenets of American nuclear strategy. Finally, it will conclude with some reflections on the future of US nuclear strategy.

STRATEGIC CONTEXT

Nuclear weapons were central to the bipolar, strategic competition between the USA and the Soviet Union during the Cold War. Following the collapse of Communism, however, nuclear weapons receded to the background. Both nuclear superpowers drastically reduced the size of their arsenals in a series of arms-control agreements and by 2010, serious people even discussed the possibility of the global abolition of nuclear weapons.[3] These deliberations made sense given the strategic context of the time. The greatest threat to US national security was thought to come from nuclear terrorism and the possibility of conflicts with nuclear powers, such as Russia and China, was described accurately as 'remote'.[4]

This reality changed in the mid-2010s. In 2014, Russia invaded Ukraine and made threats against the rest of Europe. In addition, Russia moved nuclear weapons more to the centre of its defence and military strategy. Most concerning is its nuclear 'escalate-to-de-escalate' strategy, which calls for the early use of nuclear weapons in the event of a conflict with the USA or NATO.[5] In addition, Russia is building the capabilities to support this strategy, including modernising its strategic forces and its large stockpile of non-strategic nuclear weapons. These include short- and intermediate-range nuclear-armed ground-launched missiles, nuclear torpedoes, nuclear depth charges, nuclear sea-launched cruise missiles, nuclear air-launched cruise and ballistic missiles, nuclear surface-to-air missiles for use in air defence and nuclear-tipped missile defence interceptors.[6] Furthermore, Russia is building a new generation of nuclear weapons of terror never dreamed of during the Cold War, including a nuclear-armed drone submarine, a nuclear-powered and nuclear-armed cruise missile and a nuclear-armed hypersonic missile. In short, Russia puts a nuke on almost any imaginable weapons system.

Perhaps, the greatest challenge facing the USA is the rise of China. China has also become more aggressive in recent years. Under President Xi, China has thrown away the 'hide-and-bide' strategy of Deng Xiaoping and charted a more expansionist course.[7] It is taking contested territory through brute force in the South China Sea. It is building up its military power with the goal of weakening US alliances and pushing American military power out of Asia. It is also engaging in an ambitious global strategy, including its Belt and Road Initiative (BRI) to use infrastructure investment to increase its geopolitical influence in every major world region. Fortunately, China's nuclear strategy and posture is more relaxed than Russia's, but this might be changing. The 2018 US Nuclear Posture Review (NPR) states that, despite its formal NFU pledge, China might use nuclear weapons first in a conflict in Asia.[8]

And the US government projects that China will greatly increase the size of its nuclear arsenal in the coming years.[9]

North Korea is on the verge of becoming only the third potential US adversary to possess the ability to deliver nuclear weapons to the US homeland. It is estimated to have dozens of warheads.[10] It has the ability to deliver nuclear weapons in its region and could soon have a functioning intercontinental ballistic missile (ICBM) capability. Despite years of negotiations, there are few signs that North Korea will denuclearise anytime soon and the USA and its allies must strengthen deterrence now, even as it works towards its stated goal of disarmament.

Iran currently poses a non-nuclear strategic threat to the USA and its regional security partners. Iran's foreign policy and domestic political legitimacy are predicated on resistance to the USA and resistance to the West. It is operating proxy forces in Iraq, Syria, Lebanon and Yemen. Tehran is the world's largest state sponsor of terror and has backed terror and proxy attacks against the USA and its allies for decades. It has the largest missile programme in the Middle East and is working on longer-range and intercontinental ballistic missiles. Tehran has a sophisticated, offensive cyber programme. It may also possess chemical and biological weapons.[11] Iran, therefore, has the ability to conduct a non-nuclear attack that could be nuclear-like in its strategic effects. Moreover, it has ceased compliance with the Joint Comprehensive Plan of Action and experts estimate that its dash time to a nuclear weapon might be as little as six to eight months.[12]

Nuclear terrorism also remains a concern. The threat has dissipated since the immediate post 9/11 era. The operational environment for terrorist groups, such as Al Qaeda and the Islamic State in Iraq and Syria (ISIS), has gotten more difficult. And the USA and its allies have made great strides in securing loose nuclear materials around the world. Still, if a terrorist group acquired nuclear weapons, deterrence would be more challenging (although not impossible).[13]

In short, the nuclear security environment for the USA and its allies has greatly deteriorated in the past decade. The risk of nuclear war between the USA and its nuclear-armed rivals may be greater now than at any time since the most dangerous days of the Cold War. This means that the USA must once again prioritise nuclear deterrence in its foreign and defence policy.

THE GOALS OF US NUCLEAR STRATEGY

What strategy and posture does the USA need to protect itself and its allies in this deteriorating security environment? Any good strategy begins with a clear statement of goals. At the broadest level, the goal of US nuclear weapons is to serve as the backbone of the post-1945, US-led, rules-based international system.[14] In this way, US nuclear weapons are special. Other countries use nuclear weapons to deter attacks against themselves but the USA uses nuclear weapons to defend the entire free world.[15] It extends nuclear deterrence to over thirty formal treaty allies in Europe and Asia. The twenty-eight other NATO members, South Korea, Japan, Australia and arguably others, depend on US nuclear weapons for their security. In this way, US nuclear weapons have deterred great power war and provided geopolitical stability in Europe and Asia for seventy years. This has provided the peace and stability that have allowed these regions to develop into the most prosperous and democratic in the world. In addition, US nuclear weapons underpin the NPT and the global non-proliferation regime. The USA made a bargain with its allies: do not build independent nuclear arsenals and you can rely on US nuclear weapons for your security. In the absence of these extended nuclear deterrence guarantees, it is very likely that Germany, South Korea, Taiwan and other US allies would have nuclear weapons today. So, in short, the primary objective of US nuclear weapons is to underpin the rules-based international system.

There are more specific goals as well.[16] First, US nuclear weapons deter nuclear attacks on the USA and its allies.

Second, US nuclear weapons deter non-nuclear strategic attacks on the country and its allies. It has never possessed an NFU policy and has always kept the option of using nuclear weapons first to deter attacks with non-nuclear weapons that could deliver strategic attacks that are nuclear-like in their effects. During the Cold War, the USA used nuclear weapons to deter a massive Soviet invasion of Europe. In the post-Cold War era, Washington threatened to use nuclear weapons in response to biological or chemical weapons attacks. In the future, adversaries may conduct non-nuclear strategic attacks with a wide variety of weapons systems, such as cyber, space, lethal autonomous systems or others. The recognition of a new term of art in the 2018 Nuclear Posture Review, 'nonnuclear strategic attacks' clarifies this possibility.[17]

Third, the USA uses its nuclear weapons to assure allies. As stated above, US nuclear weapons protect the entire free world. Washington does this partly out of altruism but also partly because it benefits from the peace and stability and the non-proliferation of nuclear weapons that these assurances provide.[18]

Fourth, US nuclear weapons must serve to achieve the country's objectives if deterrence fails. The primary purpose of nuclear weapons, as stated above, is to deter a nuclear attack. But, god forbid, if deterrence fails, the USA would not simply sit back and await mutually assured destruction. US leaders will not stand by and watch as tens of millions of Americans are slaughtered in a nuclear holocaust. Rather, they would do everything in their power to limit damage to the USA and its allies. This could be accomplished through offensive counterforce strikes on the enemy's nuclear forces and missile defences to blunt an enemy attack. Every enemy nuclear weapon that is destroyed in this manner is a nuclear weapon that is not landing on US territory and that of its allies. Damage limitation is also aided by America's robust ICBM forces that serve as a missile sink.[19] If an enemy is forced to employ hundreds of nuclear warheads to destroy hundreds of missile silos spread throughout America's remote interior, these are nuclear warheads that cannot be allocated to killing Americans in large population centres.

Fifth, and finally, the USA must build a nuclear force that can hedge against an uncertain future. Adversaries like China are building up their nuclear forces and the future of arms control with Russia is unclear. In addition, new strategic technologies are coming online that could affect the future of strategic stability including hypersonic missiles, directed energy lasers, space, cyber and others. The nuclear posture the USA possesses today might not be the nuclear posture it needs in ten or twenty years. It must, therefore, maintain a healthy underlying nuclear infrastructure to respond to changing security environments and deterrence requirements.

US NUCLEAR STRATEGY: TAILORED AND FLEXIBLE

How can the USA meet the above objectives for its nuclear forces? US nuclear strategy is designed to be tailored and flexible. In other words, it does not have the luxury of having a single nuclear strategy. It faces a diverse range of nuclear-armed threats. What deters Russia might not deter North Korea and China, and vice versa. The USA, therefore, requires several nuclear strategies tailored for several specific nuclear challenges. It also needs flexible nuclear forces that can back up each of these tailored strategies. The rest of this section will review the primary requirements for deterring each of the USA's strategic competitors.

At the strategic level, the USA must make it clear to Russia that any strategic attack on it and its allies would result in costly retaliation that would exceed any benefit that Moscow would hope to obtain. Perhaps the greatest nuclear threat posed by Russia currently, however, is the possibility that Russia would use nuclear weapons to escalate its way out of failed conventional aggression through its escalate-to-de-escalate strategy. This Russian limited nuclear use doctrine attempts to force the USA into a choice between 'suicide and surrender'. The USA can either back down or escalate to a large-scale nuclear exchange. To get around this dilemma, Washington has threatened that a Russian nuclear de-escalation strike will not result in American surrender, but rather costly retaliation that might include limited nuclear strikes of its own.[20] The purpose of this threat is not to fight a limited nuclear war, but to deter Russian President Vladimir Putin from going down this path in the first place. If he believes that popping off one or two nuclear weapons is an easy path to victory, US strategy aims to disabuse him of this notion.

The threat from China is more relaxed, given China's NFU doctrine and its smaller nuclear arsenal. Here, the USA can follow more of a traditional assured retaliation strategy. It makes it clear that the cost of any strategic attack by China will result in unacceptable retaliation, as judged by Beijing. Although not part of China's formal doctrine, the 2018 US Nuclear Posture Review warns that China might be tempted to conduct limited nuclear strikes in the event of a major theatre war in the Indo-Pacific.[21] As in the case with Russia, Washington, therefore, retains the option of limited nuclear retaliation in order to deter limited nuclear strikes from China.

Washington's strategy for North Korea is quite simple. It possesses clear escalation dominance over the latter at every level of conflict, including the highest, strategic levels. The USA threatens, therefore, that if Kim Jong-un conducts any strategic attack, the consequence will be the end of the Kim regime.

Iran does not currently have the ability to conduct a nuclear attack but it does have the ability to conduct a non-nuclear strategic attack, with its ties to terror and proxy groups, its large stockpile of ballistic missiles, its cyber capabilities and its possible possession of chemical and biological weapons. To deter these attacks, Washington threatens that any strategic attack on the USA and its allies will be met with an overwhelming response. It may not choose to use nuclear weapons in response to such an attack but it does leave the possibility on the table. There is no reason to assure Tehran that it can get away with these attacks without worrying about nuclear weapons. The USA seeks to deter Iran from breaking out and building nuclear weapons with a credible military option for stopping Tehran as a last resort.[22]

To deter nuclear terrorism, the USA leans heavily on deterrence by denial. It aims to make it difficult for terrorist groups to obtain nuclear material or nuclear weapons, transfer them to the USA or its allies and employ them.[23] This strategy includes counterterrorism campaigns against the largest and best organised terrorist outfits, including Al Qaeda and ISIS. The strategy is supported by continued efforts to improve the security of nuclear weapons and nuclear materials around the world. And it is bolstered by the deployment of radiation detection equipment at ports and at borders and other efforts that would make it difficult for terrorists to transport illicit nuclear materials. There is also, however, a deterrence by retaliation component of this strategy. Washington makes clear that it will hold responsible any state that assists a terrorist group in a nuclear terror attack. The credibility of this threat is enhanced by nuclear forensics and other intelligence techniques to ensure that the USA can quickly identify the perpetrators of a nuclear terror attack and those that assisted them.

Just as it has tailored deterrence strategies for potential rivals, the USA develops tailored assurance strategies for allies. Washington undertakes several efforts, including common threat assessments, dialogues, scenario-planning exercises, among others, to ensure that its allies in Europe and Asia understand and are reassured by US nuclear weapons.

US NUCLEAR CAPABILITIES

What are the capabilities that the USA requires to support its tailored and flexible nuclear strategy? Washington has plans to modernise each leg of the US nuclear triad over the coming thirty years.[24] The USA will, therefore, build and deploy new submarines, bombers and ICBMs. It also has a stockpile stewardship programme to ensure the safety, security and reliability of US nuclear warheads. In addition to its strategic weapons, the USA possesses limited non-strategic nuclear weapons with its dual-capable fighter aircraft (DCA), which can deliver nuclear gravity bombs.

The 2018 Nuclear Posture Review also introduced two 'supplemental' nuclear capabilities to enhance the country's non-strategic nuclear arsenal and to improve the credibility of its threats to deter Russian nuclear de-escalation strikes.[25] The first capability is a small number of low-yield warheads on some US submarine-launched ballistic missiles (SLBMs). The department of defence announced that these went into service in early 2020.[26] Second, the NPR calls for the development of a low-yield warhead on a nuclear-armed sea-launched cruise missile (SLCM). The USA possessed a nuclear SLCM during the Cold War but it was retired in 2010 by the Obama administration. It has decided, therefore, to resurrect this capability. Public debates on this issue have asked whether these two new low-yield weapons are necessary because the USA already possesses low-yield weapons, including the aforementioned gravity bombs.[27] But these debates are missing the point. These two new capabilities provide a low-yield capability that can be delivered promptly and that can effectively penetrate Russian air defences. The existing low-yield weapons in the US arsenal lack these attributes.

DISARMAMENT, ARMS CONTROL AND NON-PROLIFERATION

Disarmament, arms control and non-proliferation retain an important place in the US nuclear strategy. The USA remains committed to meeting its NPT Article VI requirements and working with all states on the eventual abolition of nuclear weapons. Under the administration of Donald Trump, however, Washington took a new approach towards meeting these commitments. Since the end of the Cold War, much progress was made by the USA and Russia made progress towards disarmament by reducing the size of their nuclear forces. In 1967, the USA possessed 31,255 nuclear weapons. Currently, under the terms of the New START Treaty, Washington deploys no more than 1,550 weapons.

It has become clear, however, that further nuclear reductions are not possible at the moment given the deteriorating security environment. Indeed, as the USA reduced reliance on nuclear weapons during the Obama administration, other countries, including Russia, China, India, Pakistan and North Korea, went in the other direction, expanding and modernising their forces.[28] It no longer made sense for the USA to force hardware reductions in a nuclear force that is responsible for protecting the free world in the face of increasing nuclear threats.

Instead, therefore, the Trump administration pivoted to a strategy of addressing the underlying security conditions that cause countries to want these weapons in the first place. This approach was named 'Creating the Environment for Nuclear Disarmament (CEND)'.[29] It reflects former president Ronald Regan's view that we do not fear each other because we are armed but rather we are armed because we fear each other. If we can reduce the sources of those mutual fears, nuclear reductions will easily follow. After all, the largest nuclear reductions in history came in the immediate aftermath of the cessation of Cold War hostilities. The US disarmament policy calls on all states to work together on a future peaceful security environment that will make nuclear disarmament possible.

THE US AND NFU

As explained above, the USA has never possessed a formal NFU policy. But, in a way, it has a de facto NFU for almost every state in the international system. It commits not to use or threaten to use nuclear weapons against non-nuclear states in compliance with their non-proliferation commitments. This means that the threat of nuclear use remains on the table only for America's nuclear-armed rivals (Russia, China and North Korea) and non-nuclear states in non-compliance with their non-proliferation commitments (Iran). These are the only four countries mentioned by name in the 2018 US NPR. The other roughly 200 countries in the world, therefore, already enjoy an NFU pledge from the USA.

Going further and declaring a formal NFU, however, would be ill-advised. It would essentially mean promising the four revisionist autocracies mentioned above that they can engage in aggression against the USA and its allies and not worry about America's nuclear weapons. An NFU would mean assuring these dangerous rivals that they are welcome to conduct conventional attacks, chemical and biological weapons attacks, cyber attacks or other forms of heinous aggression, but so long as they do not use nuclear weapons, the threat of US nuclear use is off the table. There is no reason to assure these states that they can get away with such aggression. A US NFU would be destabilising because it would open a space in which US rivals could be emboldened to act with impunity from the prospect of nuclear retaliation.

Indeed, NFU would be in direct contradiction to two stated goals of US nuclear strategy. An NFU would completely invalidate America's declared goal of using nuclear weapons to deter non-nuclear strategic attacks. It would also undermine the USA's ability to assure its dozens of treaty allies.

Near the end of the Obama administration, Washington considered an NFU but it was dropped largely due to opposition from US allies. Estonia, Poland, Japan, South Korea and other vulnerable front-line states have always appreciated that their conventionally more powerful neighbours must consider, and may be deterred by, America's nuclear weapons. An NFU, therefore, would weaken America's ability to extend deterrence and assure its allies.

In short, the USA's reliance on nuclear deterrence is, in part, a result of its global defence commitments. If, in the future, Washington were to retreat from its traditional security provider role in Europe and East Asia, then it could also afford to scale back its reliance on nuclear deterrence and possibly adopt an NFU. But, so long as the USA wants to uphold its global defence commitments and defend the entire free world, then an NFU does not make sense.

CONCLUSION

There are heated debates about many aspects of US nuclear policy but what might be even more remarkable is the bipartisan consensus and continuity across administrations. The US nuclear modernisation programme began under President Obama and was continued under President Trump. The Trump decision to build low-yield nuclear weapons met with controversy in the media and arms control communities but it was supported by former Obama administration defence officials.[30] And every US administration in the nuclear era, Democrat and Republican alike, has believed that the USA should leave the first use of nuclear weapons on the table to deter its rivals. We can expect US nuclear strategy to remain constant in the coming years. And that is a good thing for a special nuclear capability that provides the backbone for the rules-based international system.

NOTES

1 The White House, "A New National Security Strategy for a New Era" (Washington DC, December 18, 2017); Matthew Kroenig. *The Return of Great Power Rivalry: Democracy versus Autocracy from the Ancient World to the U.S. and China* (New York: Oxford University Press, 2020).
2 Kroenig. *The Logic of American Nuclear Strategy: Why Strategic Superiority Matters* (New York: Oxford University Press, 2018).
3 Thomas Schelling, "A World without Nuclear Weapons?" *Dædalus,* American Academy of Arts & Sciences 138, no 4 (Fall 2009): 124–129.
4 US Department of Defense, "Nuclear Posture Review" (Report, US Department of Defense, Washington DC, April 2010).
5 Kroenig, "Facing Reality: Getting NATO Ready for a New Cold War," *Survival* 57, no 1 (January 2, 2015): 49–70.
6 Hans M. Kristensen and Matt Korda, "Russian Nuclear Forces, 2019," *Bulletin of the Atomic Scientists* 75, no 2 (March 4, 2019): 73–84.
7 Elizabeth Economy, *The Third Revolution: Xi Jinping and the New Chinese State* (New York: Oxford University Press, 2018).
8 US Department of Defense, "Nuclear Posture Review" (US Department of Defense, Washington DC, February 2018).
9 Office of the Secretary of Defense, "Military and Security Developments Involving the People's Republic of China 2019" (Annual Report to Congress, Washington DC, May 2019).

10 Hans M. Kristensen and Robert S. Norris, "North Korean Nuclear Capabilities, 2018," *Bulletin of the Atomic Scientists* 74, no 1 (January 2, 2018): 41–51.

11 Alan Goldsmith, "Iran's Chemical and Biological Weapons Programs: An Under-Appreciated Threat," United Against Nuclear Iran, April 29, 2019, accessed on February 14, 2020, https://www.unitedagainstnucleariran.com/blog/irans-chemical-and-biological-weapons-programs-an-under-appreciated-threat; US Department of State, "Compliance with the Convention on the Prohibition of the Development, Production, Stockpiling and Use of Chemical Weapons and on Their Destruction" (Annual Report On Compliance with the Chemical Weapons Convention, US Department of State, Washington DC, March 2018).

12 David Albright and Sarah Burkhard, "New Estimates of Iran's Breakout Capabilities at Declared Sites Using a New, Simple-to-Use Breakout Calculator" (Report, Institute for Science and International Security, Washington DC, September 3, 2019), https://isis-online.org/isis-reports/detail/new-estimates-of-irans-breakout-capabilities-at-declared-sites-using-a-new/8.

13 Matthew Kroenig and Barry Pavel, "How to Deter Terrorism." *The Washington Quarterly* 35, no 2 (April 1, 2012): 21–36.

14 Ash Jain and Matthew Kroenig, "Present at the Re-Creation: A Global Strategy for Revitalizing, Adapting, and Defending a Rules-Based International System," (Atlantic Council Strategy Paper, Washington DC, October 2019).

15 Kroenig, The Logic of American Nuclear Strategy.

16 US Department of Defense, "Nuclear Posture Review," 2018.

17 US Department of Defense, "Nuclear Posture Review," 2018.

18 Kroenig. "US Nuclear Weapons and Non-Proliferation: Is There a Link?" *Journal of Peace Research* 53, no 2 (March 1, 2016): 166–179.

19 Kroenig, "The Case for the US ICBM Force," *Strategic Studies Quarterly* (Fall 2018): 50–69.

20 Kroenig, "The Case for Tactical U.S. Nukes," *Wall Street Journal*, January 24, 2018, sec. opinion; Kroenig, "The Renewed Russian Nuclear Threat and NATO Nuclear Deterrence Posture" (Atlantic Council, Washington DC, February 2016); Kroenig, "A Strategy for Deterring Russian Nuclear De-Escalation Strikes," (Atlantic Council, Washington DC, April 2018).

21 US Department of Defense, Nuclear Posture Review, 2018.

22 Kroenig. *A Time to Attack: The Looming Iranian Nuclear Threat* (New York: St. Martin's Press, 2014).

23 Matthew Kroenig and Barry Pavel. "How to Deter Terrorism," *The Washington Quarterly* 35, no 2 (April 1, 2012): 21–36.

24 Kroenig. "How to Approach Nuclear Modernization?: A US Response," *Bulletin of the Atomic Scientists* 71, no 3 (May 1, 2015): 16–18.

25 US Department of Defense, "Nuclear Posture Review," 2018.

26 US Department of Defense, "Statement on the Fielding of the W76-2 Low-Yield Submarine Launched Ballistic Missile Warhead," accessed February 14, 2020, https://www.defense.gov/News/Releases/Release/

Article/2073532/statement-on-the-fielding-of-the-w76-2-low-yield-submarine-launched-ballistic-m.

27 Cheryl Rofer, "Low-Yield Nukes Are a Danger, Not a Deterrent," *Foreign Policy*, February 11, 2020, accessed February 14, 2020, https://foreignpolicy.com/2020/02/11/deterrence-nuclear-war-low-yield-nukes-danger-not-deterrent.

28 Kroenig. "US Nuclear Weapons and Non-Proliferation."

29 Shannon Bugos. "CEND Establishes Two-Year Work Program," Arms Control Association. January/February 2020.

30 John R. Harvey, Franklin C. Miller, Keith B. Payne, and Bradley H. Roberts "Continuity and Change in U.S. Nuclear Policy," *Real Clear Defense*, February 7, 2018.

Chapter 12

RUSSIA'S NUCLEAR DOCTRINE JOURNEY

Petr Topychkanov

This chapter offers a look into the debates on the role of prevention in the nuclear doctrine of Russia. Based on this analysis, the text describes the doctrine as defensive. However, it is not possible to entirely exclude the military plans of preventing strikes that may simultaneously coexist with the defensive posture.

The current crisis in US–Russian arms control may make Russian authorities consider a more proactive nuclear strategy. The chapter indicates an alternative path of nuclear posture development. Instead of replacing the defensive strategy with the offensive one, Russia could return to the NFU pledge to which its predecessor, the Soviet Union, used to adhere. If several nuclear-armed states endorse this pledge and transparency and CBMs make it more credible, the NFU will not compromise Russian national security.

FROM THE SOVIET UNION TO THE RUSSIAN FEDERATION: WITHDRAWAL FROM THE NFU COMMITMENT

The Soviet Union, the predecessor of the Russian Federation, started signalling its NFU leanings at the end of the 1960s. In 1969, Soviet diplomats confidently explored the NFU commitment with their counterparts from the USA. In the 1970s, the Communist Party Central Committee instructed the country's armed forces that 'the Soviet Union will not be the first to employ nuclear weapons'.[1] In 1982, Leonid Brezhnev, the general secretary of the Central Committee of the Communist Party, sent a message to the second special session of the general assembly on disarmament, where the Soviet Union proclaimed the NFU commitment for the first time.[2]

In the West, the Soviet step was viewed as propagandistic and even endangering NATO. According to David C. Jones, the chairman of the US joint chiefs of staff in 1978–1982, the NFU policy ignored the conventional imbalance in Europe with the Eastern superiority over the Western nations and could increase the likelihood of conflict, especially in the time of high tension.[3]

The Soviet Union continued declaring its NFU policy and convincing the USA and NATO to follow its example until the collapse of the former in 1991. In the first post-Soviet military doctrinal document, 'Basic Provisions of the Military Doctrine of the Russian Federation', approved in 1993, a negative security assurance with two exceptions replaced the NFU commitment. First, Russia reserved the right to strike first under an armed attack by a non-nuclear weapons state (NNWS), being allied with a nuclear-armed state. The second case was mentioned as a joint aggressive action of an NNWS, being allied with a nuclear-armed state.[4] In both cases, it was an explicit reference to NATO as an alliance of nuclear-armed states and NNWS.

POST-SOVIET DOCTRINES—WHETHER AND WHEN TO STRIKE FIRST

For the first time, the military doctrine of Russia mentioned the concrete conditions when the country would use nuclear weapons in the version of 2000. With some changes, these conditions remained the same in the following versions. The most recent version of 2014, Russia reserves 'the right to use nuclear weapons in response to the use of nuclear and other types of weapons of mass destruction against it and/or its allies, as well as in the event of aggression against the Russian Federation with the use of conventional weapons when the very existence of the state is in jeopardy.'[5]

In the Western scientific and expert literature, it became commonplace to argue that the Russian nuclear doctrine is pre-emptive. The focus of the debate on the Russian pre-emption is on the concept of escalate-to-de-escalate; in other words, plans of the limited nuclear strike during a regional conventional conflict.[6] Russian representatives officially and unofficially refuse the existence of this concept.[7]

On the one hand, the escalate-to-de-escalate concept is doubtful in the context of the Russia—US/NATO juxtaposition in the European region. There is a common belief in Russia that any armed conflict with the USA and NATO will be quickly escalated to a global and full-fledged nuclear war.[8] In March 2018, Vladimir Putin made a statement about this in his presidential address to the Federal Assembly while commenting on the low-yield nuclear option of the US 2018 Nuclear Posture Review: 'Any use of nuclear weapons against Russia or its allies, weapons of short, medium or any range at all, will be considered as a nuclear attack on this country. Retaliation will be immediate, with all the attendant consequences.'[9]

On the other hand, there are indications showing possibilities of using nuclear weapons by Russia pre-emptively, regionally and in a conventional armed conflict. The military doctrine of 2014 portraited nuclear weapons as an essential factor of 'preventing an outbreak of nuclear military conflicts involving the use of conventional arms (large-scale war or regional war)'.[10] The 2017 naval doctrine described the following role of tactical nuclear weapons: 'During the escalation of military conflict, demonstration of readiness and determination to employ non-strategic nuclear weapons capabilities is an effective deterrent.'[11] The most recent strategic exercise, Thunder 2019, had a scenario resembling the escalate-to-de-escalate concept: 'The situation escalates along the perimeter of the Russian borders amid the persisting conflict potential, as a result of which a threat emerges to the country's sovereignty and its territorial integrity.'[12] Three examples show that Russia's pre-emptive nuclear use in a regional conflict with conventional forces involved cannot be entirely dismissed.

Meanwhile, the Russian leadership keeps describing the Russian nuclear posture as defensive.[13] It combines the elements of the 'launch-under-attack' and 'launch-on-warning' and is officially described as a 'retaliatory counter-strike'.[14]

The political statements and military documents do not contradict each other because they are two parts of strategic thinking and planning of nuclear weapons use. As Russian scholar and politician Andrei Kokoshin and Major General Valentin Larionov noted in their joint publication of 1991, 'the usual practice is to draw a line between two aspects of military doctrine: the political and military-technical aspects. Until recently, the former aspect was regarded as the more stable one, while the latter, which determines the means, forms, and methods of warfare, as the more dynamic and changeable.'[15] Russia's current nuclear doctrine may be described as defensive. In the political dimension, the prevention of war means relaxing tensions and avoiding war between Russia and the USA, NATO and other countries. There is nothing written in the doctrine that may contradict this political position.

However, the changeable military–technical aspects, not necessarily reflected in public documents, in periods of high tensions between Russian and the West could refer to the pre-emption, as it was described in Western literature about the Soviet doctrine: it 'has strong, aggressive, action-oriented overtones and is more often used in the sense of preventing by "seizing the initiative" and "preempting" to "disrupt" the enemy's attack'.[16] But this may be a temporary reaction to the growing military threats from adversaries, and if political and diplomatic efforts lead to the relaxation of tensions, these military–technical aspects will be subject to change again.

The period of high tension, in which Russia and the West exist now, means that possibility of war is higher than before, in the time of more comfortable relations between Russia, the USA and other NATO member states. It does not mean that the Russian leadership starts preferring military options rather than political and diplomatic ones. The goal of avoiding wars remains the top priority of Russia's nuclear doctrine. Hence, the nuclear doctrine remains defensive.

THE POST INTERMEDIATE NUCLEAR FORCES TREATY POSSIBILITIES—LESS RESTRAINT, MORE AMBIGUOUS?

How long the Russian doctrine remains defensive is unclear, given the demise of the 1987 Intermediate Nuclear Forces (INF) Treaty between Russia, the USA, Belarus, Kazakhstan and Ukraine in 2019.[17] The end of this agreement and the rising risk of intermediate-range missiles deployment in Europe might cause a change of Russia's defensive posture for an offensive one. Or, as a probable development, the ambiguity of the Russian nuclear posture may grow.

Two types of indicators might signal these possibilities. First, Russia has recently revealed several new offensive weapons that would deliver nuclear weapons in various scenarios, including a limited war. These weapons include nuclear-powered ground-launched cruise missiles, Burevestnik, nuclear-powered undersea drones, Poseidon, air-launched supersonic missile Kinzhal, silo-based heavy ballistic missile, Sarmat, and boost-glade system, Avangard.[18] US diplomats see these weapons as destabilising because of their potential impact on the strategic balance between the USA and Russia.[19]

Second, the ongoing debate in Russia on the nuclear weapons policy includes weighty opinions on the presumable change of the doctrine. Colonel-General (retired) Victor Esin, former chief of general staff and vice commander-in-chief of the Russian Strategic Rocket Forces, is one of them. When discussing the highly automated nuclear command and control system, Perimetr,[20] in a 2018 interview, he said that this system will not be very useful if the USA withdraws from the INF Treaty and deploys currently banned ground-launched intermediate-range missiles in Europe.[21] According to him, if this happens, the USA will be able to use long-, intermediate- and short-range delivery vehicles for nuclear weapons against Russia as well as high-precision conventional weapons of various ranges. As a result, Russia will not have many second-strike capabilities after a possible first strike from the USA.[22] This possibility undermines the primary purpose of the Perimetr, which is to initiate a mass retaliation with all the remaining means after the adversary first strike against Russia.

The argument made by General (retired) Esin is about possible consequences for Russia of the end of the INF Treaty. If existing US nuclear forces are augmented with ground-based missiles of intermediate and shorter ranges and deployed in Europe, the Russian defensive nuclear posture will become less effective in providing nuclear deterrence against the USA. If Russia is under first attack from the USA, only part of this arsenal may survive. This part would be hard enough for mass retaliation, especially if one takes into account that the first strike may include nuclear, conventional, cyber, electronic means of the USA and its NATO allies. The Russian retaliation may be limited by the USA's growing missile defence capabilities.

This risk makes the Russian authorities contemplate the possibility of replacing the defensive nuclear posture with an offensive one. The offensive nuclear posture would possibly be based on the concept of a pre-emptive nuclear strike, which is the nuclear attack being launched during conventional aggression by the adversary that has already been launched or is imminent.[23] However, the offensive nuclear posture would require carefully calibrated plans of limited nuclear use. The pre-emptive strike is expected not to provoke either a nuclear retaliation from the adversary or further escalation of conflict. As Andrei Kokoshin highlighted, the pre-emptive strike with low-yield nuclear weapons requires 'an extremely high level of strategic control on the part of all parties involved'.[24] Indeed, scholars have questioned the feasibility of maintaining such a level of control after a pre-emptive strike.[25]

Meanwhile, on 2 June 2020, a new document, 'Basic Principles of State Policy of the Russian Federation on Nuclear Deterrence', has been approved by Executive Order No. 355.[26] The publication of the document is unlikely to have a visible effect on strengthening strategic stability between Russia, the USA, their allies and other nuclear-armed states without Russia's proper outreach and the readiness of the nuclear weapons possessors for substantive and open discussions about doctrines. Clarifying some aspects of Russia's nuclear policy, the document is ambiguous about the nuclear posture, for example, regarding the use of nuclear weapons in response to a conventional attack. In the absence of symmetrical steps to reduce the uncertainty of nuclear policies with the USA, its allies and other nuclear-armed states, it is hard to expect Russia to unilaterally proceed in this direction. It explains the ambiguity of the Basic Principles language. The positive aspect of the new document, namely the fact of its publication, meaning Russian authorities care how domestic and foreign audiences perceive the country's nuclear policy, is unlikely to have an immediate impact on strategic stability relations between Russia and other nuclear-armed states. But if this fact helps to engage these countries and their allies in doctrinal dialogues with Russia, this would strengthen strategic stability and reduce nuclear risks.[27]

ALTERNATIVES TO OFFENSIVE THINKING

The possibility of a more offensive posture by Russia does not deny the fact that there are influential voices in this country to support more defensive approaches. For instance, the top leadership highlighted in 2018 that Russia considers using nuclear weapons only in the case when it receives an early warning signal about the launched nuclear attack.[28] This stance might provide grounds for the Russian return to the NFU pledge undertaken by the Soviet Union. However, the Russian decision to endorse the NFU is thinkable only as a part of complex steps, taken bilaterally and multilaterally.

Obviously, the current political conditions would not allow the creation of a legally binding NFU treaty, as proposed by the Global Zero Campaign.[29] However, there are realistic ways to make this pledge accepted by the five permanent members (P5) of the UN Security Council and even those beyond the NPT. "If China reaffirms its NFU policy and Russia returns to the Soviet NFU pledge , the USA, the UK and France will be able and eager to affirm a similar commitment."

The acceptance of the NFU policy may play either a destabilising or stabilising role, depending on the political context. For instance, if these steps are not accompanied by a comprehensive dialogue on nuclear postures and capabilities, they might be perceived as propaganda. Hence, an appropriate level of transparency on postures and capabilities of nuclear-armed states should be another part of the complex steps taken, to support the NFU pledge. It will make the renewed NFU declaration credible and stabilising.

This transparency may be achieved through strategic dialogues. There should be a dialogue between Russia and the USA, the USA and China, France, the UK and Russia, China and India, and India and Pakistan.

The P5 format and its dialogue on the doctrines have indisputable value. The glossary the P5 members compiled was a great achievement.[30] However, in the current challenging environment, it seems not to be sufficient. The P5 should continue multilateral dialogues on the changing strategic context and extend the agenda to address new challenges associated with conventional strategic systems, such as hypersonic weapons, advanced ballistic missile defences and cyberspace.

The NFU along with strategic dialogue would let the nuclear-armed states commit to no build-up of nuclear arsenals. It will not require the immediate disclosure of the numbers and compositions of their arsenals. Yet, as a product of a doctrinal dialogue, it should be based on growing transparency of nuclear postures and capabilities. As a multilateral commitment, it will play a decisive role in preventing the nuclear arms race.

Initially, to achieve no build-up, all P5 nations could put out a joint political statement promising not to extend the current levels of nuclear weapons. As a follow-up, they could promise not to add new types of nuclear weapons and to focus the modernisation plans only on replacing the ageing capabilities.

The credibility of NFU and no build-up will remain challenged if they are not supported by the pillar of arms control. Hence, the declarations and transparency and CBMs should continue with the multilateral efforts of rethinking and reestablishing nuclear arms control. This recommendation goes beyond the extension of the 2010 New START Treaty. The return of the arms control agenda is unavoidable not just due to NPT Article VI of the 1968 NPT[31] but also due to strategic stability and non-proliferation interests. In the period of the Cold War, strategic stability was found on three pillars: lines of communications, arms control and limitations.[32] Removal of one of these pillars makes international and regional security less stable and predictable. That is exactly what happened in the European region and Northeast Asia after the demise of the INF Treaty. Supporting framings such as nuclear arms control and limitations are needed to restore strategic stability in the long term.

Achieving a higher level of transparency of nuclear doctrines and planning, and strategic and non-strategic nuclear forces, their condition and development prospects are in line with both nuclear disarmament goals and strategic stability interests. Without continuous transformation and, eventually, the abolition of the postures like first strike and mutual nuclear deterrence, it will never be possible to break the nuclear disarmament deadlock.

CONCLUSION

The Russian nuclear doctrine remains defensive. However, given the post-Cold War realities related to the NATO conventional superiority, new technologies developments and a multipolar nuclear order, Russia is interested in the flexibility of its operational plans.

A new challenge emerged after the demise of the INF Treaty and the growing risk of non-distant deployments of intermediate-range missiles in Europe. In responding to the challenge, the Russian Federation may shift its emphasis from the defensive posture to the offensive one, with the development of advanced offensive means.

However, the doctrinal change in Russia will create new risks not only for the Russian potential adversaries but also for its national security. The concept of nuclear pre-emption, which is at the core of the offensive posture, triggers the rise of the unpredictability of armed conflicts. It would be overambitious for the state planning the nuclear pre-emption to pretend to control the escalation after the pre-emptive strike. Hence, instead of enhancing strategic stability, the offensive doctrine would create new challenges.

As the alternative to these developments, this chapter offers a complex of measures built around the NFU commitment. The declarations of NFU and nuclear no build-up, if supported with transparency and CBMs, including strategic dialogue and nuclear arms control, will contribute to the strategic stability and, hence, serve the national security interests of Russia.

NOTES

1 R.L. Garthoff, "Continuity and Change in Soviet Military Doctrine," in *The Dynamics of Soviet Defense Policy*, B. Parrot ed. (Washington DC: The Wilson Center Press, 1990), 159.

2 United Nations General Assembly, "12th Plenary Meeting" (Official Records, United Nations, New York, June 15, 1982), 196, accessed on April 2, 2022, https://daccess-ods.un.org/tmp/2588380.57518005.html.

3 David C. Jones, "Statement by the Chairman of the Joint Chiefs of Staff (Jones) before the Senate Committee on Foreign Relations: No First Use and Freeze of Nuclear Weapons April 29, 1982," in *Documents on Disarmament, 1982* (Washington DC: United States Arms Control and Disarmament Agency, 1985), 273–274.

4 "The Basic Provisions of the Military Doctrine of the Russian Federation," Federation of American Scientists, accessed on April 1, 2022, https://fas.org/nuke/guide/russia/doctrine/russia-mil-doc.html.

5 Embassy of the Russian Federation to the United Kingdom of Great Britain and Northern Ireland, "The Military Doctrine of The Russian Federation," (Press Release, Embassy of the Russian Federation to the United Kingdom of Great Britain and Northern Ireland, London, June 29, 2015), accessed on April 1, 2022, https://rusemb.org.uk/press/2029.

6 E. Colby, "Russia's Evolving Nuclear Doctrine and its Implications," (Report, Fondation pour la Recherche Stratégique, Paris, 12 January, 2016), 6–7, accessed on April 1, 2022, https://www.frstrategie.org/sites/

default/files/documents/publications/notes/2016/201601.pdf; Mathew Kroenig, "A Strategy for Deterring Russian Nuclear De-Escalation Strikes," (Atlantic Council, Washington DC, April 2018), 14; M.B. Schneider, "Russian Nuclear 'De-Escalation' of Future War," *Comparative Strategy* 37, no 5 (2018): 366, accessed on April 1, 2022, https://www.tandfonline.com/doi/abs/10.1080/01495933.2018.1526558?journalCode=ucst20.

7 TASS Russian News Agency, "US Claims on Russia's 'Escalation for De-Escalation' Doctrine are Wrong—Envoy," TASS, April 9, 2019, https://tass.com/politics/1052755; CSIS, "CSIS Track-II Dialogue on Liming Non-Strategic Nuclear Weapons," Washington DC, September 4, 2015, 4, accessed on April 1, 2022, https://www.csis.org/events/limiting-non-strategic-nuclear-weapons-results-track-ii-dialogue.

8 "'Ogranichennoi' yadernoi voiny mezhdu SShA i Rossiei ne budet po opredeleniyu" ("Inherently There Will Not Be a 'Limited' Nuclear War between USA and Russia"), Vesti FM, January 18, 2018, accessed on April 1, 2022, https://radiovesti.ru/brand/61009/episode/1642882/.

9 Vladimir Putin, "Presidential Address to the Federal Assembly" (Presidential Address, Kremlin, Moscow, March 1, 2018), accessed on April 1, 2022, http://en.kremlin.ru/events/president/news/56957.

10 Russian Embassy to the United Kingdom of Great Britain and Northern Ireland, "The Military Doctrine of The Russian Federation." accessed on April 1, 2022https://rusemb.org.uk/press/2029.

11 Anna Davis (trans.), "Fundamentals of the State Policy of the Russian Federation in the Field of Naval Operations for the Period Until 2030," (Russian Maritime Studies Institute, United States Naval War College, Newport, September 28, 2017), accessed on April 1, 2022, https://dnnlgwick.blob.core.windows.net/portals/0/NWCDepartments/Russia%20Maritime%20Studies%20Institute/RMSI_RusNavyFundamentalsENG_FINAL%20(1).pdf?sr=b&si=DNNFileManagerPolicy&sig=fjFDEgWhpd1ING%2Fn-mGQXqaH5%2FDEujDU76EnksAB%2B1A0%3D.

12 TASS, "Russian Strategic Nuclear Forces' Drills Not Aimed against Third Countries: Top Brass," October 14, 2019, https://tass.com/defense/1083017.

13 Vladimir Putin, "Meeting of the Valdai International Discussion Club," (Presidential Address, Kremlin, Moscow, October 18, 2018), http://en.kremlin.ru/events/president/news/58848.

14 TASS, "US Claims on Russia's 'Escalation for De-Escalation' Doctrine are Wrong—Envoy."

15 V. Larionov and A. Kokoshin, *Prevention of War: Doctrines, Concepts, Prospects* (Moscow: Progress Publishers, 1991), 13.

16 J.D. Douglass Jr and A.M. Hoeber, *Soviet Strategy for Nuclear War* (Stanford: Hoover Institution Press, 1979), 9.

17 US Department of State, "US Withdrawal from the INF Treaty on August 2, 2019," (US Department of State, Washington DC, August 2, 2019), accessed on April 1, 2022, https://www.state.gov/u-s-withdrawal-from-the-inf-treaty-on-august-2-2019/ and https://2017-2021.state.gov/u-s-withdrawal-from-the-inf-treaty-on-august-2-2019/index.html.

18 Putin, "Presidential Address to the Federal Assembly," (Presidential Address, Kremlin, March 1, 2018), accessed on April 1, 2022, http://en.kremlin.ru/events/president/news/56957.

19 Thomas G. Di Nanno, "General Debate Statement by Thomas G. Di Nanno, Deputy Assistant Secretary and Senior Bureau Official, Bureau of Arms Control, Verification and Compliance, U.S. Department of State," (Statement, 2019 UN General Assembly First Committee, New York, October 10, 2019), 2–3, accessed on April 1, 2022, http://statements.unmeetings.org/media2/21998264/united-states.pdf.

20 P. Topychkano,, "Autonomy in Russian Nuclear Forces," in *The Impact of Artificial Intelligence on Strategic Stability and Nuclear Risk, Vol. 1, Euro-Atlantic Perspectives*, ed. V. Boulanin (Stockholm: SIPRI, May 2019), 71–72.

21 Mike Pompeo. "US Withdrawal from the INF Treaty on August 2, 2019," (US Department of State, Washington DC). Accessed on May 31, 2022. https://2017-2021.state.gov/u-s-withdrawal-from-the-inf-treaty-on-august-2-2019/index.html.

22 O. Odnokolenko, "General-Polkovnik Viktor Esin: 'Esli amerikantsy vse-taki nachnut razvorachivat' svoi rakety v Evrope, nam nichego ne ostanetsya, kak otkazat'sya ot doktriny otvetno-vstrechnogo udara i pereiti k doktrine uprezhdayushchego udara'" ("Colonel-General Victor Esin: 'If Americans Finally Deploy Their Missiles in Europe, We Will Have to Replace the Launch under Attack Doctrine with the Doctrine of Pre-emptive Strike'), *Zvezda*, November 8, 2018, accessed on April 1, 2022, https://zvezdaweekly.ru/news/t/2018117102-0iaAI.html.

23 S.J. Cimbala, "Nuclear Weapons and Anticipatory Attacks: Implications for Russia and the United States," *The Journal of Slavic Military Studies* 28, no 1 (2015): 50, accessed on April 1, 2022, doi: 10.1080/13518046.2015.998121.

24 A. Kokoshin, "A Nuclear Response to Nuclear Terror: Reflections of Nuclear Preemption," *The Annals of the American Academy* 206, (September 2006): 62.

25 P. Menon, *The Strategic Trap: India and Pakistan under the Nuclear Shadow* (New Delhi: Wisdom Tree, 2018), 166–167.

26 The Ministry of Foreign Affairs of the Russian Federation, "Basic Principles of State Policy of the Russian Federation on Nuclear Deterrence" (The Ministry of Foreign Affairs of the Russian Federation, Moscow, June 8, 2020), accessed on April 1, 2022, https://www.mid.ru/en/web/guest/foreign_policy/international_safety/disarmament/-/asset_publisher/rp0fiUBmANaH/content/id/4152094.

27 Russian International Affairs Council, "Expert Opinions on Russia's Basic Nuclear Deterrence Principles" (Russian International Affairs Council, Moscow, June 23, 2020), accessed on April 1, 2022, https://russiancouncil.ru/en/analytics-and-comments/analytics/expert-opinions-on-russia-s-basic-nuclear-deterrence-principles/.

28 Putin, "Meeting of the Valdai International Discussion Club," (Presidential Address, Kremlin, October 18, 2018).

29 UN General Assembly First Committee, "Statement by Global Zero on Advancing a Bold Agenda for Nuclear Disarmament" (2019 UN General Assembly First Committee, New York, October 18, 2019), 2, https://www.

un.org/disarmament/wp-content/uploads/2019/10/18-oct-19-global-zero.pdf.

30 *P5 Glossary of Key Nuclear Terms* (Beijing: China Atomic Energy Press, 2015), accessed on April 1, 2022,, http://www.china-un.org/eng/chinaandun/disarmament_armscontrol/npt/P020150429800995728299.pdf. https://2009-2017.state.gov/documents/organization/243293.pdf.

31 UN Office for Disarmament Affairs, "Treaty on the Non-Proliferation of Nuclear Weapons (NPT)" (UN Office for Disarmament Affairs, New York, XXXX), https://www.un.org/disarmament/wmd/nuclear/npt/.

32 J.A. Russell, "*Strategic Stability Reconsidered: Prospects for Escalation and Nuclear War in the Middle East*" (Institut Français des Relations Internationales [IFRI] Proliferation Paper No 26, IFRI Security Studies Center, Paris, 2009), 19–20.

Chapter 13

LESS POSSIBLE, MORE NECESSARY? NO-FIRST-USE POLICY FOR FRANCE AND EUROPE

Damien Cusey and Olivier de France

This chapter argues that the present transformation of the international system makes GNFU policy both more desirable at the collective level and less possible to implement at the national level. The mediation efforts undertaken by French president Emmanuel Macron on Iran nuclear capabilities, backed by the United-Kingdom and Germany, are a recent highlight of the strain under which multilateral efforts have been put. The current erosion of multilateralism will have a mid-to-long-term impact on the international nuclear order and risks further undermining the legal structure inherited from the Cold War, which limits proliferation.

As Emmanuel Macron pointed to in February 2020, 'The deconstruction of international norms is part of an acknowledged logic of competition, where power politics and the reality of the balance of power take precedence. The most cynical go so far as to drape themselves in legality and a false attachment to the international order, the better to violate them with all impunity.'[1] This underlying trend has an effect on French 'defence strategy' in return. It also has both a general and specific broader impact outside France.

In the short-to-mid term, it opens up the internal politics of nuclear powers to turmoil, which is liable to have a significant effect on their external policies. In the mid-to-long term, the resurgence of great power politics makes multilateral conflict management and resolution between national states, regional powers and great powers more uncertain. Overall, the current international environment has increased the risks of great power conflicts but has also decreased the capacity to manage them, with a resulting knock-on effect on GNFU.

THE CREEPING CORROSION OF MULTILATERALISM

It would have been difficult to foresee at the turn of the century that 'cultural change would lead to an anti-liberal backlash making Orban, not Obama, the mode for European leaders'; that 'deep, fierce attachment to nation and state was not going to fade away [but] to fight back and win' so that 'illiberals, authoritarians and strongmen [...] instead of fading, kept on multiplying'.[2] Different narratives and references have been called upon to explain such trends in geopolitical terms. The emerging century has elicited a variety of comparisons to 1930s Europe,[3] the Westphalian period,[4] the restless Italian fifteenth century[5] and even to the Reformation[6] and references to the crisis of multilateralism, the return of history, the death of the West, the victory or the demise of the European normative model, the end of the transatlantic community or multipolarity without multilateralism. A rich vein of scholarship is concerned with addressing such fundamental questions in international relations theory.[7] A number of in-depth, empirical studies of populism have also been undertaken, both global[8] and localised,[9] to examine the ripple effects of a resurgence of nationalism.

The simultaneous phenomena of Brexit, the Donald Trump presidency, populism and Europe's migration crises elicited much of the empirical, political and geopolitical analysis. Following his election in January 2017, the American president wrestled the USA out of the multilateral Iran nuclear deal, the Paris climate accords, the coalition in Syria and a number of United Nations bodies including UNESCO. One tangible example of the effect it can have on the international nuclear order is the USA's retreat from the treaty on effective intermediate-range nuclear forces in August 2019, which preceded a ground-to-ballistic missile test on 18 August 2019, in California.

Within a comparatively short timescale, the former American president also threw into doubt the solidity of the transatlantic alliance and inflicted a commercial war upon his European partners. President Trump's transactional approach to world politics was the most visible symptom of an era where short-term national aims take precedence over long-term collective interest, zero-sum games over win-win diplomacy and power struggle over common solutions to international issues. The subsequent international decisions made by President Joseph Biden do not belie any great change in the American worldview. On the one hand, the USA's retreat from Afghanistan without consultation with European partners, the AUKUS Pact and the French furore over the broken submarine contract only emphasise the continuities between the Trump and Biden administrations. On the other, Vladimir Putin's invasion of Ukraine in February 2022, which is a brazen military embodiment of the corrosion of rules-based multilateralism, has forced Washington to pivot parly back to Europe.

On the Old Continent, the multilateral model embodied by the EU and its consensus-based decision-making is also coming under strain. Europe is faced both on the inside and the outside by the rise of 'strong man' leaders—from Turkey's Erdogan to Russia's Putin and Italy's Salvini—who vow to address the concerns of national electorates that fear they are losing control over their future, in the face of the perils of an increasingly unpredictable world. Back in 2014, Jean-Claude Juncker described his current five-year tenure at the helm of the European Commission as the 'last chance' of saving the European project. Two years after his prediction, British citizens across the Channel had voted to take their country out of the EU. For the first time, a portion of Europe's population had shown that the EU's political integration was reversible—a move which former president Trump publicly termed 'a great thing'.

Political Balkanisation within has also crippled the ability of the EU to come to consensus-based decisions. In the last decade, there have been strong regional tensions over the Eurozone, the debt crisis and migration issues between North and South, and significant geopolitical tensions between East and West. Power has slowly ebbed away from the European Commission towards the capitals and the European Council. On a divided continent, this makes it more difficult to create policies that bring collective added value to the common interest.

Such volatility and perceived loss of control in global and regional terms have generated political backlash at the national level, from Brazil to Poland or Italy, and from the UK to India or the Philippines. The impression that political leaders have had difficulty managing increased interdependence has led several peoples to express a wish to keep a say over their collective destinies, or at least avoid relinquishing the illusion of being able to do so—irrespective of economic consequences. These endeavours have alternatively been interpreted as manifestations of populism or as vibrant political efforts to sustain self-determination and wrestle people's political futures away from forces out of their control.

GLOBAL NO FIRST USE—LESS POSSIBLE?

This underlying trend is liable to have both a general and a particular impact. In the mid-to-long term, the resurgence of great power politics makes multilateral conflict management and resolution between national states, regional powers and great powers more uncertain. In the short-to-mid term, it can transform internal politics of nuclear powers, which are, in turn, liable to have an effect on their external policies, as in the case of the USA.

As Ullman points out,[10] the strength and simplicity of the GNFU model is also its weakness. The decision-making power rests upon individuals who can relent on their commitments—all the more so in an anarchic international system that tilts towards power politics and zero-sum logic. The doctrine is chiefly dependent on human elements and, therefore, subject to pressure and emotion in environments where political decision-making and rational choice models are largely limited.

As Ullman argues, 'Who can say what a government could do in a crisis if it feels that its existence, or its vital national interests, are under threat?'[11] The behaviour of national leaders in countries which are nuclear powers, therefore, has outsize importance on how the collective doctrine is maintained. Yet the repeal of the GNFU doctrine by any state implies the resurgence of a classic deterrence model with a risk of escalation of conflicts resulting in the use of a nuclear weapon, effectively destroying the boundary between conventional engagement and nuclear engagement.

Authors have highlighted the increased instability that could result from an NFU between states that do not believe in the commitments of their counterparts,[12] considering the balance between uncertainty and predictability (drawn from 'red lines' or 'vital interest') often described as a grounding for deterrence logic.[13] In a context of multilateral erosion and mistrust between states, the use of disinformation and the inconstancy of international leaders who feel less tied by the international legal order and are more driven by short-term interests and realistic points of view, the NFU is described as a counterproductive 'declaratory policy'.[14]

There are also strong technical, political and financial costs involved. The NFU requires 'extreme confidence not only in the survivability of its national nuclear forces, sufficient to trigger a devastating retaliatory strike but also in the effectiveness of its crisis management system'.[15] In other words, a state which accepts to be hit first, which is assumed in the NFU policy, has to show deep *resilience*, technically and socially. Adopting NFU requires investing in anti-missile defences as well as in strong and adaptable command and control and communication systems able to absorb the first strike and retaliate.[16] Political and military leaders who endorse the NFU should also be ready to assume the military, technical, demographic, economic and political costs of a nuclear strike on their territory. For states as densely populated as China and India, the question is crucial.

MORE NECESSARY? THE LONG-TERM EFFECTS OF GEOPOLITICAL POLARISATION

The global stage has witnessed the re-emergence of great power politics in a multipolar world, but without the multilateral culture, tools or robust international organisations to manage the risks of great power conflicts. As a result, geopolitical polarisation at the global, regional and national levels has arguably made GNFU less plausible but also more desirable.

The last decade has more than ever put nuclear weapons back on the international political stage, incorporating states that consider nuclear capabilities as a necessity for their sovereignty and their capacity to influence international relations, but which are perceived by Western states as threats to global security, such as North Korea and Iran. The international stage has become the scene of increasing military and nuclear proliferation. The modern equipment in North Korea, Chinese investments in the field, the exit of the USA from the INF and the issue of Iranian nuclear capabilities are all elements that suggest an erosion of the 'international nuclear order'.[17] However, if deterrence necessarily implies that nuclear weapons exist, that they can be used and that it is a good thing, the NFU would make it possible to draw an impassable line ensuring a non-passage to action in an international order that is increasingly unable to limit access to nuclear power.

Concomitantly, the legal international architecture has weakened. The doctrine of deterrence by the risk of total annihilation, which depends upon what Raymond Aron called 'the balance of terror', describes a military balance where none of the ultra-equipped powers—the USA and Russia still account for 90 per cent of the world's nuclear stockpile today—would dare to use it and risk falling into an irremediable process of mutual and total destruction. It was progressively translated into practice by the establishment of international treaties to limit proliferation (the Strategic Arms Limitation Talks [SALTs] and INF, the NPT in 1970 and then the Treaty on the Prohibition of Nuclear Weapons) and the progressive dismantling of certain arsenals. This legal framework is under question and threat, along with the strength of multilateral tools and the international organisations that underlie it.

As such, the status quo is fraying. A new impetus, a new method and a new doctrine to put arms control and non-proliferation on the agenda of nuclear powers are, therefore, welcome, even if under current circumstances it appears intellectually and politically intractable. From a symbolic and legal point of view, a doctrine such as the NFU makes it possible to make stronger international commitments and to advocate for relative disarmament. NFU would reduce the range of possibilities in the use of force but it would also provide a strong normative framework for limiting irreversible and far-reaching collateral damage.

Hybrid threats can today be exercised by indefinite and de-territorialised actors, resulting in key French contingency planning undertaken in the fields of crippling cyber and terrorist attacks. These same actors can take refuge or operate, in the case of cyberattacks, in civilian areas. In fact, French deterrence comes up against the complexity of the terrain, when it becomes difficult to use nuclear weapons in densely populated theatres or under the sovereignty of states not directly involved in the threat in question. There is also a significant risk of non-compliance with the international law of war or International Humanitarian Law (demographic and non-demographic strike discriminant). In a time of hybrid or 'grey zone'[18] conflicts, NFU would reinforce the principles of 'necessity and proportionality' at the roots of war law. It may push states to stay at the sub-nuclear level using the same means as their opponents, instead of using nuclear weapons.

THE IMPACT ON THE FRENCH NUCLEAR DOCTRINE

France undertook its research on nuclear power before the military defeat of 1940 during the Second World War and pursued part of it in England during the German occupation. It became operational at the beginning of the Cold War, at a time marked by decolonisation, the defeat of Dien Bien Phu and the Suez crisis. This historical framework has two direct implications for the French doctrine.

The first is a French willingness to access firepower capable of avoiding a major military debacle threatening state order (territory, administration, population) and ensuring national strategic autonomy. The second is the desire to maintain and affirm a status of great power by benefitting from the 'aura' that possessing nuclear weapons implies.[19] Indeed, a nuclear doctrine is not merely about deterrence but also provides a mirror through which a state sees itself as power and through it wants to be seen at the international level.[20]

The French doctrine accordingly develops firstly according to a logic of defensive deterrence, the key to which is the capacity 'to represent a sufficient retaliatory capacity for the [the enemy] to renounce aggression'.[21] Nuclear power can therefore be used first in a preventive and pre-emptive context but also used against all threats of aggression—conventional, nuclear and hybrid included. Nevertheless, French leaders typically posit that the French nuclear doctrine is driven by an interest in peace to 'prevent war', and that nuclear weapon brings its owner important moral responsibilities. France, while simultaneously maintaining its nuclear capacities, therefore, concurrently promotes the NPT, disarmament, as well as a strong diplomatic capacity and multilateral military dialogue to ensure different leverage of de-confliction in case of crisis.

It follows that the French nuclear deterrent revolves around several fundamental principles. First, it must ensure the protection of the 'vital interests of the nation' as well as sovereign autonomy by ruling out the possibility of nuclear blackmail. Second, it involves relying on a strike force capable of causing damage 'out of proportion' with the threat of aggression (the population strikes being removed that implies hitting centres considered as neuralgic at the aggressor). Third, it takes into account a potentially unfavourable and non-recoverable military relationship between France and other major powers by ensuring a strict sufficiency of nuclear means, which implies material that can be mobilised in any situation and allowing precise and powerful strategic or tactical strikes. Fourth, it is part of a context of solidarity vis-à-vis its European allies, leaving open the possibility of highlighting its nuclear capabilities in their defence. And finally, it requires the maintenance of complete independence in the decision of the nuclear engagement, in the autonome control of the the design of the nuclear armaments and its use.

Two main principles, therefore, support the use of the French nuclear weapon. One is a strict framework of autonomy decided on by the president who rejects any constraint in nuclear engagement. The other is a blend of transparency about the French nuclear doctrine[22] and strategic vagueness that leaves it to the president to define the exact perimeter of 'vital interests', as well as the degree of threat which justifies the use of the weapon. Haupais stresses for instance that 'the indeterminacy of the cases of appeal is a condition for the viability of the deterrence'. Nuclear power is thus in the hands of the president. Only he can decide to trigger a strike according to the assessment of the vital interests of the nation and the seriousness of the threat.

This personalisation of deterrence makes it difficult for the opponent to read the limits not to be exceeded in the threat or the military commitment because of their subjective definition. It also makes it difficult to identify how escalation control might be undertaken by the president after a warning strike. Lastly, personalisation is legally reinforced by the French presidential regime, which ensures the head of state to be both the leader of the armed forces and the ultimate political power in case of a crisis, such as a threat to vital interests, according to Article 16 of the French Constitution ('full powers').

In keeping with these basic principles, France has acquired the technical means that follow from its stated ambitions. It has concentrated its nuclear forces around nuclear-powered ballistic missile submarines and air–ground capability allowing for precision and speed in strategic strikes. SNLE ensure the unpredictability of the second strike in the French doctrine until the moment of the strike.[23] Finally, the concept of ultimate warning through a 'unique and non-renewable'[24] 'warning strike' is a specifically French notion aimed at restoring deterrence. This approach differs radically from the graduated response that would involve prior and increasing use of conventional forces. The French approach intends to dissuade an adversary with a minimum of means, but by threatening to cause unacceptable damage. For this to function, this, therefore, requires the possibility of resorting to an ultimate warning through the first use of the nuclear weapon in a traceable way.[25]

The main cost of this doctrine is budgetary: it involves constant investments and renewal of armaments to ensure a credible and undetectable nuclear deterrent. The 2030s will thus require significant financial investment in defence, which is under strain in several conventional areas. The largely centralised and subjective aspect of the decision resting with the president also raises the question of responsibility and morality. The triggering of the nuclear weapon rests ultimately on moral requirements, the capacities of analysis, cold blood and the information available to a single individual whose rationality is necessarily limited by lack of information, personal beliefs and external pressure.

HOW REALISTIC IS NFU FOR FRANCE AND EUROPE?

Expecting France to discuss, consider or move to NFU is an unrealistic expectation in the short to medium term for strategic, political and constitutional reasons. Firstly, the French model implies that the president is the ultimate and discretionnary decision-maker on military nuclear matters, including doctrinal orientation. As such he chairs the National Defence and Security Council which is tasked with the issue. Nuclear fire is considered the nation's guarantee of last resort against any threat to its existence. The French head of state is therefore the guarantor of strategic autonomy and the sovereignty of the French state, more so than in any other system.

In this context, a doctrine such as the NFU would amount to decisional outsourcing. In effect, the president would no longer have the monopoly of evaluation and decision-making in the face of a crisis—he would be subject to external events that would be independent of him since he would only resort to nuclear force in the setting where the enemy has initiated it. Therefore, in the context of the French doctrine, the chances of France accepting to discuss NFU appear fairly slim.

It is to escape any external constraint and to give the president full autonomy that France has 'ringfenced' deterrence at the international level, and consistently opposed all international commitments that could limit its nuclear response capability. As such, it would presently be out of step with the French diplomatic *habitus* to imagine a political commitment to the NFU, if only because it rejects the indeterminacy of the relations between states in the field of nuclear engagement by making the first decision illegal. It takes the form of an international commitment, which China and India have suggested sacralising in the form of an international treaty.

Endeavouring to eliminate the irrationality of decision-making by a framework as fixed and causal as the NFU is also a strategic position that is difficult to maintain because it amounts to forgoing a strategic advantage when conventional engagements threaten the survival of the state. As Tertrais suggests, 'deterrence is based on a subtle mix of certainty and uncertainty, which is at the root of the nuclear strategies'. By removing uncertainty, one might argue that the NFU is counterproductive for French doctrine insofar as it mitigates or nullifies its strategic nuclear advantage. French deterrence makes the defensive use of nuclear weapons possible outside a nuclear context. This implies an essential margin of manoeuvrability since France puts forward a possible answer to any form of attack that it can undergo.

This defensive format accrues more than comparative strategic advantage in the event of a conflict. The vagueness of the doctrine also partakes of a 'fascination and an aura' which is perceived as quintessential to France's status as a great power. The NFU would remove the margin of manoeuvre as well as the symbolic surplus power that nuclear weapon represents. The NFU implies breaking down the hierarchy imposed by nuclear weapons, one that is enshrined in the international order (around the Security Council and the NPT) between the nuclear-armed states and those that do not possess nuclear weapons.

However desirable this might be, such backtracking is tricky for France to accept. The NFU is a doctrine that tends to be presented in the French defence community as a strategic weakness, which embodies excessive self-restraint, as opposed to selfless moral progress. Its lack of normative dissemination and the fact that it has not been adopted by any other nuclear power since its creation does not facilitate legitimisation either, although the argument, of course, is a manner of a self-fulfilling policy. Concurrently however, France has been forced to navigate a very changeable context marked by growing Chinese ambition, Russian revisionism, as well as a longstanding, if gradual, American withdrawal from the defence of Europe, which Vladimir Putin's invasion of Ukraine in February 2022 has no doubt only temporarily reversed. The recent AUKUS Pact between the US, the UK and Australia embodies some of the repercussions of these shifts, and the strategic clarifications they occasion.

In the past decade, France has responded to this turmoil by pushing for more European strategic autonomy, in which the underlying—implicit or explicit—role of the French nuclear deterrent is key. It is difficult to predict what the reaction of European partners is likely to be in this regard. On the one hand, it may help make the French deterrent more acceptable in the eyes of some European member states. On the other hand, a modification of the French nuclear doctrine, which is over half a century old, may not be considered credible by potential adversaries. While many European member states look to Washington, such an upheaval may not be considered opportune for a political union in which, since January 2020, only one member wields a nuclear deterrent.

NOTES

1 Emmanuel Macron, "Discours du Président Emmanuel Macron sur la Stratégie de Défense et de Dissuasion Devant les Stagiaires de la 27ème Promotion de l'Ecole de Guerre," ("Speech by the President of the Republic on French Defense and Deterrence Strategy"), Paris, February 7, 2020, accessed on September 20, 2021, https://www.elysee.fr/en/emmanuel-macron/2020/02/07/speech-of-the-president-of-the-republic-on-the-defense-and-deterrence-strategy.

2 B. Judah, "Benjamin Nethanyahu Predicted Rise in Authoritarianism," *The Atlantic*, December 18, 2018, accessed on September 20, 2021, https://www.theatlantic.com/ideas/archive/2018/12/benjamin-netanyahu-predicted-rise-authoritarianism/578374/.

3 E. Traverso, "Spectres du fascisme : Les métamorphoses des droites radicales au XXIe siècle," *Revue du Crieur* 1, no 1 (2015): 104–121.

4 B. Vayssière, "Europe et souveraineté : La notion d'État, des penseurs classiques aux réalités actuelles," *Vingtième Siècle. Revue d'histoire*, no 95 (2007): 151–166.

5 N. Walton, "Sixteenth Century Lessons for Twenty-First Century Italy", *Politico*, September 19, 2015.

6 N. Ferguson, "The Roots of Today's Political Polarization" (Conference at the Long Now Foundation, San Francisco, December 18, 2019).

7 See bibliography hereunder.

8 Y. Mounk and J. Kyle, "What Populists Do to Democracies," *The Atlantic*, December 26, 2018, accessed on September 20, 2021, https://www.theatlantic.com/ideas/archive/2018/12/hard-data-populism-bolsonaro-trump/578878/.

9 T. Lochoki, *The Rise of Populism in Western Europe* (Cham, Switzerland: Springer, 2018).

10 Richard H. Ullman, "No First Use of Nuclear Weapons," *Foreign Affairs* 50, no 4 (1972): 673.

11 Ullman, "No First Use of Nuclear Weapons," 681.

12 D. Bowen, J. Gill, and A. Levesques, "Nuclear Deterrence and Stability in South Asia: Perceptions and Realities," The International Institute for Strategic Studies, May 2021, accessed on September 20, 2021 https://www.iiss.org/blogs/research-paper/2021/05/nuclear-deterrence-south-asia.

13 See for example, William A. Chalmers et. al., "Front Matter." *No-First Use of Nuclear Weapons: A Policy Assessment.* (Institute for Defense Analyses Washington DC, January 2021. http://www.jstor.org/stable/resrep29560.1. and Bruno Tertrais, "No First Use, No Deterrence," October 7, 2019, *Strategic Foresight for Asia*, accessed on September 22, 2021, https://strafasia.com/no-first-use-no-deterrence/.

14 Tertrais, "No First Use, No Deterrence."

15 Ullman, "No First Use of Nuclear Weapons."

16 See Rajesh Rajagopalan, "India's Nuclear Doctrine Debate," *Carnegie Endowment for International Peace,* June 30, 2016, accessed on September 22, 2021, https://carnegieendowment.org/2016/06/30/india-s-nuclear-doctrine-debate-pub-63950; William A. Chalmers et. al., "No-First Use of Nuclear Weapons: A Policy Assessment,"

17 Nicolas Haupais, éd., *La France et l'arme nucléaire au XXIe siècle* ("France and the nuclear weapon in the 21st century"), ed. *Biblis* (Paris: CNRS éditions, 2019).

18 Macron, "Discours du Président Emmanuel Macron sur la Stratégie de Défense et de Dissuasion Devant les Stagiaires de la 27ème Promotion de l'Ecole de Guerre. ".

19 Haupais, *La France et l'arme nucléaire.*

20 D. Bowen, J. Gill, and A. Levesques, "Nuclear Deterrence and Stability in South Asia: Perceptions and Realities," 9–10.

21 Charles De Gaulle quoted in Haupais, *La France et l'arme nucléaire.*

22 The French president, Emmanuel Macron, advocates a "clear and previsible" nuclear doctrine for France; Macron "Discours du Président Emmanuel Macron sur la Stratégie de Défense et de Dissuasion Devant les Stagiaires de la 27ème Promotion de l'Ecole de Guerre. "

23 "Livre Blanc Défense et Sécurité Nationale 2013" ("French White Paper: Defence and National Security, 2013") (ministère de la Défense, Direction de l'Information légale et administrative, Paris, April 2013).

24 Macron, "Discours du Président Emmanuel Macron sur la Stratégie de Défense et de Dissuasion Devant les Stagiaires de la 27ème Promotion de l'Ecole de Guerre."

25 Tertrais, "Le concept de dissuasion nucléaire," in *L'arme nucléaire* ("The Concept of Nuclear Deterrence", in *The Nuclear Weapon*), ed. *Que Sais-Je* (Paris: Presses Universitaires de France, 2008), 29–66.

Chapter 14

CHINA'S NO FIRST USE AS A LITMUS TEST FOR GLOBAL NO FIRST USE

Lora Saalman

INTRODUCTION

China reaffirmed its NFU pledge in its 2019 defence white paper and it serves as a potential role model for how countries may achieve GNFU.[1] Yet this pledge, which came into existence in the wake of China testing its first nuclear weapon in 1964, merits closer examination.[2] While China's NFU commitment is largely steadfast at the official level—with repeated declarations to 'never at any time or under any circumstances be the first to use nuclear weapons'—strategic experts continue to discuss the nature and verifiability of this pledge.[3] As the first country to undertake NFU and to adhere to this declaration, China serves as a litmus test for the feasibility and terms under which a GNFU pledge might form. At the same time, the conceptual and technological challenges that NFU has encountered in China's case merit greater attention, since they also indicate some of the hurdles that would need to be overcome among countries less inclined to undertake such a pledge. This chapter explores some of these challenges and provides reflections on China's potential role as a leader in pursuing GNFU.

CONCEPTUAL LEVEL

In researching NFU within Chinese-language open-source databases, what becomes immediately apparent is the limited number of domestic writings and how few elicit any critical analysis of NFU.[4] For the author, who regularly researches Chinese on postures and technologies that yield hundreds to thousands of papers,[5] the mere twenty-two Chinese-language articles found making a reference to NFU is striking. Instead, the majority of writings from Chinese experts on NFU tend to be in English and directed towards an international audience. Given that the bulk of these articles are written by Chinese arms-control experts, who are frequent participants at track 1.5 (non-official and official attendees) and track 2 (non-official and retired official attendees) strategic dialogues with foreign experts, the target audience of NFU discussion appears to be largely Western-oriented.

This could stem from three reasons. First, if NFU is a core tenet of Chinese nuclear posture, then there is less of a perceived need to explain it to a domestic audience. Second, China is engaged in an effort to convince international officials and non-officials of the veracity of China's NFU pledge and the merits of undertaking similar pledges. Third, central tenets within China's nuclear posture are not eligible for open domestic debate. Even Chinese adherents of NFU, like Major General Pan Zhenqiang, have asserted in the past that 'Within China, the no-first-use policy more or less involves important state secrets, so it is not possible to launch a nationwide public discussion about it at this time.'[6] As Senior Colonel Xu Weidi further notes in his footnotes when writing on NFU, those within China who are questioning or debating the pledge wish to remain anonymous.[7] Even following a recent speech by Ambassador Sha Zukang arguing that China should consider relinquishing its NFU pledge vis-à-vis the USA—unless the latter is willing to negotiate mutual NFU or refrains from undermining China's strategic power—other Chinese arms control experts have qualified his speech as his personal view.[8]

In China, this gap between closed and open discourse on NFU suggests that there may be more of a robust behind-the-scenes debate than the 'minority of voices' some suggest.[9] This is noteworthy in that China is actually quite transparent when it comes to technological advances and military trends.[10] Chinese television programmes and magazines on military advances are prolific and refer to both domestic and foreign military trends.[11] This differs from debate in Chinese arms-control circles, which undergoes a series of closed-door discussions before becoming part of the public discourse.[12] The rationale behind confining NFU debate to non-public spaces could have to do with an effort to avoid adding fuel to the international debate. Chinese official and non-official interlocutors learned this lesson after the release of China's 2013 defence white paper that omitted mention of NFU.[13] While denials came from domestic leadership that China's stance on NFU had changed, for documents as formulaic as China's defence white papers, such an omission attracted heightened scrutiny.[14] The international community debated China's potential alteration of its NFU pledge and expanded its discussion on whether China was seeking to 'sprint to parity' or even to shift to nuclear warfighting.[15]

Moreover, the timing of this NFU omission coincided with China's chairman and president, Xi Jinping, coming into power. His more assertive stance towards China's position in the world and efforts to streamline and empower the Chinese military—including through the 2016 conversion of the Second Artillery into the People's Liberation Army (PLA) Rocket Force[16]—made the lack of mention of NFU in an official document even more eye-catching. Despite protests to the contrary, as well as the official and non-official reiterations of NFU that soon followed, there is a political and military rationale for China signalling that US actions may trigger an aggressive Chinese response. Western-targeted strategic ambiguity serves a purpose in staying the hand of adversaries, who are unsure of how China might react in a crisis scenario.[17] This deterrent aim has been most apparent in the evolution of China's response towards the USA's pursuits and policy declarations in the past on missile defence and prompt global strike.[18] More recently, China's expansion of ICBM silo fields to allegedly house its DF-41 ICBM among other long-range missiles—and the ensuing Chinese denials and foreign debates—mark the latest extension of this trend.[19]

As these trends translate into NFU, even while reaffirming China's pledge, Major General Yao Yunzhu among others have pointed on multiple occasions to the negative impact of US military advances and arms control shifts on China's nuclear deterrent and the implications for its nuclear posture.[20] Notably, Major General Yao's analyses occur several years apart in both English and Chinese. In fact, cautioning the USA on its postural and technological developments has become part of the Western-oriented discourse among Chinese arms-control experts and interlocutors, including Shen Dingli,[21] Major General Peng Guangqian,[22] among many others.[23] Their emphasis relies on the argument that China must pursue technological development and weapons advances to address an increasingly dynamic security environment. Thus, while Chinese experts continue to reaffirm NFU, there is the potential for flexibility in its application. As just one example, some Chinese experts have privately argued that a conventional attack on a country's nuclear forces or command and control structure could be considered equivalent to 'first use', potentially compelling the victim to engage in nuclear countermeasures.

Raising potential threats to China's NFU posture has long served as a bellwether for Chinese official and non-official experts to voice the severity of its conventional and strategic military concerns. As early as 1995, General Xiong Guangkai, who at the time served in the PLA General Staff Intelligence Department and became the deputy chief of staff a year later, reportedly told a US official that China would consider using nuclear weapons in a conflict over Taiwan.[24] In 2005, Major General Zhu Chenghu, then dean of China's National Defense University, also reportedly said, 'if the Americans draw their missiles and position-guided ammunition on to the target zone on China's territory, I think we will have to respond with nuclear weapons'.[25] When combined with Major General Pan Zhenqiang's assertion in 2016 that NFU has been undergoing domestic re-evaluation over whether it is outdated, needs to be adjusted or should be abandoned, such statements carry added weight.[26] Most recently, as cited above, China's former arms control ambassador to the UN in a 2021 speech at the China Arms Control and Disarmament Association argued that China should reconsider its NFU pledge vis-à-vis the USA.[27] Even if these simply represent personal reflections and are rhetorical efforts to maintain a degree of strategic ambiguity, they merit greater evaluation in the context of China's technological advances.

Moreover, while often dismissed as the musings of a few retired officers or officials, there are indications that these views are not necessarily isolated. Such concerns highlight the long-standing issue of how China's nuclear posture pertains to such contested areas as Taiwan and Arunachal Pradesh, which it regards as sovereign territory. Over the past few decades, some international experts have argued that NFU may not apply in these locations.[28] And they are not alone. Even Chinese strategists have purportedly discussed a more tailored form of NFU, In doing so, they cite such drivers as Russia's decision to abandon its NFU policy in the face of US alliance networks; the potential for an attack on China using other forms of weapons of mass destruction; concerns over catastrophic incidents equivalent to that of a nuclear attack, such as destruction of the Three Gorges Dam; conventional attacks on China's civilian nuclear facilities and nuclear arms; alliances with China's nuclear adversary during wartime; occupation of China's territory; as well as attacks on strategic assets such as aircraft carriers.[29]

Challenges to China's adherence to NFU are likely to only grow, particularly with such newer developments as its own reaction to and version of the US Third Offset, which ushers the potential integration of a host of artificial intelligence (AI), machine learning and autonomy applications into decision-making and delivery platforms.[30] Facing US conventional and nuclear advances, Chinese experts have already begun to argue that if China's second-strike capability turns into a third-strike capability—such that Beijing is unable to effectively engage in retaliation due to nuclear decapitation—then pre-emptive countermeasures would be required.[31] While the exact nature of these countermeasures remains unclear, there is just as much the potential for a postural response as a technological one. This would mean adjustments to China's long-held nuclear postures, if not in declaration then in practice. Furthermore, inclusion in the 2018 US Nuclear Posture Review of low-yield submarine-launched ballistic missiles (SLBMs) and low-yield submarine-launched cruise missiles (SLCMs)—combined with indications that some of these programmes will continue under the Biden administration—the complexity of regional dynamics is destined to have a growing impact on China.[32]

Faced with this potential, Western discussions have centred upon whether China would consider a shift to a posture of first strike ambiguity, in which China maintains a lack of clarity on the conditions under which it would engage in nuclear first use.[33] Doing so would complicate China's alleged pre-existing stance of first-strike uncertainty in which China diminishes US confidence in its ability to decapitate its nuclear arsenal.[34] It would also effectively rank China among those countries with conditional NFU, constituting a significant postural change. For the time being, first-strike uncertainty seems to continue to dominate, as revealed in recent revelations on China's expansion of its number of ICBM silos that would complicate foreign targeting of its nuclear deterrent.[35] Nevertheless, these same technological advances also suggest that China's postural ambiguity—even on NFU—cannot be ruled out, particularly given signs that China may be shifting its stances on de-mating, nuclear arsenal size and launch-on-warning, while engaging in development and deployment of dual-capable and machine learning- and autonomy-enabled systems. Thus, while China is unlikely to fully relinquish its official NFU declaration, its pledge also needs to be weighed against the technological advances that are adding ambiguity to its strategic deterrent.

TECHNOLOGICAL LEVEL

Conducting any re-evaluation of China's NFU stance is fraught. The majority of voices both within and outside of China maintain that its NFU pledge is unshakable.[36] Nevertheless, there remains a degree of scepticism in some circles as to how NFU would apply in a conflict scenario or a severe deterioration in its security environment and territorial disputes. As just one example, experts at the global think tank RAND Corporation suggest that while China would not likely abandon NFU in the next fifteen years, it may introduce caveats or ambiguity in its discussion.[37] Rather than basing evaluation of NFU on conceptual debates based largely on statements, however, there is merit to a technology-based approach. Nuclear postures are fungible and open to interpretation, while nuclear platforms and systems are more available to scrutiny, even in a relatively opaque country like China. Thus, one of the most reliable litmus tests for China's ability to uphold an unwavering and unconditional NFU emerges in analysing its military modernisation.

Historically, China's low nuclear weapon numbers, de-mating of nuclear warheads from delivery vehicles and lack of launch-on-warning have been cited by Chinese experts as physical manifestations of its NFU pledge.[38] Chinese experts often list these alongside NFU in arguing that China has rejected a nuclear warfighting capability and does not need to maintain its nuclear weapons on hair-trigger alert.[39] However, the evolution of Chinese concerns over US advances in missile defence, prompt global strike, machine learning and autonomy have shaped not only its countermeasures but also its nuclear posture.[40] While China remains focused on its survivability and retaliatory capability, it is also engaged in a military modernisation that challenges some traditional indicators of China's NFU posture. Whether to avoid a 'science surprise'[41] through research or for actual deployment, China's technological advances require evaluation in terms of how they are impacting its nuclear posture and, in particular, NFU. They indicate that while China may be reluctant to abandon NFU, the technological indicators that shore up this pledge are shifting and, in some cases, eroding. The following five points briefly outline this phenomenon and merit greater scrutiny.

Mating of Warheads

China's storage of its nuclear warheads, apart from its delivery platforms, continues to be cited as among the technological foundations supporting China's NFU policy. For example, *China's Nuclear Forces, 2019* asserts that the country is 'thought to store most of its nuclear warheads in its central storage facility in the Qinling mountain range, and to a lesser degree at smaller regional storage facilities'.[42] This essay bases its assessment on Hans Kristensen and Matt Korda's previous works as well as those of Mark Stokes. While well-researched, the reports on which they base this analysis date between 1988 and 2006. There is certainly the potential that China will continue to manage its nuclear 'warheads in peacetime through a system that is separate and distinct from formerly known as Second Artillery missile bases and subordinate launch brigades'.[43] However, China's deployment shifts and organisational changes in forming the PLA's Rocket Force deserve greater attention before asserting that decades-old findings are still relevant. Some studies have already begun this re-evaluation, but the tendency to rely on outdated or circular references persists.[44]

Even if one were to assume that the PLA Rocket Force is identical to the Second Artillery in terms of both posture and operation, China's intended sea trials of the Type 096 nuclear SSBN, flight tests of the JL-3 intercontinental-range SLBM and expansion of its number of silos for deployment of solid-fuelled ICBMs—in particular, the MIRVed DF-41 ICBM—would be enough to challenge China's traditional de-mating policy.[45] While such platforms ensure China's ability to maintain its second-strike capability, their integration also offers Beijing a wider range of launch and policy options. Most importantly, their introduction into China's nuclear deterrent makes it difficult to assert that China's de-mating policy remains unaltered. Instead, China's policy of de-mating would need to be tailored to the specific delivery system. This operational conditionality of de-mating merits greater exploration for its impact on NFU.

Nuclear Arsenal Size

The majority of Chinese analyses continue to cite China's credible minimum nuclear deterrent as evidence of its adherence to NFU. While a limited group of Chinese experts and pundits has advocated for China to expand its nuclear arsenal size to ensure its retaliatory capability,[46] this argument of nuclear warhead number equating with strategic intent remains prevalent. As with de-mating, much of the international assessment of China's nuclear arsenal size is based off of the work of a few Western experts and foreign calculations.[47] The veracity of these estimates is debated even within China, where experts question the source of international calculations and yet offer no warhead numbers to counter these amounts.[48] Nevertheless, recent official US estimates suggest that China is sizably ramping up its arsenal growth. A 2021 US Department of Defense assessment contends that China may reach 700 deliverable nuclear warheads by 2027 and at least 1,000 warheads by 2030.[49]

Beyond Western estimates, China's alleged development of MIRVs, even if bolstered by decoys, suggests a the logistical necessity of China expanding its nuclear warhead numbers.[50] Recent allegations of China's building of further silos to house such delivery systems as MIRVed DF-41 ICBMs indicates just one avenue of this expansion.[51] Much like the MIRVs themselves, even if a portion of these silos is for deception, their numerical increase demonstrates a much-expanded foundation for nuclear warhead deployment. The same applies to China's diversification of its nuclear-delivery platform options with ballistic missile nuclear submarines (SSBNs), intermediate and long-range mobile ballistic missiles, air-launched land-attack cruise missiles, hypersonic glide vehicles (HGVs), among others.[52] Even if a debate remains as to their intended use in deploying conventional or nuclear payloads, China would still be compelled to increase its warhead numbers to meet the operational requirements of this growing range of delivery vehicles. Thus, while China's nuclear stockpile may not necessarily double over the next decade or 'sprint to parity',[53] this stockpile expansion and delivery vehicle proliferation also merit further examination for their potential impact on NFU.

Launch-on-Warning

China's focus on strategic early warning systems has caused the US Department of Defense to question whether China might adopt a launch-on-warning posture.[54] Even Western experts who tend not to question China's NFU commitments[55] have cited a 2012 article by General Wei Fenghe and General Zhang Haiyang that ended with an emphasis on maintaining 'a high alert level throughout the execution of the mission, assuring that if something happens we're ready to go'.[56] Further, in December 2013, China's Academy of Military Sciences published an updated edition of *The Science of Military Strategy* that suggested China's nuclear forces could move towards a launch-on-warning posture, such that 'When conditions are prepared and when necessary, we can, under conditions confirming the enemy has launched nuclear missiles against us, before the enemy nuclear warheads have reached their targets and effectively exploded, before they have caused us actual nuclear damage, quickly launch a nuclear missile retaliatory strike.'[57]

This is noteworthy in that the above Chinese statements appeared around the same time that NFU was omitted from China's 2013 defence white paper. As noted by a RAND report, a move towards launch on warning could undermine China's future commitment to NFU if, for example, China launched its nuclear platforms under a warning that turned out to be a false alarm.[58] Given Chinese concerns over its inability to anticipate, much less to engage in countermeasures against, a stealthy, prompt, high-precision strike—whether initiated by US space planes or other prompt global or regional strike platforms—the drivers for such a shift exist.[59] Moreover, the foundations necessary for launch on warning may be underway. As one example, following a 2014 Chinese publication on building a strategic early warning system with experimental early-warning satellites, China is alleged to have launched communication satellites to support this endeavour in 2015.[60] Combined with the 2021 discovery of new silo fields for solid-fuelled ICBMs in China, this potential shift towards launch on warning gains further traction.[61] Thus, while the conceptual shift towards launch-on-warning remains under debate, expanded infrastructure that supports its implementation could provide greater clarity and a potent future challenge to NFU.

Dual-Capable Systems

Platforms and systems that support both conventional and nuclear operations are considered to be part of China's military.[62] As China's hedging increases on the intended payload of its delivery vehicles, so do questions as to their ultimate intent. These exacerbate the chances of miscalculation and miscommunication since dual-capable platforms indicate a greater willingness to engage in first-strike ambiguity when the adversary is uncertain as to the ultimate payload in a conflict scenario. While NFU could be said to clarify that a nuclear payload would not be utilised, except in retaliation, the issue of differentiation becomes more complicated. Among the platforms cited by various Western sources as dual capable are China's DF-17 medium-range ballistic missile (MRBM), DF-26 intermediate-range ballistic missile (IRBM), DF-ZF HGV and CJ-20 air-launched land-attack cruise missile, as well as a range of unmanned aerial vehicles (UAVs) and unmanned underwater vehicles (UUVs) that are under development.[63]

As noted by some Western experts, preparations to launch or the actual launch of a DF-26 IRBM with a conventional warhead against a US base in the region could be misinterpreted as a launch of a nuclear weapon and trigger nuclear escalation or even pre-emption.[64] However, even if such platforms retain a conventional payload, there remain debates and questions over the entanglement that may occur when countries like China are thought to co-mingle their conventional and nuclear command and control systems.[65] This lack of clarity may deter an adversary from a pre-emptive launch against conventional command and control that may result in nuclear escalation, but this is a significant assumption. In a conflict scenario, conventional command and control systems would likely be targeted, potentially resulting in damage to China's nuclear infrastructure and interpretation as a nuclear first strike. This level of ambiguity could thereby render claims of NFU moot in an adversary's calculations during a crisis or conflict.

Machine Learning and Autonomy

China has leapt ahead in its development of AI, which could make significant contributions to its military, and even nuclear modernisation through military-civilian fusion (军民融合).[66] AI enhancement of decision-making and manoeuvrability of unmanned systems makes it a potent area of interest for Chinese military and civilian advances. This is particularly salient as China seeks to break through US missile defences, which have been a long-standing concern for negating China's second-strike capability.[67] There has already been a significant amount of Chinese research into neural networks and how they may improve the manoeuvrability of such HGVs as the DF-ZF, which reportedly has been deployed on the dual-capable DF-17 MRBM for anti-access/area-denial (A2/AD) military operations that are inherently more proactive and potentially even pre-emptive.[68] Other reports suggest that HGVs may be deployed in the future on the MIRVed DF-41 ICBM,[69] which is allegedly among the intended occupants of recently discovered silo fields in China. Further, China's test of an HGV coupled with a fractional orbital bombardment system (FOBS) is the latest indication that AI-enabled platforms will have a marked impact on the credibility of its nuclear deterrent.[70]

Whether intended to break through US theatre missile defence or national missile defence, China's advances in penetration and targeting suggest a strong enhancement to its nuclear deterrent. Again, these developments can be interpreted as a means of bolstering its retaliatory capability. However, hedging on the intended payload of these HGVs complicates discrimination and leads to heightened strategic ambiguity. For a country that is strongly concerned about the issue of being caught off guard by a strike and is potentially integrating strategic early warning and launch-on-warning into its nuclear infrastructure, the potential for an accidental launch or response is significant.[71] It becomes all the more important as machine learning and autonomy are built not only into the DF-ZF HGV but also the UAVs and UUVs that may imitate Russia and carry nuclear payloads in the future.

For example, Lin Yang, marine technology equipment director at the Shenyang Institute of Automation of the Chinese Academy of Sciences, has reportedly confirmed that China is developing a series of extra-large unmanned underwater vehicles (XLUUVs).[72] While not necessarily destined for nuclear payloads, China's developments in UUVs merit greater scrutiny in light of Russia's own efforts to develop such nuclear-powered and nuclear-delivery platforms as the Poseidon (Status-6), an autonomous, nuclear-powered and nuclear-armed UUV.[73] The Shenyang Institute of Automation is a major producer of underwater robots, which it supplies to the Chinese military. Furthermore, Lin developed China's first UUV with an operational depth beyond 6 km and is now the chief scientist of the 912 Project.[74] As China spends its time and resources on smaller unmanned platforms and developing swarm capabilities, the chances that these may lead to escalation through colliding with or confronting strategic platforms grows.[75]

In sum, none of these alleged technological shifts in isolation represents the death knell of NFU in China. This concept is likely to remain a fixture of China's declaratory posture and defence white papers. Chinese leadership no doubt learned a strategic lesson, given the profusion of international debate and questions raised about China's NFU and nuclear posture commitments following its 2013 omission. If changes in transparency or intent lead to international backlash, then maintaining a consistent declaratory posture, even if divergent from military advances, may be perceived in China as less destabilising. It provides a manageable level of strategic ambiguity. However, just as NFU is a bellwether for indicating Chinese concerns over US and other countries' military developments, China's technological shifts and advances must be factored into discussions of its NFU policy. Doing so would go a long way towards answering questions over verifiability that have long plagued international acceptance of NFU. Moreover, such efforts could be used to better define what a GNFU pledge would entail by offering clearer conceptual and technological indicators.

CONCLUSION

Since the 1960s, China has maintained the longest-standing commitment to NFU among nuclear-armed states. Chinese officials at the 49th UN General Assembly and leaders like Ambassador Yang Jiechi, the director of the Central Foreign Affairs Commission Office, have sought to expand the scope of NFU by calling for nuclear-armed states to sign onto a treaty universalising the pledge to further the pursuit of nuclear disarmament.[76] And China was among the five nuclear-armed states to declare in 2022 that 'a nuclear war cannot be won and must never be fought' and to 'affirm that nuclear weapons—for as long as they continue to exist—should serve defensive purposes, deter aggression, and prevent war'.[77] At the conceptual and technological level, however, significant challenges remain to China serving as a litmus test for GNFU.

If even the most faithful adherent of NFU faces ongoing questions in terms of the immutability and verifiability of this pledge, it becomes more difficult to map a pathway towards universalising such a commitment. This is particularly the case when the English-language discussion of NFU among Chinese experts is so divergent from the Chinese-language one. Mention of NFU in Chinese-language open-source databases revealed only twenty-two works, with only a third focused on China. The remainder concentrated superficially on NFU-related debates regarding India, Pakistan, Russia, North Korea and the USA. Comparing this small assemblage of domestic analyses with the profusion of English-language writings from Chinese authors suggests that NFU remains a concept largely targeted at foreign consumption. As noted by Chinese arms-control experts, NFU-related backdoor discussions and debates within China are not open to the public.

At one level, if China's NFU declaration is intended as a means of strategic assurance towards other countries, this makes strategic sense. However, this approach also makes it difficult to assess the extent to which China's NFU could be applied abroad and among other nuclear-weapon states. If there is a sense that China is not secure enough to allow its NFU discourse to emerge in open domestic discussion, much less debate, then it becomes difficult to contemplate the universalisation of an NFU pledge among countries with more robust democracies. Further, with the rapid expansion of technological, military and political shifts within China, it is difficult to argue that the underpinnings of NFU have not also changed. Instead, assuming that NFU is an immutable posture in the wake of such dynamism only exacerbates concerns that it may be simply a Chinese 'slogan' (口号). While the aforementioned challenges do not negate China's NFU pledge, they still suggest that its foundations require better articulation, beyond a formulaic declaration. This is particularly the case when it comes to China's evolution on de-mating, the size of its nuclear arsenal, launch-on-warning, dual-capable platforms and machine learning and autonomy in nuclear systems and command and control.

Moreover, the international security environment continues its drift away from realising NFU, with the USA and Russia revealing plans for fielding unmanned delivery systems and low-yield nuclear weapons, thereby lowering nuclear thresholds. As a result, even a 'lean and effective' (精干有效) example set by China would be difficult to enforce. As highlighted by Fudan University Professor Cai Cuihong, strategic stability and deterrence are more multi-valent than in the 1960s when the NFU pledge first formed.[78] As part of this, non-nuclear states and conventional forces are increasingly factored into nuclear deterrence calculations. With the introduction of emerging technologies, the evolving structure and foundation of arms control will become even more complex. These trends make the ability of countries to adhere to a GNFU pledge all the more difficult and make the role of China even more critical. China has set the gold standard with its unequivocal NFU pledge. However, until there is a willingness within China to more openly explore the complexities and evolution inherent in the technological foundations of its own NFU model, there will remain questions among foreign experts as to its verifiability, much less potential for universality.

Currently, China's declaratory NFU policy remains ossified within what even Chinese experts describe as a 'dynamic international security environment'. As a result, China is left repeating its NFU pledge and maintaining the moral high ground, but lacking traction in shaping the ever-changing international arms-control agenda. While omitting this domestic complexity and even ambiguity, however, the few Chinese-language writings available still seem to be well aware of external challenges to NFU. They lament the inability of Pakistan to adhere to NFU in light of India's conventional superiority; the alleged growing conditionality of India's NFU pledge; the US refusal to undertake an NFU pledge due to its ongoing pursuit of absolute security; and Russia's decision to relinquish NFU when faced with pressure from US regional alliance networks. Recognising these foreign trends, while remaining domestically uncritical about its challenges, makes China's own calls for others to undertake NFU commitments ring hollow.[79] This speaks to the final question of China's willingness to serve as a model for GNFU.

On this front, track 1.5 and track 2 strategic dialogues between China and the USA are illustrative.[80] For decades, Chinese interlocutors have sought to encourage the USA to undertake an NFU pledge. Their efforts have been tied to US entreaties for China to increase its nuclear transparency. Accordingly, the two sets of demands have become inextricably linked and ultimately deadlocked. Without Washington's willingness to declare mutual vulnerability and to pledge NFU through its official statements and military modernisation, Chinese interlocutors continue to argue that Beijing lacks the impetus to respond in kind with further nuclear transparency. Ultimately, the USA's role ranks paramount when it comes to China's interest in expanding its nuclear transparency to promote GNFU. Thus, with the USA and Russia moving farther and farther away from these aims—even in light of their strategic stability talks[81]—China is left with an excuse to refrain from participating in these discussions.

This does not mean, however, that China cannot serve as a model on GNFU or even lead the charge. China is uniquely positioned to undertake a central role in furthering NFU in the international community. Part of serving as a litmus test for GNFU, however, includes the need to explain how NFU has evolved both conceptually and technologically within China. Doing so would enable China to move beyond its static NFU declarations and offer a pathway towards meaningful exchanges within the international arms control community. Furthermore, if China is engaged in technological dynamism and shifts on de-mating, nuclear arsenal size, launch-on-warning, dual-capable systems, machine learning and autonomy to support its strategic aims, this dilutes China's argument of asymmetry as its key rationale for not participating in track 1 strategic talks with countries like Russia and the USA. These changes widen—rather than narrow—China's platform for engaging the international community on nuclear posture and technology.

Thus, for China to serve as the litmus test in making a case for GNFU, technology will need to play a greater part in conceptual discussions of nuclear posture. Without this, NFU will be simply a 'slogan' rather than a stance.

NOTES

1 State Council Information Office, "新时代的中国国防" ["China's National Defense in a New Era"] (State Council Information Office, People's Republic of China, Beijing, July 2019), http://www.gov.cn/zhengce/2019-07/24/content_5414325.htm.

2 Digital Archive, "Statement of the Government of the People's Republic of China" (Wilson Center, Washington DC, October 16, 1964), http://large.stanford.edu/courses/2018/ph241/shan1/docs/prc-16oct64.pdf.

3 Bin Li and Tong Zhao (eds), *Understanding Chinese Nuclear Thinking*, (Washington, DC: Carnegie Endowment for International Peace, 2016), https://carnegieendowment.org/files/ChineseNuclearThinking_Final.pdf; Ankit Panda, "'No First Use' and Nuclear Weapons" (Council on Foreign Relations, New York, July 17, 2018), https://www.cfr.org/backgrounder/no-first-use-and-nuclear-weapons; Ben Lowsen, "Is China Abandoning Its 'No First Use' Nuclear Policy?" *The Diplomat*, March 21, 2018, https://thediplomat.com/2018/03/is-china-abandoning-its-no-first-use-nuclear-policy.

4 Zhipeng He [何志鹏] and Qing Du [都青], "新时代中国国际法治思想" ["China's Thoughts on International Law in the New Era"], 国际关系与国会发学刊 [*Journal of International Relations and International Law*] 8 (August 2019): 37; Xin Zhan [詹欣], "中国与全球核安全治理" ["China and Global Nuclear Security Governance"], 当代中国史研究 [*Contemporary China History Studies*] 26, no 2 (March 2019): 119; Wei Li [李韬], "核战争的伦理思考" ["Ethical Thinking on Nuclear War"], 阜阳师范学院学报 (社会科学版) [*Journal of Fuyang Teachers College (Social Science)*] 102, no 6 (2004): 17.

5 Lora Saalman, "Fear of False Negatives: AI and China's Nuclear Posture," *Bulletin of the Atomic Scientists*, April 24, 2018, https://thebulletin.org/2018/04/fear-of-false-negatives-ai-and-chinas-nuclear-posture; Saalman, "Prompt Global Strike: China and the Spear" (Independent Faculty Article, Asia-Pacific Center for Security Studies, Honolulu, April 2014), http://www.apcss.org/wp-content/uploads/2014/04/APCSS_Saalman_PGS_China_Apr2014.pdf.

6 Zhenqiang Pan, "China's No First Use of Nuclear Weapons", in *Understanding Chinese Nuclear Thinking*, eds Bin Li and Tong Zhao (Washington, DC: Carnegie Endowment for International Peace, 2016), 68, https://carnegieendowment.org/files/ChineseNuclearThinking_Final.pdf.

7 Weidi Xu, "China's Security Environment and the Role of Nuclear Weapons," in *Understanding Chinese Nuclear Thinking*, eds Bin Li and Tong Zhao,

44–49, https://carnegieendowment.org/files/ChineseNuclearThinking_Final.pdf.

8 Based on the author's participation and exchange on the panel 'Strategic Stability: Impasse and Way Out' at the Beijing Xiangshan Forum, 25-26 October 2021. "SIPRI experts contribute to the 2021 Beijing Xiangshan Forum webinar," November 12, 2021, https://sipri.org/news/2021/sipri-experts-contribute-2021-beijing-xiangshan-forum-webinar; Juzizhoutou.net, "沙祖康大使在军控协会成立20周年纪念大会暨军控工作座谈会上的发言" [Ambassador Sha Zukang's speech at the 20th Anniversary Meeting of the Arms Control Association and the Arms Control Working Symposium], September 22, 2021, http://www.juzizhoutou.net/tianxia/guancha/2021-09-22/11242.html.

9 Pan, "China's No First Use of Nuclear Weapons", 68.

10 Saalman, "China's Integration of Neural Networks into Hypersonic Glide Vehicles," in *AI, China, Russia, and the Global Order: Technological, Political, Global, and Creative Perspectives*, ed. N.D. Wright, (Alabama: Air University Press, October 219), 153–60, https://www.airuniversity.af.edu/Portals/10/AUPress/Books/B_0161_WRIGHT_ARTIFICIAL_INTELLIGENCE_CHINA_RUSSIA_AND_THE_GLOBAL_ORDER.PDF; Saalman, "Prompt Global Strike: China and the Spear"; Lora Saalman, "Factoring Russia into the US–Chinese Equation on Hypersonic Glide Vehicles" (SIPRI Insights on Peace and Security no 2017/1, Stockholm, January 2017), https://www.sipri.org/sites/default/files/Factoring-Russia-into-US-Chinese-equation-hypersonic-glide-vehicles.pdf; Lora Saalman, "The China Factor," in *Missile Defense: Confrontation and Cooperation*, eds. Alexei Arbatov, Valdimir Dvorkin, and Natalia Bubnova (Moscow: Carnegie Moscow Center, 2013), 226–252, http://carnegie.ru/2013/04/08/missile-defense-confrontation-and-cooperation/fyab.

11 中国军网 [China Military Net], "军事期刊" ["Military Journals"], accessed on August 18, 2021, http://www.81.cn/jkhc/node_62222.htm; "CCTV-7 国防军事 ["CCTV-7 National Defense Military"], accessed on August 18, 2021, https://tv.cctv.com/cctv7; "CCTV-4 今日关注" ["CCTV-4 Focus Today"], accessed on August 18, 2021, https://waptv.sogou.com/tvshow/or3hg2dpo5ptembyhaztomyjxxy4rvnz3dl2e.html.

12 Based on the author's dissertation research, interviews and China's arms control community response following such events as its anti-satellite test in 2007.

13 国防部 [Ministry of National Defense], "中国武装力量的多样化运用" ["Diversified Use of National Armed Forces"] (White Paper, Ministry of National Defence, People's Republic of China, Beijing, April 2013, http://www.mod.gov.cn/regulatory/2013-04/16/content_4617811.htm.

14 Some Chinese arms-control experts have argued in private discussions that this omission may have been because the "Diversified Use of National Armed Forces" was a unique, stand-alone defence white paper. Rachel Oswald, "China's New Defense Paper Causes Stir over No-First-Use Nuke Policy," Nuclear Threat Initiative, April 24, 2013, https://www.nti.org/gsn/

article/chinas-new-defense-white-paper-causes-stir-over-questions-no-first-use-policy.

15 Oswald, "China's New Defense Paper Causes Stir over No-First-Use Nuke Policy"; James Acton, "Is China Changing Its Position on Nuclear Weapons?" *The New York Times*, April 18, 2013, https://www.nytimes.com/2013/04/19/opinion/is-china-changing-its-position-on-nuclear-weapons.html.

16 ChinaDaily.com.cn, "President Xi Expects Strong, Modern Rocket Force," September 27, 2016, https://www.chinadaily.com.cn/china/2016-09/27/content_26904488.htm.

17 Shulong Chu and Yu Rong, "China: Dynamic Minimum Deterrence," in *The Long Shadow: Nuclear Weapons and Security in 21st Century Asia*, ed. Muthiah Alagappa, (Stanford, CA: Stanford University Press, 2008), 176, https://books.google.ch/books?id=k-m0YnoBdwkC&pg=PA176&dq=Questions+over+China%27s+NFU+nuclear+verifiability&hl=en&sa=X&ved=0ahUKEwjj6dHs-6jkAhXEwKQKHV-bCgEQ6AEILzAB#v=onepage&q=Questions%20over%20China's%20NFU%20nuclear%20verifiability&f=false.

18 Saalman, "Prompt Global Strike: China and the Spear."; Saalman, "China & the US Nuclear Posture Review" (The Carnegie Papers, Carnegie-Tsinghua Center for Global Policy, Beijing, February 2011), https://carnegieendowment.org/files/china_posture_review.pdf.

19 Matt Korda and Hans Kristensen, "China Is Building a Second Nuclear Missile Silo Field" (Federation of American Scientists, Washington DC, July 26, 2021, https://fas.org/blogs/security/2021/07/china-is-building-a-second-nuclear-missile-silo-field/; Xijin Hu, "WashPost-Quoted Researcher Amateur To Say Suspected Silos are for DF-41," *Global Times*, July 2, 2021, https://www.globaltimes.cn/page/202107/1227655.shtml.

20 Yunzhu Yao, "China Will Not Change Its Nuclear Policy," China–U.S. Focus, April 22, 2013, http://www.chinausfocus.com/peace-security/china-will-not-change-its-no-first-use-policy; Yunzhu Yao [姚云竹], "中美军事关系：从准同盟到竞争对手?" ["China–U.S. Military Relations: From Quasi-Alliance to Competitors?"], 美国研究 [*American Studies*], no 2 (February 2019): 15.

21 Dingli Shen, "Nuclear Deterrence in the 21st Century," *Defense & Security Analysis* 21, no 4 (2005), https://www.tandfonline.com/doi/abs/10.1080/1475179052000345467.

22 Eric Heginbotham et. al., "China's Evolving Nuclear Deterrent: Major Drivers and Issues for the United States" (RAND Corporation: Santa Monica, 2017), 130, https://www.rand.org/content/dam/rand/pubs/research_reports/RR1600/RR1628/RAND_RR1628.pdf.

23 Zhibo Zou [邹治波] and Feng Liu [刘玮], "构建中美核战略稳定性框架：非对称性战略平衡的视角" ["Building a Sino-US Nuclear Strategic Stability Framework: From the Perspective of Asymmetric Strategic Balance"], *Security Strategy* [安全战略], International Security Studies [国际安全研究], no 1 (January 2019): 48–49.

24 Joseph Kahn, "Chinese General Threatens Use of A-Bomb if U.S. Intrudes," *The New York Times*, July 15, 2005, https://www.nytimes.com/2005/07/15/washington/world/chinese-general-threatens-use-of-abombs-if-us-intrudes.html.

25 Jonathan Watts, "Chinese General Warns of Nuclear Risk to U.S.," *The Guardian*, July 16, 2005, https://www.theguardian.com/world/2005/jul/16/china.jonathanwatts.

26 Pan, "China's No First Use of Nuclear Weapons," 68, https://carnegieendowment.org/files/ChineseNuclearThinking_Final.pdf.

27 Juzizhoutou.net, "沙祖康大使在军控协会成立20周年纪念大会暨军控工作座谈会上的发言" [Ambassador Sha Zukang's speech at the 20th Anniversary Meeting of the Arms Control Association and the Arms Control Working Symposium], September 22, 2021, http://www.juzizhoutou.net/tianxia/guancha/2021-09-22/11242.html.

28 Arpit Rajain, *Nuclear Deterrence in Southern Asia: China, India and Pakistan*, (New York: SAGE Publications, 2005), 303.; Alistair Millar and Brian Alexander eds, *Tactical Nuclear Weapons: Emergent Threats in an Evolving Security Environment*, (Lincoln: Potomac Books Inc., 2003); Footnote 34.

29 Pan, "China's No First Use of Nuclear Weapons," 73, https://carnegieendowment.org/files/ChineseNuclearThinking_Final.pdf; 中国时刻 [China Time Network], "中国防空火力密布三峡 防印度核武" ["China's Air Defense Firepower Densely Deployed around Three Gorges against Indian Nuclear Weapons"], August 6, 2013; Eric Heginbotham et. al., "China's Evolving Nuclear Deterrent: Major Drivers and Issues for the United States" (RAND Corporation: Santa Monica, 2017), 82, https://www.rand.org/content/dam/rand/pubs/research_reports/RR1600/RR1628/RAND_RR1628.pdf.

30 Vincent Boulanin et. al., "Artificial Intelligence, Strategic Stability and Nuclear Risk," (SIPRI, Stockholm, Sweden, June 2020), https://www.sipri.org/sites/default/files/2020-06/artificial_intelligence_strategic_stability_and_nuclear_risk.pdf>; Saalman ed., *The Impact of Artificial Intelligence on Strategic Stability and Nuclear Risk – Volume II: East Asian Perspectives* (SIPRI, Stockholm, October 2019), https://www.sipri.org/sites/default/files/2019-10/the_impact_of_artificial_intelligence_on_strategic_stability_and_nuclear_risk_volume_ii.pdf.

31 Saalman, ed., *The Impact of Artificial Intelligence on Strategic Stability and Nuclear Risk – Volume II: East Asian Perspectives.*

32 Kingston Reif, "Biden Continues Trump Nuclear Funding," *Arms Control Today*, July/August 2021, https://www.armscontrol.org/act/2021-07/news/biden-continues-trump-nuclear-funding; Saalman, "Fear of False Negatives: AI and China's Nuclear Posture"; US Department of Defense, "U.S. Nuclear Posture Review" (Final Report, US Department of Defense, Washington DC, February 2018), https://media.defense.gov/2018/Feb/02/2001872886/-1/-1/1/2018-NUCLEAR-POSTURE-REVIEW-FINAL-REPORT.PDF.

33 Susan T. Haynes, "Dragon in the Room: Nuclear Disarmament's Missing Player," *Strategic Studies Quarterly* 12, no 1 (Spring 2018): 25–47, https://www.airuniversity.af.edu/Portals/10/SSQ/documents/Volume-12_Issue-1/Haynes.pdf.

34 Riqiang Wu, "Certainty of Uncertainty: Nuclear Strategy with Chinese Characteristics" (Program on Strategic Stability Evaluation, Georgia Institute of Technology, Atlanta, August 2013), 1–35, https://www.files.ethz.ch/isn/156889/4%20Wu%20POSSEIV.pdf.

35 Yao, "China Will Not Change Its Nuclear Policy"; Yao, "中美军事关系：从准同盟到竞争对手?" [China–U.S. Military Relations: From Quasi-Alliance to Competitors?"].

36 Gregory Kulacki, "China Holds Firm on No First Use of Nuclear Weapons," Union of Concerned Scientists, July 24, 2019, https://allthingsnuclear.org/gkulacki/china-holds-firm-on-no-first-use-of-nuclear-weapons.

37 Heginbotham et. al., "China's Evolving Nuclear Deterrent: Major Drivers and Issues for the United States," 129–133.

38 Jinghua Lu [吕晶华] and Xi Luo [罗曦], "冷战后中美西太平洋军力对比的发展演变" ["The Evolution of {the} China–US Balance of Military Power in the Post-Cold War Western Pacific Region"], 美国研究 [*American Studies*], no 3 (March 2019): 95; Li and Zhao, *Understanding Chinese Nuclear Thinking*; Bin Li, "Differences Between Chinese and U.S. Nuclear Thinking and Their Origins," in *Understanding Chinese Nuclear Thinking*, 15; Weidi, "China's Security Environment and the Role of Nuclear Weapons," in *Understanding Chinese Nuclear Thinking*, 28.

39 Li and Zhao, *Understanding Chinese Nuclear Thinking*.

40 Saalman, "Prompt Global Strike: China and the Spear"; Saalman, "The China Factor," in *Missile Defense: Confrontation and Cooperation*, 226–252; Saalman ed., *The Impact of Artificial Intelligence on Strategic Stability and Nuclear Risk – Volume II: East Asian Perspectives*.

41 Li, "Differences Between Chinese and U.S. Nuclear Thinking and Their Origins," in *Understanding Chinese Nuclear Thinking*, 15.

42 Hans Kristensen and Matt Korda, "Chinese Nuclear Forces, 2019," *Bulletin of the Atomic Scientists* 75, no 4 (2019): 172, https://www.tandfonline.com/doi/pdf/10.1080/00963402.2019.1628511?needAccess=true.

43 Mark Stokes, "China's Nuclear Warhead Storage and Handling System" (Project 2049 Institute, Arlington, Virginia, March 12, 2010), 2, https://project2049.net/wp-content/uploads/2018/05/chinas_nuclear_warhead_storage_and_handling_system.pdf.

44 Anthony H. Cordesman, "The PLA Rocket Force: Evolving Beyond the Second Artillery Corps (SAC) and Nuclear Dimension" (Working Draft, Center for Strategic and International Studies, Washington DC, October 2016), https://csis-prod.s3.amazonaws.com/s3fs-public/publication/161013_China_Missile_Forces_AHC.pdf.

45 Matt Korda and Hans Kristensen, "China Is Building A Second Nuclear Missile Silo Field"; Greg Torode, "Special Report: China's Furtive Underwater Nukes Test the Pentagon," *Reuters*, May 2, 2019, https://www.reuters.com/article/us-china-army-nuclear-specialreport/special-report-

chinas-furtive-underwater-nukes-test-the-pentagon-idUSKCN1S80YB; Panda, "China Conducts First Test of New JL-3 Submarine-Launched Ballistic Missile," *The Diplomat*, December 20, 2018, https://thediplomat.com/2018/12/china-conducts-first-test-of-new-jl-3-submarine-launched-ballistic-missile; Charles D. Ferguson, "Seeking China–U.S. Strategic Nuclear Stability," Federation of American Scientists, February 19, 2015, https://fas.org/pir-pubs/seeking-china-u-s-strategic-nuclear-stability.

46 Based on interactions with Chinese arms-control experts at the Thirteenth Annual Politics and International Relations Community Conference at Tsinghua University in July 2019. The rationale for China to potentially consider expanding its nuclear arsenal also appears in Wu, "Certainty of Uncertainty: Nuclear Strategy with Chinese Characteristics," 1–35; Hu, "China Needs to Increase Its Nuclear Warheads to 1,000," *Global Times*, May 8, 2020, https://www.globaltimes.cn/content/1187766.shtml.

47 Kristensen and Korda, "Chinese Nuclear Forces, 2019," 172.

48 Based on author's interactions with Chinese arms-control experts at the "15th PIIC Beijing Seminar on International Security: Nuclear Non-proliferation and Cooperation," November 2016. Tong Zhao, "What is Driving China's Nuclear Buildup?" (Commentary, Carnegie Endowment for International Peace, Washington DC, August 5, 2021), https://carnegieendowment.org/2021/08/05/what-s-driving-china-s-nuclear-buildup-pub-85106.

49 Office of the Secretary of Defense, "Military and Security Developments Involving the People's Republic of China, 2021," (US Department of Defense, November 2021), VIII, https://media.defense.gov/2021/Nov/03/2002885874/-1/-1/0/2021-CMPR-FINAL.PDF.

50 Office of the Secretary of Defense, "Military and Security Developments Involving the People's Republic of China, 2021," VII.

51 Yao, "China Will Not Change Its Nuclear Policy"; Yao, "中美军事关系：从准同盟到竞争对手?" [China–U.S. Military Relations: From Quasi-Alliance to Competitors?"], 15.

52 Joseph Trevithick, "Four of the Biggest Revelations from China's Massive 70th Anniversary Military Parade," *The Drive*, October 1, 2019, https://www.thedrive.com/the-war-zone/30119/four-of-the-biggest-revelations-from-chinas-massive-70th-anniversary-military-parade; Panda, "Introducing the DF-17: China's Newly Tested Ballistic Missile Armed with a Hypersonic Glide Vehicle," *The Diplomat*, December 28, 2017, https://thediplomat.com/2017/12/introducing-the-df-17-chinas-newly-tested-ballistic-missile-armed-with-a-hypersonic-glide-vehicle; Minnie Chan and Zhen Liu, "China Rolls Out New Weapon Systems, Nuclear-Capable Missiles in Military Parade," *South China Morning Post*, October 1, 2019, https://www.scmp.com/news/china/military/article/3031145/china-rolls-out-new-weapon-systems-nuclear-capable-missiles.

53 Robert P. Ashley, "Russian and Chinese Nuclear Modernization Trends: Remarks at the Hudson Institute" (US Defense Intelligence Agency, Washington DC, May 29, 2019), https://www.dia.mil/News/Speeches-and-Testimonies/Article-View/Article/1859890/russian-and-chinese-

nuclear-modernization-trends; Gregory Kulacki, "China's Nuclear Arsenal: No 'Sprint to Parity' (2011)," Union of Concerned Scientists, May 2011, https://www.ucsusa.org/sites/default/files/legacy/assets/documents/nwgs/UCS-Chinese-nuclear-modernization.pdf.

54 Office of the Secretary of Defense, "Military and Security Developments Involving the People's Republic of China, 2021," 90; Office of the Secretary of Defense, "Annual Report to Congress: Military and Security Developments Involving the People's Republic of China 2019" (US Department of Defense, Washington DC, May 3, 2019), 67, https://media.defense.gov/2019/May/02/2002127082/-1/-1/1/2019_CHINA_MILITARY_POWER_ REPORT.pdf.

55 Kulacki, "China Holds Firm on No First Use of Nuclear Weapons," Union of Concerned Scientists, July 24, 2019, https://allthingsnuclear.org/gkulacki/china-holds-firm-on-no-first-use-of-nuclear-weapons.

56 Kulacki, "China's Military Calls for Putting Its Nuclear Forces on Alert," Union of Concerned Scientists, January 2016, https://www.ucsusa.org/sites/default/files/attach/2016/02/China-Hair-Trigger-full-report.pdf.

57 Kulacki, "China's Military Calls for Putting Its Nuclear Forces on Alert"; Original Source in Academy of Military Sciences ed., 战略学 [*The Science of Military Strategy*], (Beijing: Military Science Publishers, 2013), https://fas.org/nuke/guide/china/sms-2013.pdf.

58 Heginbotham, et. al., "China's Evolving Nuclear Deterrent: Major Drivers and Issues for the United States."

59 Saalman, "Fear of False Negatives: AI and China's Nuclear Posture."

60 Kulacki, "China's Military Calls for Putting Its Nuclear Forces on Alert."

61 Adam Cabot, "What Threat Do China's New Missile Silos Pose to the US?" *The Diplomat*, July 16, 2021, https://thediplomat.com/2021/07/what-threat-do-chinas-new-missile-silos-pose-to-the-us.

62 Panda, "China's Dual-Capable Missiles: A Dangerous Feature, Not a Bug," *The Diplomat*, May 13, 2020, https://thediplomat.com/2020/05/chinas-dual-capable-missiles-a-dangerous-feature-not-a-bug; James M. Acton ed., *Entanglement: Chinese and Russian Perspectives on Non-Nuclear Weapons and Nuclear Risks* (Washington, DC: Carnegie Endowment for International Peace, 2017), https://carnegieendowment.org/files/Entanglement_interior_FNL.pdf; Lora Saalman, "China: Lines Blur Between Nuclear and Conventional Warfighting," *The Interpreter*, Lowy Institute, December 19, 2014, https://www.lowyinstitute.org/the-interpreter/china-lines-blur-between-nuclear-and-conventional-warfighting.

63 Office of the Secretary of Defense, "Military and Security Developments Involving the People's Republic of China, 2021," VII, 61; Trevithick, "Four of the Biggest Revelations from China's Massive 70th Anniversary Military Parade"; Chan and Liu, "China Rolls Out New Weapon Systems, Nuclear-Capable Missiles in Military Parade."

64 Kristensen and Korda, "Chinese Nuclear Forces, 2019."

65 James M. Acton, "Escalation through Entanglement: How the Vulnerability of Command-and-Control Systems Raises the Risks of an Inadvertent

Nuclear War," *International Security* 43, no 1 (Summer 2018): 56–99, https://www.mitpressjournals.org/doi/full/10.1162/isec_a_00320; Acton ed., *Entanglement: Chinese and Russian Perspectives on Non-Nuclear Weapons and Nuclear Risks*.

66 上海市人民政府新闻办公室 [Shanghai Municipal People's Government Press Office], "上海举行推动新一代人工智能发展《实施意见》发布会" [Shanghai Holds a Press Conference to Promote the Development of a New Generation of Artificial Intelligence], November 14, 2017, http://www.scio.gov.cn/xwfbh/gssxwfbh/xwfbh/shanghai/Document/1606039/1606039.htm.

67 Saalman, "China's Evolution on Ballistic Missile Defense" (Proliferation Analysis, Carnegie Endowment for International Peace, Washington DC, August 23, 2012), http://carnegieendowment.org/2012/08/23/china-s-evolution-on-ballistic-missile-defense/dkpl.

68 Panda, "Introducing the DF-17: China's Newly Tested Ballistic Missile Armed with a Hypersonic Glide Vehicle."

69 Paul Bernstein and Dain Hancock, "China's Hypersonic Weapons," *Georgetown Journal of International Affairs*, January 27, 2021, https://gjia.georgetown.edu/2021/01/27/chinas-hypersonic-weapons; Minnie Chan, "China Fires Up Advanced Hypersonic Missile Challenge to US Defences," *South China Morning Post*, January 1, 2018, https://www.scmp.com/news/china/diplomacy-defence/article/2126420/china-fires-advanced-hypersonic-missile-challenge-us.

70 Stephen Chen, "Chinese scientists build weapon that can cause satellites to explode," *South China Morning Post*, October 21, 2021, https://www.scmp.com/news/china/military/article/3153174/chinese-scientists-build-anti-satellite-weapon-can-cause; Demetri Sevastopulo and Kathrin Hille, "China tests new space capability with hypersonic missile," *Financial Times*, October 16, 2021, https://www.ft.com/content/ba0a3cde-719b-4040-93cb-a486e1f843fb.

71 Saalman, "Fear of False Negatives: AI and China's Nuclear Posture."

72 Paulina Glass, "China's Robot Subs Will Lean Heavily on AI: Report," *Defense One*, July 23, 2018, https://www.defenseone.com/technology/2018/07/chinas-robot-subs-will-lean-heavily-ai-report/149959; Stephen Chen, "China Military Develops Robotic Submarines to Launch a New Era of Sea Power,' *South China Morning Post*, July 22, 2018, https://www.scmp.com/news/china/society/article/2156361/china-developing-unmanned-ai-submarines-launch-new-era-sea-power.

73 The Poseidon (Status-6) reportedly is an unmanned, nuclear-powered platform with intercontinental range, which has been undergoing sea trials. One of its missions is to serve as a delivery system for a nuclear payload. TASS Russia News Agency, "Key Stage of Poseidon Underwater Drone Trials Completed, Says Putin," TASS, February 2, 2019, http://tass.com/defense/1042975; Press TV, "Russia Begins Testing of 'Poseidon' Underwater Nuclear Drone," December 26, 2018, https://www.presstv.com/Detail/2018/12/26/584027/Russia-nuclear-drone-Poseidon-Putin-US.

74 Glass, "China's Robot Subs Will Lean Heavily on AI: Report."

75 Programmes on AI and autonomy receive ample government support through such funds as the Laboratory of National Defense Technology for Underwater Vehicles, the Project for National Key Laboratory of Underwater Information Processing and Control, the National Key Basic Research and Development Program, the China Aviation Science Foundation, the National Science and Technology Major Project, the National 973 Project, the National Key Laboratory Fund, the National 863 High-Tech Research and Development Program and the Ministry of Communications Applied Basic Research Project, among a number of others. Saalman, "China's AI-Enabled Offense: Hypersonic Glide Vehicles and Neural Networks," in *AI, China, Russia, and the Global Order: Technological, Political, Global, and Creative Perspectives*, ed. Nicholas Wright (Washington, DC: Air University Press, 2019), 162–167, https://www.airuniversity.af.edu/Portals/10/AUPress/Books/B_0161_WRIGHT_ARTIFICIAL_INTELLIGENCE_CHINA_RUSSIA_AND_THE_GLOBAL_ORDER.PDF; Saalman, "Factoring Russia into the U.S.–Chinese Equation on Hypersonic Glide Vehicles" (Insights on Peace and Security, no. 1, SIPRI, Stockholm, January 2017), https://www.sipri.org/sites/default/files/Factoring-Russia-into-U.S.-Chinese-equation-hypersonic-glide-vehicles.pdf.

76 Permanent Mission of the People's Republic of China to the United Nations and Other International Organisations in Switzerland, "Address by H.E. Yang Jiechi, Minister of Foreign Affairs of the People's Republic of China, at the Conference on Disarmament," August 12, 2009, http://www.china-un.ch/eng/hom/t578030.htm.

77 The White House, "Joint Statement of the Leaders of the Five Nuclear-Weapon States on Preventing Nuclear War and Avoiding Arms Races," January 3, 2022, https://www.whitehouse.gov/briefing-room/statements-releases/2022/01/03/p5-statement-on-preventing-nuclear-war-and-avoiding-arms-races.

78 Cuihong Cai, "The Shaping of Strategic Stability by Artificial Intelligence" in *The Impact of Artificial Intelligence on Strategic Stability and Nuclear Risk – Volume II: East Asian Perspectives*, ed. Lora Saalman, https://www.sipri.org/sites/default/files/2019-10/the_impact_of_artificial_intelligence_on_strategic_stability_and_nuclear_risk_volume_ii.pdf.

79 Liping Xia, "On the Evolution and Structure of China's Nuclear Strategy," *Journal of Contemporary Asia-Pacific Studies*, no 4 (April 2010): 113–127.

80 Ralph A. Cossa, et. al., "Reaching an Inflection Point? The Tenth China-US Dialogue on Strategic Nuclear Dynamics," (Issues and Insights, Pacific Forum, Beijing, China, December 2016), https://pacforum.org/wp-content/uploads/2016/09/161208_issuesinsights_vol16no20.pdf; Michael Glosney, Christopher Twomey, and Ryan Jacobs, "U.S.–China Strategic Dialogue Phase VII Report," Project on Advanced Systems and Concepts for Countering Weapons of Mass Destruction, May 2013, https://pdfs.semanticscholar.org/d2d3/bf46d7a673dcd5c92c11eca25e60aa8ac527.pdf; Michael O. Wheeler,

"Track 1.5/2 Security Dialogues with China: Nuclear Lessons Learned" (Institute for Defense Analysis, Alexandira, Virginia, September 2014), https://apps.dtic.mil/dtic/tr/fulltext/u2/a622481.pdf.

81 Office of the Spokesperson, "Joint Statement on the Outcomes of the U.S.–Russia Strategic Stability Dialogue in Geneva on September 30" (US Department of State, September 30, 2021), https://www.state.gov/joint-statement-on-the-outcomes-of-the-u-s-russia-strategic-stability-dialogue-in-geneva-on-september-30; The White House, "U.S.-Russia Presidential Joint Statement on Strategic Stability," June 16, 2021, https://www.whitehouse.gov/briefing-room/statements-releases/2021/06/16/u-s-russia-presidential-joint-statement-on-strategic-stability.

Chapter 15

CHINA'S NO-FIRST-USE POLICY AND THE PROSPECT OF THE GLOBAL NO-FIRST-USE TREATY—A CHINESE PERSPECTIVE

Zhong Ai

INTRODUCTION

China's NFU pledge has not only effectively helped it to deter nuclear attacks from other nuclear-armed states but also set China as a moderate nuclear-armed nation, which is beneficial for the strategic stability in the region. However, China's NFU has been consistently confronted with suspicions and challenges from other states, especially the USA. The USA appears to believe that China's NFU is an empty promise unless China can clarify some important ambiguities to enhance the credibility of its pledge. Besides, China's NFU pledge has been under challenge due to the development of the US non-nuclear high-precision weapons and its missile defence systems. At present, though a deliberate pre-emptive nuclear attack has become less likely, the risk of a nuclear war is growing due to the ongoing entanglement of nuclear and non-nuclear weapons. Against this backdrop, a GNFU Treaty would be desirable for China, but the USA's unwillingness to accept the mutual vulnerability with China makes China concerned about the credibility of its second-strike capability, which would discourage it to promote the establishment of the GNFU.

On 16 October 1964, China became the world's fifth nuclear-armed state after its first atomic device was successfully tested. The Chinese government announced that it would follow an NFU policy and desire a complete prohibition and thorough destruction of nuclear weapons. Unfortunately, it seems that China's NFU, without mentioning any caveat, has never been widely recognised and fully trusted by some other states, especially the USA. Since 2010, almost every Pentagon annual report to the Congress, speaking about the military and security developments involving the People's Republic of China, stated the ambiguities of China's NFU pledge. According to these reports, there are some ambiguities over the conditions under which China's NFU policy would apply: firstly, whether strikes on what China considers its territory, demonstration strikes or high-altitude bursts would constitute first use[1]; secondly, whether China might use nuclear weapons first if an enemy's conventional attack threatened China's nuclear forces and its command-and-control systems.[2]

Until now, there has been no indication that China is willing to attach caveats argued in the US annual report to its NFU doctrine. But some Chinese scholars, even though very few, suggest that China should revisit its unconditional NFU policy. For instance, Xia Liping suggests that if the US completes the worldwide deployment of the Conventional Prompt Global Strike (CPGS), one of the options China has to deal with is to revise its NFU doctrine: China could conduct a nuclear counterattack if its nuclear force is attacked by non-nuclear weapons.[3] Besides, one of the most prominent civilian nuclear expert Shen Dingli says, 'if China's conventional forces are devastated, if Taiwan takes the opportunity to declare *de jure* independence, it is inconceivable that China would allow its nuclear weapons to be destroyed by a precision attack of conventional munitions, rather than use them as a true means of deterrence'.[4] Similarly, according to Zhu Mingquan, the leading author of a Chinese government-sponsored book, *Deterrence and Stability: China–U.S. Nuclear Relationship*, China should adopt a flexible approach to the NFU policy that allows it the right to use nuclear weapons first when national security and unification face serious threats.[5]

CHINA'S DISTINCT NUCLEAR NARRATIVES

China has persisted in the policy of employing nuclear weapons only in self-defence and to deter nuclear attacks. It has been seeking assurance that the USA would not be the first to use nuclear weapons in a conflict with China, but the former's refusal to provide such assurance makes China feel that the USA is continuing to intimidate and contain China with its overwhelming nuclear weapons. As the American expert Gregory Kulacki says:

> talks between China and United States on the countries' respective nuclear programs are going nowhere and each side expresses frustration and disappointment with the other, like chickens talking with ducks, as the Chinese say ... after more than a decade of discussion, the two parties cannot seem to move past the first item on their agenda: declaratory policy.[6]

What made China's NFU unique is that it declared NFU much before it acquired credible second-strike capability. China's distinct strategic thoughts on nuclear weapons deserve serious engagement by other nuclear-armed states. There are ongoing discussions among Chinese scholars on identifying and directing various components of China's nuclear strategy.

External nuclear threats were the fundamental reason why China decided to manufacture nuclear weapons. By tracing Mao Tse-tung's nuclear thoughts and analysing the development of China's nuclear weapons, Li Bin concludes that China's nuclear strategy has been based on counter-nuclear coercion thought rather than the theory of minimum nuclear deterrence or limited nuclear deterrence.[7] Due to the influence of the nuclear taboo that discourages people from making the decision to carry out nuclear attacks, it is more practical to utilise nuclear weapons to coerce adversaries into submission. Mao Tse-tung's thoughts on nuclear weapons were to develop them to counter nuclear coercion or blackmail. In 1956, at an Enlarged Meeting of the Chinese Communist Party Central Committee Politburo, Mao said, 'not only are we going to have more airplanes and artillery, but also the atomic bomb; in today's world, if we don't want to be bullied, we have to have this thing'.[8]

Xia Liping presents a different interpretation: China's nuclear strategy has gradually evolved from counter-nuclear blackmail to a minimum deterrence strategy.[9] The core concept of counter-nuclear blackmail is a state with a tiny number of nuclear weapons and without effective second-strike capability formulates a comprehensive strategy to deal with nuclear blackmail mainly through conventional war. From 1964, when China exploded its first atomic device, to the mid-1980s, China had a counter-nuclear blackmail strategy and not a minimum deterrence strategy. This was because, in this period, China had very few nuclear weapons which were unable to deliver unacceptable damage after surviving the first nuclear strike.[10]

China's counter-nuclear blackmail strategy is essentially based on Mao Tse-tung's well-known strategic thoughts, *On Protracted War* and *People's War.* Mao's speech in 1938 *On the Protracted War* mainly discussed how weaker sides use asymmetric tactics such as guerrilla warfare to protract war into a stalemate until the will power, national power and fighting capability of the stronger side can't be maintained any longer.[11] In addition, on 23 October 1954, Mao met Prime Minister Jawaharlal Nehru in Beijing and expressed his views on the relationship between people and weapons: there is no fundamental difference between old weapons and atomic bombs; the ultimate factor deciding the outcome of the war will remain men who handle the weapon.[12]

Even though Li Bin and Xia Liping use different terms to interpret China's nuclear strategy, both the counter-nuclear coercion thought and counter-nuclear blackmail strategy are based on the 'existential deterrence' and 'first-strike uncertainty' of which the rationale is that the aggressor is not confident of a successfully disarming first strike. Specifically, China's adversaries would believe that China had nuclear retaliatory capability once it possessed the delivery vehicle and a degree of survivability, even the operability of the delivery vehicle and the survivability are merely possible.[13]

Of course, China is not satisfied with existential deterrence. Yao Yunzhu, the retired major general of the Chinese PLA, has said explicitly about the requirements of making China's nuclear arsenal a credible deterrent: 'China has to make it survivable to a first nuclear strike, even that strike is overwhelming and devastating.'[14] Similarly, Chinese scholar Wu Riqiang believes 'assured retaliation is an unshakable objective for Chinese leaders'.[15] China's first-strike uncertainty was substantially further enhanced with the successful launch of DF-21 in 1985; in 1988, China launched a carrier rocket from a nuclear submarine, which made it the fifth country to have sea-based capability. In the summer of 1995, the underground Great Wall Project was completed, which made China have a true, reliable second-strike capability.

THE CHALLENGES OF CHINA'S NFU PLEDGE

Since 1964, the core elements of China's nuclear policy have been consistently dominated by Mao Tse-tung's nuclear thinking but today, China's external environment has become more complicated. First, the USA's National Security Strategy that was released in 2017, China was labelled as one of the main challengers and 'revisionist' powers[16]; the 2018 Nuclear Posture Review (NPR) under the Trump Administration made a significant reversal from the 2010 NPR and designed a tailored strategy for China to prevent the limited use of Chinese nuclear capabilities.[17] Secondly, the technological advancement of space and cyber weapons, the development of US non-nuclear high-precision weapons and its missile defence systems complicated the US–China nuclear relationship, which has made it necessary for China to reassess its nuclear policy.

According to the theory of strategic stability, it is believed that the attempt to first use nuclear weapons could be deterred if the targeted state can conduct nuclear retaliation and inflict 'unacceptable' damage on the aggressor. In the Cold War, the then secretary of defence Robert McNamara defined the level of destruction of 'unacceptable' damage as the capability to destroy one-third of the Soviet population and one-half of its industry.[18] China didn't have second-strike capability until the mid-1980s, and even today, China's nuclear retaliatory capability is far less than the requirement of the so-called unacceptable damage. However, it would be inappropriate to use the McNamara criterion to assess the credibility of China's second-strike capability. China has its own understanding of nuclear deterrence: after surviving a first strike and penetrating the missile defence system, even a handful of nuclear weapons would be sufficient to deter adversaries from attacking China.[19]

Given the immense disproportionality of the size of nuclear forces between China and the USA, there is no need for China to achieve parity with US nuclear forces. What China needs to do is guarantee the credibility of its nuclear retaliatory capability to eliminate the aggressor's motivation to conduct a pre-emptive nuclear strike.[20] However, in the American strategic community, there are ongoing debates about whether China's nuclear retaliatory capability is credible enough for the USA to admit the mutual vulnerability. Some American strategists believe China has some nuclear retaliatory capability but this capability would not be enough to cause 'unacceptable' damage to the USA.[21] For instance, in case of a US first strike, there are discussions about the prospect of preserving US damage limitation capability against China's strategic nuclear force, which could significantly reduce the damage that China could inflict against the USA in a second strike.[22] Thus, the USA's unwillingness to accept mutual vulnerability with China might compel China to re-evaluate its NFU pledge.

The Science of Military Strategy (the third edition) published in 2013 by the PLA Academy of Military Sciences (AMS) offers some noteworthy propositions about China's nuclear deterrence, which includes:

1. Considering the big gap between China's nuclear force and that of other great nuclear powers in terms of size and technology, China should maintain a moderate degree of ambiguity, allowing an adversary to guess China's nuclear capability and the timing of China's second strike, which increases the difficulty for adversary's decision-making.[23]
2. When conditions are satisfied and when necessary, China can, after confirming the adversary has launched a nuclear attack against us, conduct counter-strike before adversaries' incoming nuclear weapons have reached their targets and exploded.[24]

These two propositions discuss that China could allow ambiguity over the timing of its second-strike capability and imply that it needs a 'launch under attack' capability so that to enhance its nuclear retaliatory capability. This discussion offers a clue from which we can explore the challenge of China's NFU.

As a consequence of the nuclear thinking adopted by Mao Tse-tung and the first generation of Chinese communist leaders, China's nuclear weapons will only be used for retaliation after China was attacked first by nuclear weapons. In addition, China currently possesses a comparatively small number of nuclear weapons, which are kept off alert, that is, the warheads are separated from the missiles.[25] As such, China has always been prioritising the survivability of its nuclear forces over the alert level and size. The US nuclear policy is one of the most important external factors urging China to rethink its NFU, and the development of the US high-precision non-nuclear weapons and missile defence systems has been increasingly calling into question China's capability to launch a credible nuclear retaliatory strike. At the same time, with the global trend of progressive reduction in the number of nuclear weapons, instead of increasing the size of China's nuclear arsenal, one of the options China has to ensure the survivability of its nuclear forces is to raise the early-warning capability.

Even though there is no indication to suggest China is planning to move towards a 'launch-under-attack' posture, this discussion about raising the alert level of China's nuclear forces should make people start to notice the escalatory risks, especially in the context of nuclear entanglement.

There are several dimensions of entanglement, including the dual-use command, control, communication and intelligence (C3I), which provides warning for both conventional ballistic missiles and nuclear attack; the co-location of nuclear and non-nuclear forces and the dual-use weapons that accommodate either conventional or nuclear warheads. The entanglement of nuclear weapons with non-nuclear weapons has been exacerbating the risk of inadvertent escalation. In the event of a conventional conflict between China and the US, the latter might attack China's dual-use C3I to gain initiative of war, but China may misunderstand this strike as a sign of attack against its nuclear assets, which could lead to an inadvertent escalation.[26]

In recent years, China has begun to pay more attention to the entanglement. Yet, so far, the debate about the danger of entanglement hasn't drawn enough attention in China. Li Bin and Tong Zhao, who led the research about the entanglement in China, point out there are two main reasons why the risk of entanglement has not been widely realised and debated.[27] Firstly, Chinese traditional military thinking has not conducted an in-depth discussion about inadvertent escalation. Instead, influenced by Mao Tse-tung's military thinking, China's security policy, to some extent, has been emphasising the importance of creating uncertainty to confuse the enemy. For instance, in 1938, Mao said, '.... creating misconceptions among the enemy and springing surprise attacks on him—mean transferring the uncertainties of war to the enemy while securing the greatest possible certainty for ourselves and thereby gaining superiority, the initiative and victory'.[28] Secondly, unlike the US and the Soviet Union, which had been involved in a lot of nuclear crises, China has had little direct experience in dealing with nuclear crises since it acquired nuclear weapons in 1964. As such, the lack of experience with managing nuclear crises has contributed to the insufficiency and reduced interest in studying how to avoid inadvertent escalation.[29]

There are some studies by Western academics that express concerns about the co-mingling of Chinese conventional and nuclear assets. For instance, given the co-location of the command and control system, it is highly likely that any attack on the conventional forces command and control system would be recognised as an attack on the nuclear forces command and control system.[30] In addition, there is some literature suggesting that China's conventional and nuclear missiles are 'operationally and geographically entangled', which exacerbates the inadvertent escalation.[31] According to Fiona S. Cunningham and M. Taylor Fravel, who interviewed several Chinese military and civilian experts working on China's nuclear strategy, most Chinese experts are more optimistic about the risk of entanglement than US experts,[32] because they believe that China's nuclear command and control infrastructures are separate from command and control facilities for conventional forces, and the open-source literature shows the majority of China's nuclear missiles are not co-located with conventional missiles.[33] Considering China's NFU pledge and the survivability of its limited nuclear forces, China has adopted very limited nuclear transparency. There is hardly any Chinese literature and publicly available documents about the specific arrangements and deployments of China's nuclear forces. It is, therefore, currently difficult to assess the risk of the entanglement of Chinese conventional and nuclear forces.

THE PROSPECT OF THE GLOBAL NO FIRST USE AGREEMENT

The NFU pledge has been widely viewed as an important first step towards complete nuclear disarmament. On the same day that China conducted its first nuclear test and declared NFU, its government also proposed the convening of a summit conference to world governments to discuss the complete prohibition and thorough destruction of nuclear weapons, and as the first step, this summit conference should reach an agreement that 'nuclear powers and those countries which will soon become nuclear powers undertake not to use nuclear weapons, neither to use them against non-nuclear countries and nuclear-free zones, nor each other'.[34] In 1995, China further declared 'not to use or threaten to use nuclear weapons against non-nuclear weapon states or nuclear-weapon-free zones under any circumstance'.[35] Even though this summit conference never convened, after the Cold War, China continued to promote the mutually agreed NFU commitment with other nuclear weapon states (NWS).

Today, although the deliberate first use of nuclear weapons has become much less likely, the risk of nuclear war due to nuclear entanglement has become more prominent. Considering the risk of entanglement has not been widely recognised, the establishment of GNFU would help mitigate the risk of inadvertent escalation. It had been expected that then US president Barack Obama would adopt NFU as his political legacy. Unfortunately, it failed due to the unwillingness of the Pentagon and its allies. What made things worse was the shift of the US nuclear policy under President Trump, who advocated more scenarios in which nuclear weapons might be used. In the backdrop of the growing US–China tension, on the one hand, China's nuclear weapons have been gradually exposed to the USA's advanced non-nuclear weapons and on the other hand, China has been increasingly concerned about the development of US capability to counteract China's second-strike capability.

Therefore, in an uncertain future, if mature capabilities of non-nuclear high-precision weapons and missile defence systems become available, in the face of a high-stakes conflict, China might be forced to downplay the NFU by introducing ambiguity over its NFU pledge. For instance, China might, without renouncing its NFU officially, send a signal that it needs to revise its nuclear policy if its second-strike capability is in doubt. In this case, China would be unwilling to actively promote the establishment of GNFU.

CONCLUSION

The NFU pledge has been one of the cornerstones of China's nuclear policy. With the revolution of military technology, the line between nuclear and conventional weapons has become blurry. Furthermore, considering China's limited nuclear retaliatory capability, its NFU policy has been under unprecedented pressure. Therefore, in the foreseeable future, China does not seem to be in a position to clarify any ambiguity and/or add caveats to its NFU pledge. China could allow some ambiguities over its NFU so that to undercut potential adversaries' confidence in initiating a conventional intervene on China's nuclear installations.

With the expansion of China's national interests, the country has been increasingly involved in international conflicts. Considering the importance of nuclear deterrence in safeguarding national security and unification[36] and US damage limitation capability to decrease China's second-strike capability, although China would be continuing to adhere to its NFU pledge, the willingness to promote the GNFU might be discouraged by US reluctance to acknowledge the mutual vulnerability in bilateral nuclear dialogue.

NOTES

1 Pentagon, "Annual Report to Congress: Military and Security Development Involving the People's Republic of China 2013," (Pentagon, Washington DC), accessed December 31, 2018, http://www.andrewerickson.com/wp-content/uploads/2015/11/DoD_China-Report_2013.pdf.

2 "Annual Report to Congress: Military and Security Development Involving the People's Republic of China 2018," (Pentagon, Washington DC, 2018), 76, accessed on November 21, 2018, https://media.defense.gov/2018/Aug/16/2001955282/-1/-1/1/2018-CHINA-MILITARY-POWER-REPORT.PDF.

3 Xia Liping, (夏 立 平), "US Conventional Prompt Global Strike Plan Under the Perspective of High Frontiers Theory," ("高边疆" 理论视阈下美国全球快速常规打击计划"), *International Review* (国际观察), no 5 (2014): 12.

4 Shen Dingli, (沈丁立) "Nuclear Deterrence in the 21st Century", *Defense & Security Analysis* 21, no 4 (2005): 424.

5 Zhu Mingquan (朱明权), "China–U.S. Nuclear Relationship" ("中美核关系"), in *Deterrence and Stability: China–U.S. Nuclear Relationship* (威慑与稳定：中美核关系), eds Zhu Mingquan, Wu Chunsi, and Su Changhe (朱明权，吴莼思，苏长和), (Beijing: Current Affairs Press, 2005), 212.

6 Gregory Kulacki, "Chickens Talking With Ducks: The U.S.–Chinese Nuclear Dialogue," Arms Control Association, September 30, 2011, accessed on November 6, 2018, https://www.armscontrol.org/act/2011_10/U.S._Chinese_Nuclear_Dialogue#1.

7 Li Bin,（李彬） "Identifying China's Nuclear Strategy," *World Economics and Politics,* no 6 (2006): 16–22.

8 《毛泽东与中国原子能事业》（*Mao Tse-tung and China Atomic Energy* (Beijing: Atomic Energy Press, 1993): 8–9.

9 Liping, "On the Structure and Evolution of China's Nuclear Strategy", *Journal of Contemporary Asia-Pacific Studies,* no 4 (2010): 113.

10 Liping, "On the Structure and Evolution of China's Nuclear Strategy," 116.

11 Mao Tse-tung, "On Protracted War," *Selected Works of Mao Tse-tung* (Vol II), (Oxford: Pergamon Press, 1965), accessed on January 8, 2020 https://www.marxists.org/reference/archive/mao/selected-works/volume-2/.

12 Digital Archives, "Minutes of Chairman Mao Tse-tung's Second Meeting with Nehru," (Wilson Center, Washington DC, 1954), accessed on October 10, 2019, https://digitalarchive.wilsoncenter.org/document/117815.

13 Wu Riqiang, "Certainty of Uncertainty: Nuclear Strategy with Chinese Characteristics," (Program on Strategic Stability Evaluation, Georgia Institute of Technology, Atlanta, 2011), 3.

14 Yao Yunzhu, "Chinese Nuclear Policy and the Future of Minimum Deterrence," *Strategic Insights* 4, no 9 (Center for Contemporary Conflict, Naval Posgraduate School, Monterey, California, September 2005).

15 Riqiang, "Certainty of Uncertainty: Nuclear Strategy with Chinese Characteristics," 6.

16 The White House, "National Security Strategy of the United States of America," (The White House, Washington DC, December 2017), accessed on July 24, 2022, https://trumpwhitehouse.archives.gov/wp-content/uploads/2017/12/NSS-Final-12-18-2017-0905.pdf.

17 US Department of Defense, "Nuclear Posture Review," (US Department of Defense, Washington DC, February 2018), 31, accessed on July 24, 2022, https://media.defense.gov/2018/Feb/02/2001872886/-1/-1/1/2018-NUCLEAR-POSTURE-REVIEW-FINAL-REPORT.PDF

18 Robert McNamara, "'Mutual Deterrence': Speech by Secretary of Defense Robert McNamara" (San Francisco, September 18, 1967), accessed on January 5, 2020, http://www.atomicarchive.com/Docs/Deterrence/Deterrence. shtml.

19 Li Bin and Hu Gaochen (李彬 & 胡高辰),"U.S. Understanding about the Credibility of China's Nuclear Deterrence," ("美国视阈中的中国核威慑有效性"), *Foreign Affairs* (外交评论), no 5 (2018): 25.

20 ZouZhiboandLiuWei(邹治波&刘玮), "ConstructingtheSino-USNuclear Strategic Stability Framework: An Asymmetric Strategic Balance Approach," ("构建中美核战略稳定性框架：非对称性战略平衡的视角"), *Journal of International Security Studies* (国际安全研究) 37, no 1 (2019): 59.

21 Bin and Gaochen, "U.S. Understanding about the Credibility of China's Nuclear Deterrence", 35–37.

22 Charles L. Glaser, "Forgoing U.S. Damage Limitation against China's Nuclear Weapons," Belfer Center for Science and International Affairs, August 2016, accessed on January 18, 2020, https://www.belfercenter.org/publication/forgoing-us-damage-limitation-against-chinas-nuclear-weapons.

23 Shou Xiaosong (寿晓松) et al., ed., *The Science of Military Science*（战略学）(Beijing: Military Science Publishing House, 2013), 173.

24 Xiaosong et. al., *The Science of Military Science*, 175.

25 "Armaments, Disarmament and International Security" (*SIPRI Yearbook 2019*, Stockholm, 2019), 11, accessed on December 26, 2019, https://www.sipri.org/sites/default/files/2019-08/yb19_summary_eng_1.pdf.

26 James M. Acton, Tong Zhao, and Li Bin, "Reducing the Risk of Nuclear Entanglement" (Carnegie Endowment For International Peace, Washington DC, September 12, 2018), accessed on January 5, 2020, https://carnegieendowment.org/2018/09/12/reducing-risks-of-nuclear-entanglement-pub-77236.

27 Tong Zhao and Li Bin, "The Underappreciated Risks of Entanglement: A Chinese Perspective," in *Entanglement: Russian and Chinese Perspectives on Non-Nuclear Weapons and Nuclear Risks,* eds James M. Acton et. al. (Washington DC: Carnegie Endowment for International Peace, 2017), 49.

28 Mao Tse-tung, *Selected Works of Mao Tse-tung* (Vol. II), (Oxford: Pergamon Press, 1965), 166.

29 Zhao and Bin, "The Underappreciated Risks of Entanglement: A Chinese Perspective," 50.

30 John W. Lewis and Xue Litai, "Making China's Nuclear War Plan," *Bulletin of the Atomic Scientists* 68, no 5 (2012): 53, 61.

31 David Cromer Logan, "Drawing a Line between Conventional and Nuclear Weapons in China," *Bulletin of the Atomic Scientists,* no 5 (2015), accessed on January 6, 2020, https://thebulletin.org/2015/05/drawing-a-line-between-conventional-and-nuclear-weapons-in-china/.

32 Fiona S. Cunningham and M. Taylor Fravel, "Assuring Assured Retaliation: China's Nuclear Posture and U.S.–China Strategic Stability," *International Security* 40, no 2 (2015): 34.

33 Cunningham and Fravel, "Assuring Assured Retaliation: China's Nuclear Posture and U.S.–China Strategic Stability," 42.

34 Digital Archives, "*People's Daily*, 'Statement by the People's Republic of China on 16 October 1964'" (Wilson Center, Washington DC), accessed on January 13, 2019, http://large.stanford.edu/courses/2018/ph241/shan1/docs/prc-16oct64.pdf.

35 United Nations, "Letter Dated 6 April 1995 from the Permanent Representative of China to the United Nations Addressed to the Secretary-General" (UN Document A/50/155, New York, April 6, 1995), accessed on January 8, 2020, https://undocs.org/pdf?symbol=en/A/50/155.

36 'Nuclear capability is the strategic cornerstone to safeguarding national sovereignty and security.' White Paper, China's National Defense in the New Era (The State Council Information Office, People's Republic of China, July 2019), accessed on January 14, 2022, http://www.gov.cn/zhengce/2019-07/24/content_5414325.htm.

Chapter 16

THE DESIRABILITY AND FEASIBILITY OF GLOBAL NO FIRST USE—AN INDIAN PERSPECTIVE

Manpreet Sethi

As few as two military detonations of nuclear weapons amply demonstrated the destructive power of the nuclear weapon in 1945. The horror of immediate death, plus the lingering radioactivity impacting human and environmental life for generations, triggered considerable thinking on how best to integrate the new weapon into military strategy. The dilemma of how to effectively use it has since persisted. The predominant understanding is that it is a weapon of deterrence. But how should one deter? What kind of a threat makes for a better and more credible deterrence strategy? Is a threat that does not shy away from using the weapon 'deliberately, immediately and unhesitatingly'[1] in the event of a military conflict more effective? Or, does the threat of nuclear retaliation seem more credible? These questions have preoccupied every nuclear weapons possessor. In seventy years of the existence of the nuclear weapon, the questions yet remain unsettled. Today, seven countries profess a first-use doctrine and two have declared an NFU doctrine.

China and India are the only two of the nine nuclear-armed nations that have publicly declared a national NFU doctrine and who advocate a GNFU as one meaningful way to move towards universal nuclear disarmament. As it stands though, neither of these countries has made the effort to explain why it considers this strategy desirable and feasible for themselves and for others. They have shied away from explaining the 'strategic logic'[2] of NFU or what in their understanding of nuclear weapons is different to enable them to buck the more prevalent trend of nuclear first use. Owing to the absence of an effort on their part to popularise, or at least to explain their position, there has been a general tendency to be dismissive of their doctrines as merely political declarations of little military significance.

The objective of this chapter is to examine the desirability and feasibility of NFU at the national and global levels. It explains why NFU is not just globally desirable for moral and ethical reasons but that it is also militarily feasible at the national level as a credible deterrence strategy. Questioning the assumptions of first-use strategies, this chapter establishes the value of NFU for a meaningful and credible deterrence, especially in the face of the contemporary reality where all nuclear dyads possess secure second-strike capabilities. In fact, as several emerging technologies begin to intersect with nuclear deterrence in new ways, it may even be necessary to adopt NFU positions to address the growing risks of stumbling into a nuclear war. The chapter, therefore, argues that a global acceptance of NFU could significantly minimise the risk of unwanted and inadvertent nuclear escalation. Moreover, in the currently crystallising post-arms-control world, a GNFU would bring down the salience of nuclear weapons by making them unusable. This would help in promoting sustainable non-proliferation and eventual disarmament.

The chapter is broadly divided into five sections. The first of these establishes the desirability of GNFU in the face of contemporary threats and as a meaningful nuclear-risk-reduction measure. It casts a look at some of the emerging technologies that will make first-use postures increasingly dangerous, and, in fact, push countries towards de facto NFU positions even if they opt not to openly declare them. The second section explores the reasons proffered by predominant nuclear doctrines for first use and suggests some ideas on how to wean them away. The third section explains the military logic of NFU, which also exposes first-use doctrines as being materially demanding, politically difficult and militarily foolish to execute. The fourth section takes a closer look at why NFU makes for a sound doctrine for India. The last section concludes that a GNFU offers several advantages for international security and strategic stability.

DESIRABILITY OF A GNFU

At this moment, none of the nuclear weapons possessors appears ready to give up nuclear arsenals. The role of nuclear weapons seems to be expanding beyond the basic or sole purpose of nuclear deterrence. A few countries like North Korea and Pakistan have shown the multi-role utility of these weapons as 'strategic equalizers' to superior conventional forces and useful bargaining chips for economic aid. The latest US Nuclear Posture Review of 2018 expands the role of nuclear weapons to include deterrence of large-scale conventional and cyberattacks besides even those of US space assets. Actions such as these tend to add value to nuclear weapons. As this impression gains further ground, non-proliferation can never hope to be a sustainable proposition.

In the contemporary world order then, evident trends include a growing reliance on nuclear weapons to meet many objectives; increasing advancements in nuclear capabilities; a fast-crumbling nuclear arms-control architecture and sentiment; and the emergence of new technologies impacting possibilities of nuclear use.[3] The last issue deserves a careful look. Development of new capabilities of cyberattacks, the blurring of lines between conventional and nuclear missiles, induction of hypersonic missiles that offer attributes of high speed and manoeuvrability, incorporation of AI and machine learning in nuclear decision-making are all likely to seriously impact nuclear deterrence in ways that are not adequately understood yet. The purpose of all these capabilities is obviously to enhance nuclear deterrence. For instance, dual-use capabilities are meant to complicate the adversary's decision-making; hypersonic missiles are meant to signal an ability to defeat missile defences; the use of AI and machine learning is meant to accelerate nuclear decision-making to bring in an assured automaticity of response.

The downside of these technologies, however, will be to raise instability during crises when each adversary is bound to believe the worst and act accordingly. This would take nations into risks of nuclear collisions due to misperceptions and miscalculations and even unauthorised launches in cases where there is delegated command and control.

None of the nuclear dyads seems inclined to actively address these threats through any confidence-building or risk-reduction measures. In fact, there does not even appear to be a common understanding of the risks, nor a willingness, to control the technological advances that may lead to the creation of new security dilemmas. However, in moments of actual crisis when facing threats that emerging technologies would inevitably bring, nations might opt for one of two possible responses—in a best-case response, one could wait out an attack to determine if it is nuclear before retaliating. Therefore, even nations professing first-use nuclear postures might, de facto, lean towards NFU to ensure crisis stability; a more dangerous response, however, could be to resort to launch-on-warning or launch under attack believing the worst and hence triggering a nuclear exchange.

Given this reality, and for the sake of international security and global stability, measures that reduce the chance of inadvertent nuclear use are urgent and imperative. Attaining a GNFU could be one significant step in this direction. If every country was to commit not to be the first to use the weapon, there would be no nuclear use, and such commitments would be especially helpful during times of crisis. This has been the experience, for instance, of crises between India and China when even during military hostilities, the threat of nuclear use is never palpable.

A GNFU would also lead to a drop in the stock value of the weapon over a period of time. In turn, this would encourage non-proliferation by sending a strong signal of the diminishing utility of the weapon and also lessen the drive of each nuclear-armed state for new and modernised nuclear arsenals. Rather, as the weapons fall into a state of disuse, they would lose their salience and hence become dispensable, aiding the move towards their eventual elimination. The question, however, is how to get all nuclear possessors to agree to NFU? The following section examines the arguments of countries that profess a preference for first use doctrines.

WHY DO COUNTRIES PREFER FIRST USE?

As it currently stands, seven of the nine nuclear-armed states have retained the option of first use of nuclear weapons. Three reasons—inferiority in conventional capability, a threat to the existence of a nation and extended deterrence commitments—are normally cited as justifications for projection of first-use doctrines. These factors need to be understood and addressed if GNFU is to become possible.

It is generally assumed that countries that are conventionally weaker than their adversary (such as Pakistan vis-à-vis India or NATO vis-à-vis Russia) or those that face existential threats (such as Israel) cannot accept NFU strategies. Surprisingly, China vis-à-vis the USA and India vis-à-vis China have not subscribed to this logic.[4] But, for the others, nuclear deterrence is premised on the idea of suggesting immediate use of nuclear weapons when faced with the possibility of being overwhelmed by the adversary's conventional superiority. Ironically, even though weaker nations may realise that it would never be rational for them to use nuclear weapons first given the inevitability of nuclear retaliation that would follow, they nevertheless believe in the need to project such a threat. It is also paradoxical that countries perceiving a threat to their very existence should find it prudent to threaten to use a weapon for the sake of their survival when the use of that weapon is sure to bring about annihilation.

While these assumptions are not easy to dislodge, they would nevertheless have to be addressed if GNFU is ever to become a reality. Insecurities of nations will need to be adequately assuaged and these may be attempted at three levels:

1. By exposing the folly of first use of nuclear weapons: If the first use of nuclear weapons is expected to make matters worse for a country that faces an adversary that has assured retaliation capabilities, such

use should actually be an unproductive step. How could it then be credible to threaten such use? A country that has already suffered conventional losses would only end up compounding them into nuclear losses and making matters worse for itself if it uses nuclear weapons without being able to make it a disarming or a decapitating strike. The first use of nuclear weapons has never been attempted, despite so many countries professing such a posture, because it is not a credible or useful strategy. Arguments that make the case for first use for weaker nations do so to derive the purportedly greater benefit of deterrence through the projection of use. But it misses the point that the credibility of action lies at the heart of nuclear deterrence.

2. By emphasising that accepting NFU would not mean giving up nuclear arsenals: Given that countries believe that they derive security insurance from nuclear weapons, renunciation of this capability is resisted. But the NFU would allow countries to retain their nuclear stockpiles while only having to commit to not using them first. This would allow them to maintain the notional sense of security as derived from the existence of nuclear weapons.
3. By finding ways of offering security assurances: Conventional asymmetry is one of the justifications for first-use postures. It would be worthwhile to find positive incentives that can address these concerns. It may be recalled that the negotiation and conclusion of the Conventional Forces in Europe Treaty played a major role in addressing the US–Soviet Union threat perceptions and enabled confidence building. Can similar arrangements be worked out in the case of the USA and China or Pakistan and India while also catering for India's threat perception from China? The proposition appears to be extremely complicated but such solutions will need to be explored to enable the acceptance of NFU.

Another reason for countries like the USA to not accept NFU is their commitment of extended deterrence. The American promise to its allies to protect them from the possibility of nuclear use by an adversary rests on the suggestion of first use of nuclear weapons against a conventional attack. The allies, therefore, resist the US abandonment of the idea of nuclear first use since they fear conventional attacks. Such sentiments were expressed when President Obama's Prague speech mentioned the possibility of the USA moving towards NFU.

If the USA can convince its allies that its conventional superiority is so far ahead of any of its adversaries that it does not need nuclear weapons to protect them, a move towards NFU may be possible.

In fact, the US ability to use its conventional capability would be higher than ever being able to use its nuclear weapons in defence of its allies. Therefore, conventional extended deterrence should be more usable and hence more credible. But, this will call for a change of mindset in the USA and its allies.

Lastly, it is argued that extended deterrence was also a measure of nuclear non-proliferation. The USA offered the nuclear umbrella in order to stop countries from acquiring nuclear weapons of their own. Hence, it is now feared that any tampering with the pledge could push nations towards building their own nuclear weapons. This argument, however, misses the point that in case the nuclear umbrella shifts to a conventional umbrella with the realisation of a GNFU, then why would nations want to acquire an unusable weapon? A GNFU would drop the value of nuclear weapons and make them less useful and hence, less attractive.

UNDERSTANDING THE DILEMMAS OF NUCLEAR FIRST USE

As a matter of training, militaries tend to incline towards offensive strategies. They like to execute *their* plan during war. Offence allows the military to stay with its pre-deliberated course of action while denying the adversary the advantage of his being able to play out his moves. As argued by Barry Posen, 'A military organization prefers to fight its war and prevent its adversary from doing so....'[5] The follow-on belief is that an army fighting a war according to its plans is likely to do better than one that does not seize the initiative.

With conventional weapons, this may be a prudent approach. Armed forces can plan an operation based on a time and place of their choosing to disadvantage the enemy. But the situation does not remain as straightforward once nuclear weapons enter the equation. In a situation where there is no nuclear monopoly but the presence of secure second-strike capability on both sides, undertaking nuclear first use/strike would require arsenals of a very high material order (quantitatively and qualitatively). Conducting a first strike would be a politically difficult decision and militarily, a self-defeating step to execute. A nuclear first-use strategy suffers from serious handicaps. Using the nuclear weapon first and seizing the initiative does not assure victory to the first user when nuclear retaliation is sure to follow. And, given the destructive potential of the weapon, the first user would only end up bringing nuclear grief upon itself for generations to bear. The following paragraphs further unpack these dilemmas of nuclear first use.

Arsenal Burden of Nuclear First Use

A country that decides to introduce nuclear weapons into a conflict could do so in two ways. The first of these would be by using a small quantity of low-yield weapons to produce limited yield against battlefield targets. This 'first use' has been described as a strategy of escalate to de-escalate. It seeks to indicate the resolve to continue towards further nuclear escalation if the conventional offensive does not stop. The best hope of the first user in such a scenario would be that the adversary would back off, or that it would retaliate with nuclear use that would be proportionate. But it is by highlighting a readiness to get into such a situation that the first user seeks to deter a larger nuclear exchange.

The second scenario of first nuclear use would be to use the weapon in a 'first strike' mode to hit as much as possible of the adversary's nuclear capability in order to reduce the quantum of retaliation. But to do so effectively, the first user must have enough intelligence inputs on the location of the adversary's arsenal, a high level of missile accuracy to destroy the adversary's retaliatory capability and sufficient capability to defend oneself against the leftover incoming nuclear attack.

In both cases, the first user is seeking the first-user advantage. In the first scenario, he is hoping to *kill the adversary's resolve to fight* and in the second, he is hoping to *kill the adversary's capability to fight.* However, neither of these are easy objectives to achieve. They require a pretty demanding slew of capabilities—a large arsenal of first-strike weapons such as accurate missiles with real-time navigational aids to ensure high precision, multiple independently retargetable vehicles to carry out multiple hits, an extremely sophisticated intelligence, surveillance and reconnaissance (ISR) network to provide real-time information on the arsenal, an elaborate and delegated command and control to enable simultaneous nuclear use against dispersed forces and a high level of active and passive defence capabilities to handle nuclear retaliation. The acquisition and maintenance of such capabilities impose a heavy strain on technological sophistication and financial resources. And yet, despite the costly investment in acquiring such an arsenal, the attainment of the military objectives of first use/ strike could remain a chimaera. There could never be a guarantee that nuclear first use would not bring back a very high cost on the first user. Meanwhile, more worrisome is the fact that maintaining nuclear arsenals on high alert to make the first use posture credible considerably raises the possibility of accidental nuclear use based on miscalculation or inadvertence.

In contrast to a highly demanding nuclear arsenal for a credible first-use posture, NFU requirements can be *relatively* smaller and easier to meet. Firstly, it does not need building large or technically very sophisticated nuclear forces to comprehensively decimate the adversary's arsenal. The focus of an NFU arsenal needs to be on ensuring survivability of enough numbers to cause damage that an adversary would find unacceptable in comparison with the political objective being sought. The delivery systems need not be extremely accurate if they have to hit population centres. Elaborate ISR is not needed and survivability can be ensured through a mix of measures that include hardening of nuclear storage sites, deception, mobility and dispersal over delivery vectors. Of course, these are not inexpensive capabilities either. Nothing in the nuclear domain is. But it is the difference in quantitative and qualitative requirements that accounts for the relative ease of one over the other. At the same time, by virtue of the nature of the response that it promises, an NFU eliminates the need for forward deployment or pre-delegation of authority of nuclear systems. This reduces the likelihood of accidental or unauthorised use.

DIFFICULTY OF POLITICAL DECISION-MAKING ON NUCLEAR FIRST USE

In a situation where both sides have secure retaliatory capabilities, a nuclear first strike, however splendid it might be, cannot rule out the possibility of nuclear retaliation. As pointed out by George Perkovich, a well-known American nuclear analyst, 'The escalatory implications of first use are at least partly why no state has tried to use nuclear weapons against a state that could retaliate in kind.'[6] In this context, the Cuban missile crisis of 1962 holds out an important lesson. Archival material declassified recently[7] reveals the extent of US nuclear preponderance and the elaborate planning on a comprehensive targeting strategy to use nuclear weapons first at that time. Yet, when President Kennedy could not be given the guarantee by his generals that there would be no Soviet nuclear retaliation after US first use, he was not prepared to take the risk of unleashing a well-considered military strategy of nuclear first strike. He dismissed every option that could bring the USA to that brink and described such choices as 'a hell of an alternative'.[8] The crisis demonstrated that despite an offensive nuclear strategy, neither could victory be assured, nor the extent of damage—owing to the very nature of the weapon—be deemed acceptable.

This understanding makes it difficult to take the decision to use the nuclear weapon first even when nations have a first-use strategy. This is a thought worth considering since conventional wisdom will have us believe that first use is politically more liberating compared to NFU.

But serious thought to the actual execution of first use/strike reveals its myriad complexities. After all, the purpose of first use should be to convey deterrence through the communication of four messages[9]:

1. I will not hesitate to use the weapon first.
2. By doing so, I would be able to substantively improve my situation.
3. My first strike will interfere with and degrade your second-strike capability.
4. I will come out of the crisis looking better after the use of the nuclear weapon than without its use.

Such communication can carry weight in case of a nuclear monopoly. But in a situation where the adversary has a survivable nuclear force, retaliation seriously complicates the calculations of the first user on how it would 'look better' after suffering nuclear damage itself. As graphically explained by a strategist, 'Engaging in a nuclear war with a nation with whom one is in a condition of mutual vulnerability would be like running a red light across a high speed, heavily travelled, multilane highway under conditions of near-zero visibility. One might make it safely across, but one could not form a reasonable expectation that one would.'[10]

Therefore, the essential question that the first user has to ask, and answer, is whether in a state of mutual vulnerability, the initiator can be in a better position than the one who retaliates. If the answer to this is in the negative, then an NFU strategy that places the onus of escalation on the adversary becomes more liberating. The political leadership is freed from the psychological pressure of making the difficult choice of having to be the first to use a nuclear weapon. And to do so with the knowledge that not only is he inflicting death and destruction on the enemy but also laying his own population open to the same fate, besides breaching a long-standing norm of non-use of nuclear weapons. The weight of this political decision is not easy to carry.

Military Illogic of Nuclear First Use

It is often argued that a possessor of nuclear weapons is likely to be provoked into using the weapon if the country faces the prospect of conventional defeat. It would then be left with no option but to use the nuclear weapon. This sense of inevitability of a nuclear response, or sense of nuclear resignation, fails to assess how the conventionally down country would gain by using this weapon. Having used the nuclear weapon, its fate would shift from being defeated-now-but-living-to-fight-another-day to one of severe damage/annihilation, depending on the state of its geographical, material and human capacities. Jonathan Schell explained this dilemma well when he questioned, 'For how can it make sense to "save" one's country by blowing it to pieces? And what logic is there in staving off a limited defeat by bringing on unlimited, eternal defeat?'[11]

Secondly, it is often questioned why a country should stick to NFU once it gets to know that the adversary is preparing for a nuclear strike. Should not nuclear pre-emption then be the right step? The answer to this lies in understanding that even preparation is no guarantee of a nuclear strike. Rather, it may well be part of a strategy of 'coercive diplomacy'. It is not a coincidence that fifty incidents of the threat of use of nuclear weapons actually intended coercion.[12] Therefore, despite the apparent show of readiness, there is, more likely than not, still a chance that nuclear weapons would not come into use. But by striking first in the face of apparent readiness being seen on the other side, a country would certainly end up inviting retaliation.

Therefore, unlike the case of conventional weapons, the first use of nuclear weapons to inflict damage on the adversary will not really protect the state. Deterrence is, in fact, the only defence against nuclear weapons. And, the message of deterrence sounds more convincing and credible when the NFU doctrine signals that:

1. I will not be the first to use nuclear weapons.
2. But any first use against me would certainly trigger retaliation to cause damage of a kind that would be found unacceptable.
3. My counter-strike will ensure that your material situation is worse off after you use the weapon first.
4. I might suffer losses but you will not escape either and you would have brought it upon yourself.

In the face of such logic, the NFU appears far more militarily sensible and credible. While a country would find it very difficult to use the weapon first, the decision of retaliation would be far easier, seemingly legitimate and more guilt-free to make. In fact, by projecting assured retaliation, a nation displays greater confidence and hence, greater deterrence credibility. By placing the onus of escalation on the adversary, while retaining the initiative of punitive nuclear retaliation, the country with an NFU lessens the possibility of deterrence from breaking down and thus aims to minimise, if not prevent, the very use of the nuclear weapon. NFU encourages the possibility of 'no use' instead of 'sure use'.

Another dilemma of military significance that the NFU alleviates is the adversary's sense of insecurity about losing his nuclear arsenal, or a better part of it, to an adversary's first use. An adversary living under the constant fear of an imminent nuclear strike would be tempted to use his nuclear force first. NFU helps to mitigate this 'use or lose' pressure and thereby lessens crisis instability. Counterintuitive though it may sound, removing the adversary from the edge where he is ready to press the nuclear trigger can make them feel more secure, a condition that is conducive for deterrence stability. The logic of this was aptly explained by Robert McNamara, 'I had no desire to face, in a period of tension, an adversary who felt cornered, panicky and desperate and who might be tempted to move irrationally.'[13] NFU naturally provides this reassurance and it significantly reduces crisis instability.

NFU FOR INDIA—SANE DOCTRINE, SOUND LOGIC

India faces a unique set of nuclear challenges from two adversaries with whom it shares contested territories. Both also have different nuclear doctrines and capabilities and are in collusion with one another. Pakistan has an intelligent nuclear strategy of using its nuclear weapons to shield against the possibility of India's conventional offensive in response to its continued use of state-sponsored terrorism. As a matter of deterrence necessity, Rawalpindi signals first use of its nuclear weapons (including what it now describes as nuclear weapons of low yield to be used against battlefield targets) to stop India from undertaking *any* use of force against the country. Maintaining a first-use posture is an imperative for Pakistan and will remain so till the state does not abandon its use of terrorist organisations to bleed India.

New Delhi responds to this first-use posture with an NFU one of its own. India contends that its NFU stabilises the situation by leaving the onus of nuclear escalation to Rawalpindi. In case India too was to profess a first-use doctrine, it would considerably lower the nuclear threshold and raise the chance of nuclear war. Rejecting the idea that nuclear weapons are militarily efficacious, India has not felt the need to move to a first-use position and has created a situation of stability. The Table 16.1 below illustrates this reality.

Table 16.1: Relationship between National Nuclear Posture and Stability

Nuclear Posture Country 1	Nuclear Posture Country 2	Nuclear Threshold	Chance of Nuclear War
First Use	First Use	Low	Very High
No First Use	No First Use	High	Very Low/Nil
First Use	No First Use	Relatively High	Low

Source: Author

As is evident from the table, through NFU coupled with the assuredness of punitive retaliation, India has tried to minimise the possibility of the use of nuclear weapons. Unless the adversary is completely irrational, has suicidal tendencies or is utterly unmindful of national survival and international public opinion, the possibility of a deliberate nuclear war should not arise.

CONCLUSION

Challenging the current conventional wisdom that tends to favour nuclear first use as a militarily meaningful deterrent strategy, this chapter has established the value of NFU on three grounds—for national security, for strategic stability between nuclear dyads and for international security. The current nuclear cacophony of hyper-nationalism must not be allowed to drown out the sane logic of NFU. It may be pertinent to conclude this essay by recalling Thucydides, who noted centuries back that, as Victor Gilinsky puts it, 'in times of war reckless audacity was equated with courage and prudent hesitation with cowardice'.[14] Those were the days before catastrophic nuclear weapons had come into play. Now that they have, it is even more important to understand that the reckless audacity of first use would not spell courage and that NFU is not about passivity and weakness. Rather, it signals the strength of prudence and confidence. Even more importantly, it makes for a credible, militarily defensible national nuclear deterrence strategy that would also contribute to international security and stability. GNFU is desirable and feasible at both the national and global levels.

NOTES

1 These words were used by American diplomat and historian George Kenan. As cited in in Lawrence Freedman, *The Evolution of Nuclear Strategy*, Third Edition (New York: Palgrave Macmillan, 2003), 63.

2 Rajesh Rajagopalan, "The Strategic Logic of the No First Use Nuclear Doctrine", ORF Expert Speak, August 30, 2019, accessed on April 3, 2022, https://www.orfonline.org/expert-speak/strategic-logic-no-first-use-nuclear-doctrine-54911/.

3 Some of these dimensions are well explained in Rajaram Nagappa and N. Ramamoorthy, "Changing Nature of Deterrence: The Challenge of Asymmetric Threats", *National Security* III, no 2 (2020): 213–231, Vivekananda International Foundation.

4 For more on this see Rajesh Basrur, "The India–China Nuclear Dynamic: India's Options", *ORF Issue Brief*, no 430, December 2020.

5 Barry R. Posen, "The Sources of Military Doctrine", in *The Use of Force: Military Power and International Politics*, eds Robert Art and Kenneth Waltz (Boulder, Colorado: Rowman and Littlefield Publishers, Inc., 2004), 24.
6 George Perkovich, *Do unto Others: Towards a Defensible Nuclear Doctrine* (Washington DC: Carnegie, 2013), 10.
7 In 2015, the US National Archives and Records Administration released a detailed list of the US targets in the Soviet Union, called "Atomic Weapons Requirements Study for 1959". It was produced by the Strategic Air Command in 1956, identifying bombers as the primary means of delivery. See Scott Shane, "1950s US Nuclear Target List Offers Chilling Insights," *The New York Times*, December 22, 2015.
8 Cited by Daryl G. Press, *Calculating Credibility: How Leaders Assess Military Threats* (Ithaca, New York: Cornell University Press, 2005), 120.
9 Some portions of this argument are derived from Manpreet Sethi, "Using Nuclear Weapons First: A Hell of an Alternative", *Air Power Journal* 8, no 4 (Winter 2013): 27–42.
10 Steven P. Lee, *Morality, Prudence, and Nuclear Weapons* (Cambridge: Cambridge University Press, 1993), 16.
11 Jonathan Schell, *The Abolition* (Stanford: Stanford University Press, 2000), 54.
12 For a comprehensive list of incidents until 1996, see Jasjit Singh, "Why Nuclear Weapons", in *Nuclear India*, ed. Jasjit Singh (New Delhi: Knowledge World, 1998), 12–13.
13 Robert McNamara, *Blundering into Disaster: Surviving the First Century of the Nuclear Age* (London: Bloomsbury, 1987), 13–14.
14 Victor Gilinsky, "What if Nuclear Weapons Are Used?" *Bulletin of Atomic Scientists*, November 16, 2016.

Chapter 17

ISRAEL AND A NO-FIRST-USE DECLARATION

Emily B. Landau

INTRODUCTION

When considering the question of an NFU policy for Israel, it is important to clarify at the outset that the situation that has developed in the Middle East over the past fifty years is unique. There is only one assumed nuclear state—Israel—that maintains a policy of nuclear ambiguity (*amimut*). This has led to the development over the years of very different rules of the game in the nuclear realm than we see in other regions, and certainly in the global context.[1] Another notable feature as far as Israel is concerned is that it has actually faced concrete existential threats from its various neighbours for decades but they are not nuclear threats. As such, this chapter will make the case that Israel's nuclear deterrent cannot be refined or even judged according to the principle of no first use of nuclear weapons.

HISTORY OF THE PROGRAMME

Israel's nuclear project began in the late 1950s under the direction of then prime minister, David Ben Gurion, to create an insurance policy that would ensure the survival of the new state. This came on the heels of the Holocaust and the War of Independence, which saw the surrounding Arab states fighting to destroy Israel before it could become a viable state. The sense of existential vulnerability in the 1950s was acute and this is what drove Ben Gurion to seek a solution. From its inception, Israel's only motivation in the nuclear realm has been *defensive*, and a special category of defence—solely for the scenario of countering an *existential threat*. This is unique in the circle of nuclear states.

Throughout the 1960s, Israel wrapped its programme in secrecy for fear that the USA would demand that Israel put a stop to it. After the American news media reported on the Dimona facility in December 1960, the USA[2] began a pressure campaign to convince Israel to open its reactor to American inspections. America's concern was that if Egyptian leader Gamal Abdel Nasser Hussein concluded that Israel was developing nuclear weapons, this would be a serious source of instability in the region. Therefore, the inspections were aimed to reassure of the peaceful nature of Israel's activities at Dimona. Israel accepted several US visits to the facility in the first half of the 1960s but did not fulfil the strict conditions that the Americans had set forth during the Kennedy administration, especially about the frequency of the visits, which the USA wanted to be biannual. The exchanges between the two countries over Dimona were a source of tension in US–Israel relations in the Kennedy administration, which continued into the next administration as well. However, President Lyndon Johnson proved to be somewhat more flexible in his approach and sought to avoid a conflict with Israel. While the USA suspected what Israel was up to at Dimona, the latter succeeded in concealing its reprocessing activities from the Americans.[3]

Tensions reached a new high in 1968 when the USA insisted that Israel join the newly formulated NPT. As the major architect and driving force behind the treaty, as well as a major advocate of nuclear non-proliferation, the USA very much wanted its Middle East ally to join.

The pressure surrounding membership in the NPT created a serious dilemma for Israel and there was some public debate over the question of joining the new treaty. At the heart of the dilemma was the desire not to further deepen the divide with the USA over the nuclear issue but an understanding of what it meant to be part of the treaty as a non-nuclear weapons state (NNWS). By September 1969, the new Israeli prime minister Golda Meir concluded that she must speak directly to the new American president Richard Nixon to clarify Israel's security concerns and calculations. She met with Nixon on the lawn of the White House, and while there is no official protocol of the meeting, Avner Cohen, in his book, *Israel and the Bomb,*[4] lays out the general contours of what was decided between the two leaders.

According to Cohen, it was agreed at the meeting that the USA would end its visits to Dimona and let up on the pressure for Israel to sign the NPT, although it would continue to call on Israel to join the treaty, which it indeed continues to do to this day. In return, Israel would not make any demonstration of its nuclear power—no test, no declaration and no explicit nuclear threats. In short, Israel would maintain a low profile in the nuclear realm, neither acknowledging nor denying the existence of a nuclear deterrent.

Since 1969, Israel's nuclear policy has been described as one of ambiguity—anchored in the understanding that was reached with the USA in 1969. Over the years, the advantages of the policy of *amimut* became clear to Israel, and its low profile also contributed to strategic stability in the region. By not openly acknowledging a nuclear deterrent, Israel did not place the Arab states in the position of having to go down the nuclear route as well. Moreover, it turns out that Israel was successful in delivering its deterrent message to the surrounding states without making it explicit. Based on in-depth research into Israel's nuclear image in the eyes of the Arab states,[5] it is apparent that the country's message of deterrence against an existential threat was understood by Israel's enemies despite its ambiguous posture. In fact, not only was it understood that this was an option solely to ensure Israel's existence but the concept of 'existential threat' was operationalised in various Arab sources, with a description of the threats that might be considered existential by Israel, in descending order of priority.

A useful example of the difference between how things have developed in the Middle East as opposed to the global context has to do with the notion of 'transparency'. In the global context, transparency has always been considered to have positive value—both for ensuring effective nuclear deterrence as well as underpinning the goal of stability in arms control efforts. As far as deterrence is concerned, transparency is considered to be essential for relaying a credible nuclear threat. In arms-control initiatives, transparency regarding nuclear capabilities is also considered to be essential—to advance strategies of reassurance and building of confidence, which in turn encourage strategic stability. But Israel, with its policy of nuclear ambiguity, over the decades, created stability without transparency; the rules of the game of restraint and responsibility were created in the nuclear realm by means of Israel's behaviour on the ground. Israel's red lines were clear to its enemies and were strengthened over the years as Israel continued to uphold them.

WHAT DOES NFU IMPLY?

An NFU policy would necessarily imply a clear declaration of Israel's nuclear status, which is not something that Israel is willing to consider, nor is there any pressure within the country to do so. It is important to understand that Israel's nuclear policy and the fact that it is grounded in ambiguity, is overwhelmingly supported by the Israeli public. Moreover, there is a quiet consensus in this regard across the political spectrum, from the far left to the far right. With all of the issues that divide Israelis, the nuclear issue is not one of them. It has never been a topic of debate ahead of elections in Israel and there is broad understanding and acceptance of Israel's need for a last resort insurance policy. The only aspect that has, in recent years, been accorded more attention in the media is the question of the safety of the Dimona facility, especially considering its advanced age.

More importantly, however, there is no need for Israel to exit ambiguity for the sake of an NFU policy. The purpose of such a declaration is to lower the risks of actual nuclear use, but Israel's policy of ambiguity is geared towards the same goal—a low-profile policy that has become the hallmark of Israel's restraint and responsibility in the nuclear realm. And Israel's restraint has been put to the test—the country has been involved in many wars since achieving the status of an assumed nuclear state, and the nuclear dimension has remained deep in the closet. Those that claim that Israel's nuclear deterrent is meaningless because it has not deterred all the conventional attacks on the country are missing the point: it is precisely the fact that the nuclear dimension has not come into play in scenarios that are not existential that is proof of Israel's responsible behaviour. Indeed, Israel has proven through its actions—that have been reinforced over the years—that if a state, or group of states, do not pose an existential threat, from Israel's point of view, the nuclear dimension is irrelevant.

THE YOM KIPPUR WAR EXPERIENCE

The Yom Kippur War in 1973 was probably the ultimate test of Israel's nuclear restraint, as it was the only instance in which Israel faced a coordinated conventional surprise attack by two of its strongest adversaries, Egypt and Syria. In its initial stage, this attack could be regarded as existential, and indeed seems to have been regarded as such by the then defence minister, Moshe Dayan, who in the first days of the war warned that Israel might be facing the destruction of the 'third temple', namely the destruction of Israel. There have been persistent reports that Israel went so far as to make some nuclear preparations in reaction to the severity of the surprise attack on what was the holiest day for the Jewish people. But even in this extreme scenario, more recent evidence has emerged that Prime Minister Golda Meir was not willing to entertain the thought that nuclear weapons would be included in Israel's war plans, thus refuting the thesis regarding nuclear preparations.

According to a January 2008 interview that Avner Cohen conducted with Arnan Azaryahu, the trusted senior aide of cabinet minister Yisrael Galili back in 1973, Israel was not on the nuclear brink in the Yom Kippur War. In this interview, Azaryahu negated the narrative that had developed over four decades, that Israel was on nuclear alert in the face of the surprise attack.[6] Azaryahu relayed to Cohen that on 7 October, when the situation at Golan Heights was looking increasingly hopeless for Israel, he was waiting for Galili outside Golda Meir's office, where some ministers had gathered to discuss the dire military situation. Shalheveth Freier, head of the Israel Atomic Energy Commission, suddenly showed up and took a seat outside the office as well. When the meeting was over, Dayan stepped out of Meir's office and casually said that he would like Meir to authorise Freier to conduct a nuclear demonstration, to save time in case there was a need to use nuclear weapons. Yisrael Galili and Deputy Prime Minister Yigal Allon both strongly opposed this idea, claiming it was premature and that Israel should base its response on its conventional capabilities. Golda Meir agreed, telling Dayan to 'forget it', and sending Freier back to Tel Aviv. This incident provides very clear evidence of Israel's nuclear restraint, a profile that it has continued to strengthen through its behaviour since that time.

Interestingly enough, it seems that Israel's message of nuclear deterrence only in the face of an existential threat was also underscored in the Yom Kippur War by the behaviour of the attacker, Egypt. While the evidence is not conclusive, a case can be made that Egypt deliberately limited its war aims in 1973 to the Sinai Peninsula, so as not to challenge Israel in a manner that it might regard as existential.[7]

IRAN'S NUCLEAR AMBITIONS UNDERSCORE THE RATIONALE FOR ISRAEL'S NUCLEAR POLICY

Over the past fifteen years, if not longer, Iran's nuclear ambitions have made the case for Israel's nuclear deterrence only that much stronger. Not only is Israel threatened by the prospect of its nuclear monopoly in the region being broken but the current contender—Iran—is itself not defensively motivated. Indeed, since the 1979 revolution, the regime in Iran has become aggressive and revisionist, seeking to actively alter the status quo in the Middle East in its favour and issuing direct threats to destroy Israel on a quite regular basis.

The desire to maintain a nuclear monopoly—often referred to as the Begin Doctrine following the attack Prime Minister Menachem Begin ordered to destroy Iraq's nuclear reactor, Osiraq, in 1981— is something that is inferred from Israel's actions, although it has never been articulated by any official source. The desire not only to have a nuclear deterrent but also to be the sole state in the region to have one, is a consequence of Israel and the Jewish people having been challenged existentially for generations. This has engendered an Israeli security culture that features two dominant and seemingly contradictory strands: an extreme sense of vulnerability to threats of destruction, together with the overwhelming and prominent strength that Israel has developed as a state. As strong as Israel has become—militarily, economically and politically—it is nevertheless plagued by an ongoing sense of vulnerability, which has deep roots in the history of the Jewish people.[8] Indeed, Israel always seeks more than 100 per cent security as it strives to overcome this lingering but acute sense of vulnerability.

While one might scoff at Israel's projection of vulnerability, it cannot be denied that Israel does continue to face threatening rhetoric of an existential nature. This rhetoric ranges from current discourse—more than Seventy years after it achieved independence—about whether Israel has a 'right to exist', to direct threats of an existential nature that are voiced regularly by Iranian leaders and military personnel. How many states have their very right to exist challenged in this manner?

CONCLUDING REMARKS

While the idea of NFU has a certain logic in the context of nuclear dyads, in the very different conditions that developed in the Middle East, it is not likely to enhance regional stability. Israel has made it clear—despite its policy of ambiguity—that these assumed weapons are solely an insurance policy against annihilation and its enemies in the region have had five decades to absorb the message and see it put to the test time and again.

When assessing nuclear principles, the relevant global and regional realities and context must be factored in. Certain principles have logic and relevance for certain nuclear relationships and realities but may be irrelevant to others. Moreover, nuclear realities are not static but rather evolve in line with the behaviour of states, as the Middle East experience has demonstrated. The fact that Israel has continued to uphold its restrained profile in the nuclear realm throughout the decades has served to strengthen its message and has engendered *reliable expectations* throughout the region which in turn have reinforced strategic stability in the nuclear realm.

If Iran were to become a nuclear state, this would be a highly dangerous challenge to regional balance and stability. It would pose a threat to Israel of a dimension that could require a revision of Israel's stance, especially if additional states follow Iran out of fear of the Islamic regime's offensive ambitions in the Middle East. Whereas Israel projected a purely defensive stance in the nuclear realm, Iran's aggressive regional posture has engendered fear among Arab states regarding its nuclear motivations and is likely to elicit a response that will severely undermine the current regional status quo.

In such a dire situation, would a GNFU policy that included all states in the Middle East make more sense? Perhaps, but it is more likely that it would not. Israel would still need to carefully assess the continued benefits of its policy of ambiguity and factor in the possibility that it could still face a non-nuclear existential threat—a scenario in which Israel's deterrent must remain strong. Moreover, a multi-nuclear Middle East would create new deterrent relationships among all the regional players, seriously complicating strategic stability. There is no guarantee that states like Iran—which had no problem cheating on explicit commitments made in the past (per the NPT)—could be trusted with any form of declaratory or written commitment regarding NFU.

The problems in the Middle East stem from highly antagonistic and aggressive regional relationships and a serious lack of trust, especially regarding states that have a proven record of cheating and deceit. From Israel's point of view, Iran cannot be trusted and its existential threats seriously complicate any consideration of mutual pledges. As for other states in the region that might follow Iran down the nuclear path, Israel would do well to devote attention to improving its relations with them. When relations are stable and mutually beneficial, a context is created within which even if nuclear capabilities are developed, they will necessarily pose less of a threat.

NOTES

1 Emily B. Landau, "Strategic Stability in the Middle East: Through the Transparency Lens," in *The End of Strategic Stability? Nuclear Weapons and the Challenge of Regional Rivalries*, eds Lawrence Rubin and Adam N. Stulberg (Washington DC: Georgetown University Press, 2018).

2 *The New York Times,* December 19, 1960.
Ariel E. Levité and Emily B. Landau. "Arab Perceptions of Israel's Nuclear Posture, 1960–1967," Israel Studies Vol. 1, no 1 (Spring, 1996), 34–59: 39

3 Avner Cohen, *Israel and the Bomb*, (New York: Columbia University Press, 1998), 175–190.

4 Cohen, *Israel and the Bomb,* 336–337.

5 Ariel E. Levite and Emily B. Landau, *Israel's Nuclear Image: Arab Perceptions of Israel's Nuclear Posture,* (in Hebrew, Tel Aviv: Papyrus Publishing House, 1994); Levite and Landau, "Arab Perceptions of Israel's Nuclear Posture, 1960–1967," *Israel Studies* 1, no 1 (Spring 1996): 34–59.

6 Cohen, "When Israel Stepped Back from the Brink," *The New York Times,* October 3, 2013.

7 Levite and Landau, *Israel's Nuclear Image: Arab Perceptions of Israel's Nuclear Posture.*

8 Emily Landau and Tamar Malz, "Culture and Security Policy in Israel" (EuroMeSCo Papers, no 21, Euro-Mediterranean Research Dialogue Advocacy [EuroMeSCo], Barcelona, March 2003).

Chapter 18

DETERRENCE UNSHEATHED—PAKISTAN AND THE PROSPECTS OF GLOBAL NO FIRST USE

Brigadier (Retd) Feroz Hassan Khan[1]

The threat of inflicting retaliatory punishment to dissuade adversaries from attacking or contemplating war has been the cornerstone of statecraft throughout the history of war and politics. However, no other revolution in military affairs has affected politics and strategy as has the advent of nuclear weapons, which have bestowed balance and stability in the last century. However, the twenty-first-century international security environment has provided a significant challenge to those conditions. Some analysts believe the mixing of emerging technologies with nuclear and conventional systems blurs the distinction between warfighting and deterrence, and rapid advances in new technologies erode deterrence, which could mark the end of strategic stability.[3] At times, referred to as the second nuclear age, the advent of nuclear capability in the mishmash of the complex regional security environment, along with the dawn of the information age, has challenged the norms and stability parameters of the first nuclear age.[4] Under these circumstances, nuclear powers are consistently re-evaluating security policies and the role of nuclear deterrence in their national security.

Under these shifting conditions in the international system, the doctrine of NFU of nuclear weapons has come under renewed debate in several countries, including in the USA. The fundamental questions surrounding the re-evaluation of a nuclear NFU doctrine relates to the impact of such a declaratory policy on the deterrence posture of the country. The GNFU idea is rooted in three distinct beliefs: that public pledge of NFU contributes to responsible stewardship of nuclear weapons creates conditions for nuclear stability and reinforces the objectives of the non-proliferation regime. A contrarian view challenges this notion, arguing that an explicit declaration of NFU erodes the robustness of deterrence, allows adversaries to exploit vulnerabilities (especially against smaller conventional forces) and weakens extended deterrence commitments to allies.

Indian Prime Minister Manmohan Singh first prepositioned the idea of GNFU in April 2014 during his keynote speech at a conference organised by the Institute for Defence Studies and Analyses in New Delhi. I was fortunate to be a participant in that event and vividly recall the animated discussion on the proposal. However, Prime Minister Singh's GNFU initiative lost momentum in the midst of India's domestic elections, especially since the Bharatiya Janata Party (BJP)—the prospective winner of the elections at the time—had little interest in the idea. During Prime Minister Modi's first term, though, there were few explicit suggestions on changing India's official nuclear doctrine on NFU; lately, though, Indian policymakers and former officials have hinted at a potential sway in Indian doctrinal thinking. They suggest reneging from its NFU pledge and even contemplate pre-emptive counterforce strikes against Pakistan.[5] In August 2019, amid the crisis in Kashmir following the eradication of the Indian Constitution's Articles 35A and 370 (which revoked the special status of Kashmir), India's defence minister Rajnath Singh reinforced perceptions of a shift in India's nuclear doctrine.[6] These subtle shifts in military and nuclear policies have impacted Pakistani security thinking, doctrinal re-evaluation and possible adjustments in its nuclear force posture.

Pakistan falls in the category of such states wherein strategic belief in the invincibility of nuclear deterrence has evolved into a 'mythical belief' that nuclear deterrence is sine qua non to national survival. In Pakistani assessment, an NFU policy exposes weaker nations to coercion and compromises their national sovereignty.[7] How might Pakistan respond to the GNFU initiative? This chapter examines Pakistan's perceptions and approach towards GNFU by addressing three questions: Is an NFU policy feasible for Pakistan? Under what conditions might NFU be acceptable? Is GNFU possible or desirable in general as a global initiative?

The analysis that follows is in four sections. The first section examines the moral and legal aspects of the use of nuclear weapons and assesses its impact on doctrinal thinking of second-tier states. The second section examines the feasibility (or infeasibility) of NFU for Pakistan by examining the factors affecting the role of nuclear deterrence in Pakistan's national security. The third section evaluates the conditions and circumstances under which NFU acceptability might be positively considered in Pakistan. The fourth and final section analyses the realistic possibility and desirability of GNFU and draws from the contemporary debate in the world, primarily in the USA. Finally, before closing, the chapter offers some concluding thoughts.

THE DEBATE: THE MORALITY, LEGALITY AND FEASIBILITY OF NUCLEAR DETERRENCE

Since the last use of nuclear weapons ended the greatest conventional war in modern history (the Second World War), vigorous debates continue on the legality, morality and feasibility of war as instruments of policy. After the end of the Cold War, there was a discernible lack of interest amongst major Western powers on the role of nuclear weapons in national security. The emergence of a weak Russia following the dissolution of the Soviet Union reduced, if not eliminated the perceived threat to the West on which the fundamentals of nuclear deterrence and its literature had evolved. The new international norms in the 1990s emphasised consensus on non-proliferation objectives, cooperative threat reductions and the diminished role of nuclear weapons in national security.[8] At this juncture, the 'second-tier states', such as India and Pakistan, were on the cusp of declaring themselves as nuclear powers.[9] The new liberal world order, spearheaded by a sole superpower (the USA), expected regional nuclear aspirants to follow the Western experience. Lessons from the Cold War suggested that conventional military capability was a useable instrument of policy; thus, states devoting resources in conventional deterrence made greater sense than investing in expensive nuclear weapons, which posed considerable downside risks, especially when deployed and deemed unusable in the end.[10] Consequently, the 1990s saw new vigour in negotiating global arms-control initiatives on weapons of mass destruction. These initiatives included chemical-, biological- and nuclear-related treaties with a regional focus—and were especially applicable to South Asia where both India and Pakistan were building nuclear weapons and delivery means.[11] India and Pakistan faced a dilemma of choosing between the immediate national security needs and prospects of good international standing. Pakistan was, however, singled out for disapproval and sanctions. It faced intense pressures from the West not only to cap but to roll back its nuclear programme and/or join the emerging global arms-control treaties on nuclear and weapons of mass destruction.

Yet, by the turn of the century, none of the states possessing nuclear weapons—neither the nuclear-armed states under the NPT nor outlier states (India, Pakistan and Israel)—were about to abandon nuclear weapons.[12] Just after the turn of the century, the USA abrogated the Anti-Ballistic Missile Treaty (ABMT), which shook the foundations of mutually assured destruction and signalled renewed salience of nuclear weapons. These shifts occurred around the time of a new era of asymmetric wars—manifested in the horrendous terror attack on the USA in September 2001.

The subjects discussed above influenced Pakistani decision-making and evolutionary thinking on nuclear doctrine, nuclear command, control and approach to global nuclear norms and arms control and disarmament initiatives. Among other determinants affecting the policy on NFU is the question of the legality of nuclear weapons as instruments of use of force. For countries pursuing nuclear capability, the legality of possessing nuclear weapons in international law is important. Unlike chemical and biological weapons, nuclear weapons are not outlawed; further, the legality of the use of nuclear weapons under certain conditions has an important bearing on doctrinal thinking and the place of nuclear weapons in national security. Israel, India and Pakistan are non-signatories to the NPT. Under the existing non-proliferation regime, their acceptance as de jure nuclear weapons states is not possible unless the three countries with nuclear weapons give them up and join as non-nuclear weapons state (NNWS)—which is unlikely.

The Legality of Deterrence: The Ambiguity of International Court of Justice

In 1996, when the International Court of Justice (ICJ) took up the examination of the question of the legality of nuclear weapons, one concern among aspiring nuclear powers was the prospect of nuclear weapons being proscribed altogether, as was the case with chemical and biological weapons. The ICJ's advisory opinion was ambiguous and stopped short of declaring nuclear weapons illegal. Newell Highsmith, the former legal advisor to the US state department, examined the legality of nuclear deterrence and noted, 'an undeniable tensions exists between nuclear deterrence strategy and the principles of international law'.[13] Additionally, he surmises, 'If nuclear deterrence is not legally defensible, then as a practical matter, the possession of nuclear weapons would not be legally defensible.'[14] Emerging powers noted the sharp difference of opinion on the legality of the threat or use of nuclear weapons. On the one hand, ICJ considered the threat or use of nuclear weapons 'contrary to international law applicable in armed conflict and against the principles and rules of international law'.[15] On the other, it also ruled, 'The court cannot conclude definitively whether the threat or use of nuclear weapons would be lawful or unlawful in extreme circumstances of self-defence, in which the very survival of a state would be at stake'.[16] Putting it bluntly, the ICJ opinion allowed both interpretations—opining that states contemplating NFU are legally and morally justified and that use of nuclear weapons is also legitimate if used in extremis for national security.

At the time of ICJ's advisory opinion, Pakistan's nuclear programme was opaque and its nuclear policy was ambiguous—neither accepting nor denying nuclear capability. After Pakistan's 1998 tests, the ICJ advisory opinion was an important development in terms of the legitimacy of nuclear weapons as well as in determining nuclear doctrine.[17] While the ICJ opinion did not *explicitly* declare possession of nuclear weapons illegal, their use, especially for states considering first use of nuclear doctrines, was open to interpretation. On the one hand, 'first-use threat' could be contrary to the principles of international law of proportionality and indiscriminate use of force; on the other hand, nuclear use in the right of self-defence and for a state's survival was considered legitimate. Though the ICJ's advisory opinion is not legally binding for states, it nevertheless sets the norm and moral obligation for states to improve their reputation as international relations as responsible stewards of nuclear capability.

The above interpretations have influenced Pakistani nuclear policy of whether or not to have a declared nuclear doctrine or to continue with the ambivalence in its policy. At the time when the ICJ opinion became public, Pakistan's official position was a denial of its military nuclear programme and there were seldom any debates in public or think tanks. Within the circles dealing with nuclear policy in the covert days, the ICJ decision reinforced the Pakistani doctrinal belief that the threat of use of nuclear weapons in extremis was justified should the state's survivability be in danger. After the nuclear tests, the debate continued within the Strategic Plans Division (SPD), which included interagency inputs from the Pakistani Foreign Office (the foreign minister is the deputy chair of the employment committee of Pakistan's National Command Authority [NCA]). The diplomatic argument focused on the 'principles of law of proportionality' aspect of the ICJ judgement. Any formal declaration endorsed in an official doctrine that made an explicit threat of use of nuclear weapons was deemed against the principles of law and against the letter and the spirit of the UN Charter, which remains a cornerstone of Pakistani foreign policy. Under President General Pervez Musharraf, the Pakistani NCA made a concerted decision not to make any officially declared nuclear doctrine. The closest Pakistan came to declare an official position on the subject was in a keynote address at a Carnegie conference on non-proliferation in June 2001. Mr Abdus Sattar, Pakistan's foreign minister, declared that Pakistan pledges 'no first use of force—conventional or nuclear'.[18]

Weighing heavily on Pakistani nuclear diplomacy at the time was also the removal—or mitigation—of nuclear sanctions as applied in 1990 under the US Non-Proliferation Law, which was Pakistan-specific (known as the Pressler Amendment in US Non-Proliferation Law).[19] Further opprobrium after nuclear tests in 1998 and the military takeover in 1999 brought Pakistan under layers of sanctions from the USA. The new military leadership in power in Pakistan made initial nuclear policy decisions as a newly emerged nuclear power under these difficult conditions and constraints.

IS NFU FEASIBLE FOR PAKISTAN

In pivotal regions, such as South Asia, three nuclear-armed powers (Pakistan, India and China) intersect and share a history of cross-border disputes overlaid with ideological and geopolitical rivalries. Situated in such a security-intensive environment, Pakistan has sought external alliances to balance against perceived threats, primarily from India; however, Islamabad soon realised that major powers (i.e., the USA and China) sought military alliances with Pakistan for their geopolitical objectives and not necessarily in agreement with the Pakistani sense of insecurity. In difficult times and crises, external allies have been capricious to Pakistan's security anxieties—as Pakistan discovered after its dismemberment in the 1971 war and subsequently when Pakistani concerns were dismissed after India's nuclear test in 1974.[20] The foundation of Pakistan's nuclear weapons quest is rooted in the deep belief that 'never again' will it endure the humiliation of 1971.[21] Since then, 'external balancing' and 'nuclear deterrence' have remained the two central tenets of Pakistan's grand strategy. In my assessment, Pakistan's policy of relying on external powers to mitigate its security predicament has been a bitter historic experience. Today, external alliance in its security policy is only a secondary factor; its primary reliance is on internal balancing involving a 'combination of conventional and nuclear deterrence to obviate conventional war'.[22]

India and Pakistan outlined their respective policy priorities about their demonstrated nuclear capability in 1998. While India preferred declaring a nuclear doctrine, Pakistani policymakers considered enunciation of their command and control system as a greater priority than the declaration of the role of nuclear weapons in Pakistani security thinking. In the Pakistani assessment, a public pronouncement of a nuclear doctrine should be ambiguous, and the real doctrine should always remain classified.

Sir Michael Quinlan, a British scholar, defined the concept of NFU as one where 'nuclear possessors would give an absolute and permanent promise that never, under any circumstances whatever, would they be the first to use nuclear weapons in a conflict'.[23] If this definition is accepted, then Quinlan considers it 'absurd' that a 'nuclear-armed state would "let itself be overwhelmed" and let its options be narrowed by past promises of a no-first-use promise made in peacetime tranquillity'.[24] Quinlan's analysis of NFU's drawback explains Pakistan's doctrinal choice dilemma.

NFU would be a natural choice for those states that have confidence in the strength of conventional forces to defeat existential threats without the need to threaten nuclear use. For such states, nuclear deterrence applies only against nuclear threats and not against conventional threats. Furthermore, a declaratory policy of NFU reinforces the principle of proportionality and nuclear use executed only under self-defence in retaliation. For example, India's conventional force has favourable asymmetry over almost all of its neighbours—except China. Thus, India can proffer declaring NFU against any conventional threats and afford considering nuclear deterrence only against a nuclear threat. In Pakistani assessment, India's nuclear capability reflects what the former Indian foreign minister, Jaswant Singh, called 'currency of power' in the international system, which is a fundamental element of India's security discourse.[25]

For states that cannot match conventional force threats at a conventional level and that also face geo-physical vulnerabilities, reliance on nuclear deterrence would be a natural course of action. Any declaratory NFU nuclear policy would dilute a state's deterrent posture designed to offset conventional force asymmetry, as was the case of the NATO facing the conventionally superior Warsaw Pact in Central Europe during the Cold War. Pakistan is in a similar predicament and seeks 'strategic equivalence' through nuclear deterrence 'to supplement conventional military capability to reassert strategic balance, regional stability and ensure peace'.[26] In addition to deterring India from the use of conventional force, Pakistan's concept of 'strategic equivalence' also aims to prevent nuclear coercion and preserve sovereignty. These factors not only preclude Pakistan from an NFU pledge, but India's limited-war military doctrine and its refinements (e.g., Cold Start/Proactive) now necessitate greater integration of nuclear and conventional force planning in Pakistan.

In the two decades since the 1998 nuclear tests, Pakistani nuclear doctrine, considering several changing strategic environments, has been in a continuum evolution. Pakistan has consistently maintained that major Indian military aggression across the international border will be met with the full defensive might of the Pakistan military, including the first use of nuclear weapons. The Pakistani security establishment is convinced that India's Cold Start doctrine, and its successors, pose a direct threat to Pakistan's territorial integrity and also that India's cross-border operations are an existential threat to Pakistan. Moreover, Pakistan has probably concluded that its 'credible minimum deterrence' posture failed to dissuade India from its objective of subduing Pakistan through military means. The lexicon of 'credible minimum' and 'minimum credible' has been used interchangeably in statements by Pakistani leaders, NCA announcements and scholarly explanations on Pakistani doctrinal discussions; however, there has been no difference in implications of the terms' usage. The common denominator, 'minimum', connotes a force posture requiring investment in nuclear weapons just sufficient to ensure credible nuclear threat in case of conventional force attack or invasion. The experience of 1971 remains indelible in Pakistan security thinking as far as India's intentions are concerned. Aware of the lack of strategic depth, Pakistani security managers observe the evolution of Indian military doctrines—particularly its military exercises. Changes in India's conventional military doctrine in the 1980s (Sunderji doctrine) and the concept of 'limited war under nuclear overhang' that envisaged 'creating space' for waging conventional war between low-intensity conflict and nuclear use has signalled India's intent to challenge Pakistan's nuclear deterrence.[27] In 2011, Pakistan declared a 'full spectrum deterrence' posture, which includes the employment of tactical nuclear weapons (TNW) along with the assortment of arsenals in its inventory. Pakistan clarified that Indian invading forces would meet nuclear weapons at all levels—tactical, operational and strategic. In several subsequent clarifications, the Pakistani NCA stated that 'Pakistan's policy of developing and maintaining full spectrum deterrence is in line with the policy of credible minimum deterrence and avoidance of arms race.'[28]

The advent of TNW in the mix of Pakistani deterrent posture will likely pose similar dilemma for Pakistani security planners, as the NATO planners faced in Central Europe during the early periods of the Cold War. Pakistani officials deny any war-fighting role of nuclear weapons other than deterring India's decision-makers from undertaking a military adventure. Pakistan intends to leverage a battlefield nuclear weapons threat to offset conventional asymmetries and raise the stakes for any conventional cross-border attacks that India might contemplate under its limited-war doctrine.[29] Pakistani assessment recognises there are challenges of deployments and employments of TNW (e.g., field security, target sets, command and control and field security issues), but strategic planners are prepared to take the risk should national security be in peril.[30] The risks to stability are severe given the incompatible nature of the two doctrines, where assumptions on escalation control are dangerously faulty. India assumes escalation control contemplating limited conventional war against nuclear-armed Pakistan by calling its nuclear bluff. In turn, Pakistan plans to deter such an attack with TNW, failing which, it guarantees the first use of nuclear weapons and to then be prepared for further nuclear exchanges. This game of chicken between two nuclear-armed rivals is what makes policymakers worldwide extremely nervous.

Escalation dangers in limited wars and TNW challenges are relics of the early decades of the twentieth-century nuclear age; in contemporary times, the regional and domestic threats are asymmetric in nature and the related role of nuclear weapons is limited. Advancements in conventional weapons and the emergence of new technologies (e.g., autonomous weapons and cyber weapons) are affecting strategy and tactics, necessitating a rethink of old tactics and offering opportunities for innovative military operations. In the new information age, emerging technologies, cyber warfare and military applications of AI are having a transformative effect and not just on social media and the national economy; they are demanding an overhaul of contemporary military operations.[31] At the time of writing this, the tension between Pakistan and India is exceptionally high following tensions in Kashmir.[32] These and other compelling security demands are affecting Pakistani nuclear doctrinal choices.

Given the above conditions in the minds of the Pakistanis, it is highly unlikely that Pakistan would be amenable to any NFU initiative. As long as conditions and the state of interstate relations between India and Pakistan remain in gridlock, it is difficult to conceive of such an outcome. Under different conditions and positive circumstances and atmospherics, is it possible that Pakistan would consider contributing to a GNFU initiative? The next section considers such conditions for a bilateral or regional NFU as a first step towards a larger global proposition if all nuclear-armed countries are amenable.

CONDITIONS IN WHICH NFU MIGHT BE ACCEPTABLE

Pakistan's concerns are primarily regional. For over four decades, it has sought a regionally based restraint arrangement with India. Given Pakistan's consistent approach in this regard before contemplating participating in any global initiative, it is unlikely Pakistan will countenance any initiative affecting its nuclear doctrine, force postures or development plans. After the 1998 test, Pakistan expected a process of rapprochement, détente and conflict resolution with India. To this end, beginning in the summer of 1998, Pakistan initiated a series of interactions with India and the USA. After several exchanges of ideas with Indian interlocutors, Pakistan proposed a formal strategic restraint regime to India and the USA. This proposal included three interlocking elements: conflict resolution, conventional force restraint and nuclear restraint. India rejected this proposal explaining that its primary concern was with China. In principle, the triangulation of political, military and nuclear factors would have helped develop a process to eventually create a peace and security architecture in South Asia.

Though India turned down Pakistan's strategic restraint proposal, Prime Minister Atal Bihari Vajpayee and his Pakistani counterpart, Prime Minister Nawaz Sharif, signed the memorable Lahore Agreement in February 1999 that included the Lahore Memorandum of Understanding of 1999. The historic 1999 summit committed both India and Pakistan to 'engage in bilateral consultations on security concepts, and nuclear doctrines, with a view to developing measures for confidence building in the nuclear and conventional fields, aimed at avoidance of conflict'.[33] Rather than gaining traction of such a promising start after the nuclear demonstrations, the region met with a series of unfortunate events of intertwined terror attacks, military crises and nuclear tensions. The subsequent two decades saw India and Pakistan drift apart. For India and Pakistan to restart a meaningful professional discussion at some point in the future, when the atmospherics are right, the structural foundation for regional doctrinal discussions are embedded in the 1999 Lahore Memorandum of Understanding.

In my view, five conditions are important for India and Pakistan to commence a serious dialogue on doctrinal issues accompanied by discussions on risk reduction. The foremost condition is a conducive political climate, which would recreate a culture of conflict resolution and reduction of tension. At the time of writing this, the regional atmosphere has been rather ugly, and any suggestion of security-related dialogue for positive ends would likely be dismissed as delusional and unrealistic. The second condition is that both countries must eschew sub-conventional strategies. At the root of the military crisis in the Indian subcontinent is the policy of applying sub-conventional strategies to perpetuate animosities. Unless both states eschew using proxies, and other forms of low-intensity conflict, serious military crises will continue to occur. The third condition, especially from a Pakistani standpoint, pertains to the nuclear and conventional force nexus, which is at the heart of doctrinal dissonance between India and Pakistan. Both states should recognise that the nuclear deterrence posture has a symbiotic nexus with conventional force balance. If the use of conventional force remains an open option, the constraining use of nuclear weapons erodes the purpose of nuclear weapons. The fourth condition is the creation of new crisis prevention institutions.

Both states should develop institutionalised mechanisms to prevent crisis triggering events. Finally, any bilateral restraint agreement between India and Pakistan should not be prejudiced in favour of either country's threat assessment of other countries. Both sides can keep open the process of assurance. As Sir Michael Quinlan expressed in a side-line conversation with me, 'Deterrence rests on a combination of accommodation and reassurance, not on nuclear threats alone.'[34]

The above five conditions would create a levelling field for meaningful discussions on regional NFU. Any regional constraint agreement, such as regional NFU, would create powerful moral authority for both countries to advocate for a global norm that is not detrimental to either Indian or Pakistani security concerns. Indeed, as explained in the next section, India and Pakistan could bilaterally declare regional NFU but would either country believe the sincerity of the other? For two nuclear-armed states, with a long and bitter history of rivalry, having true confidence in an NFU commitment is more likely to be hollow.

Pakistani leaders—both civil and military—have expressed a desire never to resort to the use of nuclear weapons unless an extreme threat to existence arises. President Musharraf, a military leader, had repeated this several times in interviews. In one such interview, he stated, 'We do not want to use nuclear capability but if our existence come under threat, what do we have these nuclear weapons for?'[35] Similar pledges have been suggested by civil leaders such as President Asif Zardari (2008–2013) as well as and current head of state, Prime Minister Imran Khan.[36] These assurances neither constitute acceptance of an NFU as Pakistan's doctrine nor are these outright nuclear threats, as some media spins suggest, which is why each time any assurance from leadership is followed by an official clarification of no shift in Pakistan's policy of ambiguity. Public assurances from Pakistan's highest offices indicate a desire to convey peace assurances to India and clarify its position to the world at large. Hoping such expression would induce confidence and prompt a peace process, Pakistani military and civilian leaders have often expressed their intent not to use nuclear weapons.

Quest for Legitimacy

For Pakistan, the legitimacy of its nuclear programme is important. India is the beneficiary of the US-bestowed civil nuclear deal, which confers India's nuclear programme with de facto legitimacy. Vergese Koithara explains the benefits of the nuclear deal:

> 'India can now upgrade and expand nuclear forces ... fissile material have now ceased to be a problem in expanding India's arsenal ...

> [these] agreements have also led to lowering the hurdles in India's path to acquire useful dual-use technologies, which can help India's missile and command and control programmes.'[37]

No such incentive exists for Pakistan. In fact, the military benefits of the civil deal, as described above, increase Pakistan's anxiety rather than dampening competition; this means Pakistan has even less incentive to eschew first use. It is unlikely that India would assure Pakistan that its increasing modernised arsenals, dual-use vectors and evolving nuclear force posture should not worry Pakistan simply because India has a declared NFU.

The best course of action to decrease regional competition and alleviate tensions would be to simultaneously make India and Pakistan members of the Nuclear Suppliers Group (NSG) and end the policy of exceptionalism. Such an incentive for both countries might create the right atmospherics for 'discussions on nuclear doctrines' as promised in the Lahore Agreement of 1999.[38] As members of the elite NSG club, India and Pakistan could demonstrate they are responsible nuclear states and adhere to regional NFU before contributing to any global initiative.

IS GNFU POSSIBLE OR EVEN DESIRABLE?

An examination of the NFU debate in advanced nuclear countries reveals there is seemingly little appetite for such an initiative at the global level. The NFU debate is perhaps as old as the first use of nuclear weapons in 1945. Within Western countries, and in particular, in the USA, the NFU debate is heating up again, wherein there have been sharp opinions on both sides of the political aisle for long. Some democrat legislators strongly support an NFU declaration. They argue, 'NFU would help us [United States] maintain our moral and diplomatic leadership in the world.'[39] Any nuclear use breaks the nuclear taboo (in place since 1945) and the consequences would be unacceptable to the public. However, as yet, no US administration has agreed to adopt an NFU policy. At best, Western democracies have adopted a policy of ambivalence that allows them to maintain a high moral ground. At the core of the debate lies the impact of an NFU pledge on deterrence, assurance and strategic stability. The advocates of NFU believe in four central benefits: stability, non-proliferation, disarmament and moral standing.

NFU advocates argue that a universal pledge of NFU would bring stability, as a mutual assurance of safety from the use of ultimate weapons would create global norms that would reinforce a nuclear taboo. Any bilateral NFU commitment among nuclear-armed adversaries would induce steps for diplomacy and the process for peaceful means of conflict resolution. Additionally, NFU advocates surmise that with emerging technologies, precision weapons and other advancements in conventional forces, the threat of the use of nuclear forces is redundant. Some argue that with missile defences and the advent of non-nuclear counterforce capabilities in advanced nuclear powers, stability from first-use nuclear threat belongs to the bygone twentieth century.[40] Any nuclear threats from new nuclear powers would result in conventional force responses, which could cause significant damage without breaking the nuclear taboo.[41] Supporters of NFU argue that the guarantee of a sophisticated non-nuclear response offers sufficient deterrence against any nuclear-armed adversary contemplating nuclear use. Therefore, the proponents of NFU consider reduced reliance on nuclear weapons but are not advocates for the elimination of nuclear weapons.[42]

Additionally, pro-NFU advocates believe this pledge is complimentary to non-proliferation and a path to global disarmament. With new advancements in lethal useable conventional weapons, nuclear-aspirant states would be dissuaded to go the nuclear route because the political, economic and security costs would be greater than the benefits of acquiring nuclear deterrence. Given the power of modern conventional technologies, should a GNFU become the norm, nuclear aspirants might be dissuaded, and those already in possession of nuclear capability might refrain from further investment in nuclear weapons and thus reduce vertical proliferation. Over time, such steps could lead to universal disarmament.

The opposition to NFU is fundamentally based on the efficacy of nuclear deterrence as a tool of national security policy. In this view, the benefits of NFU are mythical and overstated. They contest the notion that NFU commitment would bring stability. French scholar Bruno Tertrais went so far as to argue that not only does NFU give limited benefits but that it could also be costly.[43] In his 2019 article, titled 'No First Use, No Deterrence', he explains why states shy away from declaring NFU. He asks why two nuclear-armed adversaries would 'believe the other is sincere'.[44] Even if both believed each other's NFU, it would create conditions for use of sub-nuclear forces and thus create instability. The only conditions that could bring stability would be if both adversaries have an explicit 'first use' or at least one of the two has a first-use policy, and the other has an NFU policy but is not believed by the adversary. Tertrais contends that an NFU commitment is reversible in extreme conditions and no leader would hold moral grounds at the expense of reputation and or if it meant seeing his/her homeland fall to destruction and invasion.[45] Thus, an NFU is a 'severe impingement' on leadership in times of crisis as it reduces credibility.[46]

However, for great powers such as the USA, NFU impacts assurances and extended deterrence for allies. Nuclear declaratory policies cut a fine line between *positive* assurances that nuclear weapons will be used when required and *negative* assurances that they would never be used when they are not authorised.[47] The NFU policy provides negative assurances, except in retaliation of first use. Herein lies the controversy of declaring NFU. While such a declaration initially appears to secure the high moral ground, on closer scrutiny, it is not a benign moralistic policy but a deliberate strategy. States with powerful conventional forces seek conditions and space for conventional military operations against conventionally weak adversaries and to undermine the nuclear deterrence of such adversaries. More likely, those opposed to NFU would argue that any declaration of NFU would encourage adversaries to undertake measures that would subdue or impose a conventional defeat. On balance , as Sir Michael Quinlan concluded, 'NFU as a universal, unconditional, permanent promise ought not to find favour'.[48]

CONCLUSION

A GNFU is an idea worth debating in the twenty-first century, particularly because of the advent of technologies that impact strategic stability in ways never conceived of previously. The question remains whether declaratory commitments would dampen military crisis and war or create conditions of classic stability–instability paradox. Countries with nuclear weapons capabilities are increasingly acquiring dual-use vectors, and non-nuclear capabilities could undercut nuclear threats in non-lethal ways. It is debatable then whether technological advancements reduce the salience of nuclear weapons or increase incentives to be less digital and revert to analogue means of delivering nuclear warheads to deter lethal non-nuclear counterforce attacks.

Nuclear weapons are not proscribed weapons, and their possession provides unique instruments of policy and statecraft. The legal opinions on nuclear use or threat of nuclear use are not only ambiguous but also are subject to interpretations both on the illegality of disproportionate force as well as a legitimate use in self-defence in extremis. There is a consensus among realist scholars that an NFU commitment underpins deterrence and does not mitigate threats from non-nuclear forces. However, NFU provides states with high moral standing—so long as a threat does not materialise.

Pakistan remains convinced that without effective nuclear deterrence, its national security is incomplete. For smaller regional nuclear powers, like Pakistan, an NFU declaration would have implications on the credibility of deterrence, which is at the core of its national security. Pakistan is facing significant political and economic pressures at the time of this writing. The regional security situation, especially with India, is deteriorating. Like all modern militaries, the requirements to modernise its conventional forces are growing. Pakistan's relative conventional military strength vis-à-vis India will always be imbalanced, and as such, Pakistan will continue to rely on nuclear deterrence to offset the imbalance with India. It is for this reason that Pakistan remains sensitive to any NFU commitment. As explained above, even if both India and Pakistan declare and mutually assure NFU at the regional level, stability would still not resultNonetheless, the only way for détente and stability in South Asia is to eschew adversarial policies and embrace a process of sustained dialogue to rekindle the spirit of Lahore in 1999 when both countries shared a vision of peace and stability.

NOTES

1 The author is research professor in the US Naval Postgraduate School and former director in Pakistan's Strategic Plans Division. Views expressed in this paper are author's alone and do not reflect policy or position of any organisation or entity either of the US or the Pakistani governments. The author is grateful to Catherine L. Grant for her inputs, review and editing of this chapter.

2 Morton Halperin et. al., "Forum: The Case of No First Use: An Exchange," *Survival* 51, no 3 (June–July 2009): 163–182.

3 Lawrence Rubin and Adam N. Stulberg, eds, *The End of Strategic Stability? Nuclear Weapons and the Challenge of Regional Rivalries* (Washington DC: Georgetown University Press, 2018). See also Feroz Hassan Khan, "Challenges to Nuclear Stability in South Asia," *The Nonproliferation Review* (Spring 2003): 59–74.

4 Gregory D. Koblentz, *Strategic Stability the Second Nuclear Age*, Council Special Report No. 71 (Washington, DC: Council of Foreign Relations, 2014); Paul Bracken, *The Second Nuclear Age: Strategy, Danger, and the New Power Politics* (New York: St Martin's Griffin, 2013).

5 Christopher Clary and Vipin Narang. "India's Counterforce Temptations: Strategic Dilemmas, Doctrines, and Capabilities," *International Security* 43, no 3 (Winter 2018–2019): 7–52, doi: 10.1162/ISEC_a_00340. Also see Dr Adil Sultan, "India–Pakistan Crises and Evolving Dyadic Deterrence Model," *IPRI Journal* (1): 21–43 (Islamabad Policy Research Institute [IPRI], Winter 2020): 36–37, accessed in June 2021, doi: 10.31945/iprij.200102.

6 Priyanka Pulla, "India–Pakistan Nuclear Escalation? Where Could It Lead?" *Nature*, August 29, 2019, https://www.nature.com/articles/d41586-019-02578-5.

7 Peter R. Lavoy, "Nuclear Myths and the Causes of Nuclear Proliferation," *Security Studies* 2, no. 3–4 (1993); Khan, *Eating Grass: The Making of the Pakistani Bomb* (Palo Alto, CA: Stanford University Press, 2012), 5–6.

8 Muthiah Alagappa, ed., *The Long Shadow: Nuclear Weapons and Security in 21st Century Asia* (Palo Alto: Stanford University Press, 2008), 6–14.

9 India was preparing to conduct nuclear tests as early as 1995 or early 1996 when its public reporting created pressures to cause it to stop. India and Pakistan both tested nuclear weapons in 1998 and that changed the security landscape of South Asia.

10 Technological leaps in the late 1970s and early 1980s, sometimes referred to as the revolution in military affairs of the 1980s, dramatically improved conventional military capabilities. The advent of precision-guided munitions, dominance of the air force and space/satellite technologies, as well as dual-use sophisticated arsenals have reduced the significance of tactical nuclear weapons and shifted the focus of countries to enhancing conventional force deterrents.

11 Negotiations and consideration under the aegis of the UN in the 1990s in Geneva and The Hague were Chemical Weapons Convention, Biological Weapons Convention, Comprehensive Test Ban Treaty and Fissile Material Cut-Off Treaty. Also on the UN agenda under discussion were treaties on disarmament, negative security assurance, prohibition of certain conventional weapons, prevention of arms race in outer space, etc.

12 Alagappa, *The Long Shadow: Nuclear Weapons and Security in the 21st Century*, 13.

13 Newell L. Highsmith, *On the Legality of Nuclear Deterrence,* Livermore Papers on Global Security no 6 (Livermore: Lawrence Livermore National Laboratory, 2019), 2.

14 Highsmith, *On the Legality of Nuclear Deterrence*, 2.

15 Highsmith, *On the Legality of Nuclear Deterrence, 2.*

16 Highsmith, *On the Legality of Nuclear Deterrence*, 1.

17 Naeem Salik, *The Genesis of South Asian Nuclear Deterrence* (London: Oxford University Press, 2010), 235– 237.

18 Abdul Sattar, "New Leaders, New Directions," Keynote Address, Carnegie International Conference, Washington DC, June 18, 2001, *IPRI Journal* 6, nos 1–4 (2006): 41.

19 Under Pressler Amendment to the US Non-Proliferation Law, Pakistan was sanctioned in 1990 for nuclear defiance. The sanction implied that Pakistan could no longer receive military sales from the USA, which eroded Pakistan conventional capability and forced Pakistan to become even more reliant on the nuclear weapons. Rabia Akhtar, *The Blind Eye: U.S. Non-Proliferation Policy towards Pakistan from Ford to Clinton* (Lahore, Pakistan: University of Lahore, 2018): 198–213.

20 Though India called it a 'peaceful nuclear explosion', there was no question in Pakistan about the 'peaceful' intent in this event of a nuclear test. See Khan, *Eating Grass*, 68–92.

21 The 'never again' experience has affected many nations' decisions to acquire nuclear weapons, including China's humiliation in the Taiwan Straits crisis in 1955 and India's 1962 defeat in the Sino-India war. See Khan, *Eating Grass*, 68–92.

22 Pakistan Army, *Pakistan Army Doctrine 2011: Comprehensive Response*, AP 1001 E (Islamabad: Pakistan Army, 2011), 1.

23 Michael Quinlan, *Thinking about Nuclear Weapons: Principles, Problems, Prospects* (New York: Oxford University Press, 2009), 99.

24 Quinlan, *Thinking about Nuclear Weapons*, 100.

25 Jaswant Singh, *Defending India* (New Delhi: Macmillan Press, 1999), 1; Singh, "Against Nuclear Apartheid," *Foreign Affairs* (September–October 1998), accessed on January 12, 2022, https://www.foreignaffairs.com/articles/asia/1998-09-01/against-nuclear-apartheid.

26 Pakistan Army, *Pakistan Army Doctrine*, 1.

27 Walter C. Ladwig III, "Indian Military Modernization and Conventional Deterrence in South Asia," *Journal of Strategic Studies* 38, no 5 (2015): 729–772.

28 Lieutenant General (Retd) Khalid Kidwai, "Deterrence, Nuclear Weapons and Arms Control Workshop" (Keynote Address and Discussion, 7th IISS [International Institute for Strategic Studies]–CISS [Centre for International Strategic Studies] South Asian Strategic Stability, London, February 6, 2020), https://www.iiss.org/events/2020/02/7th-iiss-and-ciss-south-asian-strategic-stability-workshop; Baqar Sajjad Syed, "Pakistan to Retain Full Spectrum Deterrence Policy," *Dawn*, December 22, 2017, https://www.dawn.com/news/1378106.

29 For a detailed analysis of roles of nuclear weapons, see Feroz Hassan Khan and Peter R. Lavoy, "Pakistan: The Dilemma of Nuclear Deterrence," in *The Long Shadow: Nuclear Weapons and Security in 21st Century Asia*, ed. Muthiah Alagappa, (Palo Alto: Stanford University Press, 2008), 215–240; Mahmud Ali Durrani, "Pakistan's Strategic Thinking and Role of Nuclear Weapons" (Occasional Paper 37, Sandia National Laboratories, Cooperative Monitoring Center, SAND 2004), 33, accessed on January 12, 2022, https://www.sandia.gov/cooperative-monitoring-center/_assets/documents/sand2004-3375p.pdf .

30 For a detailed assessment of Pakistan's TNW choice, see Khan, "Going Tactical: Pakistan's Nuclear Posture and Implications for Stability" (Proliferation Papers no 53, Institut français des relations internationales, Paris, 2016), accessed on July 25, 2022, https://www.ifri.org/en/publications-papers/going-tactical-pakistanis-nucleur-posture-and Mansoor Ahmed, "Pakistan's Tactical Nuclear Weapons and their Impact on Stability" (Regional Insight, Carnegie Endowment for International Peace, XXX, June 30, 2016), accessed on July 25, 2022, https://carnegieendowment.org/2016/06/30/pakistan-s-tactical-nucleur-weapons-and-their-impact-on-stability-pub-63911.

31 Zachary Davis, *Artificial Intelligence on the Battlefield: An Initial Survey of Potential Implications for Deterrence, Stability, and Strategic Surprise* (Livermore: Lawrence Livermore National Laboratory, 2019).

32 Zachary Keck, "Billions Dead: That's What Could Happen if India and Pakistan Wage a Nuclear War," *National Interest*, February 19, 2019, accessed on July 25, 2022, https://nationalinterest.org/blog/buzz/billions-dead-thats-what-could-happen-if-india-and-pakistan-wage-nuclear-war-44682; Khan, "South Asia's Evolving Strategic Doctrines" (Panel Discussion, Henry Stimson Center, Washington DC, July 19, 2017), accessed on July 25, 2022, www://stimson.org/event/south-asias-evolving-strategic-doctrines/.

33 "The Lahore Declaration February 1999, Ministry of External Affairs, Government of India, February 1999, accessed on January 12, 2022, https://mea.gov.in/in-focus-article.htm?18997/Lahore+Declaration+February+1999.

34 Sir Michael Quinlan, meetings with the author, Wilton Park, London, July 21–24, 2008.

35 "We Did Not Build Nukes to Fire on Shab-e-Barat says Musharraf," *Times of India*, July 11, 2015, cited in Sannia Abdullah, "Nuclear Ethics? Why Pakistan Has Not Used Nuclear Weapons… Yet", *The Washington Quarterly* 42, no. 4 (Winter 2019): 157–173.

36 PTI, "Pakistan Will Not Use Nuclear Weapons First, Zardari," *India Today*, November 22, 2008, https://www.indiatoday.in/latest-headlines/story/pakistan-will-not-use-nuclear-weapons-first-zardari-33840-2008-11-22. "No Need for Nuclear Deterrents Once Kashmir Issue is resolved: PM Imran Khan, Dawn, June 21, 2021, https://www.dawn.com/news/1630650.

37 Vergese Koithara, *Managing India's Nuclear Forces* (Washington DC: Brookings Institution, 2012), 2.

38 "The Lahore Declaration February 1999, Ministry of External Affairs, Government of India, February 1999, accessed on January 12, 2022, https://mea.gov.in/in-focus-article.htm?18997/Lahore+Declaration+February+1999.

39 Brad Roberts, "Debating Nuclear No-First-Use Again," *Survival* 62, no 3 (June–July 2019): 39, doi: 10.1080/00396338.2019.1614788.

40 Andre Futter and Benjamin Zala, "Strategic Non-Nuclear Weapons and the Onset of a Third Nuclear Age," *European Journal of International Security*, February 11, 2021, accessed on July 24, 2022, https://www.cambridge.org/core/journals/european-journal-of-international-security/article/strategic-nonnuclear-weapons-and-the-onset-of-a-third-nuclear-age/91EEB3B77D348252815F9F7B59DB8A32.

41 Sadia Tasleem and Toby Dalton, "Nuclear Emulation: Pakistan's Nuclear Trajectory," *The Washington Quarterly*, (Winter 2019): 135–155, accessed on July 24, 2022, https://www.tandfonline.com/doi/full/10.1080/0163660X.2018.1558662.

42 Roberts, "Debating Nuclear No-First-Use Again."

43 Bruno Tertrias, "No First Use, No Deterrence," Strategy Asia, October 7, 2019, accessed on July 24, 2022, https://strafasia.com/no-first-use-no-deterrence/.

44 Tertrias, "No First Use."
45 Tertrias, "No First Use."
46 Tertrias, " No First Use."
47 Roberts, "Debating Nuclear No-First-Use Again," 40.
48 Quinlan, *Thinking about Nuclear Weapons*, 102.

Chapter 19

NO-FIRST-USE POLICY OF A NEW NUCLEAR WEAPONS STATE—THE CASE OF NORTH KOREA

Jina Kim

GENERAL VIEWS AND MISPERCEPTIONS ON NORTH KOREA'S NUCLEAR DOCTRINE

Scholars have paid much attention to how and when nuclear weapons are managed and might actually be employed. The case of North Korea, a new nuclear-armed state, is no exception. We pay attention to North Korea's discourse on nuclear first use as the country's nuclear weapons capabilities grow. However, methodologically rigorous research on North Korea's nuclear doctrine remains virtually absent. Due to the lack of information about North Korea in general, people tend to make assumptions based on statements that come from Pyongyang whenever major events occur. There is also a tendency to draw implications from the evolution of North Korea's nuclear weapons capabilities and predict North Korea's intentions behind these moves.

When it comes to analysing North Korea's nuclear doctrine, both factors are considered: capability and intent. The first is related to determining how great a threat North Korea's nuclear and missile capabilities pose to regional security. The second relates to determining under what circumstances North Korea will use its nuclear weapons. In this regard, it is necessary to focus on the two recent changes in the understanding of North Korea's nuclear doctrine. First, the fact that its nuclear and missile programmes are developing at an unprecedented pace appears to affect the way we understand the North's view of the utility of nuclear weapons. Second, the perception that the traditional logic of nuclear taboo cannot be applied to North Korea seems to shape our belief that the North's nuclear doctrine is different from that of the existing nuclear-armed states.

The perception of the US government and research think tanks in Washington appears to have changed considerably since 2017. US intelligence agencies present views about nuclear capabilities held by

North Korea, and there is a significant difference in their assessments compared to those made before the North's sixth nuclear test in 2017.[1] The sixth nuclear test significantly affected our assessment of its ability to make nuclear warheads. According to a report released by the Institute for Science and International Security (ISIS) in February 2015, the number of plutonium-based nuclear warheads that North Korea possesses was estimated at six to eight and the number of uranium-based arsenals at ten to twelve.[2] At the end of 2016, ISIS presented an estimate that the number of North Korea's nuclear warheads totalled thirty, assuming that enrichment facilities outside Yongbyon were operating efficiently.[3]

What's interesting is that the US intelligence agency's assessment, which has so far offered relatively conservative views, has begun to show a huge deviation from that of other research institutions. The US National Intelligence Service and the Defense Intelligence Agency assessed in 2017 that North Korea controls as many as sixty nuclear warheads, a stark contrast to the estimates of private think tanks.[4] The US intelligence agencies highlighted the gravity and urgency of the issue, presenting the opinion that North Korea would accelerate the timing of the completion of its ICBM programme by 2018.[5]

Although there is no agreement on whether the North's missile guidance and control system and reentry technology have been technically proven, concerns over the extension of its missile range have been highly influential in assessments of the North's nuclear and missile threats. After all, these discussions are believed to have had a significant impact on the prospects for North Korea's nuclear doctrine.[6] In other words, the 'speedy pace of development' that North Korea demonstrates plays an important role in predicting its future path. This is also confirmed in the remarks by Admiral Harry Harris who attended hearings of the House Armed Services Committee in April 2017 and February 2018. He said that he believes North Korea can achieve the ability to pose a true threat to the USA because it is rapidly reducing the gap between its rhetoric and capabilities.[7] Concerns regarding the level of North Korea's threat to US security were clearly expressed during a congressional hearing, which would have been reflected in the process of writing a report to Congress. The Nuclear Posture Review in 2018 argued that North Korea 'poses the most immediate and dire proliferation threat to international security and stability', and North Korea's 'expansive nuclear and missile programs suggest the potential for nuclear first use in support of conventional operations'.

A worrisome problem is that many accept the views presented without an accurate outlook due to the lack of information on the North. For example, North Korea's nuclear doctrine, presented by Vipin Narang, is determined to lie between the asymmetric escalation strategy and the catalytic strategy.[8] The logic of the catalytic strategy argument is that North Korea, facing a crisis on the Korean Peninsula, would threaten nuclear first use to draw China into joining a nuclear stand-off. The basis for Narang's catalyst strategy is China's mediating role in the denuclearisation dialogues in the mid-1990s and mid-2000s, in which China became involved in peacetime Korean Peninsula issues.

However, this line of logic does not take into account the historical context of Sino-North Korea relations. North Korea chooses self-reliance, rather than alignment when it comes to security matters. Besides, the cost of China's involvement in Korean Peninsula affairs is overlooked in his logic. North Korea–China relations in the event of a crisis would be different, given that there is a significant difference in the cost of its involvement in nuclear negotiations versus a military nuclear stand-off. The possibility cannot be ruled out that China wants to avoid a situation in which the USA and China are at odds over a nuclear crisis on the Korean Peninsula.

The argument that North Korea will pursue an asymmetric crisis strategy of 'restricting the behaviour of the other by threatening nuclear attacks', at a time when China is unable to fulfil its role as a sponsor, is also vulnerable to counterarguments. The rationale that Narang suggests is that regional countries with limited nuclear capabilities have employed such a strategy in the past. He also predicts that the North could hand over its nuclear command control to the on-site commander to use such a strategy. However, it is unclear against which country North Korea is trying to escalate tensions. In his argument, there is no distinction as to whether it is a nuclear state or a non-nuclear state. This strategy will not be able to be used against opponents whose nuclear and non-nuclear forces are incomparably superior, such as the USA, or a state under the nuclear umbrella. It overlooks that North Korea's nuclear first use is highly likely to result in severe retaliation against the regime. If North Korea uses its nuclear weapons first, it will lead to the demise, not the protection, of the regime. Questions are also raised over the assumption that nuclear control can be handed over to a field commander. The North's law makes it clear that nuclear weapons shall be used only by the supreme commander of North Korea. Therefore, it is hard to anticipate that control over a handful of nuclear weapons will be given to field commanders at the scene.

Table 19.1: Assumptions about North Korea's Warfighting Strategy

Strategy	Objective	Pattern	Logical Flaw
Catalytic Strategy	Draw China into intervening in a nuclear crisis on North Korea's behalf	Pressure the other countries with limited-weapons capabilities	Does not take into account costs associated with joining a conflict in a nuclear crisis
Asymmetric Escalation Strategy	Avoid escalation from conventional to nuclear confrontation	Compel de-escalation by threatening nuclear first use in conventional warfare	Not likely to work against nuclear-armed states

Most scholars who believe that North Korea will actively seek to take advantage of its nuclear first-use options assume that Pyongyang will perceive a great threat to the regime regardless of the nature of the conflict.[9] Therefore, they conclude that the North will want to use its nuclear capability to secure political and military advantages before its command and control capabilities are paralysed by the overwhelming advanced conventional military capabilities of South Korea and the USA. They also suggest that North Korea will have tactical nuclear weapons such as short-range nuclear missiles, nuclear artillery, nuclear landmines and nuclear torpedoes with which they could threaten a pre-emptive strike in the future.

At the centre of all these discussions is the assumption that North Korea will choose an escalation strategy. Proponents of this view argue that it is highly likely that North Korea will use a coercive strategy by threatening the use of nuclear weapons as a means to quickly end the war on its terms. There are several reasons why most adhere to the frame of a coercive strategy in predicting North Korea's nuclear doctrine. First, the intention to develop a wide range of nuclear weapons and missile options cannot be separated from the intent to use them. Second, there are concerns over the potential for North Korea's misjudgement that its nuclear capability will give it the freedom to make bold moves on a broad scale. Third, there is the assumption that nuclear weapons will be used as an actual means before the window of opportunity to use them has closed.

However, it must also be noted that such an assumption of the North's nuclear strategy invites quite a few questions. First, the intention to develop weapons and the intention to use weapons cannot be considered the same. Nuclear and missile tests are used in terms of coercive diplomacy, not coercion which is the use of threatened force, including the limited use of actual force to back up the threat, to induce an adversary to behave differently than it otherwise would.[10] Testing is a means of coercive diplomacy aimed at adding psychological pressure on the other parties. Also, North Korea keeps on claiming that the development of strategic and tactical weapons is aimed at deterring war and protecting the regime, which cannot be related to the intent to use them.

Second, the argument that the build-up of nuclear capabilities boosts North Korea's willingness to provoke makes sense only with the premise that it has been able to narrow the relative gap in nuclear power. North Korea has increased the level of its nuclear threats but the fact that the level of its capabilities is low compared to the USA and other existing nuclear powers remains unchanged. Therefore, it is still difficult for the regime to attempt provocations from a position where it is difficult to control the opponent's response.

Third, most of the arguments assume possible scenarios wherein North Korea's nuclear weapons are used not merely as a last resort but as warfighting means before the regime reaches the stage of collapse. The use of nuclear weapons will not prevent North Korea from regime collapse but will rather trigger the end of the regime. We need to reconsider this tendency to regard Pyongyang's increasing efforts to develop nuclear deterrence and the evolution of its nuclear strategy on equal terms.

Fourth, the US–South Korea military strategy is designed to de-escalate, not escalate, any situation on the Korean Peninsula until there are clear signs of North Korea's attempt to use nuclear weapons in a crisis. The fact that the alliance maintains a deterrence posture against the North does not mean that it will pre-emptively respond to major conventional threats with nuclear weapons. The alliance's policy is to focus on deterrence by denial based on the Korean Air Missile Defense (KAMD) in peacetime and swiftly bring an end to any possible conflict before a nuclear exchange can occur. Therefore, in this situation, it becomes absurd for North Korea to be threatened by the alliance's nuclear pre-emption.

However, caution should be paid to the tendency to use some of the North's rhetoric, which has drawn international attention, as a basis for reading the mind of the leadership in Pyongyang. It is necessary to examine the logic that North Korea puts forward while bolstering its nuclear capabilities, at what stage North Korea thinks it can deter the USA in a credible manner and under what circumstances North Korea claims the use of nuclear weapons is justified based on an analysis of North Korea's official statement.

AN ANALYSIS OF NORTH KOREA'S NUCLEAR STRATEGY

On 1 April 2013, North Korea passed a law further consolidating its status as a self-reliant nuclear power and has since stressed that it should fully prepare for nuclear combat by completing strategies and operations in a way that raises the pivotal role of nuclear power in all aspects of war deterrence and warfighting strategy.[11]

This law suggests that North Korea should possess the capability to make nuclear use possible on a strategic and tactical level. The law is important in that it is a document showing how North Korea has formulated and disclosed its nuclear policy both internally and externally. Overall, its focus is on the use of nuclear weapons for deterrence purposes.[12] For example, Article 2 states that North Korea's nuclear power serves the purpose of 'deterring aggression and attacks against the North and conducting retaliatory strikes against the enemy'. In addition, Article 3 says that the objective of North Korea's efforts of force enhancement should focus on 'nuclear deterrence and nuclear retaliation'. Article 4 states that the conditions under which North Korea uses nuclear weapons are 'when other nuclear powers invade or attack the North'. This stresses once again that the purpose of nuclear power is to repel and retaliate. It also states that nuclear non-use against non-nuclear states applies except under the condition that they are 'aligned with hostile nuclear states'.

An examination of this law makes clear the presence of a gap between what is understood as North Korea's nuclear strategy by outsiders and how the North's nuclear doctrine is documented by law. Still, the North's official statements highlight its nuclear weapons as the only means to prevent aggression by an external force. In other words, North Korea describes its nuclear capabilities in the context of deterrence, attaching the condition that its use of nuclear weapons can be considered in the event of an invasion or an attack against the regime. This should be supported by thorough analysis; rigorous research is lacking in previous literature.

In this chapter, discourse analysis is used as a research method to understand North Korea's official position on the utility of its nuclear weapons capabilities. There are three main issues which this paper examines. The first is the collocation of words in the text. This paper looks at what North Korea emphasises with regard to nuclear use. The second is the frequency and distribution of keywords. Frequency is a key concept in discourse analysis, and hence this paper examines statistically significant word choices. In particular, this paper looks at whether 'pre-emption' or 'deterrence' is more important in the text and whether the frequency of use varies year by year. Thirdly, it looks at the changes in the corpus and usage. It collected articles from the *Rodong Sinmun,* which is the official newspaper of the North Korean Worker's Party, to see how the frequency of expressions has changed year by year from 2012 and 2018. Then, articles that included the word 'nuclear' were selected. Next, a sub-corpus was created including 'deterrence' and 'pre-emption'.

Table 19.2: Content for Analysis

Topic	Year	Articles	Keyword	Collocation
Nuclear	2012	17,613	56,184	2,276
	2013	15,831	79,217	4,067
	2014	14,879	42,211	1,554
	2015	14,332	63.313	1,337
	2016	13,721	95,560	5,064
	2017	12,691	51,432	508
	2018	16,943	31,305	39

First, it is important to look at the concepts on which North Korea emphasises regarding its nuclear use.[13] North Korea still adheres to the principle of an immediate counter-attack on provocations by outside forces, a phrase that has been used since the early days of the Kim Jong-un regime. However, what has been added to North Korea's rhetoric is the threat of pre-emption. In 2012, the North emphasised a proportional response, mainly using the phrase 'nuclear response to nuclear use'. In 2013, it maintained its stance, while in 2014 North Korea explained the conditions of nuclear use as 'cases of any threats to survival'.[14]

One should note the interactive nature of this discourse. That is, the change in the North's nuclear doctrine is more reciprocal than unilateral. It is worth noting that at that time, Seoul and Washington put forward the concept of proactive deterrence—striking immediately after signals of North Korea's preparation of nuclear use are detected. What is noteworthy is that the term 'nuclear' is not mentioned in the phrase 'a merciless pre-emptive strike is the most correct choice'. At that time, it remained ambiguous as to whether 'pre-emptive' action means nuclear use or a conventional strike.[15]

Changes in North Korea's rhetoric centre on its response methods, not the principle of response.[16] When North Korea began to stress that it had diversified the delivery means of its nuclear weapons, words such as 'ruthless' or 'invincible' often appeared in its rhetoric. The timing of the North's frequent mention of the option of nuclear retaliation is correlated with the circumstances of its SLBM test in October 2014.[17] At that time, the North stressed the credibility of the US nuclear deterrence against South Korea, describing its deterrence capability as already complete, when explaining its possession of nuclear strike capabilities.[18]

It also became more specific when North Korea revealed the priorities of its targets. In 2012, North Korea mentioned that its strike range broadly covers 'the Korean Peninsula and the surrounding US military bases'.[19] North Korea began to mention certain targets in 2013, referring to 'the US military bases in the Pacific and the White House'.[20] North Korea again mentioned the 'US mainland' as a strike target in 2015. In 2016, North Korea revealed its priority of targets to hit, with the government agency in South Korea first, the US military bases in the Asia-Pacific region second and the US mainland coming in third.[21] In 2017, it described its capability to strike 'the entire US mainland' as there was a test launch of the Hwasong-14.

North Korea said it shifted its nuclear posture to one of pre-emptive strike, which got the attention of the international community. North Korea claimed it will counter with a precision nuclear strike if it is threatened with nuclear weapons. For example, in February and August 2016, the North warned through the Supreme Command and General Staff of the People's Army that it would launch a 'nuclear pre-emptive strike' whenever there are minor signs of aggression on its territorial land, water, or airspace.[22] North Korea also warned in March 2016 that it would react with overwhelming force if any US and South Korean troop attempts to invade its territory.[23]

The question is whether some of the rhetoric that the international community is paying attention to can represent the North's overall strategy. The North released warning statements when South Korea's 'pre-emptive strike' strategy was reported in the media and when the US–South Korea military exercises were conducted. These reactions can also be attempted in light of deterrence purposes.

Table 19.3: Major Statements

Topic	Year	Statement
Response Principle	2012	Proportional, timely response against foreign aggression
	2013	Use of nuclear force to deter, repel and retaliate against invasion and attack
	2014	Pre-emptive strike against any pre-emptive strike by the enemy force
	2015	Nuclear strike against nuclear threat, all-out war against foreign invasion
	2016	Shift to a pre-emptive strike posture (standby for nuclear strike)

Topic	Year	Statement
Target of Attack	2012	Korean Peninsula, bases of the US forces and Continental US
	2013	Stronghold of the aggressor
	2014	US White House and bases in the Asia-Pacific
	2015	Origin of provocation, forward-stationing bases, launch bases, CONUS
	2016	Blue House and the ROK government (first target) US bases in the Asia-Pacific and CONUS (second target)
Demands	2012	Conclusion of a peace treaty
	2013	Dismantlement of the UN Command on the Korean Peninsula
	2014	Suspension of the US–ROK joint military exercises
	2015	Temporary suspension of US–ROK joint military exercises Peace treaty
	2016	Withdrawal of all US forces and assets in the South Recognition of North Korea's status as a nuclear weapons state
Background Events	2012	US–ROK Missile Guidelines revision
	2013	Self-proclaimed nullification of the Armistice Treaty
	2014	Introduction of the Kill-Chain, KAMD and Korean Military Pre-emptive Retaliation Release of tailored deterrence strategy and joint exercises
	2015	Rejection of freezing nuclear tests in exchange for cancelling joint military exercises Intensified sanctions and human rights violation accusations
	2016	Joint military exercises

This paper compared the frequency of the use of the words 'pre-emption' and 'deterrence' by North Korea to see changes in North Korea's nuclear strategy. It appears that the frequency of the use of both terms significantly increased in 2013 and 2016. On the other hand, during the year when inter-Korean dialogue was attempted, the frequency of the two words decreased.

Figure 19.1: Frequency of 'Pre-emption' and 'Deterrence' in North Korea's Rhetoric (2012–2018)

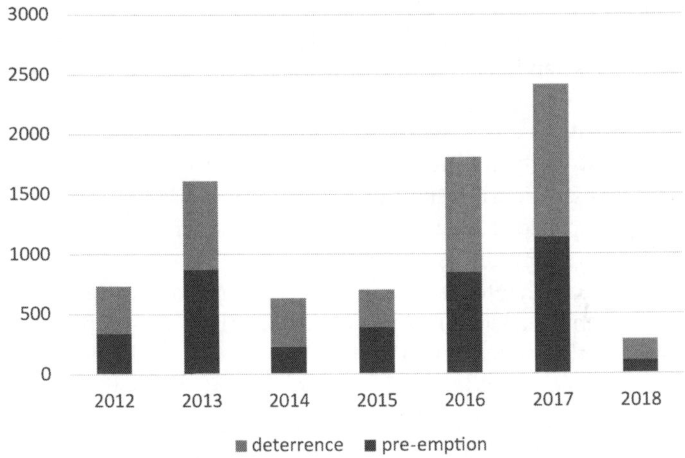

Source: *Rodong Sinmun*, 2012-2018

When the collation is carefully examined, it turns out that North Korea tends to describe itself as a 'target' of deterrence. The term deterrence was used when the North criticised pressure from the outside world to give up its nuclear deterrence. Since 2013, however, North Korea has been referring to nuclear deterrence more often than before in the context of developing nuclear deterrence capabilities. Further, the regime's confidence in its nuclear deterrence appears to have risen since 2016. For example, the appearance of the word 'deterrence' is often combined with words such as 'the strongest' and 'utmost'.

Looking at the combination of words linked to pre-emption, North Korea's rhetoric describes itself as a target of a pre-emptive strike, in 2012. In 2013, it was emphasised that North Korea had the right to make a pre-emptive strike. However, in 2016, the regime began to actively describe the pre-emptive option. The emphasis that a pre-emptive strike is not a 'monopoly of the US' and that North Korea can similarly carry out 'pre-emptive and aggressive' operations is a change from past rhetoric. In 2012, several terms were used to emphasise that nuclear deterrence is a self-defence right and criticise international demands for North Korea's abandonment of nuclear deterrence. In 2013, several terms were used to reinforce the idea that North Korea actively pursues the development of nuclear deterrence. In 2015, when the North stressed its willingness to use nuclear weapons against the USA, such words as relentlessly and pivotal were combined with deterrence. The year 2016 appears to reflect the North's confidence in its nuclear deterrence. At that time, the expression nuclear deterrence was combined with 'the strongest' and 'most powerful'. When the term pre-emptive was used, it was emphasised that North Korea is a potential target for a pre-emptive nuclear strike and that North Korea also holds the 'right' to use nuclear weapons against aggressors until 2014. In 2015, North Korea mentioned the possibility that it could engage in nuclear retaliation in response to nuclear first use by its enemies. However, in 2016, North Korea hinted that it was considering the pre-emptive option. While claiming that it is capable of conducting such pre-emptive operations, North Korea described pre-emption as 'justifiable'.

Then, this chapter examined whether North Korea prefers to use the term 'nuclear pre-emption' rather than 'pre-emptive use' of conventional options. When comparing the use of 'pre-emption' and 'nuclear pre-emption' in North Korea's rhetoric, it is noticeable that in most cases, North Korea claims the right of pre-emption, not nuclear pre-emption. North Korea continues to describe itself as a potential target of a nuclear pre-emptive strike by the USA, but the frequency of North Korea's use of the expression nuclear pre-emption is relatively low. In 2012, when North Korea emphasised deterrence as a response to a nuclear pre-emptive strike, the phrase 'nuclear response' was not mentioned. It was 2013 when North Korea first used the word 'response' together with 'nuclear weapons' against a nuclear attack. However, the high-frequency collocations of verbs and nouns show that North Korea claims that the USA threatens nuclear pre-emption whereas North Korea adheres to conventional pre-emption. In a statement to the Third Plenary Session of the Workers' Party's Central Committee held on 20 April 2018, the North said it will never use nuclear weapons unless there is a nuclear threat or nuclear provocation against it. Discourse analysis also shows that only 10 per cent of the total collocations show North Korea describing itself as an actor capable of employing nuclear pre-emption.

To sum up, until 2017, there was a marked increase in the frequency of descriptions characterising North Korea's response to US military actions in a more aggressive way. But the North still has a focus on deterrence. Although North Korea has frequently used the expression nuclear pre-emption, the subject of 'nuclear pre-emptive strikes' generally appears to be the USA.

Overall, the North's nuclear strategy places a great emphasis on deterring pre-emptive strikes against the regime and expressing its willingness to retaliate. Many experts have assumed that the North would use nuclear weapons from the outset in case of an emergency but the results of this study do not support this argument. There is no

Figure 19.2: Comparison between Deterrence and Pre-emption (2018)

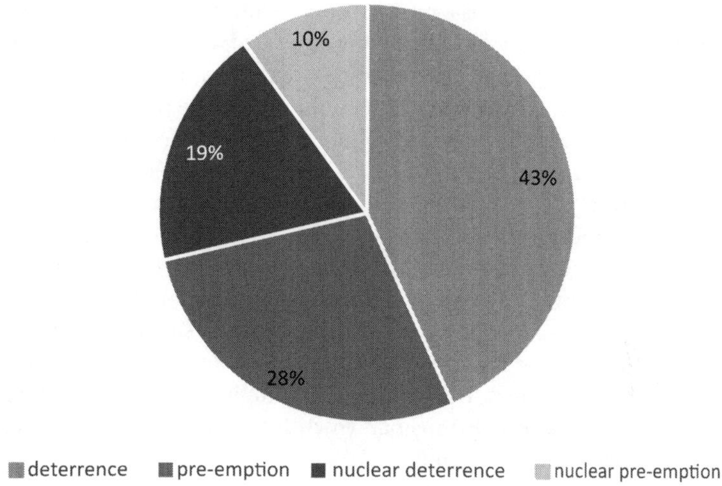

Source: *Rodong Sinmun*, 2012-2018

denying the possibility that North Korea's nuclear capability may be used as a deterrent to test the will of the USA and South Korea. However, North Korea's nuclear and missile attacks will not happen suddenly, but rather, will occur during an escalation. If convincing North Korea not to use its nuclear weapons programme is the priority of those who engage with North Korea in a crisis, then a priority should be placed on seeking ways to strengthen extended deterrence in a way that controls crisis escalation.

CONCLUSION

This chapter raised questions over some claims that North Korea's nuclear capability is directly linked to its aggressive use of nuclear weapons. It is important to prepare for the worst-case scenario in which North Korea will use its nuclear weapons pre-emptively. However, it is equally important to avoid situations that could lead North Korea to make a misjudgment that nuclear weapons should be used. Crisis management begins with accurately understanding North Korea's intention. North Korea's nuclear doctrine will continue to change as it is constructed under a specific context. The threat to the US alliance by a regional nuclear-armed state is determined in a tripartite relationship, not a bilateral one. More attention should be paid to strengthening extended deterrence through which a nuclear state expands deterrence to prevent attacks on allies. Extended deterrence aims to ensure security assurance to deter nuclear attacks on non-nuclear allies. What is important for extended deterrence to work properly is that countries that receive security guarantees must have high confidence in the nuclear deterrence provided by the nuclear ally. If a non-nuclear ally does not trust guarantees provided by a nuclear ally, this complicates extended deterrence against other nuclear states. However, given the interactive nature of military strategies between North Korea and the allied forces in South Korea, a balance needs to be struck between providing a firm defense commitment to allies and not heightening the North Korean threat perception. In the long term, efforts should be made to impose restrictions or increase transparency in the use of military force through trust-building and arms control talks with North Korea. This is a research topic that deserves more attention on the Korean Peninsula, which is facing an arms race that can even cause regional instability.

NOTES

1 James R. Clapper, "Statement for the Record: Worldwide Threat Assessment of the US Intelligence Community" (The Senate Armed Services Committee, Washington DC, February 9, 2016); Gregory S. Jones, "The Implications of North Korea Testing a Boosted Nuclear Weapon," *Proliferation Matters*, January 11, 2016.

2 David Albright, "Future Directions in the DPRK's Nuclear Weapons Program: Three Scenarios for 2020," in *North Korea's Nuclear Futures Series* (Washington DC: US–Korea Institute, 2015).

3 Albright, *North Korea's Nuclear Capabilities: A Fresh Look* (Washington DC: Institute for Science and International Security, 2017).

4 Albright, "Testimony before the Monetary and Trade Subcommittee of the Committee on Financial Services," Washington DC, September 13, 2017.

5 David E. Sanger, "Intelligence Agencies Say North Korean Missile Could Reach US in a Year," *The New York Times*, July 25, 2017.

6 Clark Mindock, "CIA Concerned North Korea Could Hit US with a Missile in a Handful of Months," *Independent*, January 30, 2018; Bruce Klingner, "Maximum Pressure and Engagement-Still Pulling Punches on US Policy toward North Korea," (Testimony before the Senate Committee on Foreign Relations Subcommittee on East Asia, the Pacific, and International Cyber Security, Senate Committee on Foreign Relations, Washington DC, July 25, 2017).

7 Harry Harris, "Statement of Admiral Harry B. Harris Jr., US Navy Commander, US Pacific Command" (House Armed Services Committee on US Pacific Command Posture, Washington DC, April 26, 2017).

8 Vipin Narang, "Nuclear Strategy of Emerging Nuclear Powers," *The Washington Quarterly* (Spring 2015): 82.

9 Taehyun Kim, "North Korea's Nuclear Strategy: Active Existential Deterrence," *National Strategy* 22, no 3 (2016); Changkwoun Park, "Military Strategy Development to Deal with Nuclear Threats from North Korea," *Weekly Defense Review*, no 1,586 (2015); Jaeyeop Kim, "Military Security on the Korean Peninsula and Nuclear Strategy," *Defense Studies* 59, no. 2 (2016).

10 Daniel L. Byman, Matthew C. Waxman, and Eric Larson, *Air Power as a Coercive Instrument* (Santa Monica CA: RAND Cororation, 1999).

11 *Rodong Shinmun*, April 1, 2013.

12 "Law on the Enhancement of North Korea's Status as a Self-reliant Nuclear Weapons State," April 1, 2013.

13 "DPRK Ministry of Foreign Affairs Spokesperson Statement," Pyongyang, August 20, 2012; "Speech by Choe Ryonghae," Director of General Political Bureau, Pyongyang, January 2013; "We Will Seek Unification without Losing Any Chance When North Korea's Dignity Is Challenged," Korean Central News Agency, February 27, 2013.

14 *Rodong Shinmun*, August 21, 2014.

15 "DPRK Government Statement," Pyongyang, January 6, 2016.

16 Korean Central News Agency, July 15, *2015*.

17 "The Successful Test of an SLBM Enables North Korea to Ensure the Effectiveness of Its Nuclear Second Strike Capabilities after US Nuclear First Use," *Rodong Shinmun*, May 18, 2015; "DPRK National Defense Committee Political Bureau Spokesperson Statement," Pyongyang, May 20, 2015.

18 "DPRK Ministry of Foreign Affairs Spokesperson Statement," Pyongyang, August 26, 2016.

19 "DPRK Ministry of Foreign Affairs Spokesperson Statement," Pyongyang, October 10, 2012.

20 "Speech by Hwang Byungseo, Rally of the Korean People's Army," Pyongyang, July 27, 2014.

21 *Rodong Shinmun*, March 27, 2015.

22 "Speech at the 81st Anniversary of the Korean People's Army," April 24, 2013; *Rodong Shinmun*, March 7, 2013; "Statement by the National Defense Committee," Pyongyang, March 7, 2016.

23 "North Korea Supreme Command Statement," Pyongyang, February 23, 2016; "Korean Peopele's Army General Staff Department Spokesperson Statement," Pyongyang, August 22, 2016; KPA General Staff Department Statement," Pyongyang, March 12, 2016.

Chapter 20

TOKYO'S RELUCTANCE OVER NO FIRST USE, FOR NOW[1]

Hirofumi Tosaki

INTRODUCTION: JAPAN'S NUCLEAR-RELATED POLICIES AND NFU

According to the latest Japan's National Defense Program Guidelines (NDPG) in December 2018, '[i]n dealing with the threat of nuclear weapons, U.S. extended deterrence, with nuclear deterrence at its core, is essential: Japan will closely cooperate with the United States to maintain and enhance its credibility…. At the same time, towards the long-term goal of bringing about a world free of nuclear weapons, Japan will play an active and positive role in nuclear disarmament and non-proliferation.'[2] These two seemingly contradictory directions—that is, relying on US nuclear deterrence while pursuing a total elimination of nuclear weapons—have often sparked debate over Japan's policies regarding nuclear issues, including NFU of nuclear weapons.

Those who advocate nuclear disarmament argue that Japan, as the only country to have suffered atomic bombings in 1945, should urge nuclear-armed states—particularly the USA, which is its ally and provide extended nuclear deterrence to Japan—to adopt NFU policies as one of the essential measures for reducing a possibility of nuclear weapons use and promoting nuclear weapons reductions, thereby strengthening Japan's national security. On the other hand, those who emphasise the importance of extended deterrence for Japan's security oppose such a proposal, arguing that the USA's adoption of an NFU policy despite the tense security environment in Northeast Asia would not be beneficial to Japan's security. They consider it is likely to have negative impacts on the effectiveness and credibility of the USA's extended (nuclear) deterrence and less likely to actually promote nuclear disarmament.

Tokyo has not unveiled its official policy on NFU. In October 2016, when a Diet (Japan's Parliament) member requested clarity on Japan's position about whether it would agree on the USA adopting an NFU policy, the cabinet's answer was that it would decline to comment on this issue.[3] However, it is widely considered that Japan has opposed the US adoption of such a policy. Tokyo, together with other US allies, reportedly urged Washington not to adopt an NFU policy on several occasions. For instance, at the US Congressional Commission on Strategic Posture, which was held in 2008–2009, with the aim to help guide a drafting of the US Nuclear Posture Review (NPR) under the Obama administration, it argued that the US adoption of NFU was contrary to Japan's security.[4] In 2016, when the Obama administration contemplated major changes to its nuclear policy, Tokyo again informed Washington of its opposition to the US adoption of NFU.[5] In addition, NFU has not been included in Japan's proposals on nuclear disarmament submitted to various fora, such as the NPT review process and the UN General Assembly.

Why has Tokyo been so reluctant regarding the US adoption of an NFU policy? Under what circumstances or conditions would it judge the USA and/or global adoption of NFU as a beneficial measure for Japan's security?

CONCERNS ABOUT UNDERMINING EXTENDED NUCLEAR DETERRENCE

One of the most important factors that affect Tokyo's expectation concerning the role of US extended (nuclear) deterrence is the security situation surrounding Japan. Throughout the 2010s, it has become more and more unstable and complicated, with diverse threats and challenges. All of Japan's neighbours, except South Korea, are nuclear-armed states that have actively modernised their nuclear arsenals and have had security issues with Japan. North Korea has repeatedly threatened to use nuclear weapons against Japan. Russia and China respectively have unresolved issues over territory and maritime interests with Japan, and their great power competition with the USA also has a significant impact on the geopolitical competition in Northeast Asia. Japan perceives that it is located in one of the most perilous regional security situations in the world.

Nonetheless, Japan has maintained a restrictive security policy. As a non-nuclear weapons state (NNWS) party to the NPT, Japan has pledged not to acquire nuclear weapons. Besides, under an interpretation of Article 9 of its Constitution, '[t]he possession of armaments deemed to be offensive weapons designed to be used only for the mass destruction of another country is not permissible under any circumstance as it would, by definition, exceed the minimum necessary level'.[6] Under the above-mentioned interpretation, Japan has considered that such 'offensive weapons' include ICBMs, long-range strategic bombers and attack aircraft carriers. Furthermore, up to the present date, Japan also does not have offensive weapon systems for the purpose of striking other countries.

In light of the security environment and policies mentioned abvoe, Japan considers relying on US extended deterrence as the only feasible and realistic measure to deter, and defeat if deterrence fails, adversaries' nuclear and other destructive attacks vis-à-vis Japan. Therefore, Tokyo has been sensitive to the possibility that a US adoption of NFU would undermine the credibility and effectiveness of extended deterrence.

The foremost important function of extended deterrence which Japan expects is not retaliation against adversaries *after* they cause enormous damage to Japan by using nuclear or other weapons, but to deter or defeat adversaries' attacks *before* incurring such damages. Japan, which lacks strategic depth, cannot tolerate any adversary's massive attacks which would poses a threat to the survival of Japan. Thus, the question regarding NFU is not whether the USA actually retaliates against Japan's adversaries on behalf of a devastated Japan, but whether the US deterrence under its NFU policy could still be credible and effective.

Japan is concerned that the US adoption of the NFU policy would have some negative implications for both extended deterrence by punishment and denial. Regarding deterrence by punishment, especially if the USA adopts NFU and simultaneously renounces the existing counterforce posture to make its NFU more credible (since retaining counterforce targeting would be seen as maintaining a first-use option), adversaries would doubt the US resolve to conduct retaliatory nuclear second strikes on behalf of Japan. Should adversaries calculate that the USA would hesitate to conduct countervalue nuclear attacks, causing highly probable mass causalities of civilians, on behalf of its allies due to legal, political and moral constraints on targeting civilians, US deterrence might fail.

Secondly, Tokyo has also been concerned that North Korea and China may consider that the adoption of the US NFU policy has made it easier for them to launch non-nuclear attacks against Japan. It is widely considered that North Korea possesses large-scale biological and, to a lesser extent, chemical weapons that can be loaded on its ballistic missiles that have the capabilities of reaching Japan. China's conventional forces, including its hundreds of dual-capable medium- and intermediate-range missiles, has been rapidly expanding, which could also pose grave damage on Japan's soil. Furthermore, the threat of massive cyberattacks has been increasing.

Proponents of NFU argue that the USA is highly unlikely to conduct nuclear retaliation against non-nuclear attacks. But adversaries cannot rule out the possibility of nuclear retaliation, which Japan expects would force them to be cautious about their escalations and, as a consequence, be deterred. As the US defence department states:

> Retaining a degree of ambiguity and refraining from a no first use policy creates uncertainty in the mind of potential adversaries and reinforces deterrence of aggression by ensuring adversaries cannot predict what specific actions will lead to a U.S. nuclear response. Implementing a no first use policy could undermine the U.S. ability to deter Russian, Chinese, and North Korean aggression, especially with respect to their growing capability to carry out nonnuclear strategic attacks.[7]

As mentioned above, whether adversaries are actually deterred or not—in other words, whether and how the US policies will affect the adversaries' perception—is much more important for Japan than whether the USA will use nuclear weapons for retaliation against non-nuclear attacks.

Clarifying a threshold of nuclear escalation—that is, under what circumstances and how a country conducts nuclear retaliation—would increase the credibility of deterrence. In addition, it is one of the effective ways to prevent adversaries' misperception, miscommunication or inadvertent escalation.[8] However, too much clarification would give adversaries a perception that its attacks below the threshold of using nuclear weapons would be permitted and might spur such attacks.

Some advocates of NFU also argue that US deterrence would not necessarily be undermined by declaring NFU because, for instance, 'whatever the U.S. declaratory policy, no adversary could ever be sure that the United States meant it'.[9] However, it is not clear whether and what such an arms-control measure has any significance. Rather, such a measure would hurt stability, particularly in a time of crisis.

Deterrence by punishment is not the only function of US extended deterrence that Japan expects. Rather, Japan considers deterrence by denial—based on counterforce or damage limitation operations by attacking the adversary's nuclear and other strategic capabilities as well as countering their strategic offensive attacks before they inflict serious damage to Japan—as more important for its security.

The USA's maintenance of a counterforce strike option does not immediately contradict its adoption of NFU since such strikes can be carried out aiming to prevent or mitigate further damage by an adversary's additional nuclear attacks after its first use of nuclear weapons. Still, Tokyo would prefer the US retention of the first-use option to limit damages Japan would suffer, or even disarm the adversaries' strategic weapons systems before they use them.

A criticism to such a policy is that the USA and/or the Japanese–US alliance conventional forces are strong enough to serve both effective deterrence by punishment and denial and to replace some of the missions that were once impossible to accomplish without nuclear weapons, such as defeating biological, chemical and massive conventional attacks. They argue that, therefore, Japan and the USA can reduce their reliance on nuclear deterrence in Northeast Asia, and thus the former can make a commitment on NFU without undermining the overall effect of the US extended deterrence provided to Japan.

However, there has been a persistent debate over whether conventional forces can provide sufficient deterrence against regional adversaries,[10] including whether and how conventional weapons can effectively destroy less vulnerable targets such as hardened and deeply buried targets and mobile ballistic/cruise missiles, or neutralise chemical and biological agents.

In addition, the US strong conventional forces as '[w]ar-winning capabilities do not always translate into war-deterring capabilities'.[11] The US 2018 NPR also stated that 'Non-nuclear forces also play essential deterrence roles. Alone, however, they do not provide comparable deterrence effects.'[12] The physical and phycological impact of conventional forces for deterrence is far less than those of nuclear forces. Besides, while the USA still maintains superiority in conventional forces, a determinative of a regional deterrence relationship is not the overall deterrent capabilities of the countries involved but the capabilities they could project, and their interests and resolve in regional contingencies, where regional countries rather than the USA are usually in an advantageous position.[13] The adversary may underestimate conventional US capabilities and/or its resolve to defend its allies.

Moreover, an overly emphasised role of the USA's conventional capabilities might rather undermine stability in a crisis where the adversary would be faced with a 'lose them or use them' choice for its strategic weapons because, from the perspective of collateral damage and morality, the adversary is highly likely to consider the threshold for a US conventional attack is much lower than that for its nuclear attack.

Lastly, Japan would be concerned that the US adoption of an NFU policy despite the worsening security situation in Northeast Asia would be interpreted by an adversary as the USA reducing its commitment to its allies and extended deterrence when its ally's vital interests are at risk. The adversary could thus calculate that it could de-couple the USA from its allies. Retaining an option of first use of nuclear weapons by the USA has been perceived by both adversaries and allies as the symbol of extended deterrence, and its change would have an inevitable impact over deterrence against adversaries and reassurance for its allies.[14]

Moreover, once declaring a commitment, the USA withdrawing the NFU pledge may not only invite blame that it is running counter to nuclear disarmament but it could also destabilise the deterrence relationship, as the adversary recognised renoucing the NFU policy as signalling a change of a more aggressive nuclear posture to the adversaries.

IMPLICATIONS FOR NUCLEAR DISARMAMENT

A proponent of NFU could argue that even if the US adoption of an NFU policy decreases the effectiveness and credibility of extended (nuclear) deterrence, Japan's security may be relatively bolstered should nuclear disarmament be promoted by such a US decision.

NFU's positive implications for nuclear disarmament, if working as expected, would include: promoting to reduce the number and roles of nuclear weapons, especially those required for first-use operations; leading to de-alerting nuclear arsenals; and reinforcing the taboo or norm on prohibiting the use of nuclear weapons. Especially adopting NFU by all nuclear-armed states, or a GNFU establishes a quasi-ban on using nuclear weapons since they do not have a chance to conduct a second use of their nuclear weapons. The proponents consider that '[a]doption of NFU would be a major step in changing mindsets with respect to nuclear weapons'.[15] The adoption of such a policy by the USA, which possesses the strongest nuclear forces and has led the international community, will particularly encourage similar actions by other nuclear-armed states.

However, as mentioned above, while Japan has strongly urged a reduction of the role and risk of nuclear weapons, its proposal for short-term disarmament efforts does not include NFU. To put it the other way around, Tokyo does not seem to count it as a nuclear disarmament measure for improving its national security under the existing regional and international security situation. Furthermore, it would consider that NFU may have negative impacts on nuclear disarmament.

Firstly, NFU as a declaratory policy would be less credible by itself. A country could covertly maintain a first-use option while officially declaring the NFU policy as was done by the Soviet Union during the Cold War. It would also easily change a declaratory policy upon its development of nuclear forces and overall security policies. Or it might decide to use nuclear weapons first despite its declaration should it face, for instance, an extreme circumstance of its national survival. 'After all, if a country is willing to use nuclear weapons, it's also willing to break a promise.'[16]

In the meantime, among the nuclear-weapon states (NWS) under the NPT, only China has highlighted an NFU policy. However, the USA pointed out: 'There is some ambiguity … in the narrative in China over the conditions under which China's NFU policy would apply.'[17] China's introduction of the new DF-41 mobile MIRVed ICBM (capable of carrying ten nuclear warheads per missile), which would be useful for counterforce operations, may cast further doubt about the credibility of China's NFU policy. If a country adopts counterforce strike options under the NFU, as mentioned above, its NFU commitment would be perceived less credible.

Secondly, the mere adoption of NFU would not promote a reduction of the number and role of nuclear weapons, or their de-alerting. Rather, a country declaring NFU might require more nuclear weapons or a higher alert status than before to maintain sufficient survivability of the nuclear weapons after receiving an adversary's counterforce or even a disarming first strike, especially conducted by conventional weapons.

Thirdly, with intensifying strategic competition accompanying the emergence of China as a global power, it could not be expected that the US declaration of the NFU would encourage other nuclear-armed states to promote and implement nuclear disarmament measures. Rather, other countries, especially those which are engaging in competition with the USA, would treat it as a sign of declining of US power or determination to defend it and its allies, and an opportunity to move aggressively for revising the current power balance and international/regional order into one that is favourable for them, by strengthening their nuclear arsenals. If the USA bolsters conventional deterrence in exchange for reducing the role of nuclear deterrence, including an adoption of an NFU policy, adversaries would respond by bolstering not just conventional but also nuclear forces to offset the US build-up of conventional forces, thus accelerating nuclear build-up that could be a negative for nuclear disarmament. At least, the USA's mere declaration of NFU would not be expected to lead to nuclear disarmament by other nuclear-armed states.

Fourthly, a deterrence by punishment posture based on countervalue targeting, that is mainly targeting civilians rather than military targets, would be contrary to the international humanitarian law (IHL) on prohibiting the direct targeting of civilians. It is also concerned that a country that does not hesitate to kill thousands of civilians might take an advantageous position in competition in coercive diplomacy over other countries which adhere to the IHL.

Lastly, it is less obvious whether the adoption of the NFU policy would strengthen the norms of the non-use of nuclear weapons. Moreover, the norm of non-use of nuclear weapons is fragile. For a world without nuclear weapons, it is imperative to establish and enhance a norm of non-use of nuclear weapons. However, at least at present, the realistic way forward seems to be to pursue a process of gradually developing a security environment in which the role of nuclear weapons can be reduced, and then underpinning this by nuclear disarmament measures, not vice versa. It might be time-consuming but there are no shortcuts.

CONDITIONS FOR CHANGING POLICY

Tokyo's current opposition to the US declaration of NFU policy will not continue forever. In the meantime, it has called NWS for providing negative security assurances (NSAs) for NPT NNWS, for instance:

> Credible security assurances by [NWS] to [NNWS] contribute to strengthening the global non-proliferation regime, building confidence among States and improving the security environment. Japan believes that effective international arrangements to assure [NNWS] against the use or threat of use of nuclear weapons (NSAs) could not only strengthen the NPT but also serve as an important intermediary step toward the ultimate goal of a world free of nuclear weapons.[18]

In the process towards the total elimination of nuclear weapons, which is Japan's strong aspiration, the prohibition of the use of nuclear weapons against any actors should become a widely adhered international norm. GNFU must be an indispensable step to reach that end.

At the same time, as mentioned above, NFU by itself is not a credible nuclear disarmament measure; rather, it has concrete meaning only when it is combined with other nuclear disarmament measures as well as security situations.

Should Japan continue to rely on US extended (nuclear) deterrence, what conditions and criteria are needed for the former to concur with the USA adopting NFU? For instance, Japan wants to have unswerving confidence that military threats which would lead to a US nuclear first-use option are significantly reduced. Or Japan might need to acquire alternative means other than nuclear weapons to deter and defeat threats against which nuclear first use has been considered vital means—and, preferably, its acquisition or adoption would not lead other countries' enhancement of nuclear forces for countering Japan's options. It is also important that prior to, or at least simultaneously with adopting the NFU, nuclear-armed states agree and implement nuclear disarmament measures, which ensure the credibility of their NFU.

Meanwhile, the international community, in particular nuclear-armed states, should commence thorough discussions on NFU, inter alia: how nuclear-armed states can collectively declare NFU beyond the asymmetry of their capabilities as well as differences in their threat perceptions vis-à-vis nuclear and/or conventional forces possessed by potential adversaries; under what situation they can declare; and for ensuring the credibility of NFU, what disarmament and security measures as well as nuclear policies the nuclear-armed states should undertake. Such discussions are also worthwhile for further promotion of nuclear disarmament.

Among others, it is imperative to contemplate ways to reduce the risks and possibilities of using nuclear weapons without eroding deterrence and Japan's security in this tremendously difficult period for promoting nuclear disarmament and improving the security situation. For instance, a nuclear-armed state (and its allies) may be able to declare that 'it possesses nuclear weapons only to respond to, and thereby deter or defeat, threat to its survival or that of its allies, particularly stemming from any use of nuclear weapons'.[19] Another important proposal is that 'the U.S. president announce a commitment to a "principle of necessity," committing the United States not to use nuclear weapons against any military target that can be destroyed with a reasonable probability of success by a conventional weapon'.[20] Participants of the Hiroshima Round Table in 2016, organised by the Hiroshima Prefecture, also recommended:

> [Until nuclear weapons] are abolished, they should be strictly subject to the principles of just war doctrine, the laws of armed conflict, and international humanitarian law. The definition of [legitimate military targets] becomes critical for appropriate application of the principles of discrimination, proportionality and, in particular, necessity. Civilian populations should never be targeted by conventional or nuclear weapons, and all efforts should be made to minimize collateral damage in any conflict. Deterrence should never mean targeting innocent civilians.[21]

In addition, Japan and the USA should continue to hold close consultations, where they discuss how, to what extent and under what security and disarmament situation can the US extended deterrence be reduced. It is also significant for them to promote dialogues with countries in Northeast Asia on nuclear disarmament and deterrence.

CONCLUSION

Reducing the role of nuclear weapons is important, but if it reduces Japan's security as well, it will be unacceptable to Japan. Nuclear disarmament cannot be allowed to undermine important national interests, especially a country's survival. Considering the security and nuclear situations in which Japan is located, more attention should be paid to envisage the negative impacts that NFU as a nuclear disarmament measure may have. For Japan, the US adoption of NFU, at least as it stands, has more strategic costs than it does benefits.

At the same time, Japan should continue to aim for a world without nuclear weapons. And the NFU is an indispensable nuclear disarmament measure in this objective. To realise those goals, it is imperative to make proactive efforts to improve the security environment and ensure concrete nuclear disarmament measures. In this context, the top priority in the current security environment is to maintain the tradition of non-use of nuclear weapons since Hiroshima and Nagasaki in 1945, until such weapons are eliminated.

NOTES

1 The final draft of this chapter was submitted in February 2020, and no major updates have been made since then.
2 Japan Ministry of Defense, "National Defense Program Guidelines for FY 2019 and Beyond" (Ministry of Defense, Tokyo, December 18, 2018), 8.
3 House of Representatives, "Answer of the Cabinet to the Question by Diet Member on No First Use of Nuclear Weapons" (House of Representatives, Tokyo, October 4, 2016), accessed on February 1, 2020, http://www.shugiin.go.jp/internet/itdb_shitsumon.nsf/html/shitsumon/b192007.htm (in Japanese).
4 Masakatsu Ota, "Japan Warned U.S. over Reductions to Nuclear Arsenal and Sought Flexible Deterrence, 2009 Memo Reveals," *Japan Times*, April 4, 2018, accessed on February 1, 2020, https://www.japantimes.co.jp/news/2018/04/04/national/politics-diplomacy/japan-warned-u-s-reductions-nuclear-arsenal-sought-flexible-deterrence-2009-memo-reveals-.XMh0ELi1tPY.
5 See, for instance, Tomoko Kurokawa, "Determinants of the Nuclear Policy Options in the Obama Administration: An Interview with Jon Wolfsthal,"

Journal for Peace and Nuclear Disarmament 1, no 2 (2018): 501–504; Josh Rogin, "U.S. Allies Unite to Block Obama's Nuclear 'Legacy,'" *Washington Post*, August 14, 2016, accessed on February 1, 2020, https://www.washingtonpost.com/opinions/global-opinions/allies-unite-to-block-an-obama-legacy/2016/08/14/cdb8d8e4- 60b9-11e6-8e45-477372e89d78_story.html.

6 Japan Ministry of Defense, *Defense of Japan 2019* (Ministry of Defense, Tokyo, 2019), 198.

7 US Departmnt of Defense, "Dangers of a Nuclear No First Use Policy" (US Department of Defense, Washington DC, April 2019), accessed on April 30, 2019, https://media.defense.gov/2019/Apr/01/2002108002/-1/-1/1/DANGERS-OF-A-NO-FIRST-USE-POLICY.PDF.

8 Forrest E. Morgan, Karl P. Mueller, Evan S. Medeiros, Kevin L. Pollpeter, and Roger Cliff, *Dangerous Thresholds: Managing Escalation in the 21st Century* (Santa Monica: RAND Corporation, 2008), xiii.

9 Harold A. Feiveson and Ernst Jan Hogendoorn, "No First Use of Nuclear Weapons," *Nonproliferation Review* 10, no 2 (Summer 2003): 6.

10 See, for instance, John C. Hopkins and Steven A. Maaranen, "Nuclear Weapons in Post-Cold War Deterrence," in *Post-Cold War Conflict Deterrence*, ed. Naval Studies Board, Commission on Physical Sciences, Mathematics, and Applications, National Research Council (Washington DC, National Academy Press, 1997), 117–119. See also, particularly in relation with NFU, James N. Miller, "No to No First Use—For Now," *Bulletin of the Atomic Scientists* 76, no 1 (2020): 8–13.

11 Robert G. Joseph and John F. Reichart, *Deterrence and Defense in a Nuclear, Biological, and Chemical Environment* (Washington DC: National Defense University Press, 1999), 21.

12 US Department of Defense, "Nuclear Posture Review 2018" (US Department of Defense, Washington DC, February 2018), 17.

13 See, for instance, Glenn H. Snyder, *Deterrence and Defense: Toward a Theory of National Security* (Princeton: Princeton University Press, 1961), 79; Paul Huth and Brice Russet, "Deterrence Failure and Crisis Escalation," *International Study Quarterly* 32, no 1 (March 1988): 29–45.

14 See, for instance, Brad Roberts, "Debating Nuclear No-First-Use, Again," *Survival* 61, no 3 (June–July 2019): 51.

15 John Carlson, "Is the NPT Still Relevant? How to Progress the NPT's Disarmament Provisions," *Journal for Peace and Nuclear Disarmament* (2019): 10–11.

16 Dominic Tierney, "Refusing the Nuke First," *The Atlantic*, September 14, 2016, accessed on February 1, 2020, https://www.theatlantic.com/international/archive/2016/09/nuclear-obama-north-korea-pakistan/499676/.

17 US Department of Defense, "Annual Report to Congress: Military and Security Developments Involving the People's Republic of China 2019," (US Department of Defense, Washington DC, May 2019), 65–67.

18 Japan, "Statement for Cluster 1: Specific Issues on Security Assurances" (Third Session of the Preparatory Committee for the 2020 Review Conference of the Parties to the NPT, New York, May 3, 2019).

19 George Perkovich, *Do unto Others: Toward a Defensible Nuclear Doctrine* (Washington, DC: Carnegie Endowment for International Peace, 2013).
20 Jeffrey G. Lewis and Scott D. Sagan, "The Nuclear Necessity Principle: Making U.S. Targeting Policy Conform with Ethics & the Laws of War," *Dædalus* 145, no 4 (Fall 2016): 62–74.
21 Hiroshima Round Table 2016, "Chairman's Summary" (Hiroshima, August 27–29, 2016).

Chapter 21

ON TURKEY'S STANCE TOWARDS NUCLEAR WEAPONS AND GLOBAL NO FIRST USE

Mustafa Kibaroglu

INTRODUCTION

The reason why Turkey's stance vis-à-vis nuclear weapons constitutes a chapter in this book, which analyses global no first use, stems from its membership in the NATO and its bilateral relations with the USA.

NATO has long been pursuing a 'first-use' strategy concerning nuclear weapons and there has been no change in its nuclear posture, despite the end of the East–West tension that was vividly experienced throughout the Cold War period.

Most recently, high-ranking NATO officials and renowned experts in the field have once again made clear what has been emphasised in the final communiqués published in the aftermath of NATO Summit meetings, which state that the Alliance will remain nuclear-capable and continue to adopt a first-use strategy as long as nuclear weapons exist in the world.[1]

Moreover, as part of the extended nuclear deterrence strategy of the Alliance, nuclear weapons, which belong to the USA, have been stationed on Turkish territory since the early 1960s. Turkish authorities show no sign of altering their stance despite mounting criticism in the West towards the USA for still keeping these weapons after the coup attempt in Turkey on 15 July 2016.

Under these circumstances, it seems highly unlikely for Turkey to join a campaign that promotes global no first use. Hence, experts in the field might consider writing and reading a chapter on this subject to be a futile exercise. Yet, it might be interesting for the larger audience to know how Turkey had its first encounter with American nuclear weapons, as early as 1961, with specific reference to the conditions under which Jupiter missiles were deployed on Turkish soil.

It might be equally interesting to discuss why the tactical nuclear weapons that were deployed in various airbases in Turkey at the height of the East–West tension remain in the country to date, despite the collapse of the Warsaw Pact and the Soviet Union more than a quarter of a century ago. With these in mind, this chapter will, first of all, discuss the role of nuclear weapons in Turkey's national security calculus, both during and after the Cold War period, with particular emphasis on the attitude of Turkish authorities regarding the value that they attributed to US nuclear weapons stationed on Turkish territory over the last six decades.

Policies adopted by Turkey, which have also fitted in with global nuclear disarmament efforts, have essentially been an outgrowth of the fundamental principles and objectives of Turkish foreign and security policy, insofar as they were not constrained by regional security considerations.

Turkey has long been committed to the goal of general and complete disarmament under strict and effective international controls. Yet, Turkish authorities also believed that this goal should be pursued with realism through a balanced approach encompassing steps relating to both nuclear and conventional weapons. Thus, in the second section, Turkey's approach to arms control, disarmament and non-proliferation issues will be presented.

Throughout the Cold War, NATO's strategic concepts have always asserted the right of the Alliance to resort to nuclear weapons at any stage of a conflict. To put it simply, the underlying concept of NATO strategies has always been and still is, a 'first-use' strategy[2] and this is also strongly supported by Turkish authorities.

In the post-Cold War era, the NATO strategy incorporated the objective of establishing cooperation with the countries of the former Warsaw Treaty Organization (WTO).[3] The military structure of the Alliance has, therefore, undergone changes commensurate with its revised strategic concept.[4] Turkey mostly welcomed these changes insofar as they could reduce the likelihood of war. Hence, in the third section, difficulties in the prospects for a change in NATO strategy to 'no first use' in the aftermath of the Cold War era will be highlighted.

The issue of nuclear armament and disarmament in general, and the status of American tactical nuclear weapons that are stationed in Turkey in particular, have started to be discussed in the political and academic circles as well as in the Turkish media more often than in the previous decades, especially during the deliberations of the 'P5+1' countries who wanted to control Iran's nuclear ambitions. Moreover, the scrapping of a major arms-control mechanism, namely the Intermediate Nuclear Forces (INF) Treaty, that was signed between the USA and the USSR back in 1987, raised concerns about the reactions of the countries in the Eurasian landscape.

Many researchers and scholars from around the world have, therefore, exhibited a keen interest in understanding Turkey's possible reactions to the developments taking place in the Iranian nuclear (weapons) capacity as well as the failure of the arms-control mechanism in lending confidence to the regional states that strategic stability could be maintained, and they have come up with various scenarios arguing that Turkey would soon follow suit by advancing its own nuclear capabilities; for instance, if Iran came closer to getting the bomb.

Turkish authorities have faced dilemmas arising from conflicts between their regional and global security concerns. The statements of Turkish president Recep Tayyip Erdoğan, on a couple of occasions in September 2019, in which he expressed his discontent with the existing nuclear order in the world that is divided as the 'nuclear haves and have-nots' has prompted a new round of discussion about Turkey's approach to nuclear weapons.[5] Hence, the chapter will conclude with an assessment of the possible courses of action of the current government vis-à-vis the demands for a GNFU of nuclear weapons and where might Turkey be heading.

THE ROLE OF NUCLEAR WEAPONS IN TURKEY'S NATIONAL SECURITY POLICY

Before embarking upon a discussion on the role of nuclear weapons in Turkey's national security, it is worth noting that the North Atlantic Treaty that was signed in Washington DC on 4 April 1949 did not involve any particular obligation on the part of the member states with respect to the deployment of nuclear weapons or any other specific weapons systems.

At the Paris Summit meeting of NATO in December 1957, it was decided to deploy long-range ballistic missiles on the territories of the allied countries in Europe. Around 1960, the US Thor and Jupiter missiles, which had ranges of about 2,500 km to 3,000 km and warhead yield of 1.5 megatons became operational in the UK, Italy and Turkey.[6]

However, some fifteen Jupiter missiles that were deployed in Turkey in 1961 had to be withdrawn only two years later in the aftermath of the Cuban missile crisis that erupted in October 1962. Nevertheless, nuclear weapons continued to play a significant role in the security policies of Turkey, both during and after the Cold War.[7]

Starting in the early 1960s, US tactical nuclear weapons in the US air force custody that could be delivered by F-100 and F-104 Phantom aircraft were deployed on Turkish territory in airbases near the cities of Eskisehir, Malatya (Erhac), Ankara (Akinci/Murted) and Balikesir.[8]

In the same vein, on 14 April 1963, the US Polaris submarine, *USS Sam Houston*, visited the Turkish port of Izmir in a display of NATO's solidarity with Turkey and its commitment to extended nuclear deterrence.[9]

The deployment of nuclear weapons in Turkey was a consequence of the country's admittance into NATO in 1952 and the geostrategic imperatives of its immediate neighbourhood. There were two main reasons for Turkey to host US nuclear weapons. First and foremost was the deterrent value of these weapons against the threat posed to Turkey by its colossal neighbour, the Soviet Union, during the Cold War era.[10]

The claims of the Soviet Union under Stalin on the Turkish Straits[11] and some of the eastern provinces of Turkey gave rise to grave security concerns among the Turkish political and security experts. Turkey's vulnerable situation in the aftermath of the Second World War and the USA's timely pledge to extend its security guarantees to Turkey marked the beginning of substantial US–Turkish bilateral military cooperation.

During the 1960s and 1970s, the Soviet threat was felt more explicitly both in Turkey and in the USA as the Soviets closed the gap in the nuclear field and increased their military presence and capabilities in both conventional and unconventional weaponry along Turkey's eastern frontier and maintained their naval presence in the Mediterranean.

The growing military presence of the Soviet Union both in quantitative and qualitative terms across the southern flank of NATO prompted the Alliance in general and Turkey in particular to rely extensively, though gradually, on nuclear forces. Therefore, Turkish authorities considered these weapons to be a credible deterrent against the Warsaw Pact in general and the huge military might of the nearby Soviet Union in particular.

Due to the overwhelming superiority of the Warsaw Pact countries in conventional weapons systems, the existence of nuclear weapons on Turkish soil meant the active presence and full backing of NATO and especially the USA regarding the contingency plans involving the WTO countries.[12]

That period also witnessed intensifying relations between the Soviets and Turkey's Middle-Eastern neighbours, such as Syria and Iraq in the military field. During the Cold War years, the Middle East was generally considered by most of the NATO countries to be 'out of area', meaning that the region was outside of the area of their responsibility to carry out military operations for defending the alliance territory.

Whereas the USA suggested the inclusion of the oil-rich Persian Gulf region in the contingency plans of NATO, the European members of the Alliance generally opposed the idea as the threat perceived from Eastern Europe was of primary importance for them[13]

Therefore, it was not clear to Turkish authorities whether or not NATO's 'nuclear umbrella' would be effective in defending Turkey in case of an attack launched by its Middle-Eastern neighbours. In the absence of US nuclear weapons in Turkey, Turkish policymakers would feel less secure against contingencies that might involve its neighbours, who had both weapons of mass destruction (WMD) capabilities and their delivery vehicles, such as ballistic missiles.

A second reason for Turkey to host US nuclear weapons has been the 'burden sharing' principle within NATO to which Turkey has forcefully subscribed since the beginning of its admittance to the Alliance. Turkey had already displayed unequivocally its willingness to share the burden of defending the interests of the Western alliance by committing a significant number of troops to the war on the Korean Peninsula in 1950, even before its membership to NATO was in sight.[14]

THE SECURITY SITUATION AFTER THE END OF THE COLD WAR

Throughout the Cold War, Turkey had enjoyed the rather privileged status of being one of NATO's sixteen nations. With its geostrategic location as a flank country and the second-largest standing army in the Alliance after the USA, Turkey became an indispensable ingredient of the security of the Western world. Turkish authorities believed they could count to a considerable extent on the USA and NATO in general, as far as the Soviet threat was concerned.

The end of the Cold War, however, drastically reduced the threat perceived from the Soviet Union and caused dramatic changes in Turkey's security environment. Newly Independent States (NIS) emerged from the territory of the Soviet Union, and the most striking outcome of this development was that for the first time in the four-century-old history of Turkish–Russian relations, the two nations were geographically separated.[15] The dissolution of common borders with the Russian-led 'Soviet empire' contributed greatly to the security of Turkey. The minimum time required for Turkey's colossal ex-neighbour to launch a surprise attack had increased to one year from a figure that used to be expressed in weeks, if not days.[16]

In the aftermath of the Cold War, Turkey continued to host US nuclear weapons on its soil, but in much smaller numbers and also limited to only one location, namely the Incirlik base, which is allocated to the USA, near the city of Adana on the eastern Mediterranean coast of Turkey.[17] All other nuclear weapons were withdrawn from the bases where they used to be deployed and moved to Incirlik.[18]

In the post-Cold war period, these weapons were believed to constitute a credible deterrent against Turkey's rival neighbours in the Middle East, such as Iran, Iraq and Syria, which used to have WMD capabilities. In addition to the existing stockpiles of all WMD categories that existed in a number of states in the Middle East, Iran's nuclear programme, which was claimed by high-level Iranian authorities to have long achieved the level of 'a complete nuclear fuel cycle', has become a source of serious concern for Turkey.[19]

Turkish officials have, time and again, expressed their views as to how a nuclear-armed Iran would be a threat to Turkey. For instance, in an interview with a journalist from the *Christian Science Monitor*, former president Abdullah Gül had said, 'You should not underestimate how seriously we take the issue of a nuclearized Iran. After all, we are neighbors and nuclear weapons would threaten us most of all. We are the first to object.'[20]

TURKEY'S STANCE TOWARDS NUCLEAR ISSUES

Regarding arms control, disarmament and non-proliferation issues, the fundamental thrust of Turkish foreign and security policy has been to become a state party to international agreements to contribute to their effective implementation. Hence, Turkey has persistently pursued a policy to become a state party to international non-proliferation agreements that sought to curb the spread of weapons of mass destruction and their delivery vehicles as well as to help strengthen the verification mechanisms and export control regimes.[21]

In the context of nuclear non-proliferation specifically, Turkey became a state party to the NPT by signing it on 28 January 1969, and subsequently ratifying it on 17 April 1980. At the NPT Review and Extension Conference held in New York in 1995, Turkey gave its full support to the indefinite and unconditional extension of the treaty. Turkey also used its influence on the Turkic republics of Central Asia and the Caucasus to induce them to do the same.

In line with its treaty obligations under the NPT, Turkey concluded a 'full-scope' Safeguards Agreement with the International Atomic Energy Agency (IAEA) in 1982. Moreover, Ankara has endorsed efforts to strengthen the nuclear non-proliferation regime and the verification mechanism of the IAEA and Turkey joined the 'Additional Protocol' in 2001.[22]

Turkey was one of the forty-seven countries that participated in the Nuclear Security Summit held on 12–13 April 2010 in Washington DC, to develop a common understanding on strengthening nuclear security and reducing the threat of nuclear terrorism. Turkey has also taken an active part in the Seoul and The Hague summits in 2012 and 2014 as well as the final summit in Washington DC, held from 31 March and 1 April 2016. Turkey will continue to be actively involved in the process, which will now be steered through international organisations such as the UN, IAEA and the Interpol.

Turkey is also part of the Non-Proliferation and Disarmament Initiative (NPDI) along with eleven other countries, namely Germany, Poland, the Netherlands, Canada, Chile, Mexico, United Arab Emirates, Australia, Japan and the two new members, Nigeria and the Philippines, which was launched in September 2010 to contribute to the implementation of the consensus outcomes of the 2010 NPT Review Conference and to take forward the nuclear disarmament and non-proliferation agenda. Turkey hosted the 4th Ministerial Meeting of NPDI in Istanbul on 16 June 2012.[23]

In accordance with its general stance against the proliferation of WMDs, Turkey has declared its support to the Proliferation Security Initiative (PSI), which was launched by the USA in May 2003. The PSI aimed at stopping the trafficking of WMDs, their delivery systems and related materials to and from states and non-state actors of proliferation concern mainly by interdiction. Turkey, while following other PSI activities, has hosted a land, sea and air interdiction PSI exercise first in May 2006 and successive years with the participation of dozens of guest nations. Turkey continues to actively contribute to the PSI.

Pursuing an active policy against terrorism, Turkey joined the Global Initiative to Combat Nuclear Terrorism (GICNT) as the initial partner state. Ankara hosted the initiative's second meeting in 2007. Turkey has also welcomed the UN Security Council Resolution 1540 regarding the prevention of the proliferation of nuclear, chemical or biological weapons and their means of delivery. To fulfil the provisions of international non-proliferation instruments and arrangements to which Turkey is a party, an enhanced system of export controls has been implemented.

Turkey has also taken several steps in the field of export control arrangements and acceded to the NSG in 1999. It has undertaken the process of adjusting its national export control regime (i.e., laws and regulations) to that of the NSG countries. Currently, the Turkish export controls system is in line with the EU's standards.

Turkish national legislation, developed in the context of the country's safeguards agreement and other IAEA protocols, provides Turkish authorities with the legal basis to control the materials and equipment covered by the list of the NSG. Nevertheless, there have been several cases of smuggling networks or individuals having used Turkey as a trans-shipment point in the past decade.[24]

Concomitantly with its application to the NSG, Turkey has undertaken the same stance towards the Zangger Committee and became a member soon after its application in 1999.[25] Turkish authorities have considered this as almost an automatic outcome of the formal accession to the NSG. Similarly, Turkey joined the Australia Group in 1999 and has taken steps to include the items on the list.[26]

Turkey also became a member of the Missile Technology Control Regime (MTCR) in April 1997. Turkish delegations have been active in participating in the meetings of member states as well as promoting new ideas to render the controls much more effective. In this context, Turkish authorities believe that it is essential to demonstrate to the actual and potential proliferators that the MTCR is a solid block of like-minded nations that are unified with the determination to fight against proliferation.

Similarly, Turkey became a party to The Hague Code of Conduct against Ballistic Missile Proliferation (HCOC) at the launching conference held in The Hague on 25–26 November 2002. Turkey considers the code as the first step towards an internationally accepted legal framework in this field.

Furthermore, Turkey is an active member of the Conference on Disarmament (CD) since 1996. As a member of the CD, Turkey joined the overwhelming majority of nations in the effort to conclude a CTBT. The complete ban on nuclear testing, the core function of the treaty, is thought by Turkish authorities to be an effective measure to control nuclear weapons technology. The international monitoring of this ban that the CTBT provides for is believed to serve as an important confidence-building measure amongst the states that are and will be a party to the treaty.

Bearing in mind that there are tons of excess plutonium and highly enriched uranium left over from weapons dismantling programmes in both the USA and Russia, the need for achieving a universal Cut-Off Treaty is obvious. Therefore, Turkish authorities fully support such an eventuality and believe that the entry into force of such a treaty will constitute another significant step towards the ultimate goal of eliminating nuclear weapons.

DIFFICULTIES IN THE PROSPECTS OF A CHANGE IN NATO STRATEGY TO NFU

At the conceptual level, a change in NATO strategy was considered by Turkish authorities to be a natural consequence of the revolutionary changes that had taken place in the Soviet Bloc, a political system to which the Alliance was conceptually opposed.[27] The original NATO strategic concept changed several times during the Cold War in response to changes and developments in the military balance between the two military blocs.[28]

NATO countries relied on their capabilities to offset the superiority of the WTO in conventional weaponry. Because it was envisaged that NATO might not win a war without resorting to nuclear weapons, whereas the WTO might, with its absolute superiority in the category of conventional weapons.[29]

In contrast to this argument, the Soviet Union declared in 1982, as part of a peace offensive, that it would not be the first to resort to nuclear weapons, and thus initiated a 'no-first-use' strategy. Turkish authorities considered the Soviet pledge to be a mere propaganda tool at the time it was initiated.

However, the tide has turned with the dissolution of the WTO and the disintegration of the Soviet Union. As NATO survived and moved towards enlargement by admitting the former Soviet republics such as Estonia, Latvia and Lithuania in the Baltics, as well as former WTO members such as the Czech Republic, Slovakia, Poland, Hungary, Romania, Bulgaria and Albania in central and eastern Europe, Russia has undergone drastic changes. The imbalance in conventional weapons area now turned more in NATO's favour, unlike the Cold War when it was in the WTO's favour.

Therefore, the Russian military authorities felt compelled to revise their NFU pledge and to declare instead, in 1993, that Russia would again reserve its legitimate right to resort to nuclear weapons in case of aggression by a nuclear-armed state or its ally, regardless of the weapons used by the aggressor.

This change in Russian policy was concomitant with the declaration of their 'near abroad' doctrine. The implication of this was that in the case of aggression, given its now inferior position in conventional forces, a feasible alternative for Russia would be to resort to tactical nuclear weapons. This could, in theory, lead to an exchange of strategic nuclear forces, that is, an all-out nuclear war.

At this point, one may ask as to whether a similar dynamic wasn't in play during the Cold War and also why Turkey believed the first-use strategy back then was credible against the Soviets when it too could lead to all-out nuclear war. The simple answer to such a question would be that during the Cold War, it was the Soviet Union that had suggested an NFU policy and declared accordingly that it adopted such a policy unilaterally, regardless of whether NATO reciprocated in kind or not.

Although simple logic might suggest that NATO, which had an indisputable superiority in conventional forces over Russia, should have adopted the NFU strategy to avoid a catastrophe, things were not so simple. A switch in NATO strategy in that direction might not, probably would not, bring about a concurrent change in Russian strategy from first use back to NFU.

Hence, knowing that Russia would not reciprocate NATO's NFU pledge, Turkey would consider advocating a similar strategy to be redundant on the grounds of the extent of the threat perceived from Russia, at a time when Turkey's relations and solidarity with its allies have been tested on many issues over the last few years.

Moreover, one should bear in mind that the Russian first-use strategy adopted in the 1990s was not only an outcome of its inferiority vis-à-vis NATO's conventional posture after the collapse of the Warsaw Pact but also a reflection of the Russian military authorities' assessment of threats from the south. According to Dr Nikolai Sokov, a former member of the Russian START negotiations team, the cumulative threat posed by nuclear weapons in China, India and Pakistan was apparently no less significant a threat to Russia.[30]

Additionally, the traumatic effects of the dissolution of the Soviet Union and the Warsaw Pact had affected the state of mind of the Russian security elites. They had lost their confidence in their counterparts in the West, especially because of the assurances that were given to them during the unification of Germany, eventually proved to be void, as regards the future composition of NATO.[31]

Therefore, even if NATO turned to NFU, Russia would probably expect further concrete steps from the West to rebuild confidence, which would be a very long process. Hence, an NFU declaration by NATO would be of limited significance at that time.[32]

On the other hand, NATO had its own constraints as far as the threat of WMD proliferation was concerned, especially in the Middle East and the Mediterranean basin. It was believed that by the early 2000s, western European capitals would be within the range of ballistic missiles based in the MENA[33] region and that the southern members of NATO would be the first to feel the political and military consequences of proliferation trends on Europe's periphery.[34]

Therefore, NATO endorsed a comprehensive approach to counter the military risks posed by such threats and this issue was explicitly cited in the communiqué released after the meeting of the North Atlantic Council in Defense Minister Session on 13 June 1996.[35]

NATO's efforts to adapt itself to meet the challenges of the new security environment have produced guidelines for appropriate responses to proliferation. The overarching principles envisaged to guide NATO's defence response were, among others, to 'maintain freedom of action and demonstration to any potential adversary that the alliance will not be coerced by the threat or use of WMD'.[36]

In view of the fact that a change in NATO strategy to NFU would not induce an immediate reciprocal change in Russia's current first-use strategy, and considering that the proliferation of WMDs in the proximity of NATO continues to constitute a serious threat, the exigency and viability of such a change seemed questionable to many experts in the West.

CURRENT SITUATION AND THE WAY AHEAD

Although dramatic and also favourable changes have taken place in Turkey's security environment, the credibility of the nuclear posture and hence NATO's deterrence policy, including the implicit first-use strategy of the Alliance, is of the utmost importance for the Turkish security elites.

Russia does not seem to have any intention to change its stance back to NFU[37] ever since the Russian authorities devised the near abroad doctrine that relies on first-use strategy even at very low levels of a hot confrontation. Therefore, as of January 2020, it would be safe to say that Turkish authorities do not see any prospect of a switch to an NFU strategy, at least for the foreseeable future.[38]

That said, however, there are reasons to be optimistic, to expect that the attitude of the current or forthcoming Turkish governments might change, hopefully in the not-too-distant future. First and foremost, the ever-rising level of the threat posed by non-state actors that seek WMD capabilities increased the level of acknowledgement among the policymakers that deterrence, especially nuclear deterrence that worked well against states and helped maintain strategic stability between the heavily armed military pacts during the Cold War period and beyond, may not, and most probably will not, work against the apocalyptic transnational terrorist organisations.[39]

The sooner the nuclear powers move towards total nuclear disarmament with the support of their allies and start by issuing NFU policies, the higher the chances of preventing non-state actors from having access to and/or developing WMD capabilities of their own that may be used in catastrophic attacks.[40] Hence, the peace-loving countries should not wait until a tragic incident that may serve, unfortunately, as a wake-up call. Turkey, being a country that has enormously suffered from terrorism for decades, would this time be among the countries that would benefit the most from a world where the possibility of WMDs falling into the hands of terrorist organisations would be much less.[41]

A second reason as to why one might expect a change in the stance of the Turkish governments is the nuclear deal, namely the Joint

Comprehensive Plan of Action (JCPOA) that was achieved between the P5+1 countries and Iran in July 2015 that enabled the international community to force Iran to become much more transparent in its nuclear activities by way of the IAEA carrying out elaborate and comprehensive inspections.

The JCPOA has shown unequivocally that talking to Iran from a position of military strength by using threatening statements alone does not help at all. On the contrary, making mutual concessions and addressing each other's concerns has shown that empathy may pave the way to an agreement.

Hence, the threat of use of nuclear force in the political discourse with Iran has so far only fuelled Iranian authorities' security concerns, thereby enabling them to use this in their threat assessment as a pretext for further advancing their nuclear programme.

There is no doubt that 'Turkey is a country that will be most negatively affected by Iran's nuclear-weapons capability, if and when it is developed.'[42] Hence, supporting an NFU policy, if not adopting it at once due to the constraints stemming from Turkey's alliance relations, may lend Iranian authorities much more confidence as well as provide them with negative security assurances that they won't need to develop nuclear weapons capabilities that might, among other things, cause a nuclear proliferation cascade in the region and further complicate the security situation for every actor, including Iran.

A third reason to expect a change in the attitude of Turkish authorities towards NATO's first-use strategy might be because of the tension that has been experienced between Turkey and some of its NATO allies with respect to the decisions of Turkish authorities concerning the acquisition of sophisticated military equipment from Russia, such as the S-400 air defence system.[43]

High-ranking military and civilian officers of some of the allied countries have occasionally harshly criticised Turkey's decisions that went beyond their domain of authority or responsibility. As a sovereign country and a proud member of the Alliance, Turkey's policies may be subject to discussion, let alone criticism, and if at all necessary only at the level of heads of state or government who convene during the NATO Summit meetings. Therefore, no less irritating an attitude of some officers was their bitter statements implying that Turkey might have to suffer the consequences of its decisions.[44]

In an unprecedented manner, Turkey and NATO in general, and Turkey and the USA in particular, have been at odds lately also on the ways and means of resolving the Syrian conflict that has been very adversely affecting the Turks in many ways. This includes the presence of nearly four million Syrians who have found refuge on Turkish territory over the last seven years, resulting in large expenditure amounting to 40 billion dollars, far beyond the capacity of a country like Turkey. There is also the challenge of the terrorist threat along the Turkish–Syrian border, posed by the YPG and PKK affiliates who were generously supported by US administrations during the tenure of both Obama and Trump.[45]

Hence, many more Turks have started to ask a very legitimate question as to what is it that NATO does in terms of sharing the burden of defending Turkey's borders as well as dealing with the threats to its national security.

There are many issues on which allies within NATO may not, and do not, see eye to eye. For instance, following the 2016 coup attempt in Turkey, there have been calls from some commentators in other NATO countries for US nuclear weapons to be removed from the Incirlik airbase. If the USA were to remove the existing nuclear bombs, Turkish authorities would not welcome this move, especially if the withdrawal of the nuclear weapons were presented as, or perceived to be, a result of a loss of confidence in Turkey.

As a reaction to such a move by the USA, Turkish authorities may consider revising their stance vis-à-vis the first-use strategy of the Alliance. Furthermore, in conformity with its foreign and security policy objectives in the new world order—where the arms control paradigm does not apply anymore, as it was signed and sealed after the scrapping of the INF Treaty in August 2019—Turkish authorities may make statements promoting GNFU a policy that may better serve Turkey's defence and security objectives.

NOTES

1 Insights gained from the author's discussions with experts and officials during the conference convened by NATO's Public Diplomacy Division, "An Integrated Approach to NATO Communications" (Brussels, Belgium, January 23–24, 2020).

2 In order to avoid any confusion or misinterpretation of the terms, it should be made clear that NATO's 'first- use' strategy by no means implies 'pre-emptive use', which refers to the use of nuclear weapons before any aggression occurs. Rather, first use implies that NATO may be the first to use nuclear weapons during an aggression, in view of the fact that no other option might provide a better way of defending NATO territory against an aggressor.

3 The Warsaw Treaty Organization (WTO) is also known as the Warsaw Pact, which will be used interchangeably throughout the text.

4 Accordingly, smaller and more flexible force units at lower levels of readiness with greater mobility are replacing the previous concept that relied on rather static linear defence.
5 Mustafa Kibaroglu, "Turkey and Nuclear Weapons: Can This Be Real", in *Turkey and Nuclear Weapons*, eds George Perkovic and Sinan Ulgen (Washington DC: Carnegie Endowment for International Peace, 2015), 127–154.
6 SIPRI, "World Armaments and Disarmaments," in *SIPRI Yearbook 1982* (London: Stockholm Peace Research Institute, Taylor & Francis Ltd London, 1982), 7.
7 Kibaroglu, "Tactical Nuclear Weapons in Europe: The Case of Turkey," in *Tactical Nuclear Weapons and Euro-Atlantic Security: The Future of NATO*, ed. Paolo Foradori (Oxon, UK: Routledge, 2013), 92–104.
8 Conversations with a retired top military commander who wished to remain anonymous, in Ankara, February 15, 2010, quoted in Kibaroglu, "Turkey and Shared Responsibilities," in "Shared Responsibilities for Nuclear Disarmament: A Global Debate" (Occasional Paper, American Academy of Arts and Sciences, Cambridge, Massachusetts, 2010), 24–27.
9 Ed Offley, *Scorpion Down, Sunk by the Soviet, Buried by the Pentagon: The Untold Story of USS Scorpion* (New York: Basic Books, 2007), 195.
10 Kibaroglu, "Turkey's Unchanging NSNW Policy," in "A Problem Deferred: NATO Non-Strategic Nuclear Weapons after Chicago," eds Malcolm Chalmers and Hugh Chalmers (Whitehall Report, Royal United Services International [RUSI], London, October 2012), 37–44.
11 The Turkish Straits of Istanbul (Bosphorus) and Canakkale (the Dardanelles) in north-western Turkey are highly strategic sea routes for countries littoral to the Black Sea. The status of the straits was agreed in the Montreux Convention of 1936.
12 Kibaroglu, "The Future of Extended Deterrence: The Case of Turkey," in *Perspectives on Extended Deterrence*, ed. Bruno Tertrais, (Recherches & Documents no 3, Fondation pour la Recherche Stratégique, Paris, 2010), 87–95.
13 The debate between the European members of NATO and the USA is not new and can be traced back to the original drafting of the North Atlantic Treaty. For a comprehensive discussion of this question, see Douglas T. Stuart and William Tow, *The Limits of Alliance: NATO Out-of-Area Problems Since 1949* (Baltimore: Johns Hopkins University Press, 1990).
14 Kibaroglu, "Reassessing the Role of US Nuclear Weapons in Turkey," *Arms Control Today* 40, no 5 (June 2010): 8–13, Arms Control Association, Washington DC.
15 If one excludes the rather distant neighbourhood across the Black Sea.
16 Interviews with Turkish military experts.
17 Hans M. Kristensen, "Status of U.S. Nuclear Weapons in Europe 2010," Federation of American Scientists, February 12, 2010, http://www.fas.org/programs/ssp/nukes/images/euronukes2010.pdf; Kristensen, "Non-Strategic Nuclear Weapons, Special Report no 3," Federation of American

Scientists, May 2012, accessed on April 2, 2022, www.fas.org/_docs/Non_Strategic_Nuclear_Weapons.pdf.

18 The Turkish air force does not have operational links anymore with the remaining tactical nuclear weapons deployed in Incirlik. Kibaroglu, "Isn't It Time to Say Farewell to US Nukes in Turkey?" *European Security* 14, no 4 (December 2005): 443–457.

19 The head of the Atomic Energy Organization of Iran (AEOI), Ali Akbar Salehi is quoted in the press on 5 December 2010, as saying "the breakthrough, using uranium ore mined in southern Iran, signified the country's full self-sufficiency in the production of uranium, cutting out the need for imported material". See Ramin Mostaghim, "Iran Says It's Now Fully Self-Sufficient at Producing Uranium," *Los Angeles Times*, December 5, 2010, accessed on January 26, 2020, https://www.latimes.com/archives/la-xpm-2010-dec-05-la-fgw-iran-nuclear-20101206-story.html

20 Global Viewpoint Network/Tribune Media Services, "Turkey's President Abdullah Gul: Iran Must Be More Transparent on Nuclear Program," *Christian Science Monitor*, September 30, 2010, accessed on January 26, 2020, https://www.csmonitor.com/Commentary/Global-Viewpoint/2010/0930/Turkey-s-President-Abdullah-Gul-Iran-must-be-more-transparent-on-nuclear-program.

21 Kibaroglu, "Turkey," in *Europe and Nuclear Disarmament: Debates and Political Attitudes in 16 European Countries*, ed. Harald Muller (Brussels: Peace Research Institute Frankfurt [PRIF], European Interuniversity Press, 1998), 161–193.

22 See the "Model Protocol Additional to the Agreement(s) Between States(s) and the International Atomic Energy Agency for the Application of Safeguards (INFCIRC/540 Corrected)" (International Atomic Energy Agency, Vienna, December 1998).

23 Ministry of Foreign Affairs, "Arms Control and Disarmament" (Ministry of Foreign Affairs, Republic of Turkey, June 16, 2012),accessed on January 17, 2022, http://www.mfa.gov.tr/arms-control-and-disarmament.en.mfa.

24 Kibaroglu, "Nuclear Security and Turkey. Dealing with Nuclear Smuggling", in *Nuclear Security: A Turkish Perspective*, ed. Sinan Ulgen (Istanbul: Centre for Economics and Foreign Policy Studies (EDAM) and Nuclear Threat Initiative, 2015), 77–94.

25 The Zangger Committee—named for its Swiss chair Prof. Claude Zangger—and the Nuclear Suppliers Group shared in common the purpose of limiting the transfer of significant material and technology to states that are suspected for being engaged in clandestine nuclear weapons manufacturing.

26 The Australia Group is an informal group of countries established in 1985 with a view to setting up a series of guidelines for effective controls of exports of sensitive and dual-use material and technologies. Currently, the Australia Groups consists of 43 members, including Australia, New Zealand, the European Commission, all 27 member states of the European Union, Norway, Switzerland, Iceland, Mexico, Japan, South Korea, United Kingdom, the USA, Canada, India, Ukraine, Argentina and Turkey.

27 Though no specification of the name of any group of countries as adversaries is found in the text of the North Atlantic Treaty. The geographical delimitation that exists in the text, however, identifies the defence commitment of the Alliance.

28 NATO's 'flexible response' strategy, designed and adopted in the 1960s, was regarded as defining the characteristic of the Alliance. It prioritised conventional responses to conventional aggression, keeping nuclear weapons as a secondary option that could be resorted to during a protracted conflict. The previous NATO strategy had relied on 'massive retaliation', according to which the immediate resort to nuclear weapons would be possible in case of an attack on the allied countries.

29 Although a clear retrospective comparison between the two military pacts is hardly possible, it was generally estimated that the Warsaw Pact member nations had a '1.5 to 1' or even '2 to 1' superiority over NATO with regard to their conventional arsenals.

30 "Conversations with Dr Nikolai Sokov from the Center Non-Proliferation Studies of the Monterey Institute of International Studies," February 1997, Monterey, California, USA. Dr Sokov worked with the Soviet Foreign Ministry in the late 1980s and participated in the START I and START II negotiations.

31 "Conversations with Dr Nikolai Sokov."

32 It could, however, contribute to confidence-building efforts between the parties. In other words, NATO's switch to an NFU strategy is considered by the Russians to be a 'necessary but not sufficient condition' of improved confidence. "Conversations with Dr Nikolai Sokov."

33 MENA stands for Middle East and North Africa.

34 Ronald D. Asmus, F. Stephen Larrabee, and Ian O. Lesser, "Mediterranean Security: New Challenges, New Tasks," *NATO Review*, no 3 (May 1996): 25–31.

35 For full documentation, see the official text of the "Final Communiqué: Meeting of the North Atlantic Council in Defence Ministers Session" on the e-library of the official NATO website, accessed on January 17, 2022, https://www.nato.int/cps/en/natolive/official_texts_25065.htm.

36 Ashton B. Carter and Davis B. Omand, "Countering the Proliferation Risks: Adapting the Alliance to the New Security Environment," *NATO Review*, no 5 (September 1996): 10–15.

37 See Abigail Stowe-Thurston, Matt Korda, and Hans M. Kristensen, "Putin Deepens Confusion about Russian Nuclear Policy" (Russia Matters, Belfer Center for Science and International Security, Harvard University, Cambridge, 25 October 2018), accessed on December 22, 2019, https://www.russiamatters.org/analysis/putin-deepens-confusion-about-russian-nuclear-policy.

38 Conversations with experts and officials, Sidelines of "Conference on an Integrated Approach to NATO Communications" (Brussels, Belgium, January 23–24, 2020).

39 Kibaroglu, "Contemporary Security Challenges: Is Classical Deterrence an Adequate Response?" in *International Security Today: Understanding*

Change and Debating Strategy, eds, Mustafa Aydin and Kostas Ifantis (SAM Papers No. 1/2006, Center for Strategic Research, Turkish Ministry of Foreign Affairs, Ankara), 205–224.

40 Kibaroglu, "Measures to Counter the Threat of WMD Terrorism," in *Technological Dimensions of Defence against Terrorism*, NATO Science for Peace and Security Series, Vol. 115, ed. U. Feyyaz Aydogdu (Amsterdam: IOS Press, 2013), 63–69.

41 Kibaroglu, "Tackling the Threat of WMD Terrorism," in *Defense against Weapons of Mass Destruction Terrorism*, eds Osman Aytac and Mustafa Kibaroglu (Amsterdam: IOS Press, 2009), 161–169.

42 Kibaroglu and Baris Caglar, "Implications of a Nuclear Iran for Turkey," *Middle East Policy* XV, no 4 (Winter 2008): 59–80, Middle East Policy Council, Washington DC.

43 Kibaroglu, "On Turkey's Missile Defense Strategy: The Four Faces of the S-400 Deal between Turkey and Russia" (SAM Papers, Center for Strategic Research, Turkish Ministry of Foreign Affairs, Ankara), no 16, April 2019).

44 See the statement made by Czech General Petr Pavel, Chairman, NATO Military Committee, Aaron Mehta, "NATO official: Turkey faces 'consequences' if purchase of S-400 completed," Military Times, October 25, 2017, accessed on June 30, 2022, https://www.militarytimes.com/land/2017/10/25/nato-official-turkey-faces-consequences-if-purchase-of-s-400-completed/.

45 YPG is the Syrian wing of PKK (Kurdistan Workers' Party) which has been designated as a terrorist organisation by Turkey and its NATO allies. See "Foreign Terrorist Organizations", on the official website of the US State Department, accessed on January 17, 2022, https://www.state.gov/foreign-terrorist-organizations/

ABOUT THE EDITORS AND CONTRIBUTORS

Bruno Tertrais is Deputy Director of the Fondation pour la recherche stratégique (FRS), a leading French think tank on international security issues. A graduate in law and politics, he obtained his doctorate under the supervision of Pierre Hassner. After working at NATO's Parliamentary Assembly, he worked for the Ministry of Defence and the RAND Corporation and joined the FRS in 2001.

He was a member of the committees in charge of the White Papers on Defence and National Security in 2007-2008 and 2012-2013. He has been a contributor to Institut Montaigne's studies since 2017 and published *Le défi démographique* (2018). His latest publications include: *L'Atlas des frontières* (Les Arènes, 2016, Prix de la Société de Géographie); *Le Président et la Bombe* (Odile Jacob, 2017, Prix du Livre géopolitique); *La Revanche de l'histoire* (Odile Jacob, 2018).

Colin S. Gray was an independent scholar, having retired as Professor Emeritus of Strategic Studies at the University of Reading. He was trained as a political scientist with a BA (Hons) from the University of Manchester, and D.Phil from Lincoln College, Oxford. He was the author of thirty books, most recently *Theory of Strategy* (Oxford: Oxford University Press, 2018).

Daryl Press is an Associate Professor of Government at Dartmouth College. His research focuses on U.S. foreign policy, deterrence and the future of war. Press has published numerous articles and two books: *Calculating Credibility* (2005), which examines how leaders assess the credibility of adversaries' threats during crises. In his second book, *The Myth of the Nuclear Revolution* (2020), he and Keir Lieber use evidence from the past seven decades to explore the central puzzle of the nuclear age: why international politics remains so competitive despite the security that nuclear weapons give their owners. Their answers shed critical light on the critical nuclear deterrence challenges of the 21st century. Press is now leading a project to create new tools of conventional force analysis, and to measure the changing military balance around the world, including in Eastern Europe, maritime East Asia, the Korean Peninsula and Taiwan.

Brigadier (retd) Feroz Hassan Khan is a former Brigadier in the Pakistan Army, with experience in combat action and command on active fronts on the Line of Control in Kashmir and Siachin Glacier and Afghanistan border. He has worked on numerous assignments in the United States, Europe and Asia. He served as Director Arms Control and Disarmament Affairs, in the Pakistan's Strategic Plans Division, Joint Services Headquarters. Khan had been a key contributor in formulating Pakistan's security policies on nuclear and conventional arms control and strategic stability in South Asia. He produced recommendations for the Ministry of Foreign Affairs and represented Pakistan in several multilateral and bilateral arms control negotiations on peace and security in South Asia and international treaties related to weapons of mass destruction.

He has published widely his most popular book *Eating Grass: The Making of the Pakistani Bomb*.

Emily Landau was a senior research fellow at INSS and head of the Arms Control and Regional Security Program, led its research, conference outreach and mentorship projects. Dr. Landau has published and lectured extensively on nuclear proliferation, arms control and regional security dynamics in the Middle East; WMD proliferation challenges in the post-Cold War era; Israel's nuclear image and policy; and developments in global arms control thinking in the nuclear realm.

Her books and monographs include *Israel's Nuclear Image: Arab Perceptions of Israel's Nuclear Posture* (co-author, 1994), a landmark study into the regional effects of Israel's unique model of nuclear ambiguity; and a major study of the ACRS talks entitled *Arms Control in the Middle East: Cooperative Security Dialogue and Regional Constraints* (Sussex Academic Press, 2006). Her most recent publications include co-edited volumes, among them: *The Obama Vision and Nuclear Disarmament* (2011); *The Nuclear Nonproliferation Regime at a Crossroads* (2014) and *Arms Control and National Security: New Horizons* (2014).

Hirofumi Tosaki is a Senior Research Fellow of the Center for the Promotion of Disarmament and Non-Proliferation (CPDNP), The Japan Institute of International Affairs (JIIA). He is an author of numerous articles on nuclear arms control, non-proliferation, nuclear strategy and deterrence, missile defense and so on. He earned his Ph.D from Osaka University.

Jina Kim is a Research Fellow at the Korea Institute for Defense Analyses, specialising in US-North Korea relations and nuclear non-proliferation. She holds a PhD in International Relations from the Fletcher School of Law and Diplomacy at Tufts University and teaches at Yonsei Graduate School of International Studies. She is on the Advisory Committee for the Blue House National Security Office and USROK Combined Forces Command, and she serves the Policy Review Committee for the Ministry of Foreign Affairs. She has authored *The North Korean Nuclear Weapons Crisis* (2014) and co-authored *Korean Peninsula and Indo-Pacific Power Politics* (2020).

Keir Lieber is Director of the Center for Security Studies and Security Studies Program, and Professor in the School of Foreign Service and Department of Government at Georgetown University.

Professor Lieber's research and teaching interests include nuclear weapons, deterrence and strategy; technology and the causes of war; US national security policy; and international relations theory. He is co-author, with Daryl Press of Dartmouth College, of *The Myth of the Nuclear Revolution: Power Politics in the Atomic Age* (Cornell University Press, 2020); author of *War and the Engineers: The Primacy of Politics over Technology* (Cornell University Press, 2005); and editor of *War, Peace, and International Political Realism* (University of Notre Dame Press, 2009). His articles have appeared in leading scholarly and foreign policy publications, including *International Security*, *Security Studies*, *Foreign Affairs* and *The Atlantic Monthly*.

Lora Saalman is Associate Senior Fellow within SIPRI's Armament and Disarmament and Conflict, Peace and Security research areas and a Senior Fellow in the Global Cooperation in Cyberspace Program at the EastWest Institute. Her research focuses on China's cyber, nuclear and advanced conventional weapon developments in relation to India, Russia and the USA. Dr Saalman completed her PhD at Tsinghua University in Beijing, where she was the first American to earn a doctorate from its Department of International Relations. Her doctoral studies and dissertation on the impact of US and European sanctions on China's and India's military modernization were conducted entirely in Chinese.

Since that time she has taught on related topics at Tsinghua University and at the Daniel K. Inouye Asia-Pacific Center for Security Studies, where she covered cybersecurity issues after having undergone technical training on hacker tools, exploits and incident handling as well as ICS/SCADA security essentials. Among the first batch of Stanton Nuclear Security Fellows, Dr Saalman was based in Beijing with the Carnegie-Tsinghua Center for Global Policy as an Associate within the Nuclear Policy Program of the Carnegie Endowment for International Peace.

Olivier de France is Research Director at The French Institute for International and Strategic Affairs (IRIS) in Paris, where he runs the

European affairs programme. He works on the political and strategic shifts affecting the Old Continent, and on the ideas that underlie them. Prior to joining Iris, he was an analyst with the European Union Institute for Security Studies (EUISS) and with the European Council on Foreign Relations (ECFR). Educated at Cambridge University in the UK and Ecole Normale Supérieure in France, he teaches political theory at Paris VII University, and European geopolitics at the Sorbonne University in Paris.

Owen Brian Toon is a Professor in the Department of Atmospheric and Oceanic Sciences for which he was the founding Chair, and a Research Associate in the Laboratory for Atmospheric and Space Physics at the University of Colorado at Boulder. He received an A. B. in physics at the University of California at Berkeley in 1969 and a PhD in physics at Cornell University in 1975. He was a Research Scientist at NASA's Ames Research Center from 1975 until 1997 when he moved to Colorado.

Brian's research group studies radiative transfer, aerosol and cloud physics, atmospheric chemistry and parallels between the Earth and planets. Brian has helped conceive, develop and lead many NASA airborne field missions aimed at understanding stratospheric volcanic clouds, stratospheric ozone loss, the effects of aircraft on the atmosphere, and the role of convective and cirrus clouds in Earth's climate system.

Manpreet Sethi is Senior Fellow, Centre for Air Power Studies, New Delhi where she heads the project on nuclear security. She is an expert on the entire range of nuclear issues having published over 80 papers in reputed academic journals. Over the last 18 years, she has been researching and writing on subjects related to nuclear energy, strategy, non-proliferation, disarmament, arms and export controls and BMD. Sethi is the author of books *Code of Conduct for Outer Space: Strategy for India* (2015), *Nuclear Strategy: India's March towards Credible Deterrence* (2009) and *Argentina's Nuclear Policy* (1999); co-author of *India's Sentinel* (2014) and *Nuclear Deterrence and Diplomacy* (2004) and editor of *Towards a Nuclear Weapons Free World* (2009), *Global Nuclear Challenges* (2009) and *Nuclear Power: In the Wake of Fukushima* (2012).

Matthew Kroenig is a Professor in the Department of Government and the Edmund A. Walsh School of Foreign Service at Georgetown University. A 2019 study in *Perspectives on Politics* ranked him as one of the top 25 most-cited political scientists of his generation.

Kroenig is the author or editor of seven books, including *The Return of Great Power Rivalry: Democracy versus Autocracy from the Ancient*

World to the US and China (Oxford University Press, 2020), which was an Amazon Best Seller, including the #1 New Release in International Relations. *The Logic of American Nuclear Strategy: Why Strategic Superiority Matters* (Oxford University Press, 2018) was selected by the US Air Force for its professional reading list and was translated into Chinese and Korean. *Exporting the Bomb: Technology Transfer and the Spread of Nuclear Weapons* (Cornell University Press, 2010) was awarded the International Studies Association Best Book Award, Honorable Mention.

Mustafa Kibaroğlu (PhD, Bilkent University, International Relations Department, 1996) is currently the Chair of the Department of Political Science and International Relations at MEF University in Istanbul. He used to be the Chair of Department of International Relations at Okan University in Istanbul between September 2011 and July 2014. Professor Kibaroğlu used to teach courses on "Arms Control & Disarmament" and "Turkish Foreign Policy" in the Department of International Relations at Bilkent University in Ankara from 1997 to 2011.

Kibaroğlu was a Research Fellow at the United Nations Institute for Disarmament Research in Geneva (1995); International Atomic Energy Agency Fellow at the University of Southampton (1996); Post-doctoral Fellow at the Monterey Institute in California (1996–97); and Sabbatical Fellow at the Belfer Center of Harvard University (2004–05).

Nina Tannenwald is Senior Lecturer in the Department of Political Science. Her research focuses on the role of international institutions, norms and ideas in global security issues, efforts to control weapons of mass destruction, and human rights and the laws of war. Her book, *The Nuclear Taboo: The United States and the Nonuse of Nuclear Weapons Since 1945* (Cambridge University Press, 2007), won the 2009 Lepgold Prize for best book in international relations.

Her current research projects include the future of the nuclear normative order, targeted killing, and compliance with, and effectiveness of, the laws of war. She has co-edited, with Matthew Evangelista, *Do the Geneva Conventions Matter?* (Oxford, 2017). Her articles have appeared in *International Organization*, *International Security*, *Journal of Strategic Studies*, *Ethics and International Affairs*, *Foreign Affairs* and the *Washington Quarterly*, among others.

Petr Topychkanov is a Senior Researcher in the SIPRI Nuclear Disarmament, Arms Control and Non-proliferation Programme. Petr works on issues related to non-proliferation, disarmament, arms control, and impact of new technologies on strategic stability. From

2006 to 2017, Petr Topychkanov was a fellow at the Carnegie Moscow Center's Nonproliferation Program. Prior to joining SIPRI in 2018, Petr held the position of Senior Researcher at the Center for International Security at the Primakov National Research Institute of World Economy and International Relations of the Russian Academy of Sciences.

Rajesh Basrur is Visiting Professor in the South Asia Programme at the S. Rajaratnam School of International Studies (RSIS), Nanyang Technological University, Singapore. He is also a Research Associate with the Contemporary South Asian Studies Programme at the Oxford School of Global and Area Studies, University of Oxford. Previously, he was Professor of International Relations at RSIS and held fellowships at various institutions of higher learning in North America, Europe and Asia. His work focuses on South Asian security, global nuclear politics, and international relations theory. He has authored five books, including (with Kate Sullivan de Estrada) *Rising India: Status and Power* (Routledge, 2017); *South Asia's Cold War* (Routledge, 2008) and *Minimum Deterrence and India's Nuclear Security* (Stanford University Press, 2006). He has also edited twelve books and journal special issues, including (with Anit Mukherjee and T. V. Paul), *India-China Maritime Competition: The Security Dilemma at Sea* (Routledge, 2019). He has published over 100 papers research and policy papers, most recently, "*India and China: A Managed Nuclear Rivalry?*" Washington Quarterly (October 2019).

Rajesh Rajagopalan is Professor of International Politics at Jawaharlal Nehru University, New Delhi. His publications include three books, *Nuclear South Asia: Keywords and Concepts* (co-authored with Atul Mishra) (Routledge, 2014); *Fighting Like A Guerrilla: The Indian Army and Counterinsurgency* (Routledge, 2008); and *Second Strike: Arguments about Nuclear War in South Asia* (Penguin/Viking, 2005). His articles (some jointly authored) have appeared in a number of academic and policy journals, such as *The Washington Quarterly, Contemporary Security Policy, India Review, Contemporary South Asia, Small Wars and Insurgencies, South Asia, South Asian Survey* and *Strategic Analysis* as well as in Indian newspapers, such as *Economic Times, The Hindu, Indian Express, Financial Express* and *The Hindustan Times.*

Sadia Tasleem is a PhD student, University of British Columbia (Vancouver, Canada), and a lecturer, the Department of Defense & Strategic Studies, Quaid-i-Azam University (Islamabad, Pakistan).

As a Robin Copeland Memorial Fellow for Nonproliferation from 2014 to 2015, she undertook a research project entitled "Creating a

Constituency for Unilateral Nuclear Arms Control in Pakistan." Also, as a core member of the Program on Strategic Stability Evaluation (POSSE) she has done extensive research on various aspects of Strategic Stability, Nuclear Learning and the implications of Knowledge Diffusion with a focus on Pakistan.

Walter C Ladwig III is Associate Professor (UK: Senior Lecturer) of International Relations in the Department of War Studies at King's College London and an Associate Fellow in Asian Security at the Royal United Services Institution (RUSI) in London. His scholarly writings on the geopolitics of the Indo-Pacific, U.S. foreign policy and South Asian security have been published in a number of academic journals including *International Security*, the *Journal of Strategic Studies* and *Asian Survey*, among others, and he is currently writing a book on Indian defence policy. He received a BA from the University of Southern California, an MPA from Princeton University, and a PhD from the University of Oxford.

Zhong Ai is a research associate working at the Research Institute for Indian Ocean Economies, Yunnan University of Finance and Economics.

INDEX

A

Air-launched land-attack cruise missile
    CJ-20, 185
American strategic community, 204
Anti-Ballistic Missile (ABM), 20, 34, 233
Anti-nuclear movement, 58
Any military structure, antisatellite (ASAT)
    technology, 40
    weapons, 40
Arab–Israeli war, 69
Arms Control Association, 116
Arms-racing effects, 39
Artificial intelligence (AI), 40
Atomic device, 200
AUKUS Pact, 167, 174

B

Balakot strikes, 56
Ballistic missile defence (BMD), 20
    nuclear submarines, 183
    systems, 20
Belt and Road Initiative (BRI), 144
Bharatiya Janata Party (BJP), 56, 232
Biological weapons, 76
British
    dependent territory, 25
    empire, 36
    virgin islands, 90

C

Central Foreign Affairs Commission
    Office, 187
Central Treaty Organization (CENTO),
    125
Chemical weapons, 76
China Arms Control and Disarmament
    Association, 180
China's declaratory NFU policy, 188
China's nuclear command, 206
Chinese Communist Party Central
    Committee Politburo, 202
Christian Science Monitor, 281
Cold War, 49, 53, 66, 68, 69, 75, 76, 85,
    104, 111, 112, 119, 123, 124, 137,
    144, 150, 161, 166, 171, 203, 233,
    237, 277, 279, 280–281, 284
    era, 277
    period, 277
    policymakers, 67
    security situation, 280–281
    system, 26
Communist Party Central Committee, 155
Comprehensive Test Ban Treaty, 34
Conference
    on disarmament, 283
Conventional Prompt Global Strike
    (CPGS), 201
Conventional wars, 18
'Creating the Environment for Nuclear
    Disarmament (CEND), 150
Cuban missile crisis, 278
Cyber warfare, 40

D

Democratic People's Republic of Korea
    (DPRK), 52
*Deterrence and Stability: China–U.S.
    Nuclear Relationship,* 201
DF-41 ICBM missiles, 179, 183, 186
Dual-capable fighter aircraft (DCA), 149
Dual-Capable Systems, 185

E

Earth system climate model, 94
East–West tension, 277
European
    commission, 168
    council, 168
External nuclear threats, 202

F

Falklands Islands, 25
Falklands War, 25, 27
Federal Assembly, 156
Firepower, 18

First World War, 24
Food Price Index, 97, 98
Fourth industrial revolution, 35
Fractional orbital bombardment system (FOBS), 186
French
- constitution, 172
- defence community, 174
- nuclear weapon, 172

G

General Staff Intelligence Department, 179
Geopolitical polarisation
- long-term effects of, 169–171
Geopolitics, 8, 11, 12
Global Initiative to Combat Nuclear Terrorism (GICNT), 282
Global no-first-use (GNFU)
- agreement, 135, 140
- desirability, 212
- model, 168
- policy, 141, 166, 230
Global Zero Campaign, 160
Great Wall Project, 203
Gross domestic product (GDP), 36
Gulf War, 115

H

Hague Code of Conduct against Ballistic Missile Proliferation (HCOC), 283
Hague summits, 282
Hiroshima firestorm, 94
Hiroshima weapon, 92
House Armed Services Committee, 251
Hyper Glide Vehicle (HGV), 20

I

India–Bhutan–China tri-junction, 37
Indian nuclear weapons, 115
India–Pakistan war, 56, 125
India's nuclear programme, 131
Institute for Defence Studies and Analyses, 232
Institute for Science and International Security, 251
Intercontinental ballistic missile (ICBM), 145
- forces, 147
Intergovernmental Panel on Climate Change, 102, 103
Intermediate Nuclear Forces (INF), 34, 158, 277
- treaty, 159
Intermediate-range ballistic missile (IRBM)
- DF-26, 185
International Atomic Energy Agency (IAEA), 281, 282
- protocols, 282
International Court of Justice (ICJ), 234
International Humanitarian Law, 171
International organisations
- IAEA, 282
- Interpol, 282
- UN, 282
Interpol, 282
Iran–Iraq War, 27
Iran nuclear deal, 167
Iraq War, 27
Israel and the Bomb, 225
Israel Atomic Energy Commission, 228
Israel's nuclear policy, 225, 226, 228–229
Israel's war plans, 227

J

Joint Comprehensive Plan of Action (JCPOA), 49, 286–287
Jupiter missiles, 276, 278

K

Kargil conflict of 1999, 25
Kargil war, 67, 72, 126
Korean Air Missile Defense (KAMD), 254
Korean War, 24

L

Lahore Agreement of 1999, 242
Launch-under-Attack, 17
League of Nations, 27
Lethal autonomous weapons systems, 40, 54
Line of control (LOC), 52
Long-range mobile ballistic missiles, 183

M

Medium-range ballistic missile (MRBM)
DF-17, 185, 186
Military-civilian fusion, 185
Military signals, 72
Missile defence systems, 205
Missile technology control regime (MTCR), 283
Montreal Protocol, 101, 103
Multiple independently targetable reentry vehicles (MIRVs), 20, 39
Mutual assured destruction (MAD), 84

N

Narang reports, 75
National Defence and Security Council, 173
National Defense Program Guidelines (NDPG), 264
National Nuclear Posture and Stability, 221
National Security Strategy, 143
Negative security assurances (NSAs), 271
Newly Independent States (NIS), 280
New Strategic Arms Reduction Treaty, 88
Nicobar islands, 53
No first use (NFU), 139
agreement, 118
commitment, 177, 241, 243
commitments, 184, 189
declarations, 140, 141, 188, 242, 245
doctrine, 136, 211
emerging security context, 131–133
India, 221–, 221–222
model, 188
nuclear policy, 237
nuclear strategies, 123
policy, 112, 113, 114, 116, 117, 118, 123, 125, 127, 129, 135, 137, 138, 143, 151, 155, 156, 160, 180, 187, 201, 224, 226, 232, 242, 244, 264, 266, 269, 270, 284, 286, 287
posture, 132
signals, 135, 136
strategy, 117, 131
Non-nuclear weapons state (NNWS), 156, 205, 225, 234, 265
Non-Proliferation and Disarmament Initiative (NPDI), 282
North Atlantic Council, 285
North Atlantic Treaty Organization (NATO), 26, 155, 156
leaders, 112
officials, 276
reaction, 30
strategy, 277, 283, 285, 286
summit, 276, 287
North Korea's nuclear strategy, 255–261
North's nuclear strategy, 253
Nuclear
acquisition, 29–30
coercion, 74–75
conflict, 100
deterrence, 23, 255
disorder, 48–50
explosion, 93
policy, 255
powers, 21, 83, 101, 171, 172
programme, 287
response, 260
retaliation, 255
revolution, 65–68
revolution theorists, 73
risk reduction measures, 57
security project, 86
security summit, 281
skepticism theory, 72
suppliers group, 242
systems, 111
terrorism, 145
war, 99, 102, 104
long-term effects of, 19
warheads, 182
weapons, 15, 17, 25, 26, 30, 31, 32, 49, 63, 68–70, 75, 77, 84, 93, 104, 115, 131, 144, 146, 150, 177, 180, 211, 214, 231, 233, 253, 264, 271, 276
free zones, 90
geopolitics, 50
programmes, 54, 103, 130
states, 91, 207, 270
in Turkey's national security policy, 277
Nuclear-armed
countries, 83
nations, 103, 211
states, 69, 70, 214
Nuclear Non- Proliferation Treaty (NPT), 16

- extension conference, 281
- review conference, 281, 282

Nuclear peace
- alternative explanations, 26–28
- analytical evidence, 25–26
- statistical evidence, 24–25

Nuclear Posture Review (NPR), 113, 203, 251

P

Paris Summit, 278
People's Liberation Army (PLA) Rocket Force, 179, 182
pledge, 206
Political communities, 11
Political error or technical mistakes, 12
Proliferation Security Initiative (PSI), 282

R

Russian
- authorities, 159, 286
- Federation, 155
- Federation on Nuclear Deterrence, 159
- military authorities, 284
- military establishment, 13
- nuclear doctrine journey, 155–
- policy, 284
- strategic rocket forces, 158

S

Sea-launched cruise missile (SLCM), 149
Second Artillery missile, 182
Second World War, 24, 27, 84, 94, 171
Shenyang Institute of Automation of the Chinese Academy of Sciences, 186
Shock waves, 93
Soviet Union, 36, 38, 86, 91, 102, 206, 233, 277, 279, 280, 285
Soviet War, 104
Space-based systems, 52
Strategic Arms Limitations Talks (SALT), 29
Strategic Arms Reduction Treaty, 34
Strategic Offensive Reductions Treaty (SORT), 87
Strategic Plans Division (SPD), 235
Submarine-launched ballistic missiles (SLBMs), 149, 257
Syrian conflict, 287

T

Tactical nuclear weapons (TNWs), 123, 128, 238
Theories of statecraft and strategy, 9
The Science of Military Strategy, 184, 204
Treaty of Tlatelolco, 90
Turkic republics of Central Asia, 281
Turkish
- authorities, 276, 277, 278, 280, 282, 283, 286, 287, 288
- export controls system, 282
- media, 277
- port of Izmir, 279
- Russian relations, 280
- Syrian border, 288

U

Ukraine, 1, 21, 27-28, 30, 88-89, 115, 144, 158, 167, 174
- *Uncommon Cause*, 19
- United Arab Emirates (UAE), 37
- United Nations Food and Agriculture Food Price Index, 98

United Nations Security Council, 24, 83, 85, 103, 282
Unmanned aerial vehicles (UAVs), 185
U.S. declaratory policy, 267
U.S. nuclear response, 267
US-bestowed civil nuclear deal, 241
US–China nuclear relationship, 203
US Congressional Commission on Strategic Posture, 265
US decision-making process, 40
US Department of Defense assessment, 183, 228
US intelligence agencies, 251
US–Israel relations, 225
US missile defence system, 52
US National Intelligence Service, 251
US Non-Proliferation Law, 236
US nuclear capabilities, 149–150
US nuclear deterrence, 257
US nuclear policy, 57
US nuclear posture review, 144, 212, 265
US nuclear strategy, 143, 147–149, 150

US nuclear weapons, 92, 146, 277, 279, 280, 288
US policy, 92
US–Russian arms control, 155
US–South Korea military
  exercises, 257
  strategy, 254
US–Soviet arms control process, 43
US–Soviet Cuban Missile Crisis of 1962, 34–35

V

Vietnam War, 104

W

Wall Street Journal, 86
War of Independence, 224
Warsaw Pact, 277, 279, 285
Warsaw Treaty Organization (WTO), 277
  members, 284
Weapons of mass destruction (WMD), 280
Workers' Party's Central Committee, 260
World order (WO), 12

Y

Yom Kippur War, 25, 75, 104, 128, 227–228

Z

Zangger Committee, 283